CISTERCIAN STUDIES SERIES: NUMBER EIGHTY-ONE

A.J. Krailsheimer

THE LETTERS OF ARMAND-JEAN DE RANCÉ

CISTERCIAN STUDIES SERIES: NUMBER EIGHTY-ONE

THE LETTERS OF ARMAND-JEAN DE RANCÉ

Abbot and Reformer of la Trappe

presented by

A.J. Krailsheimer

comprising 365 letters translated in full
together with some 1700 others
calendared with notes

Volume Two
1683–1700

Cistercian Publications
Kalamazoo, Michigan
1984

BX
4705
.R3
A4
1984
v. 2

© Copyright, Cistercian Publications, Inc., 1984

Available in Britain and Europe from
A.R. Mowbray & Co Ltd
St Thomas House Becket Street
Oxford OX1 1SJ

Available elsewhere from the publishers
Cistercian Publications, Inc.
WMU Station
Kalamazoo, Michigan 49008

All rights reserved

The work of Cistercian Publications is made possible
in part by support from Western Michigan University.

Typeset by the Carmelites of Indianapolis

Library of Congress Cataloguing in Publication Data

Rancé, Armand Jean Le Bouthillier de, 1626-1700.
  The letters of Armand-Jean de Rancé, abbot and reformer of la Trappe.

  (Cistercian studies series; 80-81)
  Includes index.
  1. Rancé, Armand Jean Le Bouthillier de, 1626-1700.
2. Cistercians—France—Correspondence.   3. Trappists—
France—Correspondence.   I. Krailsheimer, A.J.   II. Title.   III. Series.
BX4705.R3A4   1984   271'.125'024   [B]   82-19837
ISBN 0-87907-880-4 (v. 1)
ISBN 0-87907-881-2 (v. 2)

TABLE OF CONTENTS

A Note on the Letters	vii
The Letters, 1683–1700	1
Undated Letters	257
Collection of *Extracts* from the Letters	273
Index of Addresses	275
General Index	311

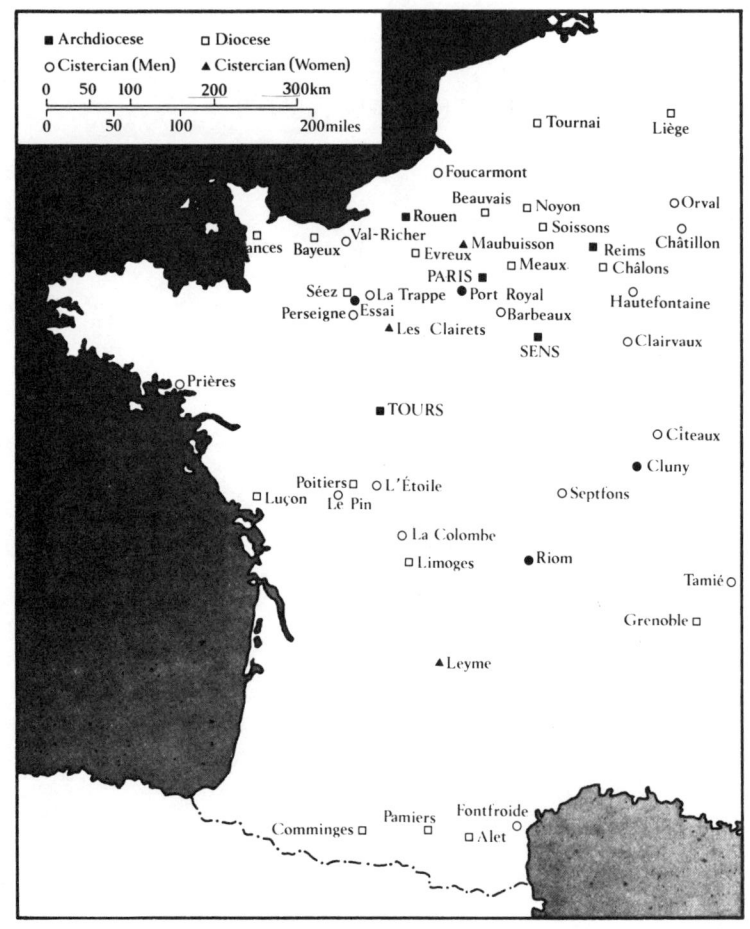

Places mentioned in the text

A NOTE ON THE LETTERS

Numbering and dating

Each letter has been given a reference number based on its date. Where the full date is known (or can be reasonably conjectured) this is given in conventional six figure form: year, month, day; and when more than one letter is attributed to the same day the second and subsequent such letters are distinguished by alphabetical serials (e.g. 821102, 821102a: letters written in 1682 on November second). When the month, but not the day, is known, the last two figures are given as '00' and letters attributed to the same month are similarly distinguished, after the first, by the use of alphabetical serials (e.g. 821100, 821100a), which have no chronological significance. Where only the year is known or can be conjectured, only the two figures for the year are used, followed by a stroke and a numerical serial for each letter (e.g. 82/1, 82/2), which also has no chronological significance.

Dates are either given in the form in which they appear in the letter, or in square brackets when the date has been established through internal or external evidence. Where a figure is wrong in the copy (a frequent occurrence) the correct figure is given in square brackets, and the incorrect one noted below. All doubtful dates, especially those involving two or more years or months, are prefixed by a query (?). Undated letters are listed separately at the end of the dated series. Minor variations have not usually been noted; many copies of surviving originals systematically give a date one day later than the original.

An asterisk (*) denotes a letter translated in full. Bold face entries are given for chronological orientation.

Styling of addressees

In most cases the original French style has been used in giving addresses, with a few exceptions (such as bishops) where translation is unambiguous. Wherever possible the full name of addressees is given, and the names of incumbents given in square brackets after their title. The form of title is often the only way in which an incomplete address can be filled out, and the distinction between M *l'abbé* (used both as courtesy title for clergy in general and also, more correctly, for commendatory abbots or priors) and RP *abbé* (used solely for regulars) cannot be adequately rendered in English. Similarly RP for regular clergy and M. or M. *l'abbé* for seculars has no English equivalent. M was used almost universally for clergy, laity, and even bishops (e.g. M. *de Meaux* for Bossuet, M. *de la Trappe* for Rancé), and *Mme* applied from royal princesses, like *Mme de Guise*, down to ordinary married women of the bourgeoisie. In the circumstances, and despite the radical inconsistency of copyists and even original correspondents, a uniform style has been used throughout for the same person. The many letters addressed simply to *religieux* or *religieuse* pose an intractable problem; some copies actually change RM into *ma soeur* (or vice versa); the same person may be addressed on one occasion as *prieure* and on another as *supérieure*, and so on. Abbesses, and abbots, are sometimes given the honorific *très-révérend(e)* or TRM, TRP, sometimes not. With the exception of the Abbot of Cîteaux (addressed as *Révérendissime* and here distinguished by being given in English) all heads of abbeys have been uniformly described as RP *abbé*, RM *abbesse*, and likewise with lesser superiors. Titles of nobility, public offices and so on have been left in the original and often have no comparable description in English. It is worth noting that Rancé reserved *très chère* for his sisters and niece, and *très cher Monsieur* or *père* for such intimates as Favier or Monchy.

Bibliographical references and abbreviations

Whenever an original ('orig.') or autograph ('aut.') has survived, this is given first and followed by references to copies in all the principal series used; when only copies survive, references are given to all the main series, but not to further single copies made from them. Printed sources, especially modern, are normally given after the MS copy, and in one or two cases only a printed source is known. MS sources have always been preferred, but it should be noted that even the best copies often omit personal postscripts found in the original, and can be shown to differ, not usually very much, from each other. In particular there is a tendency for copies to conflate or split up original letters (particularly marked in A 2606). It should be noted that MS Df 49 at the Bibliothèque Sainte-Geneviève, Paris, is a duplicate of M 1214, differing only in having correct numbering for all the letters where M 1214 has two letters 26 with consequential error thereafter; to avoid repeating 106 entries, references have been given only to M 1214.

Source Key

Manuscript

A	Bibliothèque de l'Arsenal, Paris
BN	Bibliothèque Nationale, Paris (*fonds français* unless otherwise stated)
Carp	Carpentras, Bibliothèque Municipale, MS 625,626 (the two volumes of a copy made of dom Le Nain's *Vie de Rancé* before editorial excisions, and the sole source for several letters unknown elsewhere)
CF	Clermont-Ferrand, Bibliothèque Municipale et Universitaire
L	Luçon, Archives diocésaines
M	Bibliothèque Mazarine, Paris
P	Poitiers, Bibliothèque Municipale, MS Fontaneau 65
SS	Bibliothèque de Saint-Sulpice, Paris
T	Troyes, Bibliothèque Municipale
TA	La Trappe, *Lettres originales*
TB	La Trappe, *Lettres à imprimer* (reference to page)
TC	La Trappe, *Lettres de piété* (reference to number of letter)
TD	La Trappe, *Lettres diverses* (series A,B,C)
Tour	Collection Henri Tournouër (in private hands near Alençon)
U	Utrecht, *ancien fonds d'Amersfoort, Port-Royal*
W	Windsor Castle, Royal Library, Stuart Papers

Printed Works

Autographes Troussures	*Lettres autographes de Troussures* [château near Beauvais], ed. dom Paul Denis, 1912
J-B Bossuet:	references are to the edition of his correspondence by Ch. Urbain and E. Levesque, 15 vols. Paris, 1909–12
Burnier, *Hist. de Tamié*	E. Burnier, *Histoire de l'abbaye de Tamié*. Chambéry, 1865 (contains letters, numbered serially, to Cornuty, copied from MS *Chronique de Tamié*, kept at the abbey)
Charavay	The sales catalogues of Maison Charavay, Paris, specialist dealers in autographs, still issued. An index of these, and other sales up to about 1900, can be found in the BN, MSS Department, under Fichiers Charavay (Rancé RAI-RAZ).

DBF	*Dictionnaire de Biographie française.*
Dubois	Abbé Dubois, *Histoire de l'abbé de Rancé.* 1866
Gonod	B. Gonod, *Lettres de A-J le B de Rancé.* 1846
Mug	*Lettres de piété écrites à différentes personnes par... Rancé*, vol. 1, 1701; vol. 2, 1702, published by F. Muguet
Mme de Sévigné	references are to the edition of her letters in 3 vols, éd. de la Pléiade. 1953
Sol, *ND de Saint-Bernard de Comminges*	abbé Sol, *Notre Dame de Saint-Bernard de Comminges*. Toulouse, 1923
SP	*Stuart Papers*, vol. 1, ed. F.H. Blackburne Daniell. 1902
Tans	J.A.G. Tans, 'Un Dialogue monologué; lettres à P. Quesnel, *Augustiniana*, 13. 1963 (reference to letters by serial number)

A Note on Rancé's Signature:

Up to 25 March 1643 Rancé signed his extant letters to Favier *Ab. Bouthillier de Rancé*. His signature then changed to *l'abbé de Rancé*, but starting with the letter of 14 May 1658 (after his conversion) none of his letters to Favier is signed, nor are any of those to Arnauld d'Andilly, but a letter to Andilly's son, Pomponne, of 18 February 1662 is signed *l'abbé de Rancé* and is the only signed letter from this period known to survive. After his profession he always signed *fr Armand-Jean, abbé de la Trappe*, never again using his family name, and after his resignation in 1695, when he could no longer use his hand, letters are always signed for him *fr Armand-Jean anc.[ien] abbé de la Trappe*.

THE LETTERS OF ARMAND-JEAN DE RANCÉ
(Volume Two)

*830117   BISHOP OF LUÇON [HENRI BARILLON]   17 January 16[8]3
P f.605 (wrongly dated 1673)

'You cause me great joy, Mgr, in giving me reason to hope that we may once more have the honour and consolation of seeing you. I hope that no business draws you away from your diocese, because I know how much good your presence there does, yet if providence were ever to permit you to leave it for the glory of God and the benefit of your diocese, I should certainly consider it a special fortune if la Trappe happened to be on your road. In truth it is a blessing to see with one's own eyes the enlightenment that God has been pleased to grant you, your fidelity and zeal for his service, and then you can judge the effect produced on us by all that comes from those for whom our feelings are such as you know we have for you.

We felt about the destruction of your Temple as you did, and we gave thanks to God for it. I hope that he will protect your intentions on every occasion. He has done so hitherto, and you have every cause to have complete confidence in him. You know, Mgr, that nothing leads him more powerfully to take our cause in hand than when our affairs are his, and we await the decision from him alone. I am much obliged to you, Mgr, for your good offices with the Ar[chbishop] of R[eims]. I should have found it embarrassing and difficult (for reasons which you can judge) to explain myself in letters on the matter in question. You will no doubt have seen the Bishop of M[eaux] and had the copy from him; I am sorry that you will not find in it certain passages which were changed or modified on his advice, although there is nothing essential there. I do not need to tell you, Mgr, with how much affection and respect I am yours, for I am sure that I can add nothing to what you already believe.

PS The address you ask me for, Mgr, is Abbey of la Trappe, Mortagne, Perche, and the Mortagne messenger lives at the Vallée de la Misère, at Notre-Dame de Boulogne; he is called M Baron.'

The Temple (Protestant church) at Mouchamps, a small village in Vendée, was demolished on 15 January 1683 as part of the final drive against heretics.

*830121   RM ABBESSE, LEYME [ANNE DE LA VIEUVILLE]   21 January 1683
TB 1835

'I cannot let this year go any further, RM, without telling you that I fervently hope that God will make it a happy one for you, and will give you many more of the same. It would be little enough for him to multiply your days if he did not at the same time fill them, for you know that the days of his elect must be full, and he will judge emptiness in men's lives as rigorously as iniquity. God wants us to have before our eyes only his service and his glory; it is wrong not to do that, since it means resisting his will. There is no more abiding truth, and none more indubitable, since we see in Scripture that the useless servant was treated as an unfaithful one. You make

1

such good use of God's gifts of grace, and will go on doing so with such care, that you will not incur the risk of uselessness, which is the most common and general evil, for assuredly a large number of men waste their lives doing nothing, either spending them in idleness or doing something other than what they should. I will not talk of the life we lead which, it seems to me, would be nothing remarkable if taken by itself and looked at alone. But it is true, and I cannot deny, that it is distinctive when set beside such general laxity and decadence. Yet our fathers are so far exalted above us, and are so much our masters in everything, that we never look upon them without being filled with confusion. Our consolation is that we are dealing with God, who sees our innermost hearts and perhaps sees in our intentions and desires what he does not perceive in our actions and works. Always remember me in your prayers, and please believe that it is not possible to honour you more than I do, yours' etc.

830121a   RM THÉRÈSE [BOUTHILLIER]   21 January 1683
TB 1837; TC I/129

Encouragement.

*830131   BISHOP OF LUÇON [HENRI BARILLON]   31 January 16[8]3
P f.606 (wrongly dated 1673)

'You are right when you say, Mgr, that your news regarding private [Protestant] assemblies will impress us as much as what you had already written about the demolition of the [Protestant] Temple of Mouchamps. I never doubted that God would favour your intentions, nor that the King would give you all the protection you needed. We shall not fail to thank God humbly, being obliged as we are to do so both through the Church's interests and through your personal concern.

I see that you have already made much progress in reading the manuscript; I fear (and I say this for you alone) that the remarks of the Archbishop of R[eims] may cause some fundamental distortion of principle. If that were so the work would no longer serve the purpose it should and the author would have done better to keep quiet than to speak in accordance with custom and habit and say things which pleased people but were contrary to what he practised, namely, what he took from the books of the saints. I beg you to keep an eye on that as much as you can.

It is said that the Bishop of Grenoble finds some harshness in the discussion on parents, but it seems to me that, in saying like St Basil that the monastery must provide for their needs in cases of extreme necessity, there is no longer any problem.

One of the canons of the Council of Gangra condemns the opinion of a heretic who maintained that free persons, on the pretext of a false piety, should abandon their fathers and withdraw to a cloister, however needy their fathers might be. I do not say the same thing, because I speak of persons already under a holy commitment and maintain, according to St Basil's view, that the monastery should take care of them. Nothing could be more necessary than such a view for the preservation of religious communities. I beg you to continue looking at the work, and if you do not find in it anything contrary to morality and holy doctrine, kindly give it your approval and put it in the hands of the Bishop of Meaux. It should be noted, Mgr, that the copy you have is not correct, and there are passages, which have been altered and toned down on the advice of the Bishop of M[eaux], which are not in it. Even the order has been changed in the printed copy. I am asking you not for a eulogy, but simple approval. If the Archbishop of R[eims] wanted to make any considerable changes he would spoil the work, and the printer, who is already well advanced, would be greatly inconvenienced.

I have no need to tell you, Mgr, how concerned I am at everything that affects you; you are too just towards me to doubt it. I am most respectfully yours etc.

PS I am most obliged to you for your kindness in remembering me when you spoke to the bishop of Séez. It will be most agreeable for me to have a friendly bishop.'

See 830117 on Mouchamps. R's episcopal friends did their best to tone down some of the rigour in his book, as this and later letters show, but he usually got his own way. The Council of Gangra, in Paphlagonia (c. 345), was mainly concerned with true and false asceticism. Mathurin Savary had been appointed Bp of Séez some six months earlier.

830204   PRÉSIDENT DE MESMES   4 February 1683
TB 1839

Has received books from him; praises his way of life.

830207   HENRI, CHEVALIER DE RANCÉ   7 February 1683
TB 1841

'Your life is so full of agitation and so exposed that I cannot think of it without being sorry for you.'

830207a NICOLAS PINETTE   7 February 1683
TB 1843; TC II/50

Caumartin has asked the Abbot of Clairvaux to allow la T. to retain the right to elect a prior, but should la T. fall into decadence the right would revert to Clairvaux, i.e. 'on the essential points, separation from outside people, strict silence, manual labour, hard beds . . . in diet, if they should come to use butter, eat fish, or even eggs, apart from illness or incapacity. . . . To change our present conduct could not occur without causing public scandal.'

The right, which was granted, thus depended on R's own rules, seldom so clearly stated, and going well beyond common practice in houses of the Reform.

830207b DOM PAUL, barbeaux   7 February 1683
TB 1845; TC I/175

A religious may not return to his family on grounds of health; by his profession he has renounced his family.

830211 MONSIEUR L'ABBÉ DE LA MADELEINE   11 February 1683
TB 1847

Thanks him for two boxes of preserved plums. R. resigned to thought of death.

830211a COMTESSE DE MATIGNON   11 February 1683
TB 1848

Condolences on death of her husband.

Henri Goyon, comte de Matignon, Lieutenant-General in Normandy, died in 1682.

830211b MADAME DE LA GRILLIÈRE   11 February 1683
TB 1849; TC II/45

R. has told Maupeou, her curé at Nonancourt, that she could not get through Lent just with eggs and without meat. 'This earthly body will be repaired and from its ashes will rise another, no longer subject to decay and immortal.'

Maupeou was R's future biographer. Mme de la Grillière did not die until 1690, but she was afflicted with cataracts and in poor health.

*830211c RM MARIE-LOUISE [bouthillier]   11 February 1683
TC II/308

'All the reflections which, as you tell me, you made during your retreat, my dear sister, must have been most useful, for the surest way to purify oneself before God is to destroy and annihilate oneself in one's own eyes. There are always good reasons for doing so when one looks on his divine majesty, on what one owes him for all the gifts of grace one constantly receives from him and the basic ingratitude which one retains amid so many obligations. Such a sight should cover most Christians with confusion, especially those whose profession and commitments are the same as yours. One cannot sufficiently condemn oneself when one goes into one's works in detail and looks at the particularities of one's life. For though it may be that one does not fall into gross iniquities, the number of faults one commits each day is almost infinite. Yet if that consideration humiliates, it should not overwhelm us. Together with the feeling we may have of the greatness of our miseries, we must sustain ourselves by our trust in God's goodness, who looks in pity on our weaknesses and sicknesses, when we hate them and truly grieve over not being what we should be in his eyes. He is a father who does not reject his children every time they return to him with sincere intentions of making their lives more worthy of him and more in conformity with his will, above all when this is accompanied by a firm resolve to suffer for love of him any scorn and humiliation which may come to us from men, and in peace and patience, if we do not yet have enough virtue to do so with joy.

You did well to give up all the occupations which were distracting you from God and preventing you from discharging your duties. Now that you have experienced how harmful they are to you, that is a reason for seeing that you are not replaced in them. You may well have it proposed to you, even pressingly, that you should resume them, but you will not be formally ordered to do so. Do not listen to those who would like to persuade you to adopt a docile attitude which would cost you too much, and which God does not ask of you. Although the obedience laid on you is not a sin, none the less if it brings you to sin and if it is obvious to you that you cannot achieve your salvation there, do all in your power to avoid it.

As for the measures of relief given to you on account of your poor health, just take them, but if you think that they are not necessary, point this out to your Mother Superior and then do what she says. Your obedience and simplicity will take the place of the austerity forbidden to you. In everything else be as strict as you can, and do not relax in any way your observance of the rule. Farewell, my dear sister, pray God for me and believe that no one could be more affectionately than I yours' etc.

830220   RM THÉRÈSE [BOUTHILLIER]   20 February 1683
TB 1850; TC II/24 (dated 20 January 1683)

She must submit absolutely and not make difficulties. 'You must believe because the Church so commands, and not because you have worked out by reasoning that it is in conformity with the truth. . . . The greatest advantage we have in the Catholic Church is that we are not embarrasssed as to which opinions to hold.'

830221   MONSIEUR   21 February 1683
TC II/48

X is where God wants him. M. should not change what X began or his rules for educating the young.

830224   RM LOUISE-HENRIETTE D'ALBON, TOURS   24 February 1683
TB 1854; TC I/55 (dated 21 January 1683)

She fears to lose her zeal. Pride and self-love are the source of all our faults. She should take on the most laborious and arduous tasks to cure herself of such faults.

830227 RM BÉTHUNE D'ORVAL, PORT-ROYAL, PARIS 27 February 1683
TB 1861; TC II/47

She has transferred to a stricter observance, is frightened by the silence, but will grow used to it.

This was Marie-Angélique, sister of Anne-Eléonore, Abbess of the benedictine house of Gif in 1687, whence she had come.

830227a RM ABBESSE, PORT-ROYAL, PARIS 27 February 1683
TB 1864

Reports his letter to above, with compliments.

*830311 BISHOP OF LUÇON [HENRI BARILLON] 11 March 16[8]3
P f.607 (wrongly dated 1673)

'I see, Mgr, that you have forgotten nothing for the completion of the work and have taken all possible care over it. It is one more kindness, such as you show us so often on all sorts of occasion.

All the things you noted have been corrected, unless by chance one has escaped our attention. The Bishop of M[eaux] has sent me the passage which he took the trouble to explain himself, and the explanation he supplied is absolutely right and necessary to make my ideas clear.

I have received, Mgr, the approval from the Bishop of Grenoble, and I should have liked you to have made more changes in it than you did. Indeed it always fills me with embarrassment to be praised, and I can say (at least I think so) that my heart revolts against what good may be said of me, and I recognise in myself a basic wretchedness which is plainly open to God's eyes and which acts as a counter-balance which appals me.

I think that the clarification I sent regarding the obligations of children towards their parents removes (as you say, Mgr) any difficulty there might be, since there is no assistance that the monastery cannot provide better than the children, and in that way the obligations of natural law are fully discharged. That will have to be put into a second edition. This book, which is impatiently awaited, will no doubt have very different effects. Some good people will be delighted by it, others will not be pleased, and you can imagine that the latter will be more numerous than the former. May God give it his blessing and forgive all the errors we have committed in it.

As your business is not entirely finished, it is very likely that this letter will find you still in Paris. I pray God that your business will be concluded as successfully as you hope; as it is his too and concerns his glory alone, it is for him to take care of it and reward the zeal he inspires in you. I cannot tell you, Mgr, how I honour and respect you. I feel this so keenly that I can find no words to express it.

PS Monsieur Maisne is infinitely obliged to you for doing him the honour of remembering him.'
Barillon in fact did not leave Paris until 30 March.

830324   MARQUIS DE LASSAY   24 March 1683
TC I/8

R. compares the soul drawn to God with a traveller drawn to a river's bank by the sound of rapidly flowing waters. Some people claim an intense prayer life, and in private get excited over the least thing.

830400   RM   April 1683
TC II/117

She has enjoyed God's grace since childhood, is in a strict and holy observance, and has only to await the end in peace.

* 830400a   [RM MARIE-LOUISE BOUTHILLIER]   [? April/August 1683]
TC II/309

'I am always delighted, my dearest sister, to have news of you, and I am sure that you are sufficiently convinced of all my feelings to have no doubts on that score. I praise God that you were moved by reading the book *De la Sainteté*. That shows that you love and esteem your calling, and that God has made you realise its dignity and merit. It is hardly possible that having given you such feelings, he will not also give you all those which are their result and effects. The religious are trying to attack this work with no justification. It is pure and truthful in all its principles and contains nothing but what the saints have taught.

You are lucky, my dear sister, to have Monsieur le Théologal as your superior; since God has given him so much understanding, virtue and charity, you should profit from such great learning. As for me, I am hardly able to tell you anything useful, and you can scarcely find in me what you hope for. I will say none the less that one of the first rules you must follow is to make a point of fighting against what you see as holding you back in the ways in which God wishes you to walk and to be faithful in your resolutions. Above all you must like incurring disapproval and be ready to sacrifice your own inclinations when you have occasion to do so. Nothing will be more effective in drawing God's blessings upon you. As regards trust in his providence, yours must be total. What trouble can come upon you for which you will not find consolation if you are convinced that nothing escapes him, that he rules all and arranges all things here on earth for the sanctification of the souls which are his and serve him? Secondary causes are nothing but instruments of his omnipotence and his will, and do nothing but execute his orders. Avoid contact with people in the world as much as you can, and only speak to them when obliged by necessity. They have always something one must constantly guard against, they bring with them a kind of noxious atmosphere which can hardly fail to affect even the strongest and fittest souls. The best thing is to avoid them.

Farewell, my dearest sister, I have no time to say more. Monsieur P[inette] will give you our news, and I will content myself with saying that no one could be more sincerely yours' etc.

The Théologal (canon theologian) was Pierre Courcier, who had succeeded the respected Morel on the latter's death in 1679. A doctor of the Sorbonne in 1668, secretary of the Assembly of the Clergy in 1680, Courcier died in 1713. As chief censor his powers were considerable, but he was regarded by some as lazy and not universally esteemed.

*830401 BISHOP OF LUÇON [HENRI BARILLON] 1 April 16[8]3
P f.608 (wrongly dated 1673)

'At last you are going back to your diocese, Mgr, with the satisfaction of having left it only in order to be of service and procure for it benefits and advantages which you could not have given by your presence. I can well imagine what kind of books you have had suppressed, at least I am sure that it is that catechism you spoke to me about, fit to cause nothing but disorder and confusion in your diocese. The life of a bishop as conscientious as you, striving to make himself a faithful minister, is a perpetual fight. One may say that wherever he turns he finds opposition and resistance. Your weapons, Mgr, are your zeal and your trust, and God, who has filled you with both, cannot fail to add his protection.

I am told, Mgr, as you also kindly write, that the book is beginning to appear and at this very moment is finding critics. Men being what they are, it was bound to be disapproved of by the majority and by those whose profession gives them a greater interest in it than others. Many will ask what it has to do with me, but ultimately I have spoken only of those things that concern us, and when I think that the most enduring truths would be swept away if there were no one who took the trouble to rescue them from oblivion and renew their memory, I am consoled for anything men may say about me, and hope that if they treat me still more severely and rigorously God will then look on me with more compassion and mercy. I beg you, Mgr, to pray to him for me, and to believe that your person is very present to me before him, that all my life I shall commend to him all that concerns you with all possible care, and no one could be more affectionately and respectfully yours' etc.

The suppressed catechism is quite likely to have been the Jansenist one of Raucourt, translated into French by dom Gerberon in 1677 as Catéchisme de la Pénitence.

830401a MADEMOISELLE DE [? GIF] 1 April 1683
TC I/117

She is fortunate in being inspired by God to leave the world and go to so holy and regular a house.

830402 ACHILLE DE HARLAY 2 April 1683
BN 17418,f.34 orig.
Pleased that he approves *Sainteté*, given through M. d' Etrechy. Book contains once familiar but now neglected truths.

830408 MONSIEUR L'ABBÉ DE SAINT-COSME 8 April 1683
TC I/118
Glad that he was edified by his visit to la T. R. does not recommend him at his age to change his situation.

*830415 MARÉCHAL DE BELLEFONDS 15 April 1683
BN na 12959 f.101,orig; TC II/329

'I hope, Mgr, that you found something to please you in the book sent to you on my behalf; it contains some very firm truths, but scarcely fashionable ones, and I do not doubt that they will be censured as are all those truths which are contrary to usage and custom. Sister A[nne] M[arie d'Épernon] has always lived such a pious and religious life, and has so faithfully discharged all her duties, that she will find hardly anything in the book that she has not practised. As for the wordly, it is certain that they will find much in it that they will find hard to accept, and when they put the rules beside their feelings and deeds, they will find a wide gap between the two. That does not mean that it is impossible to practise the rules, but that there are few people willing to take upon themselves what they should in order to lead a strict life among those who live in licence. However, there are some, as you know, Mgr, who do not fail to make a strenuous effort to model their conduct not on the examples before their eyes but on true principles, and who preserve a sincere piety in the midst of men. One should not imagine all the same that this is easy, for that would lead to neglect of the necessary ways, to dispensing oneself from those efforts, that diligence, that care without which one cannot resist the torrent, and it would mean remaining mixed up like others in that mass of worldly people from which one must be separated to please God. Those who think things can be painlessly acquired will not go very far; we are naturally opposed to the things that cost us dear, and no one will choose the difficult and narrow ways to go to God who has the idea that the broad and spacious ones lead to him. That is a mistake made by those who have a will, but one that is neither strong nor lively enough, so that they are very happy to spare themselves and find mitigations which satisfy them. There is nothing more common than to imagine a certain latitude in duties which they do not really have, for although they do not consist in a single point and there may be more or less, yet there are in life countless occasions in which one needs a very pure and enlightened virtue not to believe these duties to be less than they are. I am sure, Mgr, that enlightened as you are, and having as well the right dispositions of heart, you do not fail to be watchful in a place in which you know there is everything to be feared. We shall continue, Mgr, to recommend you to God, and I beg you to believe that there is nothing we offer him more than your person, your house and everything that concerns you. I am with all possible respect and fidelity yours etc.

PS I have a very humble request to make of you: M. de Tourouvre has a son whom he recently sent to sea, and who is only fourteen or fifteen. As he is on M. d'Amfreville's vessel, I should be particularly obliged if you would kindly recommend the boy to him. You know that M. de Tourouvre and I are close friends, and how I have to take an interest in all that concerns him. I hope for this favour from your kindness.'

The book is Sainteté, *which had come out in March. The boy is probably Jean-Alexandre de La Vove, born 1667. Charles-François Davy, marquis d'Amfreville (1640–92; date of birth also given as 1628) was born at Valognes, and was thus Bellefonds' near neighbor. He had a distinguished career in the navy and in January 1691 married Bellefonds' daughter Jeanne, who was then twenty-six. He died next year after the defeat at la Hougue, near his home, but not apparently as a direct result, for he lived for several months after it.*

830426   RP ABBÉ   26 April 1683
TC II/279

In deciding whether to accept office in the order, RP must go by the state of his own house. 'Your presence is necessary—the community will suffer and become less regular.' Those appointed in his absence lack authority and will not be followed. Best to concern himself solely with his own abbey.

With the General Chapter imminent (17 May) the enquiry was a natural one, and could have come from any one of R's colleagues.

830501   PAUL BARILLON   1 May 1683
TC II/105

Hopes to see Barillon one day free of duties.

*830501a   RM MARIE-LOUISE [BOUTHILLIER]   1 May 1683
TC II/183

'Concerning your doubts, I can tell you that you should never give your vote when you believe that the person is not worthy of being admitted to profession; that you may feel not bound by intellectual attitudes, that is, not enter into discussion as to whether they are lofty or ordinary, or whether they are crude or more subtle and spiritual. Often a simple religious is better and is more pleasing to God than another with more intelligence and understanding. Nor must you pay attention to certain outward imperfections when you see virtue, for charity calls us to tolerate and endure them patiently. But if you observe that someone is recalcitrant, conceited, opinionated, argumentative, opposed to humiliations, then you may be sure that she does not deserve to be admitted, and that these faults, if they have not been corrected by the trials of the novitiate, will grow as time goes on. On the pretext of showing her special charity, you will be failing in public charity by granting her entry into religion, where, according to all appearances, she will do nothing but harm. Your first obligation is to your monastery, and if you exclude from it those who give you cause, by their conduct and their present state, to believe that they are more likely to do it harm than good, do not worry, and do not be afraid of committing your conscience. Just as one must open the door to those who are called by God's spirit, so one must keep them closed when such a quality is not to be seen and when there are no signs of a true vocation.

On the other subject of your letter, I will say that it is offending God's greatness as well as his mercy not to have absolute trust in him, because there is nothing more worthy of his majesty and splendour than taking pity on souls who seek him and who, mistrustful of themselves and all their actions, hope for everything from his goodness. But what does it matter to you whether it is his greatness or his mercy which is offended when one lacks trust, since you are displeasing him to an equal degree in both cases?

Nothing, my dear sister, occupies us more in this place than praying for the King and the Queen. We have always looked on that as our principal obligation, and there is none which we discharge more scrupulously. We shall continue to do so, and to respond as far as possible to the Queen's piety, by asking God to increase it more and more, and to give her as much holiness as he has given her glory and greatness.'

830503 MGR [? LE CAMUS or BELLEFONDS] 3 May 1683
BN 24123,f.67 orig.

He cannot change what he has already said to duc de [Mazarin] and his reasons remain the same. [cf. 82091]

*830508 RP ABBÉ [? CHÂTILLON, CLAUDE LE MAÎTRE] 8 May 1683
TC II/340

'I know the state of the abbey of N., my dear Father, and although I am full of wonder that so much has been accomplished there in so little time, I cannot help observing considerable faults and sins against principles. Frequent conferences, the private conversations sometimes permitted to the brethren, theological instruction, will all soon cause a weakening of regularity and discipline, and I cannot understand how the conduct of the religious who cannot observe abstinence can be useful, whatever other good qualities he may have. As for telling people now to pray, that seems to me contrary to the Rule, which allows great freedom on that matter and requires us to act according to the way we feel the spirit of God moves us. In short, everyone has his ways of doing things, and blessed is he who has no other ways than those which God has given; to him alone it falls to prescribe the means and rules by which he wishes us to serve him.

If we had not lost religious through death, we should now have more than sixty, and we should even perhaps still have them if we had relaxed things more than we did and diminished the austerities of our life. In fact they are fortunate in having run their race in strict penitence, and every time I feel inclined to pity them and wish that they had not left us so soon, I resist it as a temptation. God committed them into our hands only so that we should give them back into his. They have consummated their sacrifices, and everything makes us believe that he has received them with pleasure as agreeable offerings. What more can we wish for them? In a word I envy their lot, and would much rather be in their place than in that in which I am.'

This letter is almost certainly to the Abbot of Châtillon, with whom R. had previously discussed life in other houses. The abbey referred to is almost certainly Orval, where reform was now fully under way, but where R. had earlier worried about the points here mentioned.

830513 [JEAN FAVIER] 13 May 1683
A 2106,f.110 vo.

Correspondence had lapsed for some time; both are in poor health and awaiting death.

830530 RM [ÉMÉLIE DE BOUILLON] 30 May 1683
TC I/110

Condolences on the death of Mlle de Bouillon.

Louise-Charlotte, sister of the two Carmelites and Cardinal de Bouillon, died on 26 April.

830530a CLAUDE NICAISE 30 May 1683
BN 9363,f.10 orig.; Gonod 59

Bossuet insisted on publication of *Sainteté* despite R's opposition. Health prevented him attending General Chapter [and thus seeing Nicaise in Dijon nearby].

830530b [JEAN FAVIER] 30 May 168[3]
A 2106,f.97 (with the impossible date 1681)

Justifies publication of *Sainteté*. True that he warns his monks against following current, and generally corrupt, monastic practice. Defends his singularity as fidelity to the true rule.

830609   RP, CHANOINE RÉGULIER   9 June 1683
TC I/119
He must examine himself carefully before accepting charge of souls.

830609a   MARQUISE   9 June 1683
TC I/29
She must not be surprised if her recent trials have upset her normal relations with God.

*830613   BISHOP OF LUÇON [HENRI BARILLON]   13 June 1683
TB/I 177; F. f.609 (wrongly dated 1673)
'It is true, Mgr, that we have had no news of you for a long time and I assure you that I should often have sought news were I not prevented by the respect I have for your occupations. I know that you do not have a moment to spare, that your love for the things you ought to love multiplies your duties and that time seems short to you when you think of the greatness and extent of your ministry. You remind me of a prelate of whom I cannot think without grief, who would say without shame or scruple as he went off to his diocese: 'Oh how bored I am going to be!' How pitiful is a man who finds himself in such a state of blindness without recognising it, and how deserving one is before men as before God when one sets oneself the aim above all of fulfilling one's obligations. It is true that these are countless, and that strictly speaking they grow in proportion to one's application to them. Never tire of working, and God will not tire of looking upon your solicitude with the eyes of compassion. Nothing more effectively elicits and influences his goodness than our perseverance, and his hands are always open upon the fidelity of those who serve him. How could you not complain, Mgr, of the distractions that come upon you in your activities, when the holy apostle himself groaned at those he found in exercising his apostolate, and confesses that he did not do all the good he wished to do? Men are men and not angels. Their strength has limits, and none has ever been seen sufficiently master of his mind and imagination to admit and retain there only those thoughts which he wished to have. Ideas about the business with which one is dealing keep coming back with importunity, and God wishes it to be so, so that we should bear and feel the full weight of our feebleness, and have reason continually to ask of him protection and strength. Please believe that you are always present in my mind, that all your interests affect me keenly and that it is not possible to add to the affection and respect with which I am yours' etc.

830614   RELIGIEUSE   14 June 1683
TC I/24
She abandoned God early on, but when she found him again did not have the fidelity to retain him. She must try to regain grace.

830627   RP ABBÉ, L'ETOILE [BERNARD DU TEILLÉ]   27 June 1683
BN 23497,orig.; Gonod 206
Sorry and surprised that book [Sainteté] arrived so late. Most people approve, except for a few monks.

830707   MARQUISE D'ALÈGRE   7 July 1683
TC I/177a
'The person who is worried about her state left through her own fault.' She must make up for her inconstancy.

Marie-Thérèse, Queen of France, dies.   **30 July 1683**

830805   RP ABBÉ   5 August 1683
TC II/301
R. more in need of urging to do his duty than of moderating supposed excesses of rigour. Openness essential in novices. 'A bad sign in a novice is to be secretive.' Monks travelling together ought to observe silence, but not if they are with seculars. A monk must always use two hands for drinking, and thus be seen to be different. If meat is given to a sick monk it should be in secret, so as not to offend the weak. RP knows all this as well as R.

830812   RM, MAUBUISSON   12 August 1683
TC II/303
She should not worry if she is not always of even temperament in her solitude.

*830817   BISHOP OF LUÇON [HENRI BARILLON]   17 August 16[8]3
P f.611 [wrongly dated 1673]
'I think, Mgr, that you will now have received the second edition of the book *De la Sainteté et des Devoirs monastiques*. You will see some additions, but they are only following up original questions. I have explained how advice became precepts for religious, I have strengthened the discussion on parents with some reflections which seem quite decisive. You will also find some additions to the sections on prayer, on charity, on death and manual labour, but there are no new principles in all that. If the work displeased some people, very many gave their approval to it, and my consolation is to know that it has borne fruit in many religious communities. I do not know whether you know that the General of the Carthusians has made it forbidden reading throughout his order.

I will not ask your news, Mgr, for I am sure you are following your usual ways and are one of those of whom it is said *ibunt de virtute in virtutem* [Ps 83:8]. Your life is one of continual progress, and you will not stop going forward until God's work is complete and you have carried out all his orders with complete fidelity. As that is what you have before your eyes alone, as in the depth of your heart, you can hardly not work at it successfully and your efforts can hardly fail to be favoured. I hope that God will give you the grace to persevere, whatever pain and difficulty you may encounter in the course of your ministry, and that at the last the master will crown the care and vigilance of his servant.

I do not doubt, Mgr, that the conversion of the two [Protestant] ministers in Angers has thrown the whole consistory into alarm and confusion. Please God that that is not the only effect, and that such an extraordinary example and its sequel produces the impression we should expect. Men are sometimes beyond converting, and are so impenetrably hard that they can be seen resisting the most urgent considerations and motives in the world. Basically it is no good speaking to them and announcing the truth to them, by deeds as by words; unless God takes a hand and sees to it that he is heard all efforts are in vain and, strive as one may, one sees anything but the effect intended. I ask of you, Mgr, to continue your accustomed kindness, which is one of the chief consolations of my life. I am sure that you will not doubt that, if you are convinced as I believe you are that no one could with more sincerity, gratitude and respect be yours' etc.

Dom Innocent Le Masson, General of the Carthusians, had for some time viewed R's activities with disapproval, and when a Paris Carthusian asked permission to go to la T. as a result of reading Sainteté *this was the last straw, hence the prohibition mentioned. The ministers, David Gilly and David Courdil, abjured publicly on 2 June 1683 and caused a major scandal among the Protestants.*

830826   CLAUDE NICAISE   26 August 1683
BN 9363,f.12 orig.; Gonod 60

Not surprised at reception of *Sainteté* in Rome. The regulars were bound to be hostile. Dom Maréchal left after three or four days and does not want to stay at la T.

830829   MONSIEUR VAILLANT, docteur de sorbonne   29 August 1683
TC I/103

A religious has discharged his obligation to his parents if he leaves them an annuity. If officials were trustworthy money could be left for schools or helping indigent girls to marry, but it is too risky. Also difficult to endow lectures on Peter Lombard. R. personally recommends leaving it to houses for female converts (Nouvelles Catholiques).

830830 PRINCESSE   30 August 1683
TC I/84

On her recent loss. She says she wants to give up everything but cannot break off obligations to the world.

The loss is probably that of the Queen, and the letter may well be to Mme de Guise.

830830a CHANOINE, GRAND PÉNITENCIER [DU SUEL]   30 August 1683
TC II/119

M's views have not changed, he still seeks peace far from the world's tumult. R. would be happy to receive him.

Du Suel, at Arras, is the only correspondent of R. known to have occupied the functions of the addressee, hence the identification.

830902 RM [DE LA ROCHE]   2 September 1683
A 2106,f.110; TC I/9

She should regard temptations as a test of humility; God will not abandon her, and has always been with her. Death should not frighten her. Recommends *Sainteté*.

830908 MADAME   8 September 1683
TC II/120

She is lucky to be bored by the world and return home weary. She would be more at ease alone, but that is not possible. Bring up her daughter in a Christian way, but no Latin; 'you would be giving her the wrong sort of spirit and making her into something unusual'.

830909 MARQUISE D'ALÈGRE   9 September 1683
TC I/137, TC II/39 (partial)

Denies using fictions or lies to humiliate his monks. There is no need, as there are always genuine occasions for correction.

830914 DUCHESSE DE GUISE   14 September 1683
BN na 12960, p. 27

He is sleeping rather better. Sends six wooden crosses.

*830914a [RM MARIE-LOUISE BOUTHILLIER]   14 September 1683
TC II/330

'You are quite right, my dear sister, to spend some time every year in retreat making up for whatever may have escaped your attention and fidelity, for it is very difficult, whatever one does, to observe in one's conduct all the justice one owes to God and oneself, as well as those with whom one is obliged to live. The subject of your conversation while you are thus in retreat should be taken from your calling and its obligations. That is the law of God which you should meditate on day and night. Think of the perfection for which he destines you, of the means he gives you for attaining it, of the happiness one enjoys already in this world if one serves him faithfully, and on the contrary of the troubles and anxieties to which one is exposed if one does not serve him as strictly as one should. Apply yourself to the things which most affect you and you will find more opportunities for meditation. The spirit that prays must be free and exempt from all constraint and turned to whatever pleases it most, so long as that is within the limits of its profession.

I see that Monsieur Pinette has talked to you about a plan which I regard as purely fanciful; we are no longer living in a time when God does such things, they are the works of past centuries and our own is not worthy. Everyone must love the place he is in, do God's will there and sanctify himself. Fr de La Grange is taking a long time to make up his mind. If he throws himself on to God's hands he should believe that he will not abandon him. God desires confidence in what he inspires, and promptness in execution once his voice has been heard.

My sister always wants to come and see us without ever coming. The main thing is that we should behave so that all of us find ourselves in God's eternity, to see each other and never be separated. Pray God for me, my dear sister, and believe that I feel for you all the affection that God demands of me and that I owe you. Assure RM Sub-Prioress of how grateful I am that she was kind enough to remember me. I commend myself to her prayers.'

Charles La Grange was a canon at Saint-Victor who became sub-prior, and was from 1683–88 superior (director) of Port-Royal. R. wrote to him in 1688, and he is known to have been a man of strict piety and, incidentally, a painter. The sister who never comes is Mme d'Albon.

830921   RM LOUISE-HENRIETTE D'ALBON   21 September 1683
A 2106,f.116 (10 pages)

She complains of a lack of fervour common to many religious. The only remedy is total submission to God's will. Advice on correcting particular passions. Concludes: religious must be completely attached to God; God's goodness is inexhaustible.

830922   RM   22 September 1683
TC II/202

Her desire to serve God more strictly praiseworthy provided she stays within her rule. Corporal mortification needs superior's permission, but spiritual does not.

18   The Letters of Armand-Jean de Rancé   830922a

830922a   [RM LOUISE ROGIER]   22 September 1683
A 2106,f.120 vo.

R's insomnia is now over, but not his fever. Not surprised at her reappointment. Asks her to help other religious to whom he has written a long letter on temptation. [830902].

She had once more in June been elected superior and was to hold office until 1689.

831008   DOM JEAN-FRANÇOIS CORNUTY, TAMIÉ   8 October 1683
MS *Chronique de Tamié*; Burnier, *Hist. de Tamié*, 9

Pleased at his news. Warns him against conduct harmful to his health.

831009   COMTESSE DE [...]   9 October 1683
TC I/51

Sorry for her in her trials.

830909a   MADAME   9 October 1683
TC I/79

Sympathies; her son has changed and wants to give up his clerical state.

831019   MADAME   19 October 1683
TC II/254

She is uncertain whether to break with the world and spend the rest of her life in retreat. She should break.

831022   MONSIEUR   22 October 1683
TC I/73

Advises person in question to change director.

*831024   MARÉCHAL DE BELLEFONDS   24 October 1683
BN na 12959 f.103, orig.; TC I/47

'If we do not often have the consolation of seeing you, Mgr, I may say that you are none the less very present to us, and no day goes by without our offering you to God with particular fervour. It is enough for me to know that you are in the world, that is, surrounded by perils, for though, knowing them as you do, you are not exposed to surprise attacks, you are exposed all the same to assaults. Often the evils we have foreseen still befall us. I do not doubt that you practise all the diligence necessary to prevent the world impressing you as it always does those who are not on their guard and behave as if they had nothing to fear.

The peace which you tell me you enjoy is the result of your detachment. If you were to give the smallest place in your heart to things which should not be there it would be filled with agitation and trouble. You know that disorderly affections cause sickness in the soul, as bad humours do in the body; that the former attack piety as the latter do health, and unless we keep our souls completely pure they fall inevitably into bitterness and languor. That is a truth that you have known from your own experience, in the very contrasting situations in which you have seen yourself in the world. I am sure that when you compare what has taken place in you since you have been in God's order and sight with what you felt when you were in the world like the rest of men, you perceive a difference that consoles you and makes you put your finger on the fact that there is no true peace and happiness but that of being in his hand, studying his will and following it. These are the ways in which his servants must walk, otherwise one could not take a step without running into traps and precipices.

What lessons, Mgr, God has been pleased to give men in the past few months in such an extraordinary sequence of events! We have seen a conspiracy against a powerful king, a great queen snatched away in a moment, at the height of her glory and in the midst of her course, an invasion of Catholic countries; all of Christendom menaced by a countless multitude of barbarians; an emperor shamefully chased out of the imperial capital. Could anything give more cause to despise the greatness and prosperity of the world, and can one attach the slightest importance to them, whatever distinction they may have, when one sees them in their true light, that is, from the angle of their fragility and inconstancy? Moses was quite right to prefer the ignominy of Christ to all the riches of Egypt, and to prefer being afflicted with God's people to enjoying a deceptive satisfaction and passing pleasure. Expectation, or rather the presence, of future rewards took from him any feeling for all the advantages and fortunes of this life. Eternity so filled him that he saw nothing worthy of him in time, nor anything to which he could respond. That is what faith does, when it is alive and animated. It brings closer evil and good things, however far they may be, whereas those in whom it is dead and languishing regard them as though they were never to happen.

It is long since, as it seems to me, that God gave you the desire and will to serve him on such occasions as have presented themselves in this campaign, and I do not doubt that it was a real joy for you to be there in support of religion and defense of the faith. God, from whom you received such feelings, will reward them. He lays to our account whatever he sees in us is real and effective, even though it does not turn out as we wanted. It is enough that you waited for God, as you say, in inactivity and silence, and held yourself ready to render him prompt and faithful obedience whenever he might let you know what he wanted from you. There is no better or more effective way of speaking to him than by the preparation of our hearts. Thus the man who is always ready and awaits the ways of providence with the sincere intention of doing whatever and going wherever God may appear to wish must not imagine that he is useless, since without that, whatever he has or does, nothing is of service or use to him.

You have much cause to praise God for the state in which your family is. Your diligence, your example and above all your prayers will obtain from God an increase in the good he has done there. You are so perfectly aware of your obligations that you do not fail to regard as the chief of them that of keeping in dependence on God those whom he has made dependent on you, and of devoting all your care to seeing that he is served by those over whom he has given you authority, and if this is not entirely as successful as you might wish, at least it is certain that some profit comes of it. In any case you will have the consolation of having forgotten nothing of what God has commanded you for the salvation of others, as for your personal sanctification. Even if you did nothing but strengthen and heighten your daughters' piety, and establishing Christ's rule in them, your efforts would be rewarded and God would have granted you much grace in using you as an intermediary for so great a work.

God must have given you great help for you to have kept a taste for retreat and prayer, and preserve you from the dissipation which is almost inevitable in the contacts, affairs, and business in which the necessities of your rank involve you. That is a pure efffect of his goodness, and if he had left you to yourself your firmest and holiest resolutions would have escaped you fifty times a day. Man moves and bends like a reed. He changes for the sake of changing, makes plans and gives them up for no reason after making them, often small difficulties prevent him from carrying out important decisions, and God alone can fix his moving and uncertain nature. That, Mgr, is something he wishes you to acknowledge and live with, and nothing is more likely to attract his mercy upon you than to abase yourself in his eyes, confess your impotence and constantly judge yourself with rigour. We shall continue to recommend to him your person, your house, and all that concerns you. We have long regarded that as one of our chief obligations. I beg you not to doubt that, and to be persuaded that nowhere in the world are you more honoured and respected than here.

PS I am deeply obliged to you for your kindness in bearing in mind the request I made on behalf of the marquis de Tourouvre's son.'

The Rye House plot against Charles II of England was discovered in June, Marie-Thérèse, Queen of France, died on 30 July, Austria and Poland were at war with Turkey, and Vienna was besieged by the Turks (14 July–12 September), obliging the Emperor to flee.

R. and his contemporaries saw nothing anachronistic in such juxtapositions as 'Moses ... the ignominy of Christ'. For them, the patriarchs and prophets of the Old Testament who proclaimed and believed in the coming of Christ thereby subscribed to the essential Christian truths as they were to be revealed in the New Testament.

831030   RM ABBESSE, DE LA COMMUNE OBSERVANCE   30 October 1683
TC I/50

Despite the mitigated observance she can still lead a proper life if she follows *In Suprema*.

831030a   RM ABBESSE   30 October 1683
TC I/46, TC I/138

She must not complain of imperfections of her community; she is on right path.

831102   [RM DE LA ROCHE]   2 November 1683
A 2106,f.121 vo.

She is still distressed and afflicted by tribulation and temptation, but must accept God's will in everything, accustom herself to the idea of death and trust in God's mercy. In accepting novices, only those with true vocations must be received.

831112   [RM MARIE-LOUISE BOUTHILLIER]   12 November 1683
TC I/37

'I see from your letter, my dear sister, how you have spent your retreat. One is bound to agree that it was in a most holy manner, and that you applied yourself during that time to those things which might be most useful to you in your profession. The main thing is to be faithful in carrying out your resolutions, for God's grace in letting you go into all the considerations which you indicate was a pure result of his mercy and you must not doubt that he will call you to account for it and that you are obliged to follow and profit from its impulses.

The most important quality for you, and the one to which you should be most attached, as being that on which your peace of mind depends, is that simplicity of heart, that indifference, which you have set yourself, in the face of all unpleasant and troubling events, that charity and mildness in enduring the faults and imperfections of your neighbour, so that far from being hurt or impatient at the real evils to be found in their conduct, you sympathise, are sorry for them, and never fail to give a favourable explanation to them by justifying their intentions, if the action itself cannot be justified. If you act like that, my dear sister, you will enjoy perfect serenity, nothing will trouble you as your life goes on, and God, who takes pleasure in communicating with patient, simple, and charitable souls, will give you in abundance the protection you need. He is faithful in his promises, his eyes are always open on those who study his will, and take it for their rule, and the surest way to walk in his ways with perseverance is to be constant in carrying out the promises you have made to him.

Nothing earns his support more than our gratitude, and all the signs of it that we give him are false if we do not make them consist in our fidelity and our works. The views and opinions you formed during your retreat come from him, they are impressions of his holy spirit, and you would be lacking in gratitude if you did not work, my dear sister, at making them effective. As he was good enough to speak to you during that withdrawal, he wants you to respond, not by words but by deeds.

The difficulty you experience in your confessions is nothing unusual for people who live under strict rules. If your conscience does not reproach you, and if you see nothing with regard to God or your sisters, or even those with whom you have some contact, in case that has occurred, do not on that account believe yourself innocent, nor imagine that your life is as pure as it should be. Humble yourself before God, pray him to lighten your darkness, and not to allow you for want of light to fail to tread the path he wants you to tread. Confess your general unworthiness if there is nothing particular for which you can criticise yourself. It is hard, however, if you examine yourself carefully, for you not to find subject for self-accusation, for in even the best actions there is always some detail open to criticism. In a word, never rest on your innocence, but on the compassion of God, who has pity on souls which wish to serve him and who always, if the preparation is genuine, forgives what may elude their weakness and infirmity. He is a strict judge, but for souls who are not strict; for those who are and take care to ask him to increase their strictness, he covers, or rather forgives, their faults, their imperfections, and even the offences which they are unable to avoid.

Do not heed all the fears which trouble you. If you have not been as faithful as you should have been in the past, if your illness has been an obstacle to doing your duties on many occasions, if in that you have sinned through negligence or even infirmity, so long as you return to God in sincere conversion, he will forget every cause you have given him for complaint, he will consider above all the grace he gave you to change your ways and adopt others quite contrary to those in which you have lived, and if your offences have produced in you marks as ineffaceable as scarlet dye, he will make you cleaner and whiter than snow. God looks on souls which are truly penitent with as much approval as those which have preserved their innocence, and as he has often given them greater signs of his affection and love, so they have more reason than others to hope that he will not subsequently refuse them the protection that he has given them or withdraw the hand he stretched out to them. Thus, my dear sister, whatever may have caused you to be less faithful than you should have been, you must still expect and hope for everything from God's goodness, since, according to his word, the hope of those who profess to be his and to serve him will never be confounded. Pay no attention to your scruples, do not let your feeling of your own unworthiness throw you into dejection. Our bad opinion of ourselves is useful inasmuch as it stiumulates and drives us to become better, but when it casts us down and discourages us, it must be regarded as a temptation and not be listened to. Humility is false when it makes us fearful, since it throws us into a dangerous state of mind, whereas when it is genuine it increases our piety and our virtue.

I am very sorry about the accident that happened to you, and I am sure that you did not fail to make good use of it. We must, as you know, use good and evil things alike, and accept each from God's hand with perfect resignation. Farewell, my dear sister, pray God for me and believe me wholly yours etc.

Please convey my respects to the Reverend Mother.'

831116   MARQUISE D'ALÈGRE   16 November 1683
TC II/317

Recent death of Mme X a great surprise, but reminded him of inconstancy of worldly things. She must remain attached to God amid all her other obligations.

831117   RM ABBESSE, DE LA COMMUNE OBSERVANCE   17 November 1683
TC I/87

Praises her resolve to see that God is served as he should be. She should quietly go over to stricter practices. Gives eight general rules for conduct of her house. Condemns admissions for money, 'the ruin of cloisters', and she must forget the rank conferred on her by birth.

The address adds 'newly elected' and a likely candidate would therefore be Marie-Madeleine d'Albert, elected abbess of Abbaye-aux-Bois, Paris, in 1684 after many years as coadjutrix.

*831203   BISHOP OF LUÇON [HENRI BARILLON]   3 December 16[8]3
P f.613 (wrongly dated 1673)

'I am very sorry, Mgr, about the indisposition which you tell me has attacked you, because in view of its nature it is not likely to pass away entirely and will affect you again from time to time. That will oblige you to keep certain rules, and accept certain restrictions to prevent the attacks being so violent and frequent. Life is full of unpleasant events and God has not failed to sow bitter things there so that we should have good reason not to love it. As you are already completely detached for the highest reasons, this event will do no more than test your virtue and patience. We shall however ask him to deliver you so that nothing hinders you in the course of your functions and exercise of your ministry.

It is true that the [Archbishop] of P[aris] told someone who came to see me that the passage you indicate had caused objections, and the Sorbonne was said to have condemned similar propositions. I wrote to him about it and told him that there were those who were determined at any price to find objectionable matter in the book, but that I was convinced that it was irreproachable both as regards faith and morals, that the Sorbonne had only condemned those who maintained that inspirations should be followed as if they were certain rules and precepts, but that I had said nothing of the kind, and that I had spoken only of a certain and recognised vocation, and in that had said nothing but what the saints had taught me. That is as far as it went, and there have been no further consequences. It occurred, nevertheless, that someone proposed in his conferences, without mentioning the book, the question of whether advice could become precept. Some say yes, others no, but no one regards the book's views as something open to condemnation. If there is a third edition soon, as the publisher thinks, there will be a big question about this matter which will remove all difficulties and show that piety tolerates no other opinion than that.

The Carthusians are still complaining and cannot swallow the discussion of their ancient constitutions. They claim that they have never considered them as statutes. I would much rather let them say what they like than have a personal dispute with them, by trying to prove that Guigues' Constitutions [1127] had all possible authority in their order. You will certainly have found many mistakes in the second edition which were not in the first. That comes from the printer wanting to make his own corrections. I pray God, Mgr, to keep you for many years to come for the good of the Church and the consolation of those whom you honour with your friendship. I do not think I deceive myself in thinking that there are hardly any for whom you have more than for me. That is a good fortune that I appreciate more than I can say. I beg you to believe me, and that no one could be with more affection and respect yours' etc.

This was the beginning of the renal colic from which Barillon eventually died. The Carthusians were (and are) justly proud of the fact that their order has never had to be reformed, and took great exception to R's opinion that the original holy austerity of Guigues' compilation had become mitigated in the course of time. Although Bruno of Cologne founded the Carthusian Order (1084) it was Guiges I (or Guigo), the fifth prior of the Grand Chartreuse, who promulgated their first Constitutions *in 1127 (PL 153:635ff).*

831206   NICOLAS PINETTE   6 December [1683]
TC I/150

RP Eloi had vowed to come to la T. when ill, and must not now, when recovered, break his vow.

The Premonstratensian Eloi le Mosle was professed as dom Bernard on 22 January 1685, causing vigorous protests from the Premonstratensian authorities. (He died in 1690).

831207   RP ABBÉ   7 December 1683
TC I/88

Religious may use only ordinary remedies, meat is not necessary for the sick. Doctor may be called if one is near. All necessary reading is supplied by Bible and Fathers, with such pastoral works as those of the Bps of Grenoble and Luçon.

831209 CLAUDE NICAISE   9 December 1683
BN 9363,f.14 orig.; Gonod 61

Discusses *Sainteté*, a MS of Ambrose to be published by Mabillon, and Santeuil's hymns.

831210 [? RM LOUISE ROGIER]   10 December 1683
A 2106,f.123; M 1214,100 (only 2 final pages, dated 3 September 1671)

Too much fear is as bad as too much presumption, and he does not share her poor opinion of herself. Religion is mere hypocrisy if based only on externals. Ends with reference to his niece's regret for bad behaviour.

The bad behaviour took place in 1671, and it looks as though a page of the earlier letter was copied in error on to the end of this, eight-page, letter on a quite different subject.

*831226 RM MARIE-LOUISE [BOUTHILLIER]   26 December 1683
TA orig.; TC II/100 (dated 13 December)

'To be brief, my dearest sister, let me say that you should sustain yourself as you see and remember your past faults by trusting entirely in God's mercy, and I repeat that all the more readily for seeing you sincerely wishing to be a better and more faithful person than you have been so far. Strive for that with every means in your power. Stir up your piety, and God will not fail to guide all your ways and give you his hand to raise you to the state of perfection to which he has destined you. You would not be as anxious to please him as you are if you were not inspired by his goodness, and you must believe that he did not grant you such a desire only to withdraw it, so long as you are resolved to use it properly.

The way your confessor has told you to go about your confessions is very good. It is little use accusing oneself so frequently of faults committed daily, either because one does not take enough care to avoid them, or because they escape our weakness through almost inevitable necessity, and that is why our confessions, for want of proper preparation, so often do us more harm than good. It would be of more use to you, my dearest sister, to lament before God your daily lapses, to work sincerely to correct yourself, to force yourself to succeed in that, and yet, although they are not absolutely matters to be confessed, it is appropriate that when you feel most keenly affected by your miseries, and so far distant from the purity in which your profession and God's design obliges you to live, that you should approach the penitential seat of judgement. It may well happen, that in favourable circumstances and state of mind, you obtain through absolution effective remedies against your ills. You must convince yourself that faults, however small, must not be neglected, and that if they do not at first cause deep wounds they still have harmful effects, if one does not take the care one should in purifying oneself from them. Nothing is small when it comes to faults and imperfections in souls from which God demands perfect things. Think often, my dear sister, of the bond you have contracted with Christ and your obligation to make yourself worthy of it. I pray him every day to give you the grace for that. Pray him too for me, I beseech you, and ask him to make me more faithful than I am in practising what I have the temerity to say and teach to others.'

831230   MONSIEUR, ECCLÉSIASTIQUE   30 December 1683
TC I/132

He must not change his profession. Having once refused promotion he dares to criticise persons far beyond him.

*831231   BISHOP OF LUÇON [HENRI BARILLON]   31 December 16[8]3
P f.616 (wrongly dated 1673)

'Allow me, Mgr, as I wish you at the start of this new year all the grace you may need to spend it in conformity with the holiness of the calling in which you find yourself engaged by the orders of divine providence, to ask for your blessing, that it may obtain for me from the mercy of Christ the help I need to discharge the duties of my profession more faithfully than I have done up to now. The winter of my life is approaching, I will soon be reaching the end of my course, and I have so far done anything but prepare myself for the exact account I shall have to give to God of all my obligations. I cannot think without grief, knowing as I do the size and extent of those obligations, how little I have bothered to meet them, and all I see in my works, when I look at them closely, are voids which fill me with dread and confusion. I have told others what I should be the first to practise, and I am sure that if I had been as I should have been, my example would have more force and success than my words. Pray God, Mgr, to give me enough fidelity to make up for the almost infinite number of faults and sins of negligence that have escaped my attention, so that I may finish my career in a spiritual state more worthy of him and me, and different from that in which I have lived. I sincerely declare my feelings to you, knowing how kindly an interest you take in what concerns me.

For the rest, Mgr, I must tell you that they are writing against the book on monastic life. The man who has become involved in this is the curé of Champrond, of whom you must certainly have heard. This man, who had approved of it at the beginning, and said that if ever it were attacked he would come to its defence, took it into his head with inconceivable eccentricity to make what he claims to be an exact criticism of it. I do not think that he will do much harm. All the truths contained in the book are so firm and established that, as it seems to me, they need not fear censure. We must wait in peace to know what he intends to say, and whether his reflections will deserve a reply, we must hope that God will give us the enlightenment necessary. It was hardly likely that a book full of principles so contrary to present usage and custom would fail to attract opposition, and that men who naturally enjoy dispute would remain silent. Favour me always with your friendship, Mgr, and believe that no one in the world could be more devotedly, faithfully and respectfully than I yours etc.

PS I forgot to say, Mgr, that those who are trying to discredit the book are the Jansenists. They are not doing so openly, but in secret are attacking it as much as they can. Monsieur Nicole finds that what I said of customs in the chapter on mitigations cannot be maintained, although I only spoke of them like St Thomas.'

The curé of Champrond (dioc. Chartres) was the firebrand J-B. Thiers, whose support did almost as much harm as his hostility. In the event his defence was not published until much later, in a different context. Ch. XXIII on Mitigations was the concluding one. The Jansenists, in fact, including Arnauld, on the whole approved of the book for its defence of asceticism.

84/1   RP ABBÉ, ORVAL [CHARLES DE BENZERADT]   [? 1684]
TC II/3

R. advises against Orval undertaking reform of a monastery in the Low Countries. Abstinence so essential a part of Cistercian rule that reform is impossible without it. Orval is making real progress, but R. thinks there should be fewer occasions for breaking silence.

84/2   RM   [? 1684]
TC II/12

She did well to put away her 'curious books' and should read in their place the ascetic works of St Basil and John Climacus.

This looks very much like the same discussion as in 840206.

840100   RP PIERRE DE MONCHY, CONG. ORAT.   January 1684
TC II/300

Monchy's reaction to illness worthy of a Christian and a priest. God has so often supported him that he will not now withhold help that is so necessary.

840115   RELIGIEUSE   15 January 1684
A 2106,f.127

Submit wholly to God's will even in affliction.

840124 ACHILLE DE HARLAY   24 January 1684
BN 17419,f.10 orig.
R. is grateful.

840124a CLAUDE NICAISE   24 January 1684
BN 9363,f.15 orig.; Gonod 62
Nicaise has recommended R. to Mgr Sluze. R. wants to keep silent in face of attacks on *Sainteté*

840201 MONSIEUR, ECCLÉSIASTIQUE   1 February 1684
TC II/284
R. wishes it were God's will that M should see him at la T. but health and advanced age are against it. R. has taken ailing men, but only when they have 'holy dispositions'.

840206 RELIGIEUSE [? DE LA VISITATION]   6 February 1684
TC I/125, TC II/101
She must trust in God's mercy. Her order does not practise physical austerity or mortification, but spiritual. Glad she has resisted the temptation of reading, there is nothing more dangerous.

840210 MADEMOISELLE DE [. . .]   10 February 1684
TC I/126
After a life of vanity she is ready to leave the world. Make a general confession, read the Bible, but never try to become learned about religion. Urges her to withdraw to Gif without delay; the abbess 'is full of zeal, piety and wisdom'.

Cf 830401. The abbess was still Anne de Montglat.

840210a DUCHESSE DE GUISE   10 February 1684
TC II/107
Sure that her surroundings do not impair God's work in her.

840212 RELIGIEUSE   12 February 1684
A 2106,f.128 vo.
Glad that she accepts her sufferings patiently.

*840214 [RM ? THÉRÈSE BOUTHILLIER]   14 February 1684
TD/A

'I received two of your letters at the same time, my dearest sister, and in one of them you tell me that you have lost three of your sisters and that the thought of death troubles you. Yet the way they died, as you write about it, should console you, and give you cause, as it seems to me, for hoping for similar mercy from God. What we must do, as you know, is to make ourselves worthy of it by a holy life, and forget nothing which we believe might obtain for us powerful protection from God in time of need; one must sow before one can reap the harvest; the crop implies previous care and preparation, and it would be in vain that we should expect from God's goodness grace to finish well a life illspent. That means, my dear sister, that we must by our works, our fidelity, and our strictness in following God's orders and doing his will, dispose ourselves for that journey which is so terrible in itself, and which none the less is regarded by souls which have loved God and been attached to his service as a time of joy, happiness, and blessings. To that end you have a most powerful means, which can even be called infallible, in the practice of our rule, since he who gave it to us, who is as far as we are concerned the interpreter of God's designs, tells us that if we observe strictly and piously what it prescribes, Christ's kingdom will be our reward and our lot. If there is anything capable of giving us confidence and stirring up our zeal and fervour, it is so advantageous a promise. It is up to us to exploit it, and to ensure, by all our conduct, that God should find nothing in us to prevent him fulfilling it and bringing it into effect. You say that you fear death. That is a natural, and almost ordinary, feeling in all men, and it should not trouble you or cause you anxiety. On the contrary the sight of God's goodness should console you. You should be convinced that all who love him have nothing to fear, but everything to hope, and that should give you complete peace of mind. The Holy Spirit assures us that those who keep the law enjoy profound peace, and cannot be troubled. I think, my dear sister, that you belong to that number, and that your chief care is to live so as never to be separated from it. We shall pray Our Lord to give you that grace; ask him for the same mercy for me and serve him so faithfully that we make him judge us in his clemency. I do not need to tell you how affectionately I am yours' etc.

The copy assigns this to Marie-Louise, but the reference to 'our rule' seems rather to suggest a fellow Cistercian; moreover between 1682 and 1685 there was only one death at the Annonciades. If it is Thérèse to whom R. is writing here, this must be the last letter she had from him, because she died before 16 February 1684, and may well never have received this.

*840216   RM MARIE-LOUISE [BOUTHILLIER]   16 February 1684
TC II/226

'I praise God, my dear sister, for maintaining you in the spirit he gave you to think only of him and have no other desire save to please him. I do not doubt that the holy season which we are entering will give you fresh ardour for his service, and that you will find yourself, as it were, kindled with a new fire. Once God has lit it, and seen that we take care to tend it, using to that end the means and grace he gives us, he not only keeps it alive, but increases it, for he never tires of pouring his gifts upon faithful souls and heaping every kind of good on them if they show him the gratitude they should. Those who strip and impoverish themselves for love of God barely notice their nakedness and poverty, because, as he never fails to fill them in proportion to their self-denial and sacrifice, their poverty is true plenty. Thus those who serve God are never so rich as when they are least so.

I do not doubt that my sister's death has deeply moved you and prompted many reflections. The most useful of all is that which will really persuade you that there is nothing stable here on earth, no moment of our lives which may not be the last, and that one must be either without faith or without reason to have other thoughts and occupations in this life than preparing to leave it, by completely separating ourselves from anything of any kind whatever which might attach us to it. The soul of religious must be quite free, depending on nothing, always free to fly to God, and expecting the moment of dissolution as that of its happiness. Farewell, my dearest sister, pray Our Lord to have mercy on me. I am with all possible affection yours' etc.

The sister whose death is referred to can only be Thérèse, to whom R. almost certainly wrote two days earlier. There exists no record of her death apart from this, another letter of 23 March to Marie-Louise, and one of April, presumably to a nun at les Clairets. She was older than R., probably born in 1622 or 1623.

840220   SÉBASTIEN LE NAIN DE TILLEMONT   20 February 1684
TC II/42

Hopes his father will soon be cured.

840303   RELIGIEUSE   3 March 1684
TC II/325

Her letters bring R. little joy. He wants to see her enjoying the peace normal to her state.

840304   SÉBASTIEN LE NAIN DE TILLEMONT   4 March 1684
TC II/43

His father is cured. [This letter and 840220 are the same except for an addition to this second text].

*840311 MARÉCHAL DE BELLEFONDS   11 March 1684
BN na 12959,f.105, orig.; TC II/2

'I hope, Mgr, that divine providence, which engages you in an employment you have not sought, will give you all the grace you need so to conduct yourself that in rendering to the earthly King the service he expects from your fidelity you do not fail in that which you owe to the heavenly King. The strictness of your life so far and your diligence in preserving in the dissipation of the world the feelings of a sincere piety is a powerful reason in God's eyes for attracting to yourself his protection. There is no reason to suppose that he will refuse it to you at the time when it is most necessary.

You know so well the misfortunes to which your present state exposes you, and the traps which surround you on every side, that you will not fail to increase your vigilance and attention and consider all your ways with unusually close care, and above all to address yourself to him without whom you know that all our efforts are of no avail, and we cannot take a single step or initiative which will be of use to us. As God is everywhere we can make churches for ourselves everywhere, that is, there is no place in which we cannot offer him our prayers; that is a sacrifice we can make to him in any situation, on any occasion, and he often receives it with more pleasure and blessing when it is offered to him in the midst of the world and in tumult, because it can only be the result of pure faith, lively religion, and real effort to break free from so many reasons and different circumstances so apt to prevent us being occupied with him, so likely to separate us from him and displease us with him. You have known by your experience the advantage of attaching oneself to him, and how his presence is full of infinite good and advantages, but we must look at him if we want him to look at us, we must try not to lose him from sight so that we can say like the prophet, 'I have constantly had the Lord before my eyes, for I knew he was at my right hand to defend me and turn away all that might harm me, that is what gave me all my trust and my joy.' [Cf Ps 120]. Such a disposition causes him never to leave us, to be our light in the darkness, our support in the most slippery places and our strength in the temptations that come upon us. There is one temptation, Mgr, that you must fear, which is to act with regard to yourself and consider yourself in the main actions, in which you should conduct yourself only in God's order, as it is declared in that of the Prince; for that is a very subtle evil in which even those who have much virtue may be caught unawares, to mix one's own glory in with what one should do solely for his interests and service. That is to say, one must renounce all love of esteem and reputation in that one of life's occasions in which one is most tempted to acquire it. I confess, Mgr, that it is easier to win battles, capture towns, discipline armies, check the insolence of soldiers, and repress others' passions than to overcome and rule one's own, particularly the one which dies last and still lives when the others are extinguished; it grows and is born, as it were, in the bosom of virtue, and is most to be feared by those who are most virtuous.

We shall not fail to recommend you to Our Lord with all the fervour in our power. You know, Mgr, how dear your person is to us and how deeply we feel everything that concerns you. I am with all possible respect and fidelity, I beg you, Mgr, to believe, yours' etc.

Bellefonds had been brought back to command in Roussillon in the war between France and Spain which began at the end of 1683. The quotation (in French in the original) looks like a very free paraphrase of Ps 120.

840312   DUC DE MAZARIN   12 March 1684
TC II/262

Mazarin's situation quite intolerable in eyes of the world, but true justice is divine, not human. Sends Association.

Mazarin's estrangement from his wife, living in England, and his daughter's marriage made him an object of general ridicule.

*840323   RM MARIE-LOUISE [BOUTHILLIER]   23 March 1684
TC II/152

'I was sure, my dear sister, that my sister's death would affect you. Those who know and have often to think, like you and me, that everything here on earth is only inconstancy and uncertainty, should take events which happen in their truth and look at them in their source: I mean in God's order, who controls their slightest movement and detail. The chief thing is that we have cause to believe that God showed her mercy. As for you, my dear sister, strive to be firmer and more constant in your resolutions. What is the good of making any unless one is faithful to them, and what is the use of planning to lead a better life if one does not take care to control one's life and correct one's ways? It is equally forbidden to all Christians ever to say anything to anyone's disadvantage, unless obliged to do so by conscience, but it is even more forbidden to people like you who are no longer in the world, who should no longer speak its language, whose every deed and word should give edification and set an example, and from whom no word should escape that is not, as it were, seasoned with the salt of wisdom. Make sure that you are never wanting in this essential duty, that you do not anger God against you and give no cause for scandal to those who hear you.

Regarding the opinion you ask of me, I can tell you that there are certain goods which one may interrupt for reasons of charity, if such an interruption gives rise to greater goods. That can be done not only without sin, but even with merit. One must be careful not to extend that so that one does evil on the pretext that good will come of it, for evil is always forbidden. The point you put to me is of that kind. Your enclosure is so important and essential to your calling that there is no reason which could oblige you to relax it. That provides your ramparts against the frivolity and vanity of the world. I well recall that a Jesuit Father, who played a major part in the foundation of your order and was fully acquainted with its spirit, when consulted on a similar point, said that your enclosure was an essential obligation for you, and distinguished you from other observances. That is to say that you are attacking the very foundations of your calling if you depart from so holy a practice. And if you are ever obliged to speak your mind on this matter, simply say that you do not believe that God wants you to buy the good proposed at the expense of so important and considerable a duty and that your conscience dictates that you cannot aspire to a good, whatever it may be, by a way that is not good. Accompany that with a mildness and humility which will show that temperament and spirit of contradiction have nothing to do with the opinion and course you are taking. A servant of God must not be obstinate, but she must be firm and steadfast when it is a question of adhering to good and avoiding evil. Farewell, my dearest sister, pray God for me and believe me yours' etc.

R. is here repeating exactly what he said in 1669 [691218]. The Jesuit is Fr Zannoni. As always, falling recruitment was being adduced as an argument for mitigating the rule of enclosure, apparently still maintained after the last dispute.

840400   RM   April 1684
TC I/170

As her observance does not allow her strict practice of the rule, her inner dispositions are the most important. 'God does not demand the impossible.'

840400a   RM [LES CLAIRETS]   April 1684
TC II/342

God instructs us most by the loss of those 'united by bonds of intimate charity.... I hope that the kindness with which you honoured my sister in her lifetime will not be so limited to her that it will not extend to me.'

This, and the two letters to Marie-Louise, is the only known record of Thérèse's death.

840416   RELIGIEUSE   16 April 1684
TC II/199

See God's will in all things. Humiliation and mortification will help her to perfection.

840420   RELIGIEUSE DE LA VISITATION   20 April 1684
TC I/36

She has been ill. She must despise the world, curb her quick temper, refuse gifts from seculars, abolish parties and presents, follow St Chantal. She is right to occupy the lowest place. May see her mother on visits.

This may be RM de Harlay.

840430   MONSIEUR L'ABBÉ DE LA MADELEINE   30 April 1684
TC II/153

Sign of friendship that M. is so responsive to R's letters.

840512   RP ABBÉ, ORVAL [CHARLES DE BENZERADT]   12 May 1684
TC I/23 (date in Le Nain)

R. exhorts him to go on as he is. The Visitor and Abbot of Clairvaux have approved. Recalls abbot's visit and edification at la T. 'No one will ever be more completely submissive to the orders of my superiors... but I know that one must obey God rather than men.'

840519   DUCHESSE DE GUISE   19 May 1684
BN na 12960, p. 33

Thanks her for news.

840529   RELIGIEUSE DE LA VISITATION   29 May 1684
TC I/85

No one, not even female visitors, should be admitted to cloister. The nuns' retreat would be compromised if everyone were admitted who wanted seclusion.

840600   RM   June 1684
TC II/204

Avoid all offices, especially those involving the conduct of souls.

840605   MADEMOISELLE   5 June 1684
TC II/323

However much it may help her sister, she must not delay her retreat if she judges such delay prejudicial to her salvation. One must not think one is solely in charge, but consult confessor, otherwise self-love returns.

840605a MONSIEUR L'ABBÉ DE LA MADELEINE   5 June 1684
TC II/213

R. wishes his letters were strong enough to protect M's will against distractions of worldly contacts. All R's friends are dying and with his poor health he is preparing too.

840605b MADAME   5 June 1684
TC II/231

'Believe me that in devotion as in the world there are what are called good cabals to which one wishes sometimes to belong without thinking any ill.' Let her serve God without talking about it. 'We are willing for everything in us to die so long as self-love lives on, which is a miscalculation of irreparable consequences.'

840606 RM LOUISE-HENRIETTE D'ALBON   6 June 1684
A 2106,f.128

She should follow her director, approved by her superior, and not seek advice from too many people. R. is still opposed to her changing her house.

840615 RM ABBESSE   15 June 1684
TC I/163

She always asks after his health as if it mattered. 'A few months or a few years more or less are not worth considering.'

840622 RELIGIEUSE   22 June 1684
TC I/169

'The more you strive the further you will go.'

840628 RM LOUISE-HENRIETTE D'ALBON   28 June 1684
A 2106,f.129; TC I/154

Things now much easier for her but her submission to God's will must not change.

840629 MONSIEUR LE PRIEUR (CHANOINE RÉGULIER)   29 June 1684
TC I/49

P. wants to retire, R. dissuades him. He would find it hard to set up a house of Canons Regular with common vestiary [that is, without private property].

840706 RELIGIEUSE DE LA VISITATION 6 July 1684
TC I/80

Her superior was right: 'the royal road to heaven is humbleness of heart'. RM X should free herself more from external things and not involve herself with family.

840720 RELIGIEUSE 20 July 1684
TC II/275

Regrets her indisposition; even if the blow is sudden it will not be unexpected.

840720a RM DE LA VIERGE, RELIGIEUSE HOSPITALIÈRE, 20 July 1684
PLACE ROYALE, PARIS
TC II/113

She is in her present post not of her own volition but on the orders of her superior. Avoid too many concessions to weaknesses of sisters and warn superior if they are slack in observing rule.

840722 RP [? DOM ALAIN, MAUBUISSON] 22 July 1684
TC I/127

He is not the superior or even the confessor of the abbess, whom he must treat with great respect: 'she is someone who requires careful handling because of her birth, and she comes from a background where spirits are lofty and humours haughty'.

The Abbess of Maubuisson had been born Princess Palatine.

840802 CLAUDE NICAISE 2 August 1684
BN 9363,f.17 orig; Gonod 63

Hopes for general peace in Christendom. *Sainteté* into third edition, admired by a Protestant but not by all Catholics.

The Protestant was Daniel Le Clerc, a distinguished doctor and medical historian.

840803 RELIGIEUSE 3 August 1684
TC I/131

Though her admission as a nun was canonically irregular, her ignorance saves her from sin. Rather than seek translation she should follow the rule where she is.

840814 MONSIEUR, GRAND PÉNITENCIER [DU SUEL] 14 August 1684
TC II/283

God gives M. a love of retreat and a desire to enjoy amidst the world the peace of those who have left it.

840902 RM   2 September 1684
TC II/326
Sympathy for her troubles; she needs patience and prayer.

840902a [RM DE LA ROCHE]   2 September 1684
TC II/315
Sorry to know she is suffering. She is lucky to have a good confessor.

840902b [? RM LOUISE ROGIER]   2 September 1684
TC II/314
Always glad to hear from her. Her virtue increases with age. RM de la R[oche] must console herself and not give way to depression.

840903 RM ABBESSE   3 September 1684
TC II/316
R. does not want to talk about his health. Whatever opposition she meets in establishing good and preventing disorder she must go on doing what God asks of her.

840903a RM   3 September 1684
TC II/57
Her renewal. See God in her [male] superior and do not love him for purely human reasons.

840903b RELIGIEUSE   3 September 1684
A 2106,f.130; TC I/173 (dated 29 December 1684)
We must not presume to lay down God's treatment of us.

840905 MADEMOISELLE DE [? VERTUS]   5 September 1684
TC I/30
She should write fewer letters, have less to do with the nuns and their affairs. Communion on Sundays and feast days not too frequent in view of the life she leads, but not a rigid rule.

   As Mlle de Vertus lived with the nuns at Port-Royal the identification seems to suit her well.

*840910 BISHOP OF LUÇON [HENRI BARILLON] 10 September 16[8]4
P f.619 (wrongly dated 1674)

'If I had known, Mgr, of the death of your brother I should not have failed to write to you, but as I have no contacts in the world, a great many things happen there without my knowing. Such a christian and edifying life could only conclude with a happy ending. His great sincerity in all he did, which in itself pleased few people, was a sign of the spirit that filled him. He is now experiencing the happiness which comes from cutting oneself off from men, shunning their principles and opinions in order to please God alone, for in truth nothing is harder than to keep a proper balance between him and men and so conduct oneself as to commit no excess, so that one gives to the world only what God wants one to give it. I am convinced that at the moment when one must leave it for ever, one always finds that one has had more consideration and respect for it than it deserved, which is why one does not have that attitude as strongly as one should. The fact is that faith is languishing, and usually events which are not present are not felt. Certainty alone is not enough, proximity too is needed, and nothing else can rouse us from our torpor. Someone with as much piety and religion as you must not be thought to need consoling at the death of a righteous man, since no one can be unaware that you have more joy at his destiny than sorrow at his loss.

I am extremely distressed, Mgr, at your indisposition. It obliges you to take care of your health and take the necessary precautions so that, if possible, nothing prevents you carrying out your functions. You discharge them with such success and blessings that we must ask God not to allow them to be interrupted by your infirmities. The life of a bishop is a perpetual sacrifice, and if he is faithful in his ministry, all he does is constantly to offer to Christ his time, his effort, his labours, his pleasures, his goods, his prayers, his very soul for the glory of his name and the salvation of the people committed to his charge. I wish you all prosperity, Mgr, in time as in eternity, and am with unbounded respect and affection yours' etc.

Barrillon's brother, Jean-Jacques, is stated in the DBF *to have died in September 1684, so that R's apology for not writing sooner is odd. A very pious man, he had died a canon of Laon.*

840929 MARQUISE D'O [MARIE-ANTOINETTE DU PRAT] 29 September 1684
TC II/280

R. has not changed his mind since telling marquis de Bonneval that, despite her past life, she would be doing God's will by spending the rest of her life in retreat.

Christophe, marquis de Bonneval (died 1685) was her son-in-law; she had been married three times.

840929a DUCHESSE DE GUISE   29 September 1684
BN na 12960, p. 36

Recommends safer way for letters than leaving them at an inn. Asks her help for daughter of a friend, desiring to place girl at Noisy, an establishment for four hundred girls under the direction of Mme de Maintenon. [Recently married to Louis XIV]

841004 RELIGIEUSE   4 October 1684
TC II/51

Sympathy in her situation.

841004a DUCHESSE DE GUISE   4 October 1684
BN na 12960, p. 21

His health is poor. He would welcome translation of St Augustine [presumably a book she had offered to send].

841009 MONSIEUR L'ABBÉ TAMIN [or famin]   9 October 1684
TC II/141

He is not being misled when told that all communications may do harm.

*841009a BISHOP OF LUÇON [henri barillon]   9 October 16[8]4
P f.617 (wrongly dated 1674)

'I learn from your letter, Mgr, that the indisposition which had attacked you has given you some respite. That comforts me, and makes me hope that it will go away completely and not prevent you from continuing your conscientious and careful conduct of your diocese. God will not deprive those whom he has put in your charge of so necessary and useful a source of assistance, and one which gives so much edification to the Church. It could be said that your solicitude, scrupulous and extensive as it is, is not limited to your province, but is widely spread and of general use from the example it gives to the world.

A third edition of the book on monastic life has been made, and will come out shortly. We shall not fail to send it to you. There are some additions to a few passages, as you will certainly notice if you take the trouble to read it. As it is nothing considerable, and only a continuation of what has already been said, it was not worth communicating it to you before sending it to be printed.

As I knew that those who tried to decry the book and stop any good it might produce have spread abroad a number of things contrary to the truth, by attributing to me meanings and thoughts that I have never had or by disputing those which I actually did have; as I had even received many particular opinions from different people, I thought that I ought to clear up the main difficulties which had arisen in order, if possible, to remove all doubts. That obliged me to make some clarifications ample enough to make up a third volume.

The Bishop of Meaux, who paid us the honour of a visit a month ago, read it and examined the whole of it carefully, changing only very little. I have charged Muguet to send you all the first sheets once he begins to print, so that you can be kind enough to make any observations that seem appropriate. We are waiting until after the holiday to show it to the Archbishop of Reims. There is nothing in all this which goes against the first principles. There are some authorities of saints, some new arguments, and I think they will all be entirely to your way of thinking. There are certainly enough to silence those who read things with sincere intentions, but as for those whose intentions are evil, you know, Mgr, that they cannot be satisfied, so that it would be bad advice to hope and undertake to satisfy them.

Monsieur Thiers has not been able to secure permission, try as he might, to have his criticism printed, and, as you say, he will have to get it printed abroad if he wants it to appear. He may take the weak unawares, and provide bad arguments to those who do not love truth, which they will not fail to employ as if they were better ones. That is to say he may cause a scandal, and do harm however good and just the cause that he is attacking. He may even carry the point, as heretics do every day writing against the clearest and firmest truths of the faith. I must say no more about it, Mgr, nor waste your time. Continue, I beg you, your accustomed kindness to me, and please believe that only my fear of disturbing your occupations sometimes prevents me asking news of you, but you are as you should be in the depths of my heart, and nothing can equal my respect and affection for you.'

Thiers (see 831231) meant well, but was highly suspect to those in authority. François Muguet published De la Sainteté *and most of R's subsequent works.*

841014   RELIGIEUSE [? RM MARIE-LOUISE BOUTHILLIER]   14 October 1684
TC I/123

She must avoid speaking ill of others, and even conversation, and prepare for her coming retreat.

841015   [JEAN FAVIER]   15 October 1684
A 2106,f.131 vo.

They are both near the end, but Favier is fortunate in having discharged his responsibilities blamelessly. A pity that things have gone so badly at Beauvais.

841019   RM [? MARIE-LUCE] 19 October 1684
TC II/53
Glad to see God's grace continuing on her.

841022   RELIGIEUSE 22 October 1684
A 2106,f.132 vo; TC I/180
Her state now better and will strengthen her against future temptation.
Probably RM de la Roche.

841023   RP PRIEUR 23 October 1684
TC II/281
Regrets state of RP's house. 'God did not order you to succeed but to work at it.' He would like to go to another congregation, but where? R. would take him but for his health. R. writes only what anyone may see: 'a principle of my conduct is not to confide readily in persons of our profession'.

841106   MADEMOISELLE DE [? VERTUS OR GOELLO] 6 November 1684
TC II/140a
'God speaks to us in many ways' by depriving us of those dear to us.

841110   RM [? DE HARLAY] 10 November 1684
TC I/102
Her retreat will be of use if God grants her the fidelity she needs. R. will pray for her mother.

*841130   MLLE DE GOELLO 30 November 1684
TC II/140
   'No one could be more affected than I by the loss you have just suffered, and I can say, Mlle, that it is one I also share, for if you lose in Mme la duchesse de [Luynes] a niece who was dear to you, I lose in her someone who honoured me, as you know, with a quite special kindness and confidence. The world is nothing, Mlle, and you are fortunate to have known this and become disabused. If there is one thing in the world able to please us, it is the delight of having friends. Yet what is solid about that delight, when there is never a moment when one may not have the sorrow of being deprived of the persons one loves? Go on loving God; you are assured that in loving him you will never lose him, and that you will find in him in time and in eternity all

that the whole world put together is unable to give. Often think that you will follow those who precede you, who only go before for a few moments, and that however long your life may last, its duration will seem but a dream to you when God is pleased to end it and finish your race, and you will find it hard to understand how men can attach so much importance to something which deserves so little. It is enough to know that there are things eternal, and to hope for them, for one to be full of contempt for passing things. I have no doubt that God, who took you by the hand and has led you with such care, has given you all the enlightenment and feelings on the subject that you need, and that all your desires, attitudes and thoughts are of the kind that will not be confounded. By that I mean that they are founded on the trust you have in his mercy. I will not cease asking him to increase it and to confirm his kingdom more and more in your heart. I do not need to say how concerned I am in all that affects you, for I am sure that you are convinced that there could be no greater cordiality and respect than that with which I am' etc.

Anne de Montbazon (1640–84), daughter of R's friend, was the second wife of Louis, duc de Luynes, son of her stepsister, the famous plotter Marie, duchess de Chevreuse, by the latter's first husband, duc de Luynes. The duke was a major protector of Port-Royal, a man of great piety, well known to R. in the early days of his conversion.

841206   RP PRIEUR   6 December 1684
TC I/74

R. had mistakenly answered a question RP had not put. Abstinence if possible Monday and Wednesday. Question of RP's election to another place.

841207   RELIGIEUSE [RM DE LA ROCHE]   7 December 1684
A 2106,f.133; TC II/142

Glad she is now happy, but if God does withdraw, she must not feel abandoned.

841207a   RM LOUISE-HENRIETTE D'ALBON   7 December 1684
A 2106,f.133 vo.; TC II/143

Her recent illness an occasion for renewal before God. though convalescence is always trying. She must accept any relief offered by her superiors.

841209   RP SIMON GOURDAN, SAINT-VICTOR   9 December 1684
TC I/75

Condemns religious going out, whether into the fields or into town to dine with friends and relations. Recommends abstinence from meat in refectory, silence, and retreat.

841211 MONSIEUR L'ABBÉ DE CORVILLY   11 December 1684
TC I/76

R. condemns Paris, but M. has now returned to his solitude. He was prevented from coming to la T. by weather.

*841220 RM MARIE-LOUISE [BOUTHILLIER]   20 December 1684
TA orig.; TC II/306

'You could not make holier and more pious resolutions, my dear sister, than those you have taken since my last letter. The chief thing is to be faithful in executing them. You ask me for the means of doing so; the only one I know and can give you is to act and practise, and to force yourself if contrary impulses and attitudes arise. To be more specific, often renew your resolutions in the presence of God. Acknowledge that you are unable to keep them by yourself and with your own strength, and ask him that, after giving you understanding, desire, and feeling, he should add special grace and protection, without which you could never keep any of the promises you have made to him. If perchance some act or word should escape you which is not in conformity with them, never fail to repair your infidelity through sincere grief at having fallen and a renewal of will, so that your commitment remains, without weakening or damage, and you discharge it as occasion arises with more piety and strictness. In a word, my dear sister, add your efforts to your prayers. That is a double means which God always looks on in his goodness, and to which he never refuses his blessing. I cannot tell you more, being indisposed for some weeks now with an inflammation on the chest. Remember me in God's presence; commend all my needs to him. I am all yours, with all the warmth I owe you, I beg you not to doubt it.

PS You forgot to put a cross at the head of your letter. The poor marquis de C is to be pitied for dying as you say he did.
I am much obliged to all your holy mothers for remembering me, for I am not worthy.'

*841230 MARÉCHAL DE BELLEFONDS   30 December 1684
BN na 12959 f.106, orig.; TC II/19

'I do not deserve the honour you do me, Mgr, in remembering me. I can however assure you that no one could be more punctilious than I in rendering before God what I owe you. No day goes by but that I offer you to him several times, and we have not failed to do so during the whole of the last campaign, according to the different events that have taken place, at least so far as we have known of them.
Some days ago the Bishop of Grenoble wrote to say how comforted he had been at receiving your visit. I see from what you tell me that the feeling was reciprocal, and that he appeared to you as rumour and reputation had represented him. Four-

teen or fifteen years of episcopacy, spent in all the fidelity that God demands of a true pastor, bring great honour before men as before God, and if he permits great things to those who have been faithful in small ones, he will necessarily heap grace and blessings on those in high places who have been careful to fulfil their obligations and respond to his intentions.

You have seen, Mgr, one of the greatest monuments of mortification and penitence remaining to us, and nothing better illustrates what the love of Christ makes men undertake than the horror of that desert, and I believe that it looked quite different from what it does now when it was settled by those whom God's Spirit used to establish it, and who, strictly speaking, were human only in form and features. It is certain that such an idea can be extremely useful to those who are involved in the world, for when they consider what has been done by men who only had the same hopes and the same goal as they, and who took paths and ways so contrary to those they follow, they cannot do less, it seems to me, than quit the languor in which they live, enliven their faith and persuade themselves that they should approach in the disposition of their hearts and a wholly inner piety those from whom they have moved away through outward exercises and practices. People find satisfaction and false security in saying that God is the master of the world, that he is everywhere and that there is no place or state in which he cannot be found. That is true, but though the sun casts its rays down indiscriminately and the heavens pour down rain and dew over the whole earth, yet there are lands which still remain sterile and unproductive because they stay dry and arid.

Thus worldly people should urgently ask God to change their natural affections, take away their hearts of stone and give them hearts of flesh [Ezk 11:20], prepare them through special protection and see that his grace should not be of no avail, but should create in them all the effect it usually has in souls which do not give way to the illusions and deceptions of earthly things, to the prejudice of what they owe him, and by a dispensation full of holy wisdom and charity render to God the things that are God's, and to men the things that are men's, that is, their innermost feelings to God and to men what the absolute necessity of society and intercourse may demand

The difficulty is to keep the balance, but in that difficulty one should realise that it is much better to tip over on one side than the other.

I am sure, Mgr, that that is your chief concern, and that being indebted to God for so much grace you fear more than anything not to respond with all the gratitude you owe him. We shall continue to pray that he keeps you always in his hand, and never allows anything to separate you from him. I wish you, Mgr, not just a year but a whole life full of blessings and prosperity. I am with all possible respect and fidelity yours' etc.

The Roussillon campaign had ended in yet another disgrace for Bellefonds, who cannot have been in a hurry to return home since he took the longest possible route by way of Grenoble. The monument is the Grand Chartreuse, near Grenoble. Despite R's strictures on the

order in Sainteté, *he could hardly deny the forbidding situation of the famous monastery which he never visited but had once thought to join, if his early biographers are to be believed.*

841230a RP ABBÉ DE L'ORDRE   30 December 1684
TC I/161

R. would like to help him but he must stay where he is and not resign.

85/1 MARQUISE DE VIBRAIE   1685
TC I/130, TC II/82

Unaware of insult offered to her. Gossip often rebounds on the wicked. Apart from formal vows she will find in the book he has sent [*Sainteté*] things which apply to her.

850102 RELIGIEUSE   2 January 1685
A 2106,f. 135

His illness has shown him how transitory are earthly things, and failure to renounce them explains prevalent tepidity of religious life.

* 850104 BISHOP OF LUÇON [HENRI BARILLON]   4 January 16[8]5
P f.620 (wrongly dated 1675) a very poor copy, and difficult to read.

'As you, Mgr, are one of the people I think about most in the world, nothing came to my mind, and my heart, at the start of this year with more force than to ask Our Lord to accord you his special blessing and give you for his service and the conduct of your people renewed zeal, vigilance, and vigour. Your views and intentions on this are so much what they should be that those who really love his glory and the good of his Church could not wish more heartily that he will preserve and increase them. Apart from the interest I take on general grounds, you know so well how many bonds and committments attach me to your person and all that concerns you that I have no need to say it.

I hope that your health will get better and better and that God will not allow you to be afflicted again by the indisposition you had last year. It would be a great obstacle to carrying out and continuing your plans, for it is hardly possible to act when in pain as great as that which you suffered. The late Archbishop of Sens was once attacked by a very similar illness, but it never returned. That makes me hope as much of yours. But you are in God's hand, and he always takes care of those who are his.

I think, Mgr, that you will now have received copies of the third edition of the book on monastic life. We shall send you at the earliest opportunity the *Clarifications* of which I spoke, so that you can kindly have a look at them. They are, as I told you, the same maxims and principles, but with different authorities and [arguments] to prove them. That will put a lot of people right, to whom some tried to give the wrong impression of the work, and all the truths of the [faith] will be seen so clearly and palpably that everyone will [want] to defend them against those who attempt at any price to combat them. Most men scarcely correct their prejudices, and if one simply shows them that they are wrong, they maintain out of chagrin and obstinancy what they can no longer maintain by reason.

I am finishing, Mgr, this letter sooner than I should have liked, but I am pressed by an indisposition which I have had for five weeks. It is a violent inflammation of the chest and [cough ?]. It allowed me a little rest last night, and that leads me to think that it may end. However my health is getting worse and cannot allow me a very long [life]. Use your offices with [God] I beg you, that he may make the end of my life better than all that has been up to now. The life of someone who is no longer of the world comprises such great obligations that whatever he may do to discharge them, he is in need of great mercy, and there is no one to whom the words of the prophet apply better than to him: *Latum mandatum tuum nimis* [Ps 118:96]. I ask for your blessing and the favour of believing that it would be impossible to add to the faithfulness and respect with which I am yours' etc.

The renal colic got worse; Abp Gondrin of Sens may have been lucky in that respect, but he was only 54 when he died in 1674. The Clarifications (Eclaircissements de quelques difficultés que l'on a formées sur le livre de la sainteté . . .) *followed closely on the third edition but far from clearing things up promoted further controversy.*

850112   CLAUDE NICAISE   12 January 1684
BN 9363, f.19 orig.; Gonod 64

Praises Nicole's book on schism [presumably *Préjugés légitimes . . . contre le Calvinisme*, of 1671]

850113   RM LOUISE-HENRIETTE D'ALBON   13 January 1685
A 2106,f.134

She owes much to RP T[. . .] and should follow his advice. The elect constantly go forward, the others slip back.

850128   RELIGIEUSE   28 January 1685
TC II/218

Hopes God will relieve her pains, and not just for this year. Accustom herself to idea of death.

850203   RELIGIEUSE   3 February 1685
TC II/327

R. only abstains from writing out of consideration for her. Her sufferings and infirmities.

850203a RM　　　　　　　　　　　　　　　　3 February 1685
TC II/209
Only advice to be given to person writing is to give herself up to guidance of someone who knows her well.

850203b RM　　　　　　　　　　　　　　　　3 February 1685
TC II/210
Hard to give advice to person writing. 'No peace or quiet to be hoped for in cloister unless one enters with the simplicity of a child.'
These two letters are by the same copyist, who clearly treats them as separate. One of the dates must be wrong.

Charles II of England dies,　　　　　　　　6 February 1685
and is succeeded by his brother, James II

850212 RELIGIEUSE　　　　　　　　　　　　12 February 1685
TC II/311
R. has had a chest infection, now better. She must be at peace and trust her confessor.

850212a RM LOUISE-HENRIETTE D'ALBON　　12 February 1685
A 2106,f.135 vo.
Confidence in God is essential in the face of all that happens. R. has heard that she is reading 'doctrinal books', than which nothing could be more harmful. She should excite her piety, not seek 'knowledge you do not need'.

*850214 RM MARIE-LOUISE [BOUTHILLIER]　　14 February 1685
TA orig
'I am most obliged to you, my dearest sister, for being so concerned about my indisposition. It is true that it was serious to begin with, and if it had continued I should have found it hard to resist. God has saved me from it by his mercy, and has just warned me to be ready for some other time, which cannot be far off. Indeed that moment is so important that if one did nothing else but think of it, one would still not be thinking enough of it. I ask for your prayers, that I might be well prepared. I do not doubt, my dear sister, that you will grant them to me. I am much more yours than I could ever show.

PS We will not fail to do what Madame La Présidente le Camus asks of us with all possible care and attention. Please assure her to that effect.

One of our brothers died two days ago; I commend him to your prayers, and to those of all your holy house.'

Nicolas Le Camus had been Premier Président since 1672. He was brother to Etienne, Bp of Grenoble. His wife, here referred to, was Marie-Elisabeth Langlois. It was dom Arsène Cordon who had just died.

850224   DUCHESSE DE GUISE   24 February 1685
BN na 12960, p. 35; Mug II/18

Sends boxwood spoons and fork and six crosses; simple gifts for a great lady. She is right to scorn wordly values.

850305   RM   5 March 1685
TC II/54, TC II/62

She is fortunate in loving silence.

850317   RELIGIEUSE   17 March 1685
TC II/339

She must patiently bear ills she cannot prevent.

* 850317a   [RM MARIE-LOUISE BOUTHILLIER]   17 March 1685
TC II/322

'As you cannot refuse the employment which those in authority over you entrust to you, so you must also work to discharge it with all the fidelity which you know God asks of you, and keep yourself, as far as possible, from the distraction which almost always goes with external occupations. If in this respect something should happen to escape you, contrary to your duty, you must acknowledge it at once, severely rebuke yourself and make new resolutions to be more vigilant and careful. It is no small thing to want God alone in one's innermost heart, and look only towards him, but it would not be enough if that feeling did not pass over into your actions and your works, and if you did not make good use of all the qualities you receive from his goodness. God wishes to find a corresponding response in those souls who have shared more than others in his mercy, and we must not give him cause to regret his gifts.

Above all, my dear sister, strive to suppress all the reasons furnished by your mind for condemning the conduct of others; and if in that you are not mistress of your emotions as much as you should be, you must be mistress of your tongue, so that it never says anything but what it should say. If you know your weakness and cannot overcome it, avoid such occasions and be careful not to expose yourself to them. The season of Lent, which is a season of silence, obliges me to be briefer than I should be otherwise. You must forgive me, my dearest sister, and be content with my assurance that we will not fail to offer all your needs to God. Pray him for me too, I beseech you, and believe me with all possible warmth yours' etc.

850328   MADEMOISELLE DE VERTUS   28 March 1685
Dubois, II pp. 342–348 (from orig. now lost)

Her poor health should remove any scruples about her way of life. Take the advice of Hamon [the Port-Royal doctor]. 'Coffee is so ordinary a relief that you can use it without worrying.'

850400   RM DE HARLAY   April 1685
TC II/236

She must not refuse all visits, nor have any peculiarity contrary to her institute. Continue looking after sick and follow superior's advice about communion.

*850409   BISHOP OF LUÇON [HENRI BARILLON]   9 April 16[8]5
P f.621 (wrongly dated 1675)

'I think, Mgr, that Muguet is going to send you the proofs of the *Clarifications* of which I have spoken to you, if he has not done so already; they have already been seen and examined by Mgr of Reims, of Meaux, and of Grenoble. Be good enough to put in the margins anything you may observe. So much has been said and spread around about the last work that it has been more or less necessary to do a second to solve the difficulties and take away the doubts raised, although they were unjust and groundless. The Bishop of Grenoble has given his approval, the Archbishop of Reims and the Bishop of Meaux have given individual approval, and we only await yours. May I trouble you to send it on to Muguet.

I have not yet thanked you for your conferences. There could be nothing finer or more useful to the Church, all the questions are treated with such purity, solidity, and scope that all one can still desire is a continuation, and it would certainly be an immense benefit and advantage for clergy, and especially pastors, if they had the whole of moral theology discuseed with similar precision.

I beg you, Mgr, to give me news of your health. You cannot doubt how keenly I feel about it. Humours usually start moving about in the spring, and I pray God that it has no ill effect on you and that nothing prevents the course of your usual cares and occupations. I ask your blessing, and the support of your prayers, of which I am much in need. Keep for me all the kindness with which you have for so long honoured me, and rest assured that you are too much present to us before Our Lord for anything to equal the fidelity and respect with which I am yours' etc.

François Muguet was R's usual publisher. From 1680 proceedings of the Luçon diocesan conferences were published at intervals, and in 1685 Barillon also published Ordonnances synodales, *to which this letter may well refer.*

850412 RELIGIEUSE 12 April 1685
A 2106,f.136; TC II/198 (dated 5 March 1685)

She is still troubled, but God will bring her safely into harbour and welcomes the prayers of his servants.

850422 RM ABBESSE [? GIF, ANNE DE MONTGLAT] 22 April 1685
TC II/186 orig.

She wants to lay down a burden that is beyond her strength, but where will she find a successor? She must not abandon the sheep and let another undo her work.

The address is erased, but as the abbess of Gif resigned in 1686, she is a likely candidate.

850422a CLAUDE NICAISE 22 April 1685
BN 9363,f.22 orig.; Gonod 65

R. would like to have gone to General Chapter [1684] and thus seen Nicaise. Recent success of Le Camus in case laid before Parlement. Criticism of R's *Eclaircissements* printed at Amsterdam.

850500 MADAME May 1685
TC II/310

The fact that she got through the winter without the help of company a clear sign of God's grace.

850509 RELIGIEUSE 9 May 1685
TC II/208

R. has four things to say: praise God, accept her present state as effect of his mercy, support superior, wait peaceably on God's will.

850509a MONSIEUR L'ABBÉ 9 May 1685
TC II/321

Always tiresome to be bound to people who follow paths one does not wish to tread.

850510 RELIGIEUSE   10 May 1685
TC II/115
In giving herself up to God she will be 'coming out of Egypt', [Ps 113:1]. Avoid too much imagination in prayer, rely rather on Scripture.

850512 CLAUDE NICAISE   12 May 1685
BN 9363,f.24 orig.; Gonod 66
Nicaise has praised the *Eclaircissements*.

850522 RM LOUISE-HENRIETTE D'ALBON   22 May 1685
A 2106,f.137; TC II/206 (dated 17 May 1685)
Delighted to know that she is now at peace, a reward from God for her past sufferings.

850526 RP, CHANOINE RÉGULIER   26 May 1685
TC II/207
He is fortunate in enjoying solitude. Abstinence from meat possible, but avoid being conspicuous. Does not know whether other canon will suit la T.

850528 MADEMOISELLE DE VERTUS   28 May 1685
TC II/65
She has been solitary throughout Lent; despite poor health she can give her heart to God.

850608 RM DE LA ROCHE, TOURS   8 June 1685
TC II/70
Sorry at her pains, but pleased at her attitude. She complains of not being calm and submissive enough. R's own health due to natural delicacy rather than imaginary austerity.

*850608a RM ABBESSE, LEYME [ANNE DE LA VIEUVILLE]   8 June 1685
TC II/71

'You tell me in your last letter that you do not know how your life will end, but that you do none of the things you want to do in this world. It is easy to reply that as there is no better way to spend it than in adversity, you have every reason to believe and hope that it will finish in happy circumstances and that God, who takes care to prepare you through the privations in which he allows you to live, will at the last moment give you powerful grace and protection.

The real way to preserve peace and tranquility is to abandon everything one wants into God's hand, to make our wills yield to his, and to be always ready to give up our best resolves when we meet invincible obstacles, and when the difficulties we encounter show that he does not wish them fulfilled. Indeed all the worries which beset us in this world derive solely from the fact that we have not become submissive to his orders and fail to abandon ourselves to his guidance. We pull, so to speak, against the dispositions of his providence, we resist it and often fight his plans without realising it. Thus, being in a situation of violence, we live without peace, in perpetual agitation. Our centre is the acquiescence or conformity of our hearts to that of God; and when that is not the case, how can we not be in confusion? God is King of peace, it has to be found wherever he reigns, and there can be only trouble and confusion where he is not master.

I am sure, and I have already told you, that one must exercise great prudence in proclamation of faults, for if they make people bitter and are done or received without charity, they will set everything ablaze, and all the information which superiors may gain from their brethren will not stop the ship foundering. One must believe that any sensible man, seeing that this exercise, holy as it is in itself, has tiresome consequences, will never fail to give it up, and seek other methods of finding out what is going on in his house. A superior is made to save souls, that is what all external discipline relates to as to its true end. When for that purpose he has acquitted himself of all the means given and prescribed by the Rule, and has omitted nothing which may depend on his own diligence, then he will be cleared before God. There are established observances from which one cannot dispense oneself, and which must be inviolably respected; there are others, such as that of proclamations, which may be suspended, or even completely given up, for reasons of prudence and charity. It is certainly a very sanctifying exercise, but it must be made acceptable if one wishes to employ it usefully. In a few words that is what I can tell you on the subject, I leave the rest to your reflections. Always do me the favour of believing that no one could be with more esteem and sincerity than I yours' etc.

*850611   BISHOP OF LUÇON [HENRI BARILLON]   11 June 16[8]5
P f.622 (wrongly dated 1675)

'This note which I have the honour of writing, Mgr, is solely to ask you, should you have read the sheets of the book which at present has finished printing and which Muguet told me he sent you, kindly to give your approval and add it to that of the Bishop of Grenoble. It would suffice, I think, to put 'signed at Luçon such and such a day', unless you wanted to go to the trouble of giving a separate approval. As the printing is done, that is the only thing we are waiting for. I shall not abuse your kindness this time, but believe, Mgr, I beg you, that no one in the world is more deeply, cordially and respectfully yours' etc.

The book in question is still the Eclaircissements.

*850617   RM MARIE-LOUISE [BOUTHILLIER]   17 June 1685
TA orig.; TC II/67

'I am always truly delighted, my dear sister, to have news from you, because it shows me your desire to belong to God and advance further and further in his service. The surest means you can adopt for that is constantly to detach yourself from yourself, and renounce it on every occasion that you can. As your present occupation did not come to you by your own choice, and is not what you wanted, you should believe that God will support you there so long as you take care to turn to him and ask for his help, without which you would not last a moment. In a word, remember him if you want him to remember you, and keep him in your memory, or rather in your heart, if you want to be in his, and as Scripture says, to be hidden in the secret of his countenance, to be protected from the different occasions when you might displease him. Distractions which come upon us despite ourselves, and despite the care we take in employment which we have only assumed through obedience, will not be imputed to us, and God is too good not to take pity on our weakness. If our souls are free from negligence and evil, they should expect everything from his mercy, and faults which merely escape our frailty are always forgivable. Farewell, my dearest sister, pray God for me and believe that no one could be more affectionately and sincerely yours than I.'

850617a   RM MARIE-LUCE [PICOT], SUPÉRIEURE, ANNONCIADES   17 June 1685
TC II/66

She is dissatisfied with herself and 'would like the wings of a dove to rise where the ardour of faith and zeal calls'.

850618   RM LOUISE-HENRIETTE D'ALBON   18 June 1685
A 2106,f.138; TC I/97

Progress in virtue essential. Practice docility and humility in imitation of Christ.

850624   MADAME   24 June 1685
TC II/68

She is back in Babylon [Paris]. R. hopes not for long, before she returns to her solitude.

*850624a   RELIGIEUSE   24 June 1685
TC I/98

'You have only to follow, Sister, the enlightenment and feelings God gives you to avoid anything contrary to his will and the duties of your profession. It is an important point that you are persuaded, as you are, that it is useful to keep silence with creatures, for since that is so you will avoid many occasions for breaking it, and when you are obliged by necessity to dispense yourself from silence, God, seeing the disposition of your heart, will preserve you from the misfortunes into which all those fall who talk because they like talking and do not know how to keep quiet. However you must remember that if you fall short of the strict rule you have prescribed for yourself on this matter, you must begin again with more care and vigilance. That is the fruit we must reap from our faults and failures, and God only permits them in persons who serve him and desire as much as you do to belong to him in order to make them better and more faithful. It is important, when the question arises of admitting or refusing entry to monasteries, to suspend prejudice and impulsive feelings and to ask God for sufficient light to avoid mistakes. Otherwise one risks excluding those whom he has called and receiving those whom he has rejected. Each of these ills is as bad as the other.

I will not say anything positive yet about your abstinence, but when you begin to observe it without the addition of fasting, you will realise what you are able to do much better than if you were to go too far to begin with. However much one trusts in God's protection and help, he often wishes us to be moderate in our conduct and not rush straightaway into what is most difficult, but to go there by degrees. There is even more humility in acting like that.

It is a considerable achievement, Sister, to have made a doctor understand that Christ's grace is a great remedy for bodily as for spiritual sickness. One must certainly avoid extremes, but there are things which those who are consecrated to God can and should practice, and which are unknown, and always will be, to people in the world.

What I said about the detachment in which a religious should live I said as something real, and proposed it as his chief obligation. He must strive for it according to all the strength and grace God gives him, keep it before his eyes as much as he can and use the means prescribed by the rule to rise to it. Thus this point must not be regarded as a mere idea or speculation, but as an essential duty to which one must adhere if one wishes to follow God's designs and live according to the truth of one's state.

In reply to your question, I will tell you what you know very well, namely, that God leads souls by ways which are very different and sometimes even contrary. We see some people embrace the most arduous and laborious exercises of the solitary life with faith and such ardent zeal that they find nothing to arrest them, or even cause them the slightest trouble. Their yoke in no way weighs upon them, and it can be said that the cross they bear offers only consolation. There are others who constantly row against the violence of the current, to whom everything seems hard, who walk, to speak exactly, through thorns and brambles, and advance only through the violence of their efforts. Those please God best and offer him the most acceptable sacrifice not who suffer least or who suffer most, but who serve him with most love and charity. For charity alone sets the price and value of all our actions.

Our brothers, since you ask, employ all the morning hours of days when they do not work in prayer and reading, and after dinner on Sundays they have a conference lasting a good hour, at which I never fail to be present, and during which five or six of them speak in succession. The subject under discussion invariably concerns matters regarding our profession and those most real to us. When a festival falls in midweek the procedure is just like that of Sunday.

It is true in the nearly twenty-four years that we have been established here many of our religious have died, but this is attributable not so much to the austerity we practise as to the situation of the place. Our monastery lies between nine or ten lakes, surrounded by forests on every side, and there is scarcely a day in the year so bright and calm that there is no mist. The winds which come to us along the lakes and woods bring harmful and penetrating cold and damp, which affect the body adversely, and since we do not have here any of those recreations and enjoyments which dispel the humours which may have been contracted in the calm of solitude, our health is certainly more under attack and liable to be compromised than it would be elsewhere. Thus we find ourselves following exactly the intentions of our fathers who, as St Bernard says, chose damp, low-lying valleys to build their houses in, so that having no assurance of good health, they should have good reason to be constantly occupied with thoughts of death. Add to that the fact that we have accepted men of advanced age, poor health and delicate constitution, and you will not be surprised at the number of monks we have lost, nor above all at the pressing prayer of nearly all of them that Our Lord will take them out of this world before he takes me. Death, when it comes, has nothing hard for those who are accustomed to have it before their eyes, and it keeps all its bitterness for those who have thought only of living. It is enough to appreciate properly the thought of death to know that the Holy Spirit declared that the way to do no sin is to have that thought ever present.'

850705   MONSIEUR L'ABBÉ LE BOULANGER   5 July 1685
TC II/263

R. approves M's attitude as he prepares for the priesthood.

850706   MONSIEUR   6 July 1685
TC I/128

Commends an abbess for work in rehabilitating her community.

850708   [JEAN FAVIER]   8 July 1685
A 2106,f.139 vo.

Favier's health much better, R's mediocre.

850712   RM   12 July 1685
TC I/167
Essential to examine postulants with great care.

850713   MONSIEUR   13 July 1685
BN 24123,f.68, orig.
Approve's M's reading programme.

850715   DUCHESSE DE GUISE   15 July 1685
BN na 12960, p. 17
Sends third volume of book on true religion [Eclaircissements].

850722   ACHILLE DE HARLAY   22 July 1685
BN 17420,f.109, orig.
R. is obliged to clear up some difficulties arising from *Sainteté* [in the *Eclaircissements*].

*850802   MARÉCHAL DE BELLEFONDS   2 August 1685
BN na 12959,f.109, orig.; TC II/235

'I did not think that the *Eclaircissements* I have been obliged to give would change the minds of those who made difficulties about the book on *Monastic Life*, but rather that some people would be very pleased that I should answer the arguments that had been advanced to make the book no use to them and prevent them deriving from it profit and consolation. My own consolation in this is that I have spoken only about the matters of my profession, that I am convinced I was doing nothing that was not in the order of God, and that I know there are souls on whom the book produced impressions and effects which were full of blessing and salvation. It is true that men need to have perfection put before their eyes, for whatever they do they always fall far short of their duty. Nothing is more dangerous than to take too narrow measures when what is at stake is something as Important as eternity. Anyone who wanted to cross an abyss would leave behind him as much ground as possible and would never say that it is enough to have one's foot on the edge. On that matter, Mgr, you see as clearly and fully as you should, and I do not doubt that this helps you in the conduct of your life. What God's Son said regarding the broad way and the narrow way [Mt 7:13–14] is frightening when one looks at it closely, I mean for both those who are no longer in the world and those who are. The only means of obtaining peace and calm in this is to love him more than everything, and in all the circumstances of life to regard him as the goal to which everything must be related. I pray God, Mgr, to give you all the fidelity necessary, and to see that in all the diverse affairs and commitments in which you are through the necessity of your position nothing takes place

which does not accord with what he wants of you, and with all the grace you have received from him, for which, as you know, he will ask you to account most exactly. We shall be awaiting you impatiently, Mgr, I beg you to believe as you should be sure of all the respect and fidelity with which I am yours etc.
I am sending you the route from la Trappe to Chambord.'

The Eclaircissements *came out in June, in an attempt to meet some of the objections raised against successive editions of* Sainteté *(which R. usually described as the 'book on monastic life').*

* 850806   RM ABBESSE [LEYME; ANNE DE LA VIEUVILLE]   6 August 1685
TC II/109

'It is a long time since I had the honour of writing to you. I cannot blame myself, because I really wanted to ever since receiving your last letter; the only reason has been my bad health and state of exhaustion. I assure you that if I did not very much have providence before my eyes, I would be distressed at my state and would find it hard to bear, seeing how much better is the situation of those who live in the depths of the cloister, separated from men and with no other occupation but thinking about themselves, or rather thinking solely of God and how to serve him. The weight overwhelms me, and I shall carry it until I die, with the desire to rid myself of it without ever managing to do so.

No one could be more sorry for you, RM, than I, nor feel more keenly your troubles. You will be free of them if you make every effort to bring the souls under your charge into God's ways and keep them there. But if your diligence is not as successful as it should be, he will not hold you to account for a work which is more in his hands than yours. Your duty is to watch and exhort, but not to persuade; he alone gives virtue to words, and without him it comes to the same whether one speaks or keeps silence, except that speaking to no purpose and without effect is most tedious. It may well be that those who acquit themselves of that ministry will find in the next world the reward they do not have in this. One often sows on barren ground in time seed which will produce an abundant harvest in eternity for whoever cultivates it. That is a feeling given us by faith, and it should be our chief consolation.'

850806a   RP   6 August 1685
TC II/343

R. very sad that RP had to leave; he must offer God his incapacity and intention together.

850812   RELIGIEUSE   12 August 1685
A 2106,f.140 vo.

She is still beset with temptations and stress, but must put her hope in Christ.

850819   LOUIS-FRANÇOIS LEFÈVRE DE CAUMARTIN   19 August 1685
TC II/83

R. glad at sentiments inspired in Caumartin by God and hopes that the seed sown in his heart will not be choked.

*850821   RM MARIE-LOUISE [BOUTHILLIER]   21 August 1685
TA orig.

'I see from your letter, my dearest sister, that your feelings continue to be the right ones. As they come to you from God, as you perfectly well acknowledge that fact, and take great care to address yourself to him, I have no doubt that he will preserve and increase them, for you know that a Christian, still less a religious, must not stay in the same state, but must make every effort to advance in God's service, having no other business in the world than that. As your present employment did not come to you by your own choice, but it is obedience that puts you there, if you are faithful, God will give you the necessary grace to avoid the distraction which is always encountered when one is obliged to think of something other than oneself.

I am very pleased that you find pleasure and comfort in the book of which you speak. It is not surprising that it has its opponents; that always happens to truths when they are little known or practised, but they remain true despite opposition from men. Let men say what they will, we must follow God's spirit and act according to the rules which are his, according to the teachings of his saints, and if men do not speak like them, they do not deserve to be heeded.

We shall not fail to commend to Our Lord Mlle de La Vove; she would do well to settle in your house, and since she wants to leave the world she could hardly find anything better. Farewell, my dearest sister, pray Our Lord for me, and please believe that no one could love you more tenderly than I.'

Mlle de La Vove must be one of the children of the marquis de Tourouvre, R's neighbour. There were three unmarried daughters, but the only one of likely age is Marie, who did not in fact take the veil (1668–1726).

850823   RELIGIEUSE   23 August 1685
TC II/84

Too much reading merely distracts nuns' spirit and weakens their heart. 'Fight your natural inclinations, especially those to which you are most prone.'

850826   RP PIERRE DE MONCHY, CONG. ORAT.   26 August 1685
TC II/99

Monchy's health seriously undermined. 'I can only look on you as a man on the point of reaching harbour after a successful voyage.'

850830   MONSIEUR [? LE BOULANGER]   30 August 1685
TC I/4
R's views on status of ecclesiastics. Example of St Martin.

850830a   RELIGIEUSE   30 August 1685
A 2106,f.140 vo.
She must thank God for his mercies.

850913   RELIGIEUSE   13 September 1685
TC II/260
Her decision to give herself wholly to God will help her make progress.

850920   [JEAN FAVIER]   20 September 1685
A 2106,f.140
R. now realises the frailty of his constitution: 'my life is a spark which a drop of water may extinguish'. He has been saying this for ten years, but it will soon come true.

851000   RP GÉNÉRAL, FEUILLANTS, [J-B PRADILLON]   [October 1685]
Grenoble, C 3554
The Feuillant fr Jacques de Saint-Gabriel has come to la T. and R. does not doubt that 'he needed a more withdrawn life and stricter discipline than is observed in your congregation'.

   The General's reply was acid; he ordered the young man (age 17) to return at once, and in August 1686 obtained a papal brief prohibiting any further migration.

851003   RP PRIEUR, PERSEIGNE   3 October 1685
Tour. orig.
He can give up cider for wine, more suitable for his infirmities. Dom P[aul] must be careful. Why should RP go to Barbeaux when he has his own monks to look after? Keep the monk from Fontaine-Daniel until authorised to send him on. R. will not send prior of la T. [Eustache Picot] as that would only cause trouble.

   Fontaine-Daniel was a house of the Common Observance in the diocese of Le Mans. Dom Paul was advised not to come from Barbeaux to la T. on health grounds [780222]. The prior at Perseigne was still probably Robin Couturier, though there is no documentary evidence after 1681.

Revocation of Edict of Nantes   **18 October 1685**

851018   RM LOUISE-HENRIETTE D'ALBON   18 October 1685
A 2106,f.141 vo.; TC I/164

Perfection is obtainable in any order provided the rule is observed. Interior dispositions are what counts.

851018a   RELIGIEUSE   18 October 1685
TC II/261

She still suffers but God still sustains her.

851022   MONSIEUR, ECCLÉSIASTIQUE   22 October 1685
TC I/44

R. encourages M. who has just reluctantly accepted a benefice.

851025   RELIGIEUSE   25 October 1685
TC II/274

Very sorry that her troubles come from a source from which she might have expected consolation.

851028   CLAUDE NICAISE   28 October 1685
BN 9363,f.26, orig.; Gonod 112

Second edition of *Eclaircissements*. R. thinks a Latin version of *Sainteté* would be approved in Rome. 'What the King is doing to extirpate heresy is a prodigy.' Destruction of Protestant temple at Charenton a kind of miracle.

851104   RELIGIEUSE   4 November 1685
TC II/258

Forget the past, concern herself with present. 'There is no doubt that you should avoid unnecessary talk, but there would be some inconvenience in reducing this to yes and no. Charity demands a little more expansiveness.'

851104a   MADEMOISELLE DE VERTUS   4 November 1685
TC II/195

Her numerous visitors have not made her like the world and its contacts any more. 'You endure what you cannot prevent. . . . Your practice of not taking communion the day after some major diversion is praiseworthy, but one should not often be so obliged. . . . It is sometimes useful to stay away, but only to come back with more holiness.'

851108   RP PIERRE DE MONCHY, CONG. ORAT.   8 November 1685
TC II/73a

Death of the Chancellor [Michel Le Tellier] in Monchy's arms. Praises his 'love of justice, and constant equity.'

He had been Chancellor since 1677 (born 1603).

851113   RM [? DE HARLAY]   13 November 1685
TC I/139

She should report laxity to superior and then to visitor. She was right to avoid confidences. Prefer public interest to her own. Discusses her 20th Constitution.

The 20th Constitution laid down by St François de Sales concerns 'extraordinary confessors', recommended four times a year and permitted when any distinguished person is available, though undue reliance on outside confessors is discouraged. In no case should this lead to austerity greater than that practised by others.

851115   MARQUISE D'ALÈGRE   15 November 1685
TC I/99

Promises her his prayers and sympathy.

851119   RP, DE LA COMMUNE OBSERVANCE   19 November 1685
TC I/100

RP has been misinformed by those who say that he can be saved just as well where he is as in a stricter house. Condemns in detail laxity of RP's house and is ready to welcome him.

851121   RM LOUISE-HENRIETTE D'ALBON   21 November 1685
TC II/259, TC II/324 (dated 1686)

God sends pains to try our faith and patience without any need for us to produce extraordinary ones ourselves. 'Self-love is everywhere, and pride is often encountered in humiliations as in actions of vanity.'

851122   RP CONG. ORAT.   22 November 1685
TC II/32

Pinette has shown R. a brief restoring marriage of Mme X who should never have left the convent where she was novice. She still has 20,000 livres.

*851125 MARÉCHAL DE BELLEFONDS   25 November 1685
BN na 12959,f.111, orig.

'I feel obliged to make a request of you, Mgr; the Abbot of Clairvaux is trying to establish as much as possible with the means at his disposal good order in the abbey of Montier, which belongs to the abbé de Villars, your nephew, who has already lent his support to some arrangement enabling this to be achieved, but the Abbot of Clairvaux advises me that if he does not agree to the construction of a certain enclosing wall all that has been done so far will be of no use. I wrote last year to Mother Agnès about it, and she was kind enough to take it up, and now, Mgr, I turn to you, having no doubt that the abbé de Villars treats with the consideration he should anything coming to him from you. It is certain that if the religious are not separated and their communications with seculars not cut off, it is not possible to establish regularity or discipline among them. I should be particularly obliged, Mgr, if you were kind enough to see that the Abbot of Clairvaux has not been wasting his efforts, and for my part I confess that I should be really delighted if my intervention were not without use to him, especially on an occasion contributing to God's glory and concerning his service. I thought that I could not do better than send you the letter of the Abbot of Clairvaux, and a plan to show you what is at issue.

I cannot refrain from mentioning, Mgr, the consolation it is to see the destruction of error, and the prompt return to the bosom of the church of those who had separated from it and hitherto shown insurmountable resistance to every effort made to reduce them; it is a quite miraculous event, and scarcely anything has occurred since the birth of the Church which is greater and more surprising than what the King is doing today.

I have just had a letter from the Bishop of Luçon, telling me that of eight thousand Huguenots who were in his diocese all have been converted in less than a fortnight, with the exception of two or three hundred scattered over the countryside, but who are following the example of the others as they return to their homes. You no doubt know what the Bishop of Grenoble has done for his part; in those parts it is harder, and men are more obstinate and intractable.

Do me the honour of maintaining me in your favour, and be sure that no one could be more gratefully and respectfully yours' etc.

See 820423; RM Agnès was the aunt of abbé de Villars. For comments on the effect of the Revocation, see letters to Barillon and Mme de Guise, among others.

*851129 MARÉCHAL DE BELLEFONDS   29 November 1685
BN na 12959,f.113, orig.

'It must be admitted, Mgr, that God's mercy has resources that men cannot understand. When it pleases him one can return to him from the ends of the earth, and there is no aberration, however great, that should take away our hope and make us think that it is not possible to return.

I could not read Monsieur le P[rince's] letter without adoring God's goodness in thinking of those who do not think of him and dispelling the densest darkness in those whom he wishes to enlighten with the light of his truth. The character and style of the letter show that its writer is touched and speaks from the heart without affectation. All those who love Christ's glory must urgently pray him to confirm his work, and not allow it to remain imperfect. This conversion appears to me so great and at the same time so useful to the church that there is hardly anything I so ardently desired.

The Prince de Conti's death has surprised all those who knew the circumstances, yet those which you tell us are reassuring and consoling, for there is reason to believe that God had not given him feelings so contrary to the life he had led, nor desires such as he was able to show you, except by some special disposition of his mercy.

God sometimes takes pleasure in snatching from the devil those whom he thought to have taken from God. He saves them against every kind of rule to show that he is master, and holds in his hands the fate and destiny of men. These are among the extraordinary acts he performs to prevent despair, but not to encourage impenitence. Nevertheless men are so wretched and unjust that they abuse his goodness instead of using it properly, and what ought to make them more loath to offend him only makes them bolder to displease him.

Thus it is that David's sudden and prompt conversion created incomparably more sinners than penitents. I have always thought that there is a secret between God and a few souls whom he does not wish to lose, and that he hides it from men because it would harm them to know it. We shall not fail to offer our prayers to God, together with what little penance we can do, in order to satisfy his justice and make it more favourable to one to whom he has refused the usual means of becoming worthy of his mercy.

I do not think that M de Maz[arin] will be coming here. He has sometimes told me that he very much wanted to, but there are always things happening to deter him. I did not know of the marriage of which you speak. You are fortunate, Mgr, to seek only to be detached and in peace, for I know that the peace you seek is not of this world, but that which can only be expected from God. We must have it to serve him, for when earthly things occupy and worry us, we are remote from the state in which we must be to enjoy heavenly things. Whatever one may say, it is hard to combine them, and strictly speaking only those who enjoy earthly goods without loving them and becoming attached to them can aspire to those of the other world. Although I believe you to be perfectly convinced of this, Mgr, I shall still ask God to strengthen you in this sentiment and allow nothing to weaken it, but to make it the unshakable foundation of all your conduct.

I am returning the note you were good enough to send me and which I read with the greatest consolation.'

Monsieur le Prince was Condé, who after a notoriously debauched youth, spent his last years in study and piety, but the letter referred to, if by him, is not obviously identifiable. Louis-Armand de Bourbon, prince de Conti, (Condé's nephew) had married Marie-Anne, the subsequently legitimised daughter of Louis XIV and Mme de la Vallière. The young man (1661-85) had also been worldly, and from this letter died piously.

*851129a   BISHOP OF LUÇON [HENRI BARILLON]   29 November 16[8]5
P f.622 (wrongly dated 1675)

'Your honoured letter, Mgr, fills me with joy. One would have to be heedless of the interests of Christ, the glory of his church and the salvation of those who are signed with the mark of his children, not to be deeply touched to learn that those who had left her bosom, who had risen against her and persisted so obstinately in their revolt, are at last returning to their duty with a readiness that can only be considered as a true miracle. For what connexion is there between this present fear and docility and the insuperable audacity which led them into the excesses and violence of the past? Such a change comes purely from God, and it is obvious that he has inspired the King, and given him the firmness necessary to undertake so great a matter and liberated him from all the political arguments and considerations which had stopped his royal predecessors.

I cannot tell you, Mgr, how much I share in your consolation, for I am sure that, having the heart of a true father and shepherd, you see the return of these sheep who have strayed in the holy spirit which, according to Christ's word, should be found in those charged with their conduct. I do not doubt that the work will be completed, and that the small number, which, you tell me, still holds out will give up in the end and follow the others' example.

As I imagine that you know what the Bishop of Grenoble has done, I will not tell you. It is his preaching, his care, and God's blessing that have reunited his diocese, and all the circumstances seem to me so happy that one cannot think about it without being deeply impressed. In his diocese those who bring terror with them have not been seen, and yet all have submitted.

You are no doubt going to work, Mgr, at strengthening spirits and those conversions which are still very shaky. There is every reason to believe that when souls seduced for so long by the wickedness and ignorance of their teachers come to know the truth, they will embrace it in good faith, all the more so as they will be unable to ignore the fact that they have been deceived and been given quite false ideas of the belief, principles, and conduct of Catholics. We shall not fail to redouble our prayers to give God humble thanks for looking in his mercy on our brothers, to ask him to complete what he has begun with such success, and to fill the King always with all blessings. I do not need to tell you, Mgr, how dear your person is to us. I am sure that in that you do me all the justice I deserve, and know very well how devoted I am. Ultimately it could not be a more entire and sincere devotion, any more than the respect and affection with which I am yours etc.

PS I must tell you that apart from the reasons for which I was so interested in the Chancellor's appointment, your brother was one of the main ones, and as a necessary consequence, you yourself, Mgr, for it is a great help to you in any affairs you may have that that door should be open to you.

I do not know if you know that a criticism of the book on monastic life has been printed at Cologne; the most slashing and violent thing possible. In a word it is the author who is attacked in respect of his life in the world, not the truths he put forward. Some people of the same stamp as the one who wrote it have been delighted, but apart from them it is true that it has been generally scorned and badly received, and even those who do not wish me well have condemned it like the others.'

The readiness with which Protestants were accepting conversion a month after the Revocation was hardly miraculous or reassuring. Louis' grandfather, Henri IV, a former Protestant, had no doubt granted the original Edict for political reasons, but Louis' action was no less political for corresponding with the wishes of his religious advisers. The dragoons had brought terror, being forcibly billeted on Protestant households in the final stages of the campaign of intimidation leading up to the Revocation. Dauphiné apparently escaped this shame. Such forced conversions were worth what one might expect, but it is to the credit of many bishops and clergy that they genuinely and humanely tried to win hearts and minds.

Louis Boucherat had just become Chancellor. His daughter, Catherine, was the wife of Barillon's brother, Antoine de Marangis, Intendant at Caen in 1685.

The Cologne book was Les Véritables motifs de la conversion de l'abbé de la T. . . . , *a scurrilous libel by the Protestant Daniel de Larroque, notable for apocryphal details concerning Mme de Montbazon's death and its effect on R.*

851130   MADEMOISELLE DE VERTUS   30 November 1685
Dubois II pp. 342–348 (from lost orig.)

'God knocked at the door . . . but passed on, being content to tell you and warn you to be on your guard.'

851205   RELIGIEUSE   5 December 1685
TC II/269

Give herself up to God in all her ills of body and spirit.

851206   MATHURIN QUÉRAS   6 December 1685
T 1066,f.75 orig.

Warm praise for book sent by Quéras. Hopes it meets a receptive public.

851220   MONSIEUR L'ABBÉ LE BOULANGER   20 December 1685
TC I/101

R. will pray for M. in a situation he has accepted out of obedience. Comments on dignity of priests of former times.

860101   DUCHESSE DE GUISE   1 January 1686
BN na 12960, p. 23; TC I/136: Mug II/19
The way to salvation 'for princes of the earth as for shepherds' is that of the Cross.

860103   RM [? DE HARLAY]   3 January 1686
TC II/185

Unexpected temptations should not surprise her. It is sometimes easier to overcome them with gentleness than violence.

*860121   [RM MARIE-LOUISE BOUTHILLIER]   21 January 1686
TC II/298

'I wish, my dearest sister, that God may continue to look on you in his mercy, not only for this year, but up to the moment when he has resolved to show his whole mercy to you, for I do not doubt that you share in it as much as you could wish by following the feelings and guidance he has given you on your calling. Madame de Fieubet is fortunate to have gone to God after serving him and leading such a Christian life. Her fate, as you say, is much better than that of those she has left behind on earth. You do well not to love life, for it is not agreeable, and only the hope of soon ending it and finding a better one can make it tolerable. I could not be more obliged to Monsieur le Théologal for his friendship towards me, and I beg you to tell him that I appreciate it as I should.

It is not, my dearest sister, out of natural feelings that you should be sorry at the evil you hear spoken of me, but because you are a Christian you love those whom God bids you love, and calumniators and speakers of evil offend him. If you find such people, pity them for their blindness, tell them very mildly and charitably that Christ forbids us to speak to the prejudice of our neighbour, especially of those who serve him, and that you would think yourself guilty of the sin they commit if you were not disgusted and repelled by what they tell you, and pray God for them. We must hate evil, but not the evildoer. Above all have no confidence in them, and never take their advice as regards your spiritual direction. Although a calumnious priest is in a state of mortal sin, his absolution is valid, but avoid confessing to them as far as possible. You can tell Monsieur le Théologal about your difficulty, and even what I have told you on the subject. The world is full of occasions obliging us to detach ourselves constantly from ourselves, and ceaselessly sacrifice ourselves to God's will. Pray God for me, my dearest sister, and ask him to make me faithfully observe the knowledge he has given me of my calling. Such knowledge is true, and there is no other, whatever may be said to the contrary.

I have seen the book of which you speak, and the fact is that I took no notice of it, and did not think that I ought to take up my pen for a moment in reply. He is a man who wants to do so much harm that he does none. I have been told that someone answered him some time ago, that the answer was generally current, but I have not seen it. I have also been told that there were others who wanted to reply, but it is God who answers for his servants when they are unjustly attacked by men. Let us not worry about what they say and let us only be concerned with pleasing God. I am yours more than I can say, please do not have any doubt on that score.'

The wife of Gaspard Fieubet, a close friend of R., was Marie Ardier, a cousin of Gaspard who married him as her second husband. The comtesse des Hameaux, her aunt, was one of the convent's chief benefactors. It was not long before the widower began to think of retiring from the world. The book referred to is that by Larroque, and an answer had been published in 1685 by Pierre de Maupeou, later R's biographer.

860130   CLAUDE NICAISE   30 January 1686
BN 9363,f.27 orig.; Gonod 68

Eclaircissements sent to Sluze. Alleged '*hemina*' of Monte Cassino no reason to relax rule. Sudden extinction of heresy an act of God through the King.

The much disputed hemina *is the measure used in the Rule (Ch. 40) for the daily wine ration.*

860131   RELIGIEUSE   31 January 1686
TC I/179, TC II/116

R. praises her conduct, 'one must never do wrong, but as regards good, one must sometimes abstain'. She is too weak to observe Lent. Respects to RM Superior.

*860131a   BISHOP OF LUÇON [HENRI BARILLON]   31 January 16[8]6
P f.625 (wrongly dated 1676)

'Only someone with as much kindness as you, Mgr, would remember a person like me amid your continual cares and occupations. I receive your blessing in spirit at the beginning of this year and pray Our Lord to spread his blessing over all your ways so that you do not labour in vain and have the consolation of seeing with your own eyes the fruit and effects of this solicitude.

I take more interest than I can say in the conversions in your diocese, and although I have already had the honour of writing so to you, I cannot refrain from expressing it again over the new progress of the faith with regard to the nobility, who were more obstinate and persevering in their error.

It is a surprising thing that reason, powerful as it is, should have had so little power over rational creatures until they had come to the last extremities, instead of going to meet the happiness that was being offered them and being delighted to find an opportunity for extricating themselves from the false path on which they were engaged.

The main thing, Mgr, is that they are now listening to what they would not hear, and there is every reason to hope that they will grow used to the truth when it is shown to them plainly and when they see it free from all the imaginary attributes with which they had so falsely endowed it. Time itself will soften the remaining bitterness and resentment in the hearts of those who took the step with less sincerity than they should have done, and they will come to see that the cruelty which they allege has been used towards them was really only charity. I do not know if I am mistaken but it seems to me that such a prompt and general return is one of the greatest things to happen in the Church since its inception.

I do not doubt, Mgr, that your tireless application and the special grace you have received from God to draw souls to his service will contribute more than anything to confirm the work, and that your gentleness and patience will smooth the ways for people who need to be supported and whose conscience cannot but be still confused. We do not fail to commend to Our Lord both flock and shepherd. You are too well aware of how deeply we are moved by all that concerns you.

The book of which you speak, Mgr, has fallen quite flat. Those who have read it have felt only contempt, and I think that the author is not a little mortified to see that he has not even had the prompt approval given to all scandalmongers. I did not think it worth a stroke of the pen. By God's mercy I shall always be as ready to abandon my person as to attempt to defend truth when it is under attack. You will be sent as soon as possible the *Clarifications* in the second edition, which has just finished printing; there are a few minor additions.

I thought that the conversions in the diocese of Grenoble were more complete than you tell me. God, whose intention is to test the zeal of the Bishop of Grenoble, does not want him to get away so lightly. What is to be feared is that as he is obliged to act alone, he will succumb to the weight of the task, and it is true too that God is the protector of his saints and that they find in him infinite resources. I am, Mgr, with a gratitude, affection and respect I cannot express yours' etc.

The book that fell flat was Larroque's; it did not fall quite as flat as R. says and was (and even is) quoted freely by R's critics. Le Camus continued to have grave difficulties with Protestants in his diocese.

860214   DUCHESSE DE GUISE   14 February 1686
BN na 12960, p. 24; Mug II/21

Encourages her in her impending retreat; nothing should deflect her from her chosen path.

860215   HENRI, CHEVALIER DE RANCÉ   15 February 1686
TC I/45

Avoid occasions of evil, treat neighbour as oneself.

860215a RM [? MARIE-LUCE]   15 February 1686
TC II/190
'It is better to deprive oneself of self than of outward things.'

860216 DUCHESSE DE GUISE   16 February 1686
BN na 12960, p.28; TC I/178 (dated 17 January 1686); Mug II/22
She must pursue her resolve without turning away or being deflected by others.
The BN series is usually the more reliable, but in this case the January date is the more likely.

860220 MONSIEUR ANJUBAULT, COLLÈGE DE MAYENNE   20 February 1686
BN 24123,f.69 orig.
R. always interested to hear from him. Recent brief worthy of the King's zeal in converting heretics.

860221 RM [? DE HARLAY]   21 February 1686
TC II/191
Contentment comes from leaving everything to God. Spiritual simplicity important.

860224 MADEMOISELLE DE VERTUS   24 February 1686
Dubois II/pp.343-348 (from lost orig.)
Detach herself from all earthly bonds.

*860225 MARÉCHAL DE BELLEFONDS   25 February 1686
BN na 12959,f.115, orig.
  'I am writing, Mgr, to the duc de Gesvres to tell him that we are very far from using against him the note he gave us, and, to keep you informed of the matter, I am sending you a memorandum about it. However, I am informing the duc de Gesvres that since we cannot maintain our right without harming his interests, we are withdrawing, and would not wish for anything in the world to draw any advantage from the consent he gave us. I can assure you most truthfully that I have written several times to Paris asking that he should be advised of our attitude about this and that I would not abuse his kindness towards us or do anything against the respect I owe him. I beg you, Mgr, to tell him yourself whatever you deem appropriate.
  The converts in these parts are extremely hard. They are some distance from us and do not come as far as our area, with the exception of a neighbouring gentleman who is no less Huguenot after his abjuration than he was before. Bellême and Alen-

çon are two towns that have distinguished themselves above all others for their obduracy. All we can do is pray God to touch their hearts and soften them. I hope that you find things better disposed in Normandy, and that the workers you take there with you are working there with blessing and success. I cannot believe that God has done so great a thing just to leave it unfinished and not put the finishing touch to it. I shall be really mortified if la Trappe is not on your itinerary. I do not need to tell you, Mgr, how present you are to us, and how carefully and diligently we offer you to Our Lord. I am sure that you are quite convinced of all the feeling and respect we have for you.

PS If you do not mind I am addressing the duc de Gesvre's letter to you.'

Léon Potier, duc de Gesvres (1620–1704), was at that time Governor of Perche (where la T. is) and in 1687 became Governor of Paris and a leading figure in the royal household. The case concerns an annual payment to la T. (going back to the Middle Ages) of 14,000 barrels of herring in respect of rights at Pont-Audemer. In a letter of 1681 Gesvres recognised this right, which was confirmed by the Parlement at Rouen in 1684. Gesvres then suddenly challenged the due, and in December 1686 obtained a reduction to 9,000 barrels. The monastic chronicler is in no doubt that la T. was in the right, but notes that R. was unwilling to pursue the case (Inventaire de la T. MS 304, pp. 624–6). It should be added that the herrings were not for the monks, who never touched fish, but for sale.

R. repeatedly refers to the obduracy of Protestants in the region and Mme de Guise organised several missions to Alençon.

860228 [JEAN FAVIER] 28 February 1686
A 2106,f.142 vo.

R. would be delighted to see him once more, but failing health makes him look more to death.

*860304   RM MARIE-LOUISE [BOUTHILLIER] 4 March 1686
TC II/188

'I could not answer your last letter sooner, my dear sister, being prevented by my ailments, which do not diminish, as you can imagine, and my usual occupations. All I see in it is a continuation of the situation in which it has long pleased God to place you, that is, one of temptations and sufferings, and with that your constant will to accept his orders and submit in all things to the dispositions of his providence. The more you embrace them the more he will give you the peace you need, and the more you will move him to take care of your person and all that concerns you. The shortest and surest way to do well in his eyes what we have to do is to hand over the care to him, without neglecting anything which we know he asks of us, for it would be no way to please him to put trust in him while remaining useless and negligent. You are quite right to renew your zeal and revive your piety, for one certainly always goes downhill unless one takes care, the weight of nature drags us down towards the ground, and unless we constantly wake ourselves up, we cannot help falling into torpor, a serious evil for those whose profession obliges them to live in continual vigilance. If you have some difficulty in the strictness you prescribe for yourself, remember that it cannot last long and that it will produce for you benefits and blessings which will never end. You tell me that you are depressed, and I say to you that you must banish all sadness from your heart. It is so great a fortune to serve Christ and be specially consecrated to him, that the mere thought of it should fill you with comfort and joy. In short, my dear sister, hope in him, his goodness is without limits and your infidelities are limited, great as they may be and you may believe them to be. I wish you, dear sister, all the grace you need, and beg you to believe that no one could be more interested than I in all that concerns you.'

860314   RELIGIEUSE [? DE LA ROCHE]   14 March 1686
A 2106,f.142

Trust superiors and find inner peace.

860315   RM   15 March 1686
TC II/296

Best way to fight human impulses is to turn one's mind away.

860317   PIERRE MAUPEOU   17 March 1686
Maupeou, *Vie* I, p.511

Asks Maupeou not to undertake his defence [against Larroque].

860324   MONSIEUR L'ABBÉ   24 March 1686
TC II/337

Once past the midpoint the rest of life is steady decline. M's province is in a terrible state: 'public calamities are like storms'.

Without identification of the address the province in question is unknown, but famine was afflicting much of France.

860328   CLAUDE NICAISE   28 March 1686
BN 9363,f.32 orig.; Gonod 69

Nicaise is in Paris. Criticism of *Sainteté* continues.

860402   RELIGIEUSE   2 April 1686
TC I/77

Only accept charge of souls if obliged. Praises RM superior. Advice on electing a sister.

860404 MADEMOISELLE DE VERTUS   4 April 1686
TC II/121; Dubois II/pp.342-348 (from lost original)

She fears death; R. reassures her. He is sure she received God's visit [in her illness] as a sign of his justice and goodness.

860406 DUCHESSE DE GUISE   6 April 1686
BN na 12960, p. 19

Commends her support of an upright man unjustly attacked [? Bp of Séez]. Her recent retreat must have made her see the world in different colours.

860509 RELIGIEUSE   9 May 1686
TC I/182

Since her infirmities continue, and neither cure nor sudden death is likely, she must abandon herself to God.

860512 RELIGIEUSE   12 May 1686
TC I/77a, TC I/181

Forget the past.

860512a [?]   12 May 1686
U 863

A Carthusian, dom D., having taken all his vows, wanted to come to la T. but R. was unable to receive him. After leaving his order the man has written to R. whose conscience is clear.

There is no address, and no indication even of whether the recipient is a man or a woman.

860515 CLAUDE NICAISE   15 May 1686
BN 9363,f 248 orig., Gonod /0

RP B[occone] wants to come to la T. R. encloses letter for abbé Régnier.

François Régnier des Marais (1632-1713), perpetual secretary of the Académie française from 1684, was a noted stylist and grammarian.

860523 RP CHANOINE RÉGULIER   23 May 1686
TC II/295

RP was right to avoid direction of souls; his strict principles would give him trouble with young monks. He may accept a simple benefice, but would do better to live and die in a cloister.

*860523a   BISHOP OF LUÇON [HENRI BARILLON]   23 May 16[8]6
P f.624 (wrongly dated 1676)

'I have just learned, Mgr, with extreme sorrow the loss that you have suffered in Monsieur de Morangis. As soon as I heard the news I thought of you, and I did not doubt how much you would take it to heart. God robs you of a brother whom you loved tenderly and who deserved your love. I am sure that he will not have failed at the same time to give you the necessary feelings not only to endure with patience such a harsh blow and one so unexpected, but also to make use of it in a holy way. If there is anything capable of detaching us from things on earth, it is seeing and experiencing the fact that they have neither duration nor consistency and elude us when it seems least likely that they will be taken from us. The best we can do for our peace of mind is to be always ready to hand back to God what he may ask of us at any moment. That is, we must separate ourselves from our self as from others, and not consider ourselves with regard to this present state, which is a mere vapour, which is why it deceives all those who look in it for a stability which it does not have and is not of this world. I share in your distress, Mgr, beyond all I can express. I say nothing of my own, which is what it must be after a friendship going back forty years. You know how I have always looked on your house. I pray God, Mgr, to be your consolation, I beg you to believe that I commend you to him more than all else, with all that concerns you, and no one in the world is yours with more heartfelt affection and respect than I.'

Antoine de Morangis died on 18 May.

860526   MADEMOISELLE DE VERTUS   26 May 1686
Dubois II/pp.342–348 (from lost orig.)

'In your present state God alone should speak to you and men should keep silent.... God appears to you as judge, he appears as charitable father, and I am sure his clemency ... will greatly outweigh his rigour and severity.'

860527   RP   27 May 1686
TC II/297

R. sorry that RP has to attend such unsuitable recreations and mix with persons of every condition and sex. Better to go to a smaller community than be obliged to have contact with women.

860530   MADAME   30 May 1686
TC I/183

'Believe that the days remaining to you are days of blessing and mercy.'

860530a RM PRIEURE   30 May 1686
TC II/146
If she is really sure that she lacks the qualities needed, then in conscience she must not accept the abbey offered.

860605 DUCHESSE DE GUISE   5 June 1686
BN na 12960 p.18
She is quite right but must beware of hostile people. The faithful can sometimes serve God only by suffering.

860606 RELIGIEUSE   6 June 1686
TC II/194
Her state is so deplorable that she needs prayer more than advice. 'If God is dead in your heart he can revive there again.' She should change her order if she can.

860611 DUCHESSE DE GUISE   11 June 16[8]6
BN na 12960 p.12 (wrongly dated 1676)
Missions to Protestants not having hoped-for success. R. thinks it would have been much better after their abjuration if they had been instructed and 'very gently' induced to approach the altar, not forced to do so.

Asks her when she comes to bring as few ladies as possible. 'Their curiosity is never satisfied and our brethren find them in every corner of the house.'

*860613 RM MARIE-LOUISE [BOUTHILLIER]   13 June 1686
TA orig.
'It is a great joy for me, my dear sister, to learn from time to time that you still have the feeling given you by God of wanting to be his alone, and separating yourself from anything that might prevent you from attaching yourself to him as much as you should. That duty, as you know, has no limits, so you could not renounce too many things, so long as that renunciation is according to your rules and consistent with your profession.

Do in simplicity all the good you can, without heeding judgements that may be passed on your conduct, and follow the impulses given to you by God. Those who think that the love of God consists in desiring to love him are not mistaken, so long as these desires are genuine and lively; for love is, as it were, in the feelings of the heart like their principle and source; and if one has it in this way, these desires spread over into effects and works, and do not run out in mere speculation. In truth it is when occasion arises that one knows whether one loves him or not, for the person who claims to love God and does not do what he ordains does not know himself, and does not know what it is to love.

Your understanding of your imperfections will be of use to you, provided it does not throw you into confusion and worry and gives you a will to be better and more perfect. That is the goal to which all our feelings about ourselves should tend, and whatever they may be, they are of no good to us unless they bring us to God, make us come nearer to him and increase our fidelity in his service.

Act with simplicity in any doubts that may come upon you; you have enough knowledge and understanding to embrace what is right in events, so long as your intentions are pure, and there is nothing against God's law and your Rule. Walk confidently and without fear or hindrance, for otherwise you will live in continual perplexity.

Farewell, my dear sister. I pray God to speak to you himself, and take particular care of your conduct; love him and you will find all you seek.

PS Assure Monsieur le T[héologal] of my gratitude doing me the favour of remembering me; please tell him that no one could honour him more than I. It would give me great joy to tell him so in person.

You sent me a letter from Madame d'Albon. Please send her on my reply.'

860616   RELIGIEUSE   16 June 1686
TC II/234

Whoever told her to forget her languor must have been inspired by God. Our physical state imposes on our souls.

860707   RM LOUISE-HENRIETTE D'ALBON   7 July 1686
A 2106,f.143 vo.

She should have followed advice of RP T. in giving up external penances. What she needs is inner mortification.

860711   RP   11 July 1686
TC II/47

If his monks are willing to live by the Rule 'you must sacrifice not only your peace . . . but your health and your own life for the salvation of your brothers and accept the yoke imposed on you'. Otherwise he must refuse.

860725   RP, CONG. ORAT.   25 July 1686
TC II/149

RP should not leave place to which God's will called him.

*860812   BISHOP OF LUÇON [HENRI BARILLON]   12 August 1686
P f.626

'I can assure you, Mgr, that it would hardly be possible to think of you more than I do. The loss of your brother, of the clergy of your diocese whom you needed so badly, and above all your poor health come into my mind more often than I can tell you, and never without feeling for you in your difficulties and pains. What we can do is to commend to God all that concerns you, and pray him to be himself your strength and consolation.

I wish you could find some remedy for your usual indispositions, for I confess that it would be most distressing if you, who are able to do all possible good in your diocese through your diligence and care, should find yourself in such a state as to be unable any longer to act. I hope that God will have pity on your people, and I cannot convince myself that he has given you all the qualities of a great bishop only to make them of no avail to you. However, Mgr, you know that he sometimes acts in ways impenetrable to men and the best one can do is to await the dispositions of his providence in a spirit of perfect submission. It is in that alone that we can find here on earth any peace of mind, for anyone who makes that depend on events will spend his life in agitation and anxiety and will never have a stable situation, whatever he may do.

I do not doubt that your brother will do all he can to make a stay in Paris, but I do not know if that will be in his power. The post he holds involves commitments of which he may well not be master. I beg you, Mgr, to do us the honour of coming to see us since God put the idea into your head. You will spend a few days in retreat and solitude to refresh yourself a little from all your fatigue. I cannot tell you how much joy that would give me nor the good it would do me, that is beyond any words of mine. Do me the justice of believing, Mgr, that no one could add to the affection, gratitude and respect with which I am yours' etc.

Barillon had lost M Boisdavid, his senior archdeacon, on 23 April, M Vainet, an archdeacon, on 2 May, and then his brother on 18 May. The surviving brother was Paul, ambassador to London.

860813   DUCHESSE DE GUISE   13 August 16[8]6
BN na 12960 p. 11 (wrongly dated 1676)

Everyone is complaining about the new converts. 'Those who are compelled to approach the sacraments are no better for it, but on the contrary most have exceeded all bounds by sacrilege.'

860814   MADAME DE LA GRILLIÈRE   14 August 1686
TC II/85

'God allows your outward eyes to grow weaker, but you must console yourself with the fact that your spiritual eyes are all the more open to your needs and wretchedness.'

She had cataracts.

860818   RP SIMON GOURDAN, SAINT-VICTOR   18 August 1686
TC I/143 (dated 1689); [Gervaise], *Vie de Gourdan*, p. 60

Danger of living in lax observances. Fatal blow given to Congregation of Saint-Victor by their fathers. Gourdan should go. R. would welcome him at la T. but there is not much choice; he has seen 'men of prayer' come and become 'cold as ice'.

860825   DUCHESSE DE GUISE   25 August 1686
BN na 12960 p. 13

R. has always striven to keep out of party disputes.

860908   MADEMOISELLE DE VERTUS   8 September 1686
TC II/86

Though she has no hope of a cure, it is a consolation for R. to know her submission to God's orders. People criticise her for living in too great seclusion, but let them talk.

860912   DUCHESSE DE GUISE   12 September 1686
BN na 12960 p. 16

God moves in a mysterious way. Hopes her health will soon improve.

*860913   BISHOP OF LUÇON [HENRI BARILLON]   13 September 1686
P f.627

'You can imagine, Mgr, my joy at the news you did me the honour of telling me. The Pope has given to the Bishop of Grenoble a rank in the Church of which he has surely shown himself worthy through all his life and conduct, and all right-minded people must rejoice to see him distinguished by such an eminent dignity as he was already by his sanctity and merit.

I do not doubt, Mgr, that God who has supported him up to now by a special and quite manifest protection will fortify him with renewed spirit and vigour so that he may meet the demands of so exalted a place, and one which exposes him much more than before. Those who care about him must diligently commend him to God, and I am sure that you will not fail to do so in accordance with the affection I know you bear him.

You do not say, Mgr, what you think about coming to see us on your return as you had given us to hope. I wish more than I can say that God would once more grant me that consolation before I die. However that may be, do me the honour and justice to believe that no one could be with more gratitude, sincerity and respect than I yours' etc.

Le Camus had just been promoted cardinal, to the intense annoyance of Louis XIV, who had unsuccessfully proposed Abp Harlay of Paris. Barillon had gone to Paris on family and other business, but did manage to call at la T. on his way back in May 1687.

860919   DUCHESSE DE GUISE   19 September 1686
BN na 12960 p. 2
Glad she is cured, but hardly thanks to him.

860921   RELIGIEUSE   21 September 1686
TC II/87
Wishes God would lighten her pains. 'Your pain is hard and long, but God, who is master, does not want it shorter or lighter.'

860923   CLAUDE NICAISE   23 September 1686
BN 9363,f.21 orig.; Gonod 71
Approves of Nicaise's journey to Paris.

860926   DOM PAULIN DE L'ISLE, OSB   26 September 1686
Lambert, L'Idée d'un vrai religieux, p. 60
So far Vannists have had little success at la T. but if dom Paulin is resolved to surrender wholly to providence, let him come and try.

861003   DUCHESSE DE GUISE   3 October 1686
BN na 19960 p. 20
Recent attacks on *Sainteté* have been contemptible; he does not know the author. 'The main thing is that truth prevails and all right-thinking people are convinced that I am right.' The book printed in Cologne, sold in Amsterdam.

This is Larroque's scurrilous book of 1685.

861007   DOM PAULIN DE L'ISLE, OSB   7 October 1686
Lambert, L'Idée d'un vrai religieux, p. 64
R. regrets so many obstacles to Paulin's translation, but his patience will eventually be rewarded with joy.

861007a   RM LOUISE-HENRIETTE D'ALBON   7 October 1686
A 2106,f.143
Pleased at Le Camus' promotion to cardinal. She should not scruple to read attacks on R. which are self-defeating. Le Camus too is under attack.

Louis XIV had been infuriated at Le Camus' promotion.

861008 RM ABBESSE   8 October 1686
TC II/40

R. knows how hard it is to destroy inveterate abuses in religious communities. She must not participate but try to show the nuns their duty.

861010 RM LOUISE-HENRIETTE D'ALBON   10 October 1686
A 2106,f.144 vo.; TC II/205

She should not complain of being left without a cross to bear. Now is the time to strengthen defences against her passions in calmness. Avoid singularity and make up in the heart for lack of bodily penitence.

861014 BISHOP OF GRENOBLE [ETIENNE LE CAMUS]   14 October 1686
TC I/145

Congratulations on promotion to cardinal. He should not change his way of life and should avoid courts both of France and Rome unless absolutely obliged to go.

861022 COMTESSE DE LA FAYETTE   22 October 1686
BN 24123,f.62; TC II/69

Tréville has misled her into thinking R. might be able to help. His motives for leaving the world: 'I hated it because I did not find what I sought there'. At first R. thought of living in his country house [Véretz] but God willed otherwise. This is the first time he had told anyone and she must respect the secret.

Her use of the word 'motive' suggests that her question was prompted by Larroque's scurrilous Les véritables motifs . . . *of 1685. This not very revealing letter has been reproduced in almost all biographies of R.*

861024 CLAUDE NICAISE   24 October 1686
BN 9363,f.29 orig.; Gonod 72

Nicaise is still in Paris. R. is pleased at promotion of both Le Camus and Sluze. Discusses *hemina* again [cf 860130].

* 861102 BISHOP OF LUÇON [HENRI BARILLON]   2 November 1686
P f.770

'No one could feel for you more than I, Mgr, in all your ills and troubles. God tries you in many ways, and I am sure that you look on all these unpleasant events as gifts of grace and do not fail to make good use of them. I hope that at the moment of speaking you have got out of this predicament, and that we shall soon have the joy to which we have for so long aspired. I think it will be the last time that I have the honour, for you can well imagine, Mgr, that my health is not increasing with my age. Ask God, I beg you, that I should employ the moments remaining to me better than I have those which are past. I admit that when I look at myself, all I see in my conduct gives me much cause for fear, and only my trust in God's goodness, which is without limit or measure, raises and sustains me from the dejection in which the sight of my wretchedness would cast me. I wish you, Mgr, a renewal of strength and blessings on the occasion of the great feast which we are still celebrating, and pray God that you may be one of those who have had the greatest share in the abundant grace spread by heaven upon earth. I am with a gratitude, affection and respect which I cannot express yours' etc.

861106   FRANÇOIS DE L'ISLE   6 November 1686
Lambert, *L'Idée d'un vrai religieux*, p. 68

R. has not forgotten visit of de l'Isle to la T. His brother [dom Paulin] has no choice but to await brief from Rome.

This brother was a canon of Notre-Dame de Châlons.

861110   MONSIEUR L'ABBÉ   10 November 1686
TC II/287

M is not obliged to convert people, but God's will is that he should try.

861111   CLAUDE NICAISE   11 November 1686
BN 9363,f.31 orig.; Gonod 73

Nicaise has sent a portrait of Le Camus.

861114   RP SUPÉRIEUR   14 November 1686
TC I/34

R. barely able to advise. Encourages vocation of a priest who has hitherto been a director; but one should not refuse oneself to the public for a quieter, but rather for a more austere, life.

861121   DUCHESSE DE GUISE   21 November 1686
BN na 12960 p. 4

They are praying for the King at la T. R. sends a book on religious life [probably *Instructions de Saint Dorothée*, just published].

861121a MADEMOISELLE DE VERTUS 21 November 1686
Dubois II/pp. 342–348 (from lost orig.)
She has been near death and must not now become too attached to life. Perseverance wins grace from God.

861125 RP [? SANTEUIL] 25 November 1686
TC II/88
RP must judge whether composing hymns or prose sequences makes him arid, but if it does he should give it up.
The address is to a Canon Regular, and Santeuil fits best among R's known correspondents.

861128 DUCHESSE DE GUISE 28 November 1686
BN na 12960 p. 1
R. is sending a letter to Mme de M[ornay] urging moderation but not indicating that anyone else had suggested it.
This may be the Mme de Mornay who, on being widowed in 1688, tried her vocation at les Clairets.

861201 COMTESSE DE LA BARGE 1 December 1686
TC II/270
R. thanks God for inspiring her to think more about herself than before. She has been ill for a long time, has an excellent confessor, has just taken communion and has asked for R's prayers.

861205 DUCHESSE DE GUISE 5 December 1686
BN na 12960 p. 22
Still praying for the King; thanks her for telling King.

*861207 BISHOP OF LUÇON [HENRI BARILLON] 7 December 1686
P f.628
'Allow me, Mgr, to ask for your news. You were ill last time you wrote, and intending to come and see us as soon as you were better. I am too genuinely interested in all that concerns your person, and especially your health, not to feel some anxiety and desire to know how you are. I admit that I should be much consoled if nothing were to prevent you passing by here on your return, for I have never had so many things to tell you, and such a need to talk to you. It will be however as God wills, for you know that the ideas of men are often not his.

I do not doubt, Mgr, that you were afflicted by the death of Father de Monchy. You were one of those he most honoured in the world. The poor man, holy as he was, feared death, to the extent of being disturbed and upset about it, and God (as I am sure you know) gave him perfect serenity ten or twelve hours before he passed away. I wish you, Mgr, both a long and a happy life, and pray God to pour on you all the gifts of grace, prosperity, and blessings which you need. I am with affection and deep respect yours etc.

PS I have to make a request of you, Mgr: Madame de Tourouvre [?] has made one to Madame de Morangis, asking her to use her good offices with Monsieur de Barillon to obtain for her a bed at the Incurables, which is about to fall vacant, on behalf of a lady in whose family I am much interested. As that has to go through your hands, as I understand, I should be deeply obliged to you, Mgr, if you could see to it that Monsieur de Barillon gives his consent. The lady is called Mlle de la Croix, of very good family, but poor and in distress. I will say no more about her because I know that Madame de Morangis has already spoken of her.'

Monchy, one of the closest friends of both R. and Barillon, died on 8 November. 'M.B.' is Paul, Mme de Morangis Antoine's widow. The reading 'Tourouvre' is doubtful; Mlle de la Croix is not identified.

861216   DUCHESSE DE GUISE   16 December 1686
BN na 12960 p. 3

Still praying for King's complete recovery. Praises his piety.

861219   MADAME   19 December 1686
TC II/253

R. driven to reflect on death of Condé [11 December]: 'It is much more advantageous to win battles over oneself than against outside enemies.'

861219a   DUCHESSE DE GUISE   [? 19] December 1686
Mug II/26

Death of Condé; approach of Christmas.

861225   DUCHESSE DE GUISE   25 December 1686
BN na 12960, p. 14

Improvement in King's health.

861227 COMTESSE DE LA FAYETTE 27 December 1686
BN 24123,f.63 vo.; TC II/69 (partial, dated 14 December)

Glad she enjoyed *Saint-Dorothée*. Mme de Saint-Loup not reliable on subject of R. as her charity leads her to extol her friends.

*861229 BISHOP OF LUÇON [HENRI BARILLON] 29 December 1686
P f.770

'Monsieur Pinette has told me, Mgr, how much care you took over my request, and I cannot dispense myself from expressing my gratitude. As I was extremely anxious that the matter should be successful, and was obliged to participate for quite urgent reasons, I appreciate all that you have done more than I could ever say. I hope to assure you myself more personally when we have the honour and pleasure of seeing you. Meanwhile I wish you a happy year and a renewal of health and holiness at once, and we shall continue to ask God to make you more and more in accordance with his heart. I beg you to grant me your blessing and be kind enough to believe that it is not possible to add to the respect, affection and gratitude with which I am yours etc.

PS Please be good enough to tell Madame Barillon how much I appreciate her kindness in nominating the person we desired. She could do no greater act of charity. Assure her that I have all possible respect for her.'

Barillon made retreats at the Institut de l'Oratoire, where Pinette lived and knew him well. There is no hint as to R's request. On the PS, see 861207.

861230 MADEMOISELLE DE VERTUS 30 December 1686
Dubois II/ pp. 342–348 (from lost orig.)

On frequent communion.

861230a DUCHESSE DE GUISE 30 December 16[8]6
BN na 12960 p. 8 (wrongly dated 1676); Mug II/30

Complete recovery of King. God counts our intentions and submissions, not our success.

87/1 MADEMOISELLE DE VERTUS [1687]
TC II/11

She is deprived of someone she trusted [? Hamon]. R. deeply sorry for her.

87/2   DUCHESSE DE GUISE [1687]
BN na 12960 p. 42

If only everyone did his duty all would be well but she must be forgiving. M de S[éez ?] to be pitied for receiving such a blow from such a quarter.

The allusion seems to be to the bp, and presumably to the continuing quarrel over jurisdiction.

87/3   RP SUPÉRIEUR 1687
TC I/185

R. not surprised in difficulty RP has had in trying to visit la T. He should not abandon his present charge nor accept the other one offered.

870116   DUCHESSE DE GUISE 16 January 1687
BN na 12960 p. 5

We follow Christ, not our works, and their success is unimportant. R. suffering a chest infection.

870118   COMTESSE DE LA BARGE 18 January 1687
TC II/80

Glad that her feelings are stronger and that she is persevering in her intention of belonging to God. She must trust not in her own strength but in God alone.

870125   DUCHESSE DE GUISE 25 January 1687
BN na 12960 p. 7

Sends some thoughts for her retreat. They sang *Te Deum* for the King's recovery. The bitter cold is not helping R's health.

870130   RM LOUISE-HENRIETTE D'ALBON 30 January 1687
A 2106,f.145

R. had no time to answer her request for advice, but is deeply sorry that her election obliges her to move so far, among strangers who may be hostile to her ideas. He urges charity and prudence, to temper the 'vivacity of your zeal'.

She had just been elected superior at Riom, in Auvergne, near her sister, Mme de La Barge (who must have had a hand in it) and Favier, against strong opposition from her own superior (RM Louise Rogier). She took up the post in May.

*870202   RM MARIE-LOUISE [BOUTHILLIER]   2 February 1687
TA orig.

'I do not think I wrote to you, my dear sister, that it was not a good thing to make retreats, but rather that it was not the main thing, and that it was of little use unless one took care to bring into one's works whatever resolutions one might have made, for it is not from one's frame of mind during retreat that one should judge one's state, but from its consequences and effects. It happens to many people that they are strict and regular for ten days, and then resume for the rest of the time the habits they had interrupted. My thoughts went that far and no further. I had no other intention than to oblige you to make some reflection which might be useful to you.

I am very glad that what you read in the book on monastic life causes you neither fear nor trouble, and that you appreciate the truths contained there. It is certain that anyone who examines those truths without prejudice and in a christian and pious frame of mind will find there a utility which those who read it in another spirit could never meet.

I pray God, my dearest sister, more and more to increase the feelings he has given you to love those things that come to you from creatures which might repel and to make all your happiness consist in pleasing him and living in such a way that there is nothing in your conduct that he will not find agreeable. Pray him for me, my dearest sister, and believe that no one could be more yours' etc.

*870206   RM MARIE-LOUISE [BOUTHILLIER] [?]   6 February 1687
TC II/81

'I should like you, my dear sister, to be wholly free from the thoughts that are occupying you, so as to be more able to put yourself in God's hands and ready to let yourself be guided purely by the dispositions of his providence. He has been pleased to deprive you of health, and you must believe, as I have often told you, that that is in order to purify you from many things which have no doubt escaped you against your duties, and thus make you stricter, better and more faithful than you have been hitherto. That is what will happen in you, provided you keep faith and patience, and remain in the state in which a true religious should be. For the rest, my dear sister, take care to keep yourself from all envy, all jealousy, and any other emotion which you know to be contrary to the feelings that God wants you to have for all the people with whom he has united you. The trouble that your ills may cause you inevitably arouses suspicions in you, and makes you imagine that people have an unfavorable view of you, or will find it hard to put up with you in your infirmities, but in this matter do not trust any of your thoughts, and listen to none to the detriment of the opinion you ought to have of all your sisters, especially your superior. It is the only means you have of winning from God all the consolation you need. We shall not fail to commend your needs to Our Lord as much as we can, I beg you not to doubt it.'

870206a CLAUDE NICAISE   6 February 1687
BN 9363,f.34 orig.; Gonod 74
Acknowledges receipt of document concerning Nicaise.

*870211   MARÉCHAL DE BELLEFONDS   11 February 1687
BN na 12959 f.117, orig.

'The best news you could give us, Mgr, is that of the King's complete restoration to health. God has granted it in response to the needs and prayers of the people, and never was anything more desired and requested than this.

It is a great good fortune that you keep your taste for a life of retreat in the midst of the world; it is a sign that that feeling has grown deep roots in your heart, and it is a most rare grace, especially at the present time when people do all they can to combine heavenly affairs with earthly ones, and to find pious peace in the agitation and tumult inseparable from the occupations undertaken in that lower region in which we are never secure unless God's order engages us there.

It is inevitable that worldly people, charitable as they are, take different views and attitudes about you, but they must have their say. The truth is that, as they have no certain knowledge, their decisions are always either false or rash, and one should consequently not be embarrassed by them or lay too much store by them. We do not fail to recommend to Our Lord, Mgr, your person and all that concerns you, I beg you not to doubt this.

PS I have received the writings you sent me. What I have already read seems to me so powerful, so elevated, and so enlightened that I do not think anyone has spoken better on these matters. All the principles are solid, pure, and fully developed. The treatises on penitence are incomparable; equally so is what is written on the subject of death and the attitude one should have towards it. Such opinions will not prove acceptable to everyone, and I do not doubt that, firmly founded though they are, there will be those who regard them as just personal opinions. I confess that they have moved me more than I can say. So far I have had to make only a few slight corrections. As soon as I have finished going over it I will send it back. The printed work may be very useful for women in religion but lacks the force of the manuscript.'

On 18 November 1686, Louis had undergone an operation for anal fistula, generally regarded as having been very serious.

The writings referred to in the PS *are the spiritual works of Bellefonds' aunt, Laurence Gigault de Bellefont [sic], foundress and superior of an abbey at Rouen. On the death of his parents she had been largely responsible for his upbringing and their relations had been close. She died on 31 October 1682. In 1686 the Jesuit, Dominique Boubours published a* Vie de Mme de Bellefont *in Paris, and alluded to the project of publishing some of her works later. It appears that Bellefonds and his other aunt, the Carmelite* RM *Agnès, found Boubours' approach somewhat controversial (his book, though relatively restrained, contains a violent at-*

tack on Port-Royal and identifies Mme de Bellefont with Jesuit interests in an unmistakably partisan way), and for whatever reason sent the MS to R. As printed, the essay on penitence covers three chapters, that of death another three, amounting in all to 282 pages, and five more chapters on various spiritual themes complete the work in 444 pages. The 'printed work' is her Considérations religieuses, written for her nuns and published at Rouen in 1674, comprising some 175 pages devoted to religious duties and concluding with brief acts of devotion. These were included at the end of the Œuvres spirituelles published in 1688 (and reprinted at Rouen separately in 1698). Also included, with separate pagination 1-24 at the beginning, were some early verse works, mostly paraphrases of psalms and the like. R's admiration is not misplaced; the essays on death and penitence show a woman of great sensibility, originality, and learning. From Boubours we learn that she had also published an anonymous translation of Edmund Campion's Decem Rationes (his ten reasons in defence of the Catholic faith). See also 870309.

870213   DOM JOSEPH MONTAIGNAC, FONFROIDE   13 February 1687
TC II/89

R. glad that Joseph still feels as he did despite opposition from his brethren.

870213a   DUCHESSE DE GUISE   13 February 1687
BN na 12960, p. 9; Mug II/31

R. is sure her retreat has been profitable.

870227   DUCHESSE DE GUISE   27 February 1687
BN na 12960 p. 6

R. sends a picture representing transitory nature of worldy goods and showing charity alone worthy of respect.

870227a   DUCHESSE DE GUISE   27 February 1687
BN na 12960 p. 15

Praises purity of her intentions. Great care is needed in selecting missionaries [among ex-Protestants].

The date may be wrong, or two sheets of the same letter may have been copied separately by mistake.

870227b   [JEAN FAVIER]   27 February 1687
A 2106,f.146 vo.

Favier's health is better. At sixty R. must feel his own end is near. On Mme X who wants to renounce the world for a christian life: 'the world is full of half-conversions', trying to combine earthly and heavenly values.

870302   MADEMOISELLE DE VERTUS   2 March 1687
TC II/167; Dubois II/ pp. 342–348 (from lost orig.)
Sympathy on her loss of Hamon; 'he was good for the soul as well as the body'. God tries us with suffering.
Hamon, physician of Port-Royal, had just died. See 87/1

870304   DUCHESSE DE GUISE   4 March 1687
BN na 12960 p. 26
Has seen pastoral letter of Le Camus. Sorry that such contradiction of the King's strict orders has been published rather than just orally discussed. Such tolerance good in itself but impolitic. Edifying death of the Abbess of Essai. His own end so imminent that he cannot contemplate the work she suggests.

Le Camus had mitigated the royal orders regarding forced attendance at sacraments of ex-Protestants in sending instructions to his clergy. Françoise Trotti de la Chétardie is recorded as dying on 10 June, so this letter is either based on false information or the date is wrong (probably July).

870306   DUCHESSE DE GUISE   6 March 1687
BN na 12960 p. 25
R. commends her choice of missionaries for A[lençon]. Gentle approach much better than a triumphalist one.

* 870309   MARÉCHAL DE BELLEFONDS   9 March 1687
BN na 12959,f.119, orig.

'I am sending back, Mgr, the manuscript which Mother Agnès addressed to me on your behalf, and the two little pieces you left with me when you were here; I have had them copied and corrected because they were full of mistakes. I have changed a few words here and there. I hope the work has been done exactly enough to satisfy you. It certainly contains opinions, reflections, and thoughts of the most remarkable kind, and people will find it hard to understand how a woman could have gone so far. We are sending you two prefaces for the memoranda you left with us. The first is a brief and succinct account of the life of the person in question, the other goes into it at rather greater length; no name has been included. You can put Madame or Mother as you deem appropriate. There is also a letter for the printer, more or less in the sense you indicated. I put in the phrase Christian Hours because that is what I thought you said; it can easily be changed if I am mistaken.

I have nothing new to tell you, Mgr. The large number of persons who leave this earth every day gives us no time to forget that it is not worth becoming attached to; everything there runs away too easily, and the best one can do is to turn one's eyes and desires towards those things which are more sure and substantial. We must love the things that cannot be lost if we wish to retain them and make every necessary effort to do so. We do not cease, Mgr, to recommend you and all your interests to God. I beg you not to doubt this, any more than the deep respect with which I am yours' etc.

The MS *is that referred to in 870200; the 'little pieces' are probably the poems mentioned in the note to that letter. This letter appears to be the sole, but conclusive, evidence that R. was the author or editor of material never hitherto attributed to him. In 1688 the* OEuvres spirituelles de Mme de Bellefont *were published in Paris by Hélie Joset, and dedicated to Mme la Dauphine. Since the word 'Hours' appears in the dedicatory letter ostensibly signed by the printer (referring to an earlier work similarly dedicated), and since a brief foreword (four pages) is followed by a longer biographical sketch (thirty-two pages), exactly as described in this letter, there can be no doubt that R. was the author of all three. The life in particular, with its reluctant recognition that in the unusual case of Mme de Bellefont studies had done no harm and its statement that she had always felt aversion for 'loose principles' (contemporary shorthand for Jesuit moral theology), is wholly characteristic of R. and neatly reverses the values of Bouhours' biography. Moreover the work itself is amply provided with marginal notes and such comments as 'belle phrase' ('fine phrase'), with which R. should also be credited. The volume came out with approval from Pirot (director of the Carmelites) dated 1 October 1687, from Bossuet (10 July 1688), the Bp of Coutances (Bellefonds' diocesan; 26 June 1688) and finally the official censor D'Arnaudin (15 July 1688).*

870316   DUCHESSE DE GUISE   16 March 1687
BN na 12960 p. 35

Desirable that there should be agreement on how to treat new converts. Truths are more likely to be acceptable if offered 'without the contentious manner which usually makes them odious'. The new converts everywhere are becoming more obdurate. R. has heard good things of C[uré ?] d'A[lençon ?].

870324   CLAUDE NICAISE   24 March 1687
BN 9363,f.37 orig.; Gonod 76

Nicaise's lawsuit. Hopes to see him after Easter.

870327   DUCHESSE DE GUISE   27 March 1687
BN na 12960 p. 29

Few men are concerned with doing their duty to God. Good wishes for mission.

*870329   BISHOP OF LUÇON [HENRI BARILLON]   29 March 1687
P f.771

'It would be a painful mortification for me, Mgr, if you went back to your diocese without giving me the honour of seeing you after hoping so long for it, for indeed if I do not have that pleasure at this juncture, I can no longer expect it in my lifetime, with my health being as poor and precarious as it is. The subject which keeps you in Paris is so worthy of your piety and the rank you hold not only in your family but in the Church, that you cannot refuse the time and effort you deem necessary to maintain peace between persons who ought to dwell in perfect union and understanding. I do not doubt, Mgr, that God will bless your diligence. My extreme concern with all that affects you, your person, and your house, makes me wish that more fervently than I can say. Keep for me always your accustomed kindness, and rest assured that I am with all possible respect and affection yours' etc.

The family affairs presumably concern settlement of the estate of Antoine, but the nature of the quarrel is not known.

870407   RM DE HARLAY   7 April 1687
TC II/168

She should be grateful for God's goodness, and her brother for God's enlightenment. She should write to him from time to time because he has confidence in her.

Her brother was Nicolas-Auguste Harlay, comte de Bonneuil, a conseiller au Parlement.

870504   RP   4 May 1687
TC I/158

R. has two certain principles: prefer public edification to private interests, and mistrust men of affairs. He has always refused money for masses, and prefers, as recently, to give it to the poor.

870504a   PIERRE COURCIER, THEOLOGAL, PARIS   4 May 1687
TC I/42; U 863

Case of a lady who withdrew sum offered at her religious profession. R. condemns the action, quoting St Charles.

This case aroused much controversy at the time. Louise-Catherine de Grignan entered the Carmelites in 1686 and renounced her heritage in favour of her father, comte de Grignan (whose second wife was a daughter of Mme de Sévigné) so that her sisters could have more from him. For reasons of health she left after eight months and the Carmelites then lost the pension her father had given them in return for her renunciation. (see Sévigné, Lettres, vol. III: p. 262).

870504b DUCHESSE DE GUISE   4 May 1687
BN na 12960 p. 10
R. has just heard of the indisposition which made her cut short her retreat.

870509 DUCHESSE DE GUISE   9 May 1687
BN na 12960 p. 32
Glad that her fever has abated.

870519 RELIGIEUSE   19 May 1687
TC II/151
R. has prayed as requested for a young woman and also for her mother.

870520 MADEMOISELLE DE VERTUS   20 May 1687
Dubois II/ pp. 342–348 (from lost orig.)
R. sends latest *Relations, Saint-Dorothée*, and *Dissertation sur les Humiliations*, a wooden spoon and some crosses.

870522 MADEMOISELLE DE VERTUS   22 May 1687
TC I/40
No hope of her recovery, but R. consoles her.
This date is suspect because of the previous letter.

870526 DUCHESSE DE GUISE   26 May 1687
BN na 12960 p. 30
R. not surprised at her disappointment over the new converts. 'Time, gentleness, and careful instruction might overcome their prejudices, but it very much looks as though too much pressure does them more harm than good.' Men should follow God's actions, not anticipate them.

870529 RM LOUISE-HENRIETTE D'ALBON   29 May 1687
TC II/334
Strongly advises her against becoming superior.
Since she actually began as superior at Riom in May this date must be suspect.

870601 CLAUDE NICAISE 1 June 1687
BN 9363,f.38 orig.; Gonod 77

M Ouvrard, canon of Tours, came with Nicaise to la T. but was in such a hurry that Nicaise could stay no more than two days.

870604 FRANÇOIS DE L'ISLE 4 June 1687
Lambert, *l'Idée d'un vrai religieux*, p. 76

Paulin is now a novice, in perfect health, always mindful of his brother.

870610 DUCHESSE DE GUISE 10 June 1687
BN na 12960 p. 43

Recent heat has made R. very tired, but he feels better now. Wonders who will take place of Abbess of Essai.

It was in fact her sister, Marie Trotti de la Chétardie.

870614 MATHURIN QUÉRAS 14 June 1687
T 1066,f.76 orig.

The two religious in question are not at la T., though as soon as anyone disappears that is where people look. Four Vannists [including dom Paulin] are there, but with their superiors' permission. Warm praise for Bp of Troyes [François Bouthillier de Chavigny, R's cousin].

870620 [? RM LOUISE-HENRIETTE D'ALBON] 20 June 1687
TC I/39

Sees his friends less and less and writes less and less. Would do anything for her and her mother, but cannot consent to what he has always refused.

Presumably a visit, permitted only to women of royal standing.

870629 FRANÇOIS DE L'ISLE 29 June 1687
Lambert, *L'Idée d'un vrai religieux*, p. 80

Paulin, just professed, enjoying deep peace and tranquillity; does not write himself from respect for the rule.

870703 [JEAN FAVIER] 3 July 1687
A 2106,f.147 vo.

R. is sorry about his niece's translation, but praises her exact and even severe conduct. Wishes he were worthy of Favier's opinion of him.

*870703a BISHOP OF LIMOGES [LOUIS D'URFÉ] 3 July 1687
TC I/71

'Mgr, the ideas which you believe to have been effaced more than forty years ago are still very much alive and present, and I well remember having noticed in you from your most tender youth a wisdom and maturity which were the manifest signs of the hand of God and of his design for putting you one day into the top ranks of his church. Indeed, as his providence has used you in such a post, by charging you with the conduct of a great diocese, which you only reluctantly accepted, submitting to the opinions of those who told you that you could not refuse it without resisting his orders, you have reason to hope that he will fill you with that vital spirit and give you all the protection necessary for bearing a burden whose weight you know full well. God leads his ministers when it is he who chooses them, and as all appearances lead one to believe that you have been placed by his hand, it must not be doubted that he will be met with in all your ways and that he himself will be your guide and your light. I am convinced, Mgr, by all the evidence reaching me, that your life sheds all the edification and odour of sanctity which that of a true bishop should. I know too that it is exempt from the pomp and spirit usually encountered in those whose vocation is not as pure as yours. But the main thing is that you give yourself entirely to the flock whose sanctification has been entrusted to you by the first of shepherds and regard that occupation as your sole task.

It is true, Mgr, that although I withdrew from the world in order to be entirely forgotten by it and devote myself to eternal silence, against all my views God has allowed that what I wrote for the instruction of my brethren should become public, and as in that I had confined myself solely to what concerns my calling, it may be that he has given it some blessing. But it would not be the same thing if I went beyond the bounds he prescribed for me, and you will permit me to say, Mgr, that what you desire of me exceeds my strength and ability, and does not befit a man of limited intelligence, a religious, or a sinner, such as I am, *nec ignaro in promptu, nec monacho in ausu, nec poenitenti in affectu.* These words of St Bernard [Ep 89.2] seal my lips, set my duty before my eyes, and prevent me from forgetting it. So what we can do is to offer our prayers to God for those whom he exposes in his church, who constantly have their weapons in their hands and who, so to speak, bear all the burden and heat of the day [Mt 20:12-13]. I feel under all the more obligation to do so for knowing that dissipation is not to be avoided even in the holiest of functions.

I did not deserve the honour of being remembered by you nor your kindness in giving me such proof. I humbly beg you to believe that I am as appreciative of your grace as I should be. I shall try as far as I can to acknowledge it before God, praying him with special fervour to bless your efforts and solicitude and to finish making you a pastor wholly according to his heart. I ask your blessing, and beseech you to be sure that no respect could be greater than that with which I am yours' etc.

The reference to forty years is odd: the Bp had made a long retreat at la T. in 1676, on his appointment as Coadjutor, but the period before 1647 would go back to his childhood at court, and presumably some prophetic conversations. It sounds as though publication of Sainteté had prompted a renewal of correspondence.

870710   RP CHANOINE RÉGULIER   10 July 1687
TC II/290

No need to study theology; morals of the Fathers enough not only for directing a parish, but for ruling the largest diocese. Avoid offices not conducive to salvation. Do not give in to blindness of superiors.

870717   CLAUDE NICAISE   17 July 1687
BN 9363,f.41 orig.; Gonod 79

Nicaise is writing an account of his visit to la T. Greetings to abbé de La Chambre.

Nicaise was persuaded not to publish his excessively fulsome account. La Chambre was curé of Saint-Barthélemy, Paris, and died in 1693.

870814   DUCHESSE DE GUISE   14 August 1687
BN na 12960 p. 37; Mug II/35

She must accept the frustration of her plans for good as God's will.

870814a   CLAUDE NICAISE   14 August 1687
BN 9363,f.43 orig.; Gonod 80

Death of Cardinal Sluze.

870823   DUCHESSE DE GUISE   23 August 1687
BN na 12960 p. 41

R. has been ill for a week with a chest infection, fever, and general lassitude, but has been better for past two days. People have not supported her, and her plans have not succeeded, but God will not blame her.

870829   MADEMOISELLE DE VERTUS   29 August 1687
Dubois II/ pp. 342–348 (from lost orig.)

No hope of recovering her health. 'You must regard yourself as a victim already on the altar ready to be sacrificed.'

870831 DUCHESSE DE GUISE   31 August 1687
BN na 12960 p. 39

R. hopes to see her. His health is a bit better. Hopes mission in October will have more success. Old established Catholics need it as much as new converts.

870900 MONSIEUR DE [. . .]   September 1687
TC II/273

Long illness gives best idea of world's wretchedness. God has been gracious to M.

870904 ABBÉ COMMENDATAIRE   4 September 1687
A 2106,f.148 vo.; TC II/95

Monsieur supervises training of priests for England and Ireland, an admirable use of Church funds. A commendatory abbot must see that his monks have enough food to do their duty if not to fill them, and then help the local poor and see to other religious purposes.

870911 CLAUDE NICAISE   11 September 1687
BN 9363,f.47 orig.; Gonod 83

Death of Sluze. Comment on 'extravagant and impious doctrines attributed to Quietism'.

870918 RM LOUISE-HENRIETTE D'ALBON   18 September 1687
A 2106,f.149 vo.

He is not surprised at the difficulties she is encountering. She must be patient and moderate, win gradually what cannot be won at once. Let her nuns read François de Sales and Rodriguez if they do not like saints of the distant past. Superiors need God's help more than anyone.

Rodriguez was a Jesuit spiritual writer (1526–1616) whom R. frequently recommended. Cf. 881213.

870918a MADAME   18 September 1687
TC II/196

'God wants you to be attached to nothing, like a bird on the branch which is always ready to fly away.'

870921 RM ABBESSE, 21 September 1687
LES CLAIRETS [FRANÇOISE-ANGÉLIQUE D'ETAMPES DE VALENÇAY]
A 3389,f.23

R. answered her first letter saying that his bad health did not allow him to do what she asked. The decision now rests with Abbot of Clairvaux.

The abbess on election had written to ask R. to take direction of the abbey over from Val-Richer. There is no trace of his earlier letter, nor of two later ones (noted in MS *as written on 3 December 1687 and 8 April 1688) in which he continued to refuse.*

870924 DUCHESSE DE GUISE 24 September 1687
BN na 12960, p. 45

R. still feels tired, but fever has gone. He is more and more affected by seasons. Hopes to be well enough to see the Grand Duchess [of Tuscany; Mme de Guise's sister] on her return journey. Regrets emigration of Protestants but if they had been approached more gently and gradually they might have been won over. A consistent policy would have prevented the present deteriorating situation.

870930 DUCHESSE DE GUISE 30 September 1687
BN na 12960 p. 44

We must accept frustration of our best plans as God's will. 'It is true that I am easily deceived, for, since during my time in the world I had the wretched rule of always believing evil in order to believe the truth, because of my poor opinion of men's sincerity, it seemed to me that I could best repair the distortion to which I had been so prone by following completely the opposite course.'

* 871005 BISHOP OF LIMOGES [LOUIS D'URFÉ] 5 October 1687
TC II/355

'I see that you are not satisfied with yourself, Mgr, and that your conception of the greatness of your duties makes you believe yourself to be falling far short. You are receiving a special grace from God in being as diligent as you are in his service, in giving to it all your time, presence, and mind [?], and yet considering yourself a useless servant. That is the way to bring the Prince of shepherds to support and increase your fidelity. For you know that nothing pleases and touches him more than the humility of his ministers when it is accompanied by their solicitude. I know, Mgr, that yours is continual, that you deny yourself everything so as to give yourself to those to whom you belong, and that your only care is to make yourself useful to the people whose guidance it has pleased God to give you. It can hardly be that, following as much as you can his orders and intentions, and seeking only to please him, you are not working for yourself by working for others . I do not doubt, however, that in all your diligence in acquitting yourself of what God demands of you, you feel the anxieties of those who have ardent charity and affection for those he has entrusted to them, and say like the apostle *quis infirmatur et non infirmor? quis scandalizatur et ego non uror?* [2 Co 11:29] But I do not doubt either that his merciful hand sustains you, convinced as you are that he takes note of the dispositions of the hearts of those who serve him and that their works are often most full when they believe them to be most empty.

If the book on monastic life edifies you, Mgr, it is the pure result of your piety, and you must have much piety in the rank you occupy in the church to find in monastic instructions, made only for simple religious, something applicable to yourself. It is true that mention is made there of vigilance in superiors, of prayer, charity, humility, and penitence, which are the principal virtues and qualities of those fortunate enough to belong to Christ, but this is done in so ordinary a manner, so ill befitting the excellence of the subject, that what is said is much more likely to weaken the subject than show it in its true light. It is easy to see, Mgr, that all that concerns the glory of God is precious to you, and I confess that I should be rewarded already in this world for the time I spent on that work if there were something in it of some importance or use to you.'

871009   DUCHESSE DE GUISE   9 October 1687
BN na 12960, p. 38; Mug II/49

R. wishes she had more cause to be satisfied with people, but she must observe charity.

871015   DUCHESSE DE GUISSE   15 October 1687
BN na 12960, p. 40; Mug II/40

R. deplores men's obduracy, but we must accept what we cannot change. Better authority in the hand of one person than continuation of divisions that have caused such scandal of late.

871016   PIERRE NICOLE   16 October 1687
BN 17755 orig.; Nicole, 1718 *Lettres*, I/ p. 566 (dated 1689)

R. is used to fine work from Nicole. Praises his last work, in particular reply to Jurieu [Protestant polemist].

871027   MGR RANUZZI, NUNCIO   27 October 1687
TC I/20

Refers to recent letter from superior of Theatines and whole question of religious of other orders accepted at la T. Justifies reception fifteen or sixteen years before, of Celestines whom he could not send back 'to the middle of a shipwreck'. Praises Maurists but condemns decadence of Celestines.

871028 [JEAN FAVIER] 28 October 1687
A 2106,f.150 vo.
Delighted at news of his niece, and Favier's approval of her efforts. Her reply to her sister [Mme de La Barge] is edifying, and promises well. Asks Favier to recommend her to go gradually.

From surviving letters we know that Mme de La Barge had tried to persuade her sister that her daughters had a religious vocation, about which Louise-Henriette was most sceptical.

*871030   BISHOP OF LIMOGES [LOUIS D' URFÉ] 30 October 1687
TC I/83

'It is true, Mgr, that it would have been an appreciable consolation for me if nothing had frustrated your plan to honour our desert with your presence. God has deprived us of it, and has only wished us to be obliged to you for having thought of it. I cannot help wondering at the restlessness of most men, who with good intentions upset those with still better ones and often unconsciously fight against impulses and desires which are God's. I speak thus in our own interest, for the mere sight of a person of your dignity, on whom God has bestowed so much grace, would have benefited us more than I can say. The main thing is that we can be sure that we have some part in your remembrance, especially before Our Lord.

You must be persuaded, Mgr, that the austere life you lead will not fail to be censured. It is enough that a man should not follow the way of the majority and walks with the minority. The broad and spacious paths win the vote of the world outside, but not that of God, who taught us that the gate is strait and will be opened only to a few. Since men fortunately do not judge us in the last resort, they must be allowed to have their say, when one has truth on one's side. To be content and indifferent to their opinions it is enough that one should please God. I do not see anything blameworthy in the conduct of a bishop who withdraws from all useless contacts and frequentations, who gives himself solely to his calling and who sustains by himself those whom he must use in the holy functions of his ministry. Is it not right that he should know them in order to apply them, that he should know the degree of their virtue, piety, and learning, so as to avoid mistakes in giving them tasks of which they are incapable? As the society in which you live is the most cherished portion of the flock, and that which should contribute to the sanctification of your diocese, you could not have it too much under your eye, and when you reflect that the disorder within the church and the disruption one sees among the people come from the incapacity of its ministers, nothing will divert you from the conduct you are following. It is unusual, but completely healthy and appropriate to your profession.

I perfectly understand, Mgr, what you say, and I confess that in your calling more suffering can come in a moment through events which God allows to occur, than in years or through the most rigorous mortifications in places of solitude. That is why, when I set the life we lead, hard and severe as it may appear, beside the tribulations exercising those who are in the world, I am far from believing our life to be as people imagine. Yet I cannot help acknowledging my infinite obligation to the goodness of God who, seeing me feeble as I am, withdrew me to shelter so as to protect me from countless vexatious occurrences to which I should have succumbed. I have this confidence in his mercy that, providing I am faithful in acquitting myself of the duties with which he has charged me, he will not fail to count my intentions as something and judge me in his compassion.

You owe to God alone, Mgr, the feelings you have about yourself and the greatness of the task with which you are charged. There is no better way of preserving yourself from the negligence of those shepherds who have only the most banal views on so exalted and difficult a position, and who, for want of knowing what God demands of them, have anything but the care and vigilance they should have for the preservation and increase of the flock whose conduct it has pleased God to entrust to them, and pay no attention to the fact that he will look to their hands for the blood of the least of the sheep lost through their neglect. That means, Mgr, that a pastor will only be clear when he has given himself entirely to those to whom Jesus Christ gave himself, when he looks to Christ as his model and in imitation of him works for the salvation of the souls he governs on Christ's behalf and in his name by his solicitude, his words, his example, his prayers, so that, with the prophet, he can say, of those who stray despite his diligence and efforts, *justitiam suam non abscondi in corde meo, veritatem tuam et salutare tuum dixi, ipsi autem contemnentes spreverunt me* [Ps 39:11].

That is all too much for a person who has all the charity and enlightenment you have. I pray God to increase it continually, and by his grace see that you do not cease in his service, and that the words and different thoughts of worldly people do not delay you for one moment or one step in your course. I am with deep respect yours' etc.

The society in which the Bp lived was the diocesan seminary.

871030a HONORÉ COURTIN, CONSEILLER D'ETAT   30 October 1687
TC II/189

R. believes that God wants Courtin where he is; Courtin has seen close friends die and must prepare for his own end.

871106 RM LOUISE-HENRIETTE D'ALBON   6 November 1687
A 2106,f.150

Urges her again to go gently, to seek to persuade in private as well as in public. If gentleness fails, then try severity, and if that fails too, give up and return to Tours.

871109 RM ABBESSE   9 November 1687
TC II/289

Since her efforts to restore order have been vain, and things are now worse, thanks to protection given to recalcitrant nuns, all she can do is go; 'it is a Babylon which you must leave'.

871115   RP CHANOINE RÉGULIER   15 November 1687
TC II/271

Though his community is not strict, RP must do what he can to follow strict penitence, even if it means being different.

871119   RP PRIEUR   19 November 1687
TC II/46

He should refuse post offered, sure to be dangerous. Follow his rule, vigil, fasting, and silence.

The date 4 February 1682 also appears on the copy and is almost certainly correct. See 820224.

*871122   BISHOP OF LUÇON [HENRI BARILLON]   22 November 16[87]
P f.14 (wrongly dated 1673)

'No one could be more delighted than I, Mgr, that your [cure ?] was successful, and to learn that the waters were fully as effective as you expected. I hope that your health will improve as a consequence; it is necessary to so many people that God will no doubt preserve it for their good and consolation. The bad climate of your region always makes me afraid, and I confess that when I consider the great number of persons you have lost, and your difficulty in finding replacements, I share all your worries and feel them more than I can say. You are in the hand of God, Mgr, and dependent on him, and I am sure that you look on all the orders of his providence with perfect submissiveness.

I received a few days ago a letter from Cardinal Le Camus saying how pleased he was with your visit. The steadiness of his conduct is most edifying. God gives him counterbalances to keep him in a consistent position, and prevent the effects which could easily arise from the situation in which he is. He assures me that nothing escapes his control and he profits from everything that God allows to happen to him.

I have seen the brief sent to him by the Pope, which amounts to public justification of him. We do not cease, Mgr, to offer you to God and commend to him your health and sanctification. Nothing comes more constantly to my mind than what concerns you. I beg you to believe this, as well as all the affection and respect with which I am yours' etc.

Le Camus was not made cardinal until 1686, and as the close collaborators of Barillon referred to in this letter died in 1686, and Barillon took the waters and then spent a week at Grenoble in 1687, the proper date for the letter would seem to be that year.

871123   BISHOP OF MEAUX [J-B BOSSUET]   23 November 1687
Bossuet, *Correspondance*, III p. 447

R. is attacked on all sides. Visits of Mme de Guise proof of his loyalty.

871200 DUCHESSE DE GUISE   [November/December 1687]
Mug II/43
Her letter brought by a gentleman who intends to give himself to God and leave the world.

*871214 BISHOP OF LIMOGES [LOUIS D'URFÉ]   14 December 1687
TC I/35

'I believe, Mgr, since you order me to tell you my opinion, that the chief penance open to a person appointed to high dignity in the church is to afflict himself before God for not doing, whatever he may do, all that he should to acquit himself of the duties of the charge imposed upon him and, at the same time, for the fact that those with whose government he has been entrusted respond neither to his efforts nor his desires. I am sure that there are none in the place you are in who do not find the people lacking in docility, the ecclesiastics negligent, and who do not have constantly before their eyes reasons for just and legitimate grief. It is a hard and heavy cross to bear for those who have a pastor's charity and really have at heart the salvation of souls. There are numerous other unpleasant and trying incidents which God allows to occur in the course of their lives, in order to test and increase their virtue, and we must believe that they are obliged to accept them not only with patience but with a resignation worthy of the perfect calling in which they are engaged. A common virtue is enough for ordinary people, but for those called by God to consummate piety, the virtue must be eminent.

Apart from the spiritual hardships they must endure and the different obstacles put in their way by men who treat them unjustly and judge their actions without understanding or equity, there can be no doubt that they must of their own accord seek particular penances, and while these should not go as far as those of persons devoted to retreat, they must be really felt and the sacrifice made to God must cost them something. That is something they can accomplish by depriving themselves of the pleasures to which people living in the world become habitually attached, as of the table, carriages, furniture, conversation, and by reducing themselves to a simplicity which is not too extreme, but is still fitting for those who must continually instruct others by their example as well as by their precept. Such moderation may be called a penance, and such retrenchment has something painful about it at a time when it can be said that luxury, vanity, profusion, and pomp reign more than ever. To that may be added, Mgr, if God is in one's mind and feelings, a hard bed to lie on, which has its uses, as long as health permits, and that is necessary for a prelate to discharge his functions, which are always laborious and arduous if they are done properly, and fasting on Saturday, less noticeable than on another day, because more usual. That seems to me to be enough, unless God for special reasons or by special inspiration moved you to do more. The main thing is to animate the body with action, and to ally to it the spirit, without which all outward things are without value or merit in the eyes of him who rejects all victims unless the heart offers and sacrifices them.

I see, Mgr, that I am going on too much, but I do so only because you wanted it, and in accordance with my desire to give you at every opportunity signs of my respect and obedience.'

871214a   CLAUDE NICAISE   14 December 1687
BN 9363,f.31 orig.; Gonod 83

Nicaise has sent some Latin poems which R. would once have enjoyed but on which he used to waste time which he must now make up.

871218   RM LOUISE-HENRIETTE D'ALBON   18 December 1687
A 2106,f.151; TC II/90

Her gradual methods are at last bearing fruit. Avoid admitting more nuns, as this would make dowry necessary, which would be wrong. Try to reduce visits from outside; seculars only cause trouble.

871228   PIERRE NICOLE   28 December 1687
BN 17755 orig.; Nicole, *Lettres*, 1718 I/ p. 562

Thanks Nicole for latest volume of *Essais de morale*.

871229   RM   29 December 1687
TC II/197

She asks if God will forgive her past aberrations. In her strict observance she has every hope of salvation. No need for unusual penances, the ordinary ones will do.

88/1   DUCHESSE DE GUISE   [1688]
Mug II/59

R. sorry for the people she speaks of, who went off without a word of thanks.

88/2   DUCHESSE DE GUISE   [1688]
Mug II/60

She did well to use the people sent for from Le Mans.

88/3   DUCHESSE DE GUISE   [1688]
Mug II/64

As she did not strictly keep her resolve, she did well to put off her communion. R. hopes to see the Grand Duchess as she passes through.

88/4 DUCHESSE DE GUISE [1688]
Mug II/65
She is in Paris. Life assuredly full of unpleasant events.

88/5 COMMANDEUR DE MALTE [1688]
TC I/27
R. sends rule of life requested; from first rising every action should be accompanied by prayer.

This is either Commandeur de Laval or de Mareuil; his relations with each were similar and belong to about the same time.

88/6 MARQUISE DE LA SABLIÈRE [1688]
Menjot d'Elbenne, *Mme de La Sablière*, 14

We should not leave the situation in which God has put us without good reason; 'the difference between temptation and inspiration is the disturbing effect of the first and the calm of the latter'.

The attribution of this fragment is not absolutely certain. Mme de La Sablière's first extant (copied) letter of March 1687 shows that R. has already written to her, but no letters from him can be identified before 1688.

880101 DUCHESSE DE GUISE 1 January 1688
TC I/148
New Year greetings.

880100 DUCHESSE DE GUISE January 1688
Carp, p. 606; Mug II/54
R. will obey the Queen of Spain [who had written asking for a letter].

880115 RM ABBESSE [? GIF] 15 January 1688
TC I/134

If resignation has not brought her the peace she wanted, it is because it was her own decision for which God may be punishing her.

Anne-Victoire de Montglat resigned as abbess in 1686, becoming prioress in 1687, and is almost certainly the person addressed.

880115a CLAUDE NICAISE 15 January 1688
BN 9363,f.53 orig.; Gonod 85
Nicaise is right to long for retreat.

*880115b BISHOP OF LUÇON [HENRI BARILLON] 15 January 1688
P f.629

'There is never a day, Mgr, when I do not think many times of you; your cares, your difficulties, the losses you have suffered in your diocese often come into my mind, and always with much regret. I hoped that your health would be a little better, and that taking the waters would have restored it, but I learn that you are suffering your usual attacks. I confess that I am much distressed to hear it.

I fully understand, Mgr, the state in which you may be, knowing your zeal for those whom it has pleased God to entrust to your charge, and the way you have been deprived of the workers necessary for aiding your plans. I add to that many other things, and all I can say (alas, I tell you what you practise perfectly well) is that you will have no peace and consolation in this world except inasmuch as you submit to God's orders. He is the master, who makes of men anything he pleases, and often leads them to the only good they desire and hope for by ways unknown to them. We must love his providence, worship it without examining or seeking its reasons. It is enough to know that it is just, *non delectatur in perditionibus nostris* [Job 3:22], he wants only the salvation of those who serve him and sincerely intend to be his. I am certain that you belong to that number, small as it may be.

We shall not fail, Mgr, to commend to God your person and all that concerns you, with all possible diligence, and to ask him to give you happy days. It must be admitted that this life is a slight enough thing, whether because of its uncertainty or its short duration.

I have just learned of the death of the poor Président de Mesmes, who was, as you know, one of our oldest and best friends. He was struck down with apoplexy and lived only two or three hours.

Do me the honour of continuing your friendship and please believe that no one could add to the affection and respect with which I am yours' etc.

Jean-Jacques de Mesmes came of a long line of distinguished magistrates and was a member of the Academy.

880118 MARQUISE D'ENTRAIGUES 18 January 1688
TC II/169

He is sure she has already taken steps to implement the feelings inspired by God. She must find a good director.

She was the half-sister of Sr Louise de La Vallière.

880118a RP ABBÉ, VAL-RICHER [DOMINIQUE GEORGES] 18 January 1688
Maupeou, *Vie* I, p. 529

R. refers to Mège's commentary on the Rule.

880120 MONSIEUR 20 January 1688
Carp, p. 625
Floods of visitors at la T.

880200 DUCHESSE DE GUISE [January/February 1688]
Mug II/48
Thanks her for the *Life of Saint Louis*. The poor lad who came to try his vocation stayed only four days.

*880128 BISHOP OF LIMOGES [LOUIS D'URFÉ] 28 January 1688
TC II/98

'I never doubted, Mgr, that you were perfectly well informed about all the things concerning which you ordered me to write, and better able than anyone to give lessons to those who did not know them; but I am sure that you have also learned from your own experience, for it is hardly possible that, having left the broad and spacious ways to walk as you do in the narrow paths, you should not find opposition from those who do not follow the same route as you. Good is no more than a goal for those who do not do it. Those who do not have it in themselves cannot bear it in others, and men very commonly condemn those who are better than themselves. One would have less to complain about if one only had to cope with those who have declared themselves against the good, but what is more trying is that often those who profess it are no more just and equitable, and can be seen deciding against persons whom they ought to approve as freely as though they did not know that rash suspicions and judgements will be condemned no less serverely than homicide. Never have consciences shown less embarassment over such excesses as at the present time. People attack without scruple anything they do not like and say the hardest and most offensive things about a man as if they were saying that he has a poor complexion or looks unwell. That is the degree of men's malice nowadays. With all that, Mgr, those who belong to Christ must follow their path without turning aside for a step or a moment, their firmness must be constant, they must find in their hearts that peace which the whole world together cannot take from them, and by their fidelity in following God's will they must make themselves fit to receive from his goodness the strength and consolation they need. You are engaged in practice and use of these things, and as you are on a great stage, you cannot help being more exposed than those in lesser places. But if the Prince of shepherds was the object of envy and hatred in those who should have felt for him only deep respect and submission, you may, looking at the insults inflicted on him, find cause for consolation for any injustice done to you. Besides, if one is blameless in the circumstances of a given attack, there are many other circumstances when one is blameworthy and which are passed over in silence. Finally when one finds oneself innocent on every point, what can a servant do better than to resemble his master and keep his patience?'

*880202   RM MARIE-LOUISE [BOUTHILLIER]   2 February 1688
TC II/170

'I pray God, my dearest sister, to give you new zeal and new fervour for his service and for your perfection, and to increase your fidelity as your years are multiplied. You should not be surprised at finding contradictions in the good you have to do, but you must fight against them, grace must overcome, and you must make yourself superior to anything that may prevent you going to God as promptly as you should. It would not be right for these obstacles met on your path to halt you, they must be useful to you and help you go forward. Do not listen to all the terrors of which you tell me. We must fear, but that feeling, which should accompany the religion of all who go towards God, must not reach the point you indicate. That should be a reason for you to be more careful in your ways, behave with more caution and vigilance, but not to cast you into trouble or deprive you of the peace enjoyed by all souls who put all their trust in God's goodness. Ask him to tear from your heart everything which his hand has not put there, and which could therefore not be pleasing to him. Add strictness to trust and be at peace.'

880210   MONSIEUR   10 February 1688
TC II/333

M. is not suitable for the profession for which he is intended; he has been badly advised. 'It is for God to choose his ministers.' See Pinette.

880210a   RM HENRIETTE DE SAINT-SAUVEUR,   10 February 1688
RELIGIEUSE DU PRÉCIEUX SANG
TC II/171

Anxious as she is to repair the past, R. is sure she will be given grace to do so. 'There is a fruitless, or rather a harmful, grief that God's spirit can neither endure nor approve.' She should practise all possible penitence if superior agrees.

880218   RM LOUISE-HENRIETTE D'ALBON   18 February 168[8]
A 2106,f.152; TC II/250 (dated 15 July 1688, a possible date)

Two nuns have protested unjustly against her conduct, but she must keep calm. She would do well to go back to Tours.

880219   MADAME DE SAINT-LOUP   19 February 1688
TC II/172

Her troubles are signs of God's care for her salvation, and should make her glad.

880226   DUCHESSE DE GUISE   26 February 1688
TC I/186; Mug II/49
He had thought that Mlle de Guise was better, but one should not wait for the end to prepare for salvation.

Marie, Mlle de Guise, was the aunt of Mme de Guise's late husband (1615–88).

*880228   RM MARIE-LOUISE [BOUTHILLIER]   28 February 1688
TA orig.

'We will not fail, my dear sister, to pray God for Madame de Saint-A. and say the novena you request. It is very strange that having all the qualities needed to be a true religious, as she has, she should have lacked the will and succumbed to temptations excited by the devil to prevent her carrying out her intention. That spirit of evil never attacks us so furiously and stubbornly as when he sees us on the point of committing ourselves further to God's service, and he would do anything to upset our resolutions and make them fruitless. She must revive her zeal, ask God for fresh strength, and be convinced that her salvation is attached to her firmness and constancy. She must believe that God will call her to account for the grace given to her, and although she has promised him nothing, she will not be acquitted before his judgement seat unless she has done all in her power to make her vocation succeed.

As for you, my dear sister, I have no other advice to give you than to abandon yourself to God and put your fate in his hands. He knows perfectly well what you need, and will not refuse it if you ask him with confidence. All your fears will only serve to shrink and squeeze your heart and make it less receptive to God's goodness. You know that he only gives himself to our souls in proportion to their breadth, and that our weak capacities bear no relation to his generosity, which is infinite. Farewell, my dearest sister, let us pray God for each other, I do not think we could do anything better and that is what God asks of people who follow the calling which we both do.'

Mme de Saint-A. is very likely the duchesse de Saint-Aignan, second wife of the duc, aged seventy when he married her, and of very humble birth. He died in 1687, and she lived a very retired life, which earned her much respect. She may well have contemplated entering a convent, but never did so (1642–1728).

880229   RM MARIE-LUCE [PICOT], PRIEURE, ANNONCIADES   29 February 1688
TC II/174

'Your ardour increases with your days'; she wants only to complete her sacrifice.

880229a   CLAUDE NICAISE   29 February 1688
BN 9363,f.56 orig.; Gonod 86
Hopes that Nicaise will not be one of those who never implement their resolves. 'St

108   *The Letters of Armand-Jean de Rancé*   880300

Teresa is a mistress who has prescribed rules which cannot be too highly esteemed and followed.'

880300   DUCHESSE DE GUISE   [March 1688]
Mug II/53

Death of Mlle de Guise [3 March].

880308   RM LOUISE-HENRIETTE D'ALBON   8 March 1688
A 2106,f.153 vo.

Repeats warning about admission of outsiders. Family gifts should be shared; sorry for all her troubles.

880329   RP CHANOINE RÉGULIER   29 March 1688
TC I/160

Whenever there are two paths in a community, however much one preaches the narrow way, the broad path is always present. He should not go into town or country, or pay visits.

880404   RM LOUISE-HENRIETTE D'ALBON   4 April 1688
A 2106,f.154 vo.

She must try to persuade her nuns to want more strictness. Keep X out if possible; superiors will surely not force her to admit him/her.

880408   CLAUDE NICAISE   8 April 1688
BN 9363,f.57 orig.; Gonod 87

Dom Boissard needed penance to repair the scandal he caused and his order is too charitable not to permit this.

He was sacristan of the Carthusians in Paris who allegedly sought a (quite illegal) benefice and was linked with attacks on R.

880415   RP PRIEUR   15 April 1688
TC I/159

Anyone as conscientious as RP would want to lay down office. A novice master is depressed or discouraged by the way the example of seniors effaces the impressions he tries to make on the young. R. had said all this to a prior of canons regular before.

880415a [JEAN FAVIER]   15 April 1688
A 2106,f.154

Unfair attacks on Favier. His niece's firmness impressive. He has urged discretion on her. A pity that Favier's age makes it impossible for him to meet her. Many monks have died, but now that conditions at la T. are so widely known any relaxation would cause public scandal. 'The honour of Christ must be maintained at the cost of our lives.'

880415b RP PRIEUR   15 April 1688
TC II/288

He must give up preaching, either for a long time or for ever, in reparation of past faults. He was right to give up his office as superior, which was too heavy.

880417   MONSIEUR, ECCLÉSIASTIQUE   17 April 1688
Archives Nationales M 825, orig.

M. should go to Saint-Victor if it is as he has been told, or even if there is a hope, 'as to your mother'. In any case he should join those with common training.

Despite the title Monsieur, this seems to be a Canon Regular.

880422   PIERRE NICOLE   22 April 1688
BN 17755 orig.; Nicole, *Lettres* 1718 I p. 563 (dated 1689)

R. thanks him for latest works and expresses usual approval.

880422a MADEMOISELLE DE VERTUS   22 April 1688
TC I/158a; Dubois II/ pp. 342-348 (from lost orig.)

Her fever and lassitude signs of the end. She must submit to God's will. 'Above all make sure that any regrets for your past life give way to confidence: that is what will open the gates of Christ's kingdom to you.'

*880424 BISHOP OF LUÇON [HENRI BARILLON]   24 April 1688
P f.629

'Allow me, Mgr, to go no longer without asking for your news. Your health is so uncertain, and so dear to me, that I cannot help feeling really anxious every time I think about it. This winter has been so trying, and the weather is still so cold and damp, that I do not doubt that the climate in your part of the country is even worse than usual. I hope that God, in whose service you are so useful, will take particular care to preserve you, and I can assure you that there is never a day but that I ask that of him.

I have no news to give you from these parts. News from the world rarely reaches here, as you know, and in fact all we hear of it only incites us to raise our hands and eyes incessantly to heaven to ask that peace may be granted to the Church, and that God will establish in it that unity and harmony which should be inviolable among those who belong to him and profess to serve him.

I do not know, Mgr, if your new converts continue to be converts in good faith, as they seemed to at the beginning, at least from what you told me. There are very few around here who do what they ought to. It is to be hoped that the bad ones will go off and that their children will be better and more christian than their fathers.

I ask of you, Mgr, your blessing, the continuation of your accustomed kindness and beg you to believe that no one could be more affectionately and respectfully than I yours' etc.

880427   CLAUDE NICAISE   27 April 1688
BN 9363,f.58 orig.; Gonod 88
Praises Latin elegance of a friend of Nicaise.

880502   MONSIEUR DE LOGERIE,   2 May 1688
         SUPERIOR OF THE SEMINARY, PÉRIGUEUX
Charavay catalogue, 1888, 1889, orig.
A priest has been accepted, a Benedictine has gone.

880509   MADAME   9 May 1688
T 1689,f.205
R. criticises Bp of Tournai [Gilbert de Choiseul] for allowing Abbess of Saint-Sauveur, Laon [his niece] to leave her monastery to take the waters. R. had once told the Abbot of Clairvaux to refuse similar permission to his own sister [Thérèse]. 'She was the same one who came to within a league of here with her abbess and whom I would not see. It is never permissible on any occasion to authorise what is not right.'

880513   RP CHANOINE RÉGULIER   13 May 1688
TC II/293
The only way to restore a lax house is to reintroduce practices and regularity of old. R. condemns 'distractions, games, social contacts, luxury, superfluity'. It is hard to convert people to a vegetarian diet but simple food would be enough.

*880513a   BISHOP OF [LIMOGES, LOUIS D'URFÉ]   13 May 1688
TC II/294
'I should have been really distressed, Mgr, if the last letter which I had the honour

of writing you had had on you the effect you report, and had prevented you from giving your people the instruction they needed. I know that you will never be content with your works, and far from believing them complete, will find in them gaps which frighten you. Yet, Mgr, if you imitate the saints in the poor opinion you have of yourself, and in the severity with which you treat yourself, you must also imitate them in the rest, and as such a holy disposition did not close their lips, so that they still spoke and taught, you must not remain silent. If the low opinion we have of ourselves was a reason to be quiet, since the saints never think of their own conduct except unfavourably, they would have forbidden themselves to speak, and so only those who are not saints would have done so, which would have been the greatest of ills. You say, Mgr, that you very nearly spent the festival [Easter] without speaking to your people, although in your heart you had the truths you had to preach to them, and I tell you, without wishing to sing your praises, that not only are they in your heart, but they are in your hands and, without realising it, you act as you think. I am convinced, whatever you say, that when you condemn good living, idleness, love of pleasure, avarice, vanity, luxury, and all the other disorders to which those who love the world abandon themselves, you must not be afraid of incurring the reproach which Christ made to those who charged others with excessively heavy loads. Saint Bernard, saint though he was, called his life monstrous and looked on himself as a man given over to sin, but God has allowed his true servants to express themselves thus for the consolation of those who do not see in themselves all the virtue they desire. Either their humility conceals from them what they are, or they do not yet have it in the degree and as perfectly as their perseverance will achieve.'

Easter 1688 fell on 18 April. The letter of 28 January seems hardly likely to have produced so violent an effect, so that there must be at least one letter missing.

880527   RM LOUISE-HENRIETTE D'ALBON   27 May 1688
A 2106,f.156 vo.

Her perseverance is at last effecting changes. She is right to prevent outside contacts.

880530   MONSIEUR L'ABBÉ   30 May 1688
Carp p. 607

R. comments on a new ritual [presumably that which came out after lengthy discussion in 1689 with the Abbot of Cîteaux's approval].

880600   MADAME   [before 13 June] 1688
T 1689,f.208 vo.

R. regards Bp of Tournai 'as my master and superior in rank' and would not wish to argue with him openly, but is still against religious going away to take waters.

In between 880509 and this letter from R. the bp had written to the unidentified lady on 26 May a long letter recalling R's initial horror at the idea of becoming a monk (expressed at Comminges) and then his change of heart when they met in Paris in 1663. The bp would find R. 'inhuman' if he did not like and respect him so much.

880603   CLAUDE NICAISE   3 June 1688
BN 9363,f.59 orig.; Gonod 89

R's rheumatism is worse. Mabillon should not quote at second hand. Discusses case of Canons Regular [in an argument about precedence].

880607   BISHOP OF LUÇON [HENRI BARILLON]   7 June 1688
P f.771

'One of my close friends, Mgr, has asked me to commend to you the ecclesiastic who will hand you this note. I do not know him personally, but I hope that he has the qualities which will oblige you to honour him with your protection. Allow me to use this opportunity to assure you that no one in the world is with more fidelity and respect than I yours etc.

PS The ecclesiastic's name is Monsieur Tesson.'

880609   RM ABBESSE,   9 June 1688
               LES CLAIRETS [FRANÇOISE-ANGÉLIQUE D'ETAMPES DE VALENÇAY]
TC I/108

Dom Jacques de Lanchal, the confessor, has given good reports. They must both want and do good.

*880613   BISHOP OF LIMOGES [LOUIS D'URFÉ]   13 June 1688
TC I/109

'We should be happy, Mgr, to bring you some comfort and in some way relieve the continual labours of your life of toil. I call it thus because the princes of the people who see, as you do, the true origin of their obligations perceive only the thorns and briars, and God so skilfully conceals from them the best of what they do for the establishment of his glory that they constantly regard themselves as useless workers in his house. Yet if God afflicts them on the one hand, he sustains them on the other, and if he humiliates them by the feelings he gives them about themselves, he also inspires holy trust in them, which prevents them becoming dejected at the sight of what they consider as deep wretchedness. The shepherds who really belong to God always believe themselves guilty and fear everything. The others imagine themselves to be righteous and have no apprehension. Fear protects the former from the dangers threatening them, and the others succumb, giving way to a deceptive assurance. When I think of this countless multitude of souls entrusted to you, I share all the worry and difficulty which such an extensive inspection causes you. When I consider that you make this your only business, the object of all your cares, I do not doubt that God will bless your fidelity and fervour, and that you are one of those servants whose zeal and vigilance will receive a crown. You will only know the value of your works, Mgr, when you have put the final touch to them. God will conceal their goodness and merit up to the moment of reward. Thus all you can do is to await it and persevere until it comes, giving yourself up to the promise made to us by Christ that he would make eternally happy those who stay firm and constant in his service. That, Mgr, should be your hope and peace together. Be charitable enough, I beg you, to remember me before Our Lord, as someone who most needs it and most respects and honours you.'

880621   RELIGIEUSES, LES CLAIRETS   [21 June 1688]
TC II/60 (date from Le Nain)

Their joint letter a sign of their zeal. The mitigation in their house is of the body, not the heart.

They were still begging R. to become their superior.

880628   CLAUDE NICAISE   28 June 1688
BN 9363,f.60 orig.; Gonod 90

Tells Nicaise not to go to Holland at his age. In any case he would never convert his friend if he did go.

880629   RP LA GRANGE, CHANOINE RÉGULIER   29 June 1688
TC I/107

'The study of theology . . . means the extinction of piety', except for Franciscans and Dominicans destined for it. Monasteries have not erred in faith but in morals. A leading scholar who found monks at la T. reading moral works of SS Augustine and Gregory thoroughly approved.

880712   CLAUDE NICAISE   12 July 1688
BN 9363,f.63 orig.; Gonod 91

Glad that Nicaise has abandoned plan to go to Holland. Comments on new book on Lérins [from Anisson].

*880719   BISHOP OF LIMOGES [LOUIS D'URFÉ]   19 July 1688
TC II/251

'I do not know, Mgr, whether my letter will find you on your visitations. I hope that God will have given his blessing to them, and that, since you have him before your eyes as much as you have, he will have granted special efficacity to your preaching and solicitude. Knowing perfectly well the greatness of your duties, you are wholly devoted to them, and I do not doubt that you discharge them with all the zeal of a faithful servant who is always ready, since he cannot be certain when it will please his master to call him to give an account of his conduct. If there is anything capable of making those who are not conscientious become so, and those who are retain so rare and so necessary a disposition, it is having such a view always before one's eyes. For surely the reason why those who have the chief authority in the church take so little trouble to make the use of it for which it was entrusted to them is that they do not think either of the punishments or the rewards prepared for them by God, according to whether they have neglected or executed his orders. It can be said that in all callings and professions men leave the obligations with which they are charged as if they did not affect them, and live as though they were never to die and had left God's hand never to return. The best thing one can do is to attach oneself to him in unshakable dependence, study his designs, love them, express them in one's conduct and make of that alone all one's peace and all one's happiness. Apart from that, whatever one may do, one is deceiving oneself, and engaging with deliberate perversity in a conduct reparable only by repentance which cannot be certain. Keep for me, Mgr, your habitual goodness, and believe that there is no one in the world more respectfully yours' etc.

880723   RP, CLUNY   23 July 1688
TC II/111

Can only answer briefly because of a cold and chest trouble. 'Monks must not possess anything but the superior must give them what is necessary.'

880727   [JEAN FAVIER]   27 July 1688
A 2106,f.156

Despite his niece's good news, R. expects her to return to Tours after her three years. Pities his niece, de La Barge, for putting her daughters so imprudently into religion. She is risking her own salvation by risking that of her children so indiscreetly.

880730   MARQUISE DE LA SABLIÈRE   30 July 1688
Menjot d'Elbenne, *Mme de La Sablière*, 11

'I will lose no time doing what would bring you the peace you so rightly desire.'

880809 BISHOP OF COMMINGES [LOUIS DE RECHIGNEVOISIN] 9 August 1688
Sol, ND de St Bernard de Comminges
R. officially approves fr Dosithée.

In 1682 a shepherdess, Madeleine Serre, aged twelve, had a series of visions of the Virgin at Alan (dioc. Comminges). Shortly afterwards Pierre Cathiény, from Chur in Switzerland, passed by Alan and was later professed at la T. as fr Dosithée. In 1688 he was so haunted by what he had heard of the vision that R. gave him leave to return to the Pyrenees and supported his application to the bp to build a chapel. After much opposition he secured permission, began building in October 1688 and a year later persuaded the bp to say the first mass. Pilgrims soon began to come, but the girl Madeleine was kept under close control until her death at the cistercian house of Fabas in 1739. The whole episode was handled with remarkable discretion and without damping pious enthusiasm. The chapel still stands and has been restored to use.

880810 MADEMOISELLE [? DE LA BARGE] 10 August 1688
TC I/33

When he first heard from Mme N of Mlle's proposal to become a religious without real vocation he told her that this was wrong, but now that he has heard from Mlle direct he encourages her.

The circumstances fit so well those of R's great-niece that the identification is almost certain.

880810a MONSIEUR L'ABBÉ DE MONTIGNY 10 August 1688
TC II/216

For those works which come from God the best thing is to follow the intentions of founders used by God. RP Barré's work will be of use as long as it keeps its original purity, but once the Paris house becomes rich it will cease to be fruitful.

Nicolas Barré (1621–86) had founded several christian and charitable schools. The one in Paris, founded 1676, was run by the Dames de Saint-Maur. In 1694 Montigny published a collection of Barré's spiritual maxims.

880818 RM LOUISE-HENRIETTE D'ALBON 18 August 1688
A 2106,f.157; TC II/211

She is afflicted from inside and outside her convent. The malice of men matters less than God's service. In the words of St François de Sales she must accept crucifixion as her life.

880820 RM ABBESSE, 20 August 1688
        LES CLAIRETS [FRANÇOISE-ANGÉLIQUE D'ETAMPES DE VALENÇAY]
A 3389,f.32

R. will now accept the charge of being Visitor.

After Val-Richer's visitation in June, the abbess, prioress and community had each written to beg R. to reconsider his refusal, and the abbess wrote again on 13 August, representing that everyone now regarded her as R.'s spiritual daughter.

880900   DUCHESSE DE GUISE   [? September 1688]
Mug II/70

They have sung a *Te Deum* for the King's victory and the preservation of Mgr [the Dauphin].

This suggests the capture of Heidelberg in September 1688.

880905   CLAUDE NICAISE   5 September 1688
BN 9363,f.64 orig.; Gonod 92

A letter of R. [unidentified] has been published in part.

880914   RP ABBÉ, VAL-RICHER [DOMINIQUE GEORGES]   14 September 1688
Maupeou, *Vie* I p. 594; Dubois II p. 204

Remarkable reconciliation of factions at Les Clairets [where the abbot had just concluded his visitation].

880924   RM ABBESSE,   24 September 1688
            LES CLAIRETS [FRANÇOISE-ANGÉLIQUE D'ETAMPES DE VALENÇAY]
A 3389,f.34

The only reason R. changed his mind was from personal consideration for her.

880924a   RELIGIEUSES, LES CLAIRETS   24 September 1688
A 3389,f.35 vo.

R. delighted at their letter. They must now act as though observing the rule in its original fervour and be united under their abbess.

880926   MADEMOISELLE DE VERTUS   26 September 1688
TC II/144

'I see two things . . . the continuation of your ills . . . and fear of not following God's order . . . by taking more care of yourself than you should.' But that is natural after so long an illness.

*881001   MARÉCHAL DE BELLEFONDS   1 October 1688
TC I/157

'God must be giving you powerful protection, Mgr, to resist the temptations which can arise in a soul like yours. God must have made it entirely subject to him for you to find the peace which I believe you have, while the rest of the world is afflicted with movement and agitation. That obliges you, Mgr, to be very grateful and to profit from the moments that God gives you; I mean to confirm you in your awareness of the vanity of all passing things and in the attachment you have long felt for what is not subject to the changes and chances of fortune. Such an attitude must constantly grow in those who truly belong to God, for unless they raise themselves and come closer to him, all that they leave behind them diminishes and recedes from their sight, and they no longer have eyes to see the sole good to which they aspire. That is a truth which I am sure you experience, and the further forward you go the more you will become aware of it, careful as you are to set aside all that could divert and distract you. One must be as it were outside the world to be able to pass solid and equitable judgement on what it is, for if one is at all fond of it, what one sees there speaks in its favour and prevents us treating it with the harshness it deserves. You owe an infinite debt to God in his goodness for destroying or fixing in you the natural activity which moves most men about, and for giving you the grace to look so moderately, or rather indifferently, on those things which in them cause such strong and violent passions. They are in truth slaves of what they desire; possession only tightens the bonds, and when they lose these things their greed only increases. Thus they are always the same in enjoyment as in deprivation, and spend their lives in shameful servitude. You would be one of them and would live in subjection like the others if divine mercy had not freed you. I pray God, Mgr, to be in all your ways, to bless them and never allow you to do anything that does not match all the marks you have received of his concern for your person and all your conduct. I am with deep respect yours' etc.

881008   MADAME DAGUESSEAU   8 October 1688
TC I/156

She is not satisfied with herself. Seek peace in God.

*881013   BISHOP OF LUÇON [HENRI BARILLON]   13 October 1688
P f.630

'I cannot dispense myself, Mgr, from asking news of you from time to time. It is enough that your health is as dear to me as it is, and that I know it is uncertain. I have even learned recently that you had had attacks of your usual trouble. I beg you to believe that I feel for you, perhaps even more than I would my own ills.

I have nothing to report from these parts. The Dutch fleet has appeared off the coast of Normandy. That is a storm which God will disperse by that great protection that he has long accorded to France by making her victorious over all her enemies. That does not prevent us from taking particular care to double our prayers and ceaselessly address them to him who holds the destinies of men in his hands. The chief obligation of those who live in retreat and solitude like us is to speak to God of the needs of the world to the point of being importunate. You know, Mgr, and you have frequently been a witness, how carefully and diligently we offer to God the person of the King.

Monsieur le C[uré] de Saint-J[acques] was here for a few days. You can imagine with what pleasure we talked about you. Keep for me, I beg you, Mgr, all the friendship with which you have for so long honoured me. Please believe that you are very present to me before God, and that nothing can exceed the affectionate and profound respect with which I am yours' etc.

William of Orange had been invited by his supporters to come to England in May, and actually landed at Torbay in November, which explains the naval activity. Louis Marcel was still curé of Saint-Jacques.

881014   RP SIMON GOURDAN, SAINT-VICTOR   14 October 1688
[Gervaise], *Vie de Gourdan*, pp. 76–85

Long and detailed criticism of Saint-Victor, but R. will send back fr Gueston if his vocation is not proved.

The young man in question had gone to la T. against the orders of his prior, but after an acrimonious exchange between R. and the prior, Gourdan intervened in more pacific terms. In the end the young man proved unable to stand the austerities and was sent back.

*881016   BISHOP OF LUÇON [HENRI BARILLON]   16 October 1688
P f.772

'The religious, Mgr, who will have the honour of bringing you this letter has spent eight months with us, and although he has spent that time with edification, none the less, since he is convinced that God is not calling him to the solitary life, but wants him to serve him in his original vocation, we have not been able to keep him, however much we wanted to, but as the observance he left is extremely lax and that the necessary means of achieving his salvation do not exist there, I thought of that house in your diocese of which you have told me so much good and thought that charity demanded that I should try to gain him entry to it. I would be most obliged if your protection could open its doors to him. As God has sent him to me, I have an urgent reason for taking an interest in his salvation, and I therefore recommend him to you with all my heart. I have nothing to add to my humble request on his behalf, and will content myself with assuring you, Mgr, that no one could be with deeper respect than I yours' etc.

This religious is almost certainly the same as that of 890117, q.v.

*881017 MARÉCHAL DE BELLEFONDS   17 October 1688
TC I/78

'I see, Mgr, that you forget nothing in order to render unto God all that is God's, that you give to men only what you cannot refuse them and that in all this you observe strict justice. It is a difficult division to make, and one that can only be achieved successfully if God takes a hand. On this point, as in so many others, he accords you special grace, and I do not doubt that you are fully aware of it. It is the most powerful means you could have to oblige him to continue thus. I admire the calm you appear to enjoy in these stormy times when everyone is in a state of agitation. God alone can calm the emotions of our hearts, like the waves of the sea. That is an effect of his voice which makes itself heard by all his creatures, and which, when it pleases him, none fails to obey. It is in him that you put all your trust, and he has hitherto given you, as you rightly remark, so many evident signs of his protection that you can only throw yourself upon it without reserve. I am sure that when you go over all the circumstances of your life there is no place in which you do not perceive it. That is a great support in the different events by which it may be affected. For what greater consolation could there be for someone who has religion and faith, as you have, than to see by such apparent signs that God's eyes are open to all your ways, above all the eyes of his mercy?

Our parts have been in alarm, as you doubtless know. The Dutch fleet, which had sailed past the coast of Normandy, seemed to threaten the whole province, and people said such different things about it that fear began to spread on every side. It has not really come as far as us. It is certain that persons consecrated to God, who are concerned solely with lifting their hands and eyes to heaven for the preservation and defence of the world to which they no longer belong, should have put their fate into his hands in such a way that no earthly matter should cause them the least apprehension or anxiety.

All that is going on at present, Mgr, is a great book, but few people bother to study it, and that is why men profit so little from the lessons that God gives them. He reveals himself in thousands and thousands of ways, but it is a language that men do not understand because they do not want to understand it. However there is nothing he omits to say to both great and small in such pressing situations. Do me the honour of believing, Mgr, that no one could be more affectionately and respectfully yours' etc.

It was to be another month before William landed at Torbay, but R. evidently shared the excitement and apprehension of everyone to judge from his frequent allusions to naval movements.

881017a MONSIEUR   17 October 1688
TC I/7

M has resolved to withdraw from the world. Should follow decisions made in his third retreat: 1. repentance for past life, 2. mortification of the flesh, 3. submit to God's will, 4. love the poor. Follow his director as regards sacraments, but frequent communion a great source of strength.

881022 RP ABBÉ   22 October 1688
TC II/150

If his monks are incapable of sanctification under reasonable moderation 'leave this unruly flock which does not heed the voice of its shepherd' just as St Benedict and St Robert [of Molesme] did.

881100 DUCHESSE DE GUISE   [October/November 1688]
Mug II/74

Hopes that James II rallies support, but William of Orange may win support of dissidents.

William did not land until 15 November, and this seems to be written before that.

881102 CLAUDE NICAISE   2 November 1688
BN 9363,f.67. orig.; Gonod 94

All R. wants is to be left alone, yet people keep talking about him.

881107 [JEAN FAVIER]   7 November 1688
A 2106,f.158

Favier's health is so good that R. expects to go first; he is already afflicted by rheumatism and a bad cough.

881108 RELIGIEUSE   8 November 1688
TC II/200

R. glad to see that her desire to belong solely to God increases day by day.

881111 BISHOP OF COMMINGES   11 November 1688
         [LOUIS DE RECHIGNEVOISIN]
Carp p. 608; Sol, *ND de St Bernard de Comminges*

Approves fr Dosithée's initiative in building a chapel.

See 880809.

881118 DUCHESSE DE GUISE   18 November 1688
TC II/154
It is easy to leave God when circumstances are hard.

881122 CLAUDE NICAISE   22 November 1688
BN 9363,f.70 orig.; Gonod 95; TC I/155
R. rejects ill-informed criticism of la T. Novices should give their money to the poor unless their parents are in need. Attacks standards of parish clergy. Praises Bossuet's recent *Histoire des Variations des Églises Protestantes.*

881125 LAZARE BOCQUILLOT   25 November 1688
BN 17755; *Vie de Bocquillot,* Lettre 51 (dated 13 October 1688)
His esteem for Bocquillot's *Homélies,* and regrets misunderstanding over first volume, which a mutual friend had erroneously judged hostile to R.
Abbé de Cantorbie was the culprit; volume I appeared in 1686.

881128 RM SUPÉRIEURE   28 November 1688
TC I/174
God counts our will for the deed.

881128a RM   28 November 1688
TC II/37
God awakens her attention from time to time. Her poor health and use of sickness.

*881129 RM MARIE-LOUISE [BOUTHILLIER]   29 November 1688
TA orig.

'I am very sorry about your indisposition, my dearest sister, but as you are at the source of the remedy against that sort of ill I am sure that you are now quite rid of it. Life is nothing but a succession of tiresome events, one has hardly left one behind before another occurs. God allows life to be so in order to prevent us loving it, and to give us loftier feelings and desires. Our souls, however, are so earthbound that, despite all the care God takes to make them worthy of their first origin, I mean the state in which they were when they left his hand, they think only of lowering themselves and work ceaselessly at their own degradation. We must follow the impulses of God's spirit, my dearest sister, forget forever transitory things and attach ourselves to those which do not change. That should be the sole occupation of a christian soul, but much more so of a religious one, since by its profession it has contracted much greater and stricter obligations than those which have remained in contact with the world. I leave the rest for you to reflect upon, my dearest sister. I do not doubt that it will give you abundant insights on so extensive a subject. Keep peace amid all the temptations that may arise in you and put your fate in the hands of God. You are his, you want to be so still more; he never fails to take care of those who belong to him. Farewell, my dearest sister, pray Our Lord for me, and believe that no one could be more yours than I.'

881130 RM LOUISE-HENRIETTE D'ALBON 30 November 1688
A 2106,f.166

Things so difficult for her that R. advises her to go back to Tours as soon as she can in the face of so much hostility.

881202 COMMANDEUR DE LAVAL 2 December 1688
TC II/268

Most people must be edified at Laval's conduct. Advantage of the vow of a Knight of Malta to give blood and even life in service of Christ is that he must always be ready to die.

881210 RM ABBESSE 10 December 1688
TC II/104

Visitors may be admitted for their edification, but better not. Example of visiting abbot who spoke to a monk who had been two years at la T. but left two days later as result of this conversation, apostasised, and spent more than ten years in the army.

Le Nain confirms this story with details (Carp II/p.82).

881213 CLAUDE NICAISE 13 December 1688
BN 9363,f.69 orig.; Gonod 96

Discusses books by abbé Régnier (translator of Rodriguez, *De la Perfection chrétienne*), by Quesnel and RP V.

Régnier translated De la Perfection chrétienne, *a much admired moral treatise by Alfonso Rodriguez, SJ, in 1675.*

881200 LAZARE BOCQUILLOT [December 1688]
Vie de Bocquillot, lettre 53

Glad that Bocquillot accepts R's explanation and thanks him for volume II [cf 881125].

881224 RELIGIEUSE   24 December 1688
TC II/299
R's only advice is that she should close her eyes to the woman causing her such pain. As for the [male] superior, it is not up to her to examine what he does or does not do.

881229 PREMIER PRÉSIDENT DE BRETAGNE   29 December 1688
TC II/252
New Year wishes.

*881229a BISHOP OF LUÇON [HENRI BARILLON]   29 December 1688
P. f.631
'Allow me, Mgr, to begin this year by asking for your blessing, and at the same time assuring you that I have offered my prayers to God to continue to pour his grace upon you and all your conduct, or rather to inspire you with new ardour and zeal for his service, since I do not doubt that you are always finding new difficulties in your way.

Such a diligent shepherd as you needs much protection, whether to succeed in the things he undertakes for God's glory, or to preserve consistent serenity in those things which do not succeed quite as he might wish. God does not fail to try those he loves, and as you belong to that number, I am sure that trials, so to speak, arise on your path and that he exercises you in many different ways. I assure you, Mgr, that nothing here on earth is worthy of consideration or attachment. The fate of the King of England, and his Queen, who has just arrived in France in a state that you will know, is a strange lesson which God affords to all those who love the world and seek after its benefits and fortunes. No one applies it to himself, however, and people live without heeding events at all, remarkable as they may be, as if God's design were not to use them to tear us away from all that is transitory and without any assured state of substance. Men have never been blinder or harder of heart than they are now and have never had more cause to ask God to give them feelings and light, for one without the other could not be of much use.

I think many times a day of your brother's situation and how difficult it is. Only God can sustain him, for human prudence, extensive as it may be, is indeed short in such disorder and confusion as that obtaining in that abandoned and wretched kingdom. I wish you, Mgr, limitless and endless prosperity, for that prosperity which has limits does not deserve to be desired. Remain always my friend, I beg you, and do me the justice of believing that no one could add to the affection and respect with which I am yours' etc.

All R. knew at the time of writing was that the Queen of England and her infant son had escaped to France on 21 December, and that James had been deposed (see 890105 below).

Since Louis XIV continued to recognise James II as King of England, the French ambassador, Paul Barillon, the bp's brother, also had to flee from London and was not, in fact, appointed to another post, preferring the ease of retirement. He reappeared at court in the first week of 1689.

89/1   DUCHESSE DE GUISE [end 1688/early 1689]
Mug II/75

Extraordinary fate of the Queen of England.

Mary of Modena, who arrived in exile in France in December 1688 with her baby son.

89/2   DUCHESSE DE GUISE [1689]
Mug II/80

She has still not found an assistant priest for her parish [in Alençon].

89/3   DUCHESSE DE GUISE [1689]
Mug II/81

Importance of humility for the great.

89/4   RELIGIEUSE, VISITATION [? RM DE HARLAY] [1689]
TC I/31

Sends advice requested taken from writings of St François de Sales.

89/5   MONSIEUR [after April 1689]
TC II/56

R. justifies publication of *Explication* by pressure of friends; took him three months. Bossuet praised it, Maisne gave it to the publishers Fosse and Muguet for six hundred livres; R. would have liked it to sell for nine francs rather than twelve and a half. 'Thousands are waiting impatiently for this work and will bless its appearance.' Proceeds to go towards a charitable school.

R's explanation of the Rule of St Benedict came out in April 1689.

*890105   MARÉCHAL DE BELLEFONDS 5 January 1689
TC II/110

'I wish you, Mgr, a happy new year, and I pray God that among the graces you receive from his goodness will be that of growing in the love he has already given you for a life of retreat and contempt for worldly things. I cannot understand how people can attach any weight to them, if one has time to consider how uncertain is their possession and, whatever their nature and quality, how easy it is to lose them. We have at the present moment a lesson on the subject to which one could not pay too much attention. I mean the situation of the King of England. I do not doubt that his disaster affects you keenly, knowing your feelings for him and the favour and esteem in which he holds you. Who could have believed that a prince of his merit and value should be chased from his throne by a usurper, inferior to him in so many ways, and by so general a conspiracy of all his peoples that he should find himself abandoned and betrayed by those who ought to be most inviolably attached to his person, and all without anyone having occasion to draw his sword?

I do not know, Mgr, whether he is under arrest in the Tower of London, as we have heard, or whether he perished in the storm. Either of these events, from any normal point of view, is the ultimate calamity. Yet if one looks at it with the eyes of faith, he is a Catholic prince who, preferring to lose his life and his kingdom to losing Christ, will receive from his hand the greatest of all blessings, that of martyrdom, and, to go still further, he is a Christian who prefers to reign for ever in heaven to reigning for a few moments on earth. Such are the true reflections inspired by Christian piety on the fortunes of this poor prince; they are consoling, but they do not stop us feeling his disgrace. You must at present have before your eyes a sad spectacle in the person of his Queen. I confess that although I see it only from afar and my profession makes me less sensitive than other men, yet it makes the deepest impression on my heart. I think and think again about it incessantly, and all these different considerations lead me to ask God to draw glory from it and sanctify those on whom he has been pleased to lay his heavy hand. There is something for everyone to learn from such a revolution. In it God speaks clearly, and both small and great can find infinitely useful lessons. The greatest of all evils is that God is not heeded, and we do anything but what we should with the instruction he carefully provides. Instead of applying and reducing to our own conduct such remarkable dispositions of his providence, we look at them so superficially and indifferently that their memory is almost immediately effaced. I will leave it at that, Mgr; you will discover more in a moment by your own lights than I could tell you in whole volumes.'

James II had fled from England to France on Christmas Day, never to return. His Queen and infant son had escaped on 21 December. R. was soon to learn the news. James suffered for his faith only because he showed more zeal for the Catholic cause than even his allies and Catholic friends thought prudent or necessary, but it is probably true that even if he had shown more discretion he would sooner or later have had to choose between his throne and his faith.

890105a   TRM [? PRIEURE, GIF]   5 January 1689
TC II/264

She judges herself severly as usual. Right to want to give up present post and take up another purely supervisory one under orders. Refers to 'abbess'.

The title, and reference to abbess, make it virtually certain that this is to the former abbess of Gif, Anne de Montglat, who had become prioress after her resignation.

890113   RP ABBÉ, VAL-RICHER [DOMINIQUE GEORGES]   13 January 1689
Maupeou, *Vie*, I p. 530 (dated 1684 in error).
Reference to Mège's book.

890113a   CLAUDE NICAISE   13 January 1689
BN 9363,f.72 orig.

Nicaise has seen R's sister [? Mme d'Albon]. He hopes for conversion of Mme de la Rongère.

Tournouer attributes this letter to Maisne, who wrote quite often to Nicaise and had in fact first raised the subject of Mme de la Rongère (wife of a courtier) in 1687, but inspection shows that it is by R. (though written by Maisne). Since all correspondence, and most visitors, passed through Maisne's hands, and since he, as a secular, was free to make what contacts he chose, orally or in writing, it becomes increasingly difficult with the years to distinguish between letters genuinely dictated by R. and those sent on Maisne's initiative. Even before 1694, when R. lost the use of both hands for writing, one cannot be sure that absence of a signature necessarily indicates that a given original letter is by Maisne rather than R. Maisne clearly enjoyed his contacts with the great, Bellefonds, for example, to whom he wrote several extant letters, and was equally clearly encouraged by Nicaise to provide material for gossip.

* 890117   BISHOP OF LUÇON [HENRI BARILLON]   17 January 1689
P f.632

'I have just received one of your letters, Mgr, from which I see that you have not yet had the one I wrote you seven or eight days ago. I told you how sorry I was about your brother, on the occasion of the troubles in England, but I have just learned this minute that he is due in Paris and expected there. He has found himself on a great stage and has seen at close hand what is more likely than anything to cause disgust for worldly things. Can anyone love them, uncertain as they are? The state in which the King of England finds himself is a powerful lesson, but the human heart is of bronze and impervious to everything.

I am most obliged to you, Mgr, for the good Franciscan father whom I had commended to you. He has written to tell me of all your kindness, and Father Le Balleur is taking all possible care of him out of consideration for you.

I will do what I can to address myself to the work proposed. I need time and health, and have very little of either; in a word I am beginning my sixty-fourth year with attacks of rheumatism which will not slacken in the course of the winter. What grieves me is having passed my life so uselessly and having done so little in solitude to make up for the many evils I committed in the world.

As for you, Mgr, you have only to continue in the situation in which God has placed you. You are employed solely in his service, your functions are quite holy, and the use that people get from them is a recommendation to which God can refuse nothing. I am sure that he receives with pleasure those works which satisfy you so little and that he judges you very differently from the way you judge yourself. Yet you are right to condemn yourself rigorously, since there is no surer way to oblige God to look on you in his mercy, which the saints need no less than others.

It is true, as you have been told, that I did some months ago a commentary on the Rule of St Benedict, which will appear, I think, very shortly. You can be sure that you will have it the moment it is given to the public.

Please believe, Mgr, that nothing is dearer to me than your person, I do not cease commending it to God, and no one will ever be more affectionately and respectfully than I yours' etc.

The delayed letter must in fact have been 881229, written some seventeen or eighteen days earlier. The Franciscan is almost certainly the religious mentioned in 881016. Fr Joseph Le Balleur, OFM, was one of the leading figures in Franciscan reform at the time, and the connexion here established with R. is of more than passing interest. In 1667, when Guardian of La Rochelle, Le Balleur was appointed by the Minister General, at the request of the King and a committee which included Jouaud, to undertake the task of reforming the widely differing and constantly bickering branches of the Franciscans in France. He made an extensive visitation throughout France, but despite all his efforts failed to bring the notoriously unruly great house in Paris to heel. The record of his visitation and litigation in Paris is preserved in BN 15776. Returning to his province of Touraine-Pictavienne in 1672, he persuaded the Bp of La Rochelle to allow him to set up a reformed custody (small group of houses) in the diocese, and was also active in the neighbouring diocese of Luçon, where he evidently enjoyed good relations with Barillon. In 1680 a house of recollection (a house of prayer to which friars could withdraw for a time or permanently to live a strictly regulated life) was set up at les Robinières (see below 890317) in the diocese of La Rochelle and another at Olonne in the diocese of Luçon. In about 1681 Le Balleur retired to les Robinières, where he remained until his death on 7 February 1700. His obituary speaks of him as being, if not the founder, then the mainstay of the house (see A. de Léon, OFM 'Couvents de Récollection de la province Touraine-Pictavienne', in Etudes franciscaines, 36 [1924] 624–40, esp. 630.) His career and influence in his own Order closely resemble those of R. in his, and it is quite exceptional to find R., who normally treated all Mendicants with the greatest caution, actively collaborating in an attempt to settle a friar in a suitable Franciscan house.

* 890126   BISHOP OF LIMOGES [LOUIS D'URFÉ]   26 January 1689
TC II/265

'I do not doubt, Mgr, that your chief concern in this time of trouble and confusion is to raise your hands and eyes to heaven to pray God to have pity on the world. All that is happening today fills rightminded people with fear and grief. Nothing is more to be desired than to see cast down the pride of the man who is trying to raise his throne above the clouds to the North [William of Orange], who declares himself against God's law, and who supports so boldly and insolently the enemies of His name. It is true that we enjoy great peace here and live in great silence, but it is also true that it is difficult to make of this the use that we should, and to respond to such special grace. When we think that God separates us from men only to unite us more closely to himself, and see our weaknesses and languors, we cannot fail to be overwhelmed by the weight of our wretchedness. The truth is that we ought to spend our days groaning before God at being so little what he wants us to be. That is an obligation affecting me more than the rest of our brothers, because I am much more exposed than they, and whatever I do to reduce myself to a stricter solitude, countless occasions arise to take me out of it. Thus my daily resolutions to restrict myself to what solely concerns me, in the heart of those whose conduct it has pleased God to give me, remain useless, and I cannot deny myself to the outside affairs which providence sends my way, short of wanting to break off all contact with men, which I am told I must not do in the calling I follow. Although I have forbidden myself all communications which are of no use, those which I cannot abandon still affect me as they no doubt would not if all my occupations were limited to what seems to me my sole duty, and God grant that I am not mistaken in following the advice of those who believe that I should not prescribe for myself such strict limits.

I wish you, Mgr, infinite prosperity and blessings. Those of this world are so little worthy of being desired, so subject to change and revolution, that they are not worth thinking about. What has happened before our eyes to the King of England is a lesson only to be understood by applying it to oneself, but unfortunately this event, great and visible though it is, will only make a superficial impression on most people, for it can be said that the heart of men, which is of wax for everything likely to pervert it, is of bronze for those things capable of contributing to their salvation. I ask your blessing, Mgr, and beg you very humbly to believe that it is not possible to honour you more than I do nor have more respect than I have.'

890208 DUCHESSE DE GUISE	8 February 1689
TC I/64	

She has asked for Lenten exercises. The sight of James II of England exiled, the death of the Queen of Spain [Marie-Louise d'Orléans, niece of Louis XIV] teaches us that there is no real greatness on earth, everything passes in a flash.

Mary II and William III proclaimed joint sovereigns of England.	13 February 1689

890217   CLAUDE NICAISE   17 February 1689
BN 9363,f.74 orig.; Gonod 97

Nicaise has at last got rid of his benefices and is free to leave Babylon for the promised land [retreat].

890220   MARQUISE DE [. . .]   20 February 1689
TC I/12

R. is sure she has made more progress than she thinks. The two essentials are humility and dependence on God.

890300   DUCHESSE DE GUISE   [March 1689]
Mug II/92

God is above the counsels of men.

890302   MADEMOISELLE DE VERTUS   2 March 1689
Dubois II/ pp. 342-348 (from lost orig.)

No reason why she should not communicate as often as she does: 'your sufferings and separation from the world are genuine preparations'.

890303   CLAUDE NICAISE   3 March 1689
BN 9363,f.250 orig.; Gonod 98

Nicaise still in Babylon [Paris] in connexion with an essay on *Explication d'un ancien monument*.

890307   COMMANDEUR DE MAREUIL   7 March 1689
TC II/187

R. declines to give any further instructions or he will be accused of wanting to reform everything.

* 890317   BISHOP OF LUÇON [HENRI BARILLON]   17 March 1689
P f.772

'I was just about to write to you, Mgr, about the ecclesiastic from your diocese who has been here nearly a month, for I would not receive him and give him the habit until you had granted your consent, and I do not doubt, Mgr, that in beginning his sacrifice with your blessing he would consummate it successfully, and with all the benefits for which he hopes. He is strongly inclined towards penitence, and believes it to be necessary, he is sensible, reserved and shows by all his conduct that he has been brought up in the right place and has had a strict education. If it should happen that he cannot persevere, or if we should not find in him all the necessary qualities, we should take care to send him back to you, and I do not doubt that this attempt would completely stabilise him in his original situation and even make him better able to discharge his functions. It will be a real consolation for him to be assured that you will see him, should he return, only with more approval, and I personally am much obliged to you for that.

The Franciscan father who had gone to the convent of les Robinières under your protection came here in the greatest distress, because his fathers will not consent to his translation. It is cruel to exclude him from a place and a life which seem absolutely necessary to his salvation. These good fathers make it a point of honour never under any consideration to let go those who have once joined them.

I fully understand, Mgr, all your difficulties, and those which constantly arise. They are the result of your care and vigilance. The greater it is the more difficulties you will find, and only those whose conduct is superficial and do not go to the bottom of things fail to meet difficulties on their way. I am even convinced that your health suffers much from the continuous run of your occupations.

What we can do, Mgr, is to take an interest in them before God and commend to him all your spiritual and bodily needs as far as we are able. I look on that as one of my chief obligations.

How much we should have to say to you, Mgr, if we could talk to you. That is a joy which it pleases God to deny me, but at least I have the joy of knowing that you honour me with special kindness. That is a blessing which no one could appreciate and recognise more than I do. I am with an affection, fidelity and respect which no words can express yours etc.

PS Your brother wrote to me some time ago. Monsieur Pinette, who has been very ill and is now better, tells me that he had told him that he would come and see me in better weather. Would to God that you were free, but the way things are at present gives me no cause for hope. Those who occupy important posts will not stop.'

Les Robinières (see 890117) was near Courçon, only a few miles from the diocesan boundary of Luçon, but not actually under Burillon's jurisdiction (see note on the house in Revue d'Histoire Franciscaine, *6 (1929) p. 302). It seems as though opposition to translation came from the man's province of origin, not from les Robinières, but the French is ambiguous. The friar must have been of some branch of the Order different from the Observants, who would not have opposed such a move.*

890400   RELIGIEUSE, VISITATION [? RM DE HARLEY]   April 1689
TC I/32

Thanks her for sending him *Life*. Discusses SS François de Sales and Jeanne Françoise de Chantal, and application of principles contained in his book to Visitandines.

890400a DUCHESSE DE GUISE   [? April 1689]
Mug II/93
Her zeal for religion, the state, and the King so great that she constantly inspires them to prayer.

* 890414   BISHOP OF LUÇON [HENRI BARILLON]   14 April 16[8]9
P f.659 (wrongly dated 1699)

'The ecclesiastic, who has been here nearly two months, has had to go. It is not for want of courage or will, for no one could have a better one or more inclined to good than we have seen in him. However, his melancholic temperament and natural excitability made him unable to bear the austerity and great solitude in which we live. He left here with much sorrow and the intention of going to see you and doing whatever you order. He has given up, from what he tells me, his idea of taking his Baccalaureate, so as to avoid the involvements which always occur when one is in contact with people in the world. I assured him of the kindly dispositions which you had told me you would have towards him.

I understand, Mgr, that this is not a time when you can leave your diocese and we cannot hope for the honour of seeing you under present circumstances. Although your part of the world is at peace and the new converts show no signs of stirring, your personal presence is still necessary to prevent them doing so. It is not that the state of affairs in England is anything but very liable to hold them in check and make them lose all their fantasies, for there is every reason to think that the Prince of Orange will achieve anything but what he intends. The King's party grows stronger every day and his weaker. People withdrawn as we are must never cease commending the needs of the world to God; that is our chief duty.

Your brother still intends to come and see us; you can imagine how impatiently we look forward to it. That may be when you will come in for criticism. Nevertheless we must follow in all things the dispositions of providence and desire what is pleasing to God.

I am sending you, Mgr, an *Explication de la Règle de Saint Benoît*. You will see in it opinions and principles which you have approved in the book on monastic life, and I shall be really delighted if I learn that it has not displeased you. There came out a year ago a commentary on the same rule, written by a religious of the Congregation of Saint-Maur called Father Mège; it is full of lax opinions and principles completely opposed to those of the saint. I do not know if it has fallen into your hands, but I am sure that you would not read it without indignation. It is right that you should see the approval of one of the doctors [of the Sorbonne] who approved it; I am sending you an extract. The audacity of the author must be considerable for him to dare to use an approval of that kind. If I were the only one attacked, it would be nothing. If his fathers had been more sensible and better advised than they are they would have prevented publication of a work which can only cause them shame and confusion. I do not need to tell you, Mgr, how much you are honoured here, I do not doubt that you are convinced of all the respect and affection with which I am yours' etc.

The ecclesiastic is the one referred to in 890317. There were fears that former Protestants would act as a sort of fifth column for William, by now at war with France, and a Protestant rising in the Cévennes was ruthlessly suppressed. R's optimism regarding James' success was wildly misplaced.

Mège's work came out in 1687, and was clearly opposed to R's interpretation, already completed in MS by then. It was the approbation given by Fr Alexandre, OP, that R. enclosed. R. was supported in his enterprise of commenting on the Rule by Bossuet and, under pressure from the latter, by the Maurist authorities, who thought Mège had gone too far and in 1689 banned his book.

* 890422   RM MARIE-LOUISE [BOUTHILLIER]   22 April 1689
TA orig.

'I have only time, my dearest sister, to tell you briefly that you were quite right not to give my letter to Sister [. . .]. I only wrote to her in accordance with what she told me, and it was really not possible for me to give her any other advice, at least according to her account of her situation; I praise God for turning her heart, and giving her feelings so different from those which she had. I am writing to her and saying nothing about the letter she did not receive, and even letting her think that I had not replied. Farewell, my dearest sister, I pray God for you every day of my life, do the same for me, I beg you, and please believe that it is with all affection that I am yours' etc.

890428   ACHILLE DE HARLAY   28 April 1689
BN 17423,f.21 orig.

Glad that Harlay approves of book [*Explication*] R. has sent.

890429   MADEMOISELLE DE VERTUS   29 April 1689
TC II/145

'I see that God prolongs your days and your sufferings . . . but preserves the peace he has given you'.

890502   RP ABBÉ, VAL-RICHER [DOMINIQUE GEORGES]   2 May 1689
Maupeou, *Vie* I p. 531

The Benedictines are unwilling to allow R's *Explication* to be read in their houses.

* 890507   MARÉCHAL DE [BELLEFONDS].   7 May 1689
SS orig.

'It is too kind of you, Mgr, to remember us, and to be so concerned about the preservation of our health. Although our persons are entirely devoted to you, we are so little use to you that we do not deserve the least of your attentions. I will confess, Mgr, that the remedies which we have so far been able to take for the curing of our ailments have had no effect, and if those which you were kind enough to send have, as I hope, more effect, I shall attribute it to you and shall think that God has desired to attach a special blessing to the marks which you have kindly given us of your charity. I do not need to tell you how grateful we are, but will simply assure you that our gratitude is as sincere and profound as it could possibly be. I pray God, Mgr, to continue to bestow on you the grace you have had up till now, and to give you such feelings and dispositions of heart that you do not become accustomed to the world in which you live. So long as the world does not please us, it need not be feared, but when we begin to become more familiar with it, and nothing in it seems strange to us any more, then it becomes dangerous and we need to be on our guard. I wish you, Mgr, all kinds of prosperity and blessing, and beg you to believe that one of our chief obligations is to offer you to Our Lord, and to recommend to him your person and all that concerns you. I am with deep respect yours etc.

PS Allow me to say that we do not know just how to use the water you sent us, nor in what way and in what quantity to take it.

We are profiting from the opinion you kindly gave us. We shall be more reserved and circumspect in our words than we have been.'

* 890623   RM MARIE-LOUISE [BOUTHILLIER]   23 June 1689
TA orig.

'Poor Mother Luce, whose death I learn from you, is very fortunate. God has taken her away because she had done her work in this world. She was a simple, faithful soul, tender for the affairs of God, who loved him and did what she could to love him more. This is an example, my dearest sister, which should both move and instruct you. We have not failed to pray God for her with every possible care and attention. I am personally much obliged to her for the confidence she had in me. Farewell, my dearest sister, pray Our Lord for me and please believe that no one could be more yours than I.'

RM Marie-Luce Picot had been prioress several times, and R. was in correspondence with her at least from 1682–88. She died on 13 June, aged 80, having been professed in 1626, and was sub-prioress at her death.

* 890627   MARÉCHAL DE BELLEFONDS   27 June 1689
BN na 12959,f.121, orig.

'I am sending you, Mgr, the memorandum about the religious of whom I had the honour of speaking to you. It is true that I should be greatly consoled if his health could be restored and a life preserved which has so far been to every one of us most edifying. If he recovers from his illness, God will permit it rather for love of us than for love of himself.

I do not tire, Mgr, of thinking about the grace that God bestows on you. As you are perfectly aware of it, your gratitude cannot fail to obtain not only the continuation but also the increase of this grace, since it pleases God to communicate himself and extend his presence in souls where he finds gratitude. It is no mistake to say that men only lose God because they are not as responsive as they should be to the effects of his mercy; he loves and wishes to be loved, and nothing causes him more distaste and estrangement from those to whom he has given most signs of his goodness than when they do not have the fidelity to respond; that is to say he breaks off contact with those who neglect to maintain contact with him. We shall not fail, Mgr, to recommend to him your person and all that concerns you. You do indeed do me justice when you believe that I consider that one of my chief obligations, and that nothing can equal the respect and fidelity with which I am yours etc.

PS The *Relation* of the Grenadier's death is not yet written.'

Dom Muce Faure, the former grenadier, died on 13 May, and R. wrote a longer account than usual of his death. A version of this was published in Paris in 1690 without R's permission as Instructions sur la mort de dom Muce *(ninety-one pages) and was usually referred to as* Mort du Grenadier. *It provoked both controversy and incredulity.*

890630   RP ABBÉ, VAL-RICHER [DOMINIQUE GEORGES]   30 June 168[9]
Maupeou, *Vie* I p. 531 (wrongly dated 1684)

Further comment on *Explication.*

890630a   CLAUDE NICAISE   30 June 1689
BN 9363,f.76 orig.; Gonod 99

Approves Bp of Tripoli.

890703   ACHILLE DE HARLAY   3 July 1689
BN 17423,f.37 orig.

The Lietenant-General at Mortagne has reported Harlay's care for R's interests.

Mortagne was the nearest judicial centre to la T.

* 890704   MARÉCHAL DE BELLEFONDS   4 July 1689
BN na 12959,f.123, orig.

'We have received what you sent, Mgr, and express our deepest thanks. I must tell you of an incident which occurred with the dropsy remedy. Although the bottle was tightly corked, we noticed that the liquid still ran out, and we thought it right to expose it to the air and open it because the cork was too tight. At the moment of opening the liquid gushed out violently and went almost up to the ceiling, continuing to pour out with the force of the fermentation as if from a pipe, so that part was lost, but we were able to save a lot by putting a vessel underneath, so that there will be enough left for curing the patient.

I am not surprised, Mgr, that the ideas formed by long habit come back when we would like them to be completely effaced. We are not masters of our minds or imaginations, things stay there despite us. That is an effect of our fragility, and God wants us to be aware of it, so that we bear within ourselves a perpetual cause of humiliation, and recognise in his eyes our weakness and impotence. The main thing is to guard one's heart, and if the fidelity we owe him does not prevent us suffering some wounds, at least it should stop them being too deep and ensure that the impression made is slight. The surface of the water may be moved, but the bottom should remain, if possible, in an untroubled and uninterrupted calm. That is a grace we should constantly ask of God, because it is rare though necessary, when one is within range of business and contacts because those who wish to belong wholly to God must take care not to be divided between creator and creature. It is very right to belong solely to the former, and not to take away what belongs to him on the basis of so many claims and reasons.

Do not doubt, Mgr, that we recommend to God your person and all that concerns you as fervently as we can. You know with what fidelity and respect I am yours etc.

PS We ceaselessly pray God for the world and nothing is more present to us than the person of the King and the needs of the State.'

* 890709   MARÉCHAL DE BELLEFONDS   9 July 1689
BN na 12959,f.125, orig.

'I must report to you, Mgr, about the remedies you sent, since you so desire and your charity wishes to go into details. The one who had a tumour round the throat and other ailments that you know about has been taking waters since you left here and the three doses of powder which you sent, according to the note, and that has really been so successful that all the tumours have dried up, his face has gone back to normal, and I have never seen so swift a change in so serious an illness. I do not doubt that if he is given some kind of purge which suits him and which he can use regularly he will be completely cured, which would be a most extraordinary cure. On that we await your kind instructions.

As for the one who was coughing blood, that has ceased, but he still coughs in the mornings and part of the night. He took the powder only once, because with the coming of the hot weather its effect was hardly perceptible. As for the dropsy patient, he is cured, and indeed as his cure happened almost at a stroke and before we had received your remedies, we have kept them for some other similar occasion, for there is no lack of them in these parts. God takes great care to prevent us losing from sight what men should constantly have before their eyes. I mean the moment of death. It is a road on which we see ourselves constantly through our infirmities, be they serious or slight. The saints say that God knocks at the door when he makes men ill and the first thing a Christian should do, if he has faith, is to be ready to open it, in case God's will is to call his soul and bring it out of its prison. That is a thought which hardly occurs to those who love the world; since they find pleasure in present things, the future causes them no concern, and they are no more worried about it than if it were never to be and if life, uncertain as it is, had for them a solid and assured character.

We learn little of the world here, but what news we do have gives us continual cause to pray God and ask him with all our might to confound the wicked, break up their plots, overturn all their plans and their undertakings. That is the chief occupation and business of those who live in retreat. I do not need to tell you, Mgr, how diligently we offer you to God, for I do not doubt that on that point you do us the justice we deserve. I am with all possible devotion and respect yours' etc.

890716   CHEVALIER DE MALTE [LAVAL *or* MAREUIL]   16 July 1689
TC II/103

Now that he recognises the grace received he must live up to it. Difficult to follow God when surrounded by people of different views.

* 890718   RM MARIE-LOUISE [BOUTHILLIER]   18 July 1689
TA orig.

'I have received your last letter, my dear sister, and at the same time had news of you from Monsieur le Théologal, who seemed to me perfectly satisfied with you and all your views; it is certain that he takes as much interest in everything that concerns you as one could wish, and I confess that that gave me great delight. I will not say anything on all that you tell me, except what I think I have often written to you, which is that your peace of mind consists solely in abandoning yourself into God's hands, in the care you take to avoid becoming involved in things which do not concern you and with which you are not charged, and in other things to say, where you are obliged to speak, what you think according to your lights and the prompting of your conscience and then hold your peace. As for the temptations and difficulties which you will meet on your way, you must believe, my dear sister, that they are effects of providence, that God allows them not only to try you, but to sanctify you. God wants his elect to resemble his Son, to walk in ways which are like an imitation of those by which he wished to lead him, and it would not be conforming to his intentions to desire other ways. Thus what we must do in pressing situations is to address ourselves to Christ, our only strength, and ask him to make us superior to the ills that we feel; he is faithful, as you know, he has promised to hear our prayers when we take care to offer them to him in our needs and when they are accompanied by our trust. Do not doubt that he will keep his word, and that we shall find in him all the help we hope for.

I am sending you my answer to the letter Father Tourné wrote me, which was full of evidence of his friendship. Please tell him in a word that I could not be more moved by it. From the way Monsieur le Théologal spoke of you, I have every reason to believe that he will always do everything possible for your consolation. Farewell, my dearest sister, pray for me, and please believe that no one could be more yours than I.

PS I have not seen the gentleman from Avignon you mention.'

890719   BISHOP OF COMMINGES   19 July 1689
         [LOUIS DE RECHIGNEVOISIN]
Carp p. 608; Sol, *ND de St Bernard de Comminges*

Thanks God for blessings on chapel at Alan.

890720   BISHOP OF [GRENOBLE, ETIENNE LE CAMUS]   20 July 1689
Nouvelles de la République des Lettres, mai-juin 1710, pp. 488–519, 628–661

The bishop has asked 'for weapons with which to defend' R., his old friend, against the unjust attacks of the Carthusians, who claim that R's criticism is unfounded. R. ends by saying that the Carthusians are less decadent than most contemporary religious, but should not claim 'an immutability that is not of this world'.

This letter, really a pamphlet 'in reply to the difficulties raised by dom Innocent Le Masson', General of the Carthusians, goes into great detail to refute the General's defence of the state of his Order in the face of R.'s strictures on its decline from primitive austerity in matters of diet and the like. The draft probably was sent to Le Camus, but never published in the lifetime of R. or his opponent, in obedience to a royal prohibition on continuing the dispute.

890726   COMTESSE DE LA BARGE   26 July 1689
TC I/184

R. has learned that she wants to put her [three] daughters into religion, and does not mind where. 'The interest I take in your salvation and that of your daughters obliges me to warn you that you are drawing the wrath of God on yourself and all your family if you commit them to being religious without being sure that they are called to it.' Unless she chooses the convents with care 'you make your daughters for ever wretched'. In writing thus R. has broken all his resolutions to give no more advice.

R. had learned in detail what was going on from Louise-Henriette at Riom, and as her correspondence with Favier on the same subject is extant, it is clear that his misgivings were well founded. The reason was probably financial, and it is clear that M de La Barge was the prime mover.

* 890728 MARÉCHAL DE BELLEFONDS   28 July 1689
BN na 12959,f.127, orig.

'We are much obliged to you, Mgr, for so many tokens of your goodness and remembrance. I hope that God will give his blessing to the remedies that you send. The brother who had such a tiresome and uncomfortable ailment has been taking your waters for eighteen days and feels very well. All the open sores have dried up and the tumours quite reduced. As I saw that the effect was so beneficial, I put off for a few days the last dose of powder but made him go on with the waters; the delay will not be for more than three or four days.

We shall see that the one who was coughing blood takes the purgative powder, for although he has now stopped coughing blood for the last month, he still has a little cough which makes me fear a relapse. We shall not fail to tell you what effect it has.

One takes great care, Mgr, to preserve the body, which is the least part of us, and often the care of the soul is so neglected that we attach no importance to it, and it seems a matter of indifference whether it is sick or well, or, to be more accurate, we prefer it to be sick rather than well, since we do all we can to keep it sick and almost nothing to make it well. You know so well the wretchedness and fragility of humanity that you never fail to be constantly occupied with the means of preventing yourself being taken unawares by it. It must be agreed that our safety depends on our attention, and once one ceases to watch oneself one exposes oneself. Our vigilance excites that of God, and if anything can make him forget us, it is being forgetful of ourselves. We pray him, Mgr, not to close his eyes on your person and all your conduct, and that he will not only indicate the ways in which he wishes you to walk, but give you the strength and fidelity to follow them, without which it would be of no avail to know them. I wish you all kinds of prosperity, I humbly beg you not to doubt that, any more than all the respect and gratitude with which I am yours' etc.

890809   MONSIEUR, ECCLÉSIASTIQUE   9 August 1689
TC I/120

M has tried in vain to join Carthusians but must persevere. In answer to person seeking advice: even in Common Observance of Cîteaux, obedience to *In Suprema* can bring salvation. If superiors fail to set a good example, religious must follow their own conscience. Benediction must be accepted, even from someone unworthy. A religious is to be pitied if not disposed to approach sacraments frequently.

890812   RELIGIEUSE   12 August 1689
TC II/336

R. has not written for a long time, he realises how ill she is. She is worried at not loving her neighbour enough but must try.

* 890815 MARÉCHAL DE BELLEFONDS 15 August 1689
BN na 12959,f.129, orig.; TC II/176

'I have just received your honoured letter of the 6 August. I saw in the copy of the King of England's letter what you observed, that is, the character of a simple and upright man who looks only to God in all he does. These are very rare attitudes in a person of his rank; God must have become master of his heart to an unusual degree. However God sometimes delivers those whom he loves most and who are united to him by the most lively faith and piety to the greatest persecutions. The history of England offers considerable examples. It is true that the consolation of a king, when God permits irresistible tempests to rise up against him, is to know that the King of kings has said that his kingdom is not of this world. Finally they are disciples of Jesus Christ like all the others, and the lot of a disciple has never been better than that of his master. That is something men do not understand, and do not want to understand. That is what makes me often say that there are many fewer Christians than one thinks, for since the only true ones are those who bear this feeling in their innermost heart and strive to express it in their works, and since no traces of this can be seen in the conduct of Christians, it would seem that faith has been almost extinguished among them, and that they live in complete ignorance of their most essential obligations. This is cause for grief in those who love Christ, who are jealous of his glory and would like to see his house filled only with servants worthy of him. Those who hold the truth must preserve it most carefully and take care that their religion does not become weakened through contact with those who are content with the name and appearance and do not bother with the reality and effect. Such reflections are useful and may preseve us from such a universal evil.

One hears, as everywhere else, much uncertain and varying news. For my part, I count solely on the protection of God, and I always hope that the perfidy of the man who has been prime mover in this great conspiracy will bring down God's curse on his person and on all those who have supported his designs. God acts, as you know, by means unknown to men, and he is often found where he is least expected. In a word, he is the God of hosts and battles, and whatever action men take, whatever confidence they may have in their worth, their power, and the multitude of those who serve their passions, they are the simple executors of his orders and do only exactly what he intends them to do. I pray God, Mgr, to confirm more and more what he has put into your heart, and make you completely understand that nothing is to be preferred to the peace one finds in the life of retreat. I am with all possible devotion and respect yours' etc.

890826 PIERRE NICOLE 26 August 1689
BN 17755, orig.; Nicole *Lettres* 1768, I p. 564

Thanks him for his latest work, but would have preferred continuation of *Essais de morale*.

The four volumes of Réflexions morales sur les épitres et les évangiles *had appeared 1687-88, and had been sent to R., who approved them, and according to Dubois the work here referred to was Nicole's edition of the works of Jean Hamon (1617-87), physician and solitary of Port-Royal.*

890829   MADEMOISELLE DE LA TRÉMOUILLE   29 August 1689
TC II/175

She is convinced she should leave the world but recognises faults which prevent her doing so. R. encourages her.

890829a   RP NICOLAS MALEBRANCHE, CONG. ORAT.   29 August 1689

P. Le Brun, *Hist, critique de pratiques superstitieuses* 1701, III, p. 177

Malebranche has consulted R. on alleged properties of a divining-rod used by a peasant in Dauphiné; R. admits possibility of discovering water, metal etc. as being in the natural realm, but any claim to identify thieves, or other non-physical questions, can only come from the devil.

* 890903   MARÉCHAL DE BELLEFONDS   3 September 1689
BN na 12959,f.133, orig.; TC II 173

'It is too kind of you, Mgr, to think of my health; it is of so little use that it does not deserve to be in anyone's mind. I will, however, do as you wish, those are easy remedies and, as they only require one to be a little careful, they do not lead to painful subjection.

It is true, Mgr, that the present state of affairs offers matter for much reflection. The world is a great and ever open book in which all may read, and the strange thing is that some find in it powerful lessons which teach them to despise all that is transitory and without certain solidity, while others on the other hand find only reasons for exciting their ambition and attaching them to the world, as if it could bring them solid advantages capable of making them happy. Such diverse events are quite incomprehensible; most men regard them as strokes of fortune, but the wisest and most enlightened consider them as dispositions of providence, which rules all things and without which the forests do not lose one of their leaves. In truth, if that is so, as cannot be doubted, can one stop at the goods of this world, and not put one's fate solely in the hands of God by abandoning oneself in genuine peace to his will and following it as the rule of one's life and conduct? That is the only means of being rich and happy, whatever happens, and achieving a tranquility which will never be disturbed. A Christian's peace comes from staying within God's order, and being exactly what he wants one to be, and anyone who is so ill-advised as to withdraw from it, if his life is full of bitterness and tribulation, is seeking to feed on his own imagination and projects, but he is flattering and deluding himself, for whether he has or has not, his greed is always the same and he can never satisfy it. These are truths which one must continually tell oneself, for fear of forgetting them or weakening them. Unless they are deeply engraved in the hearts of those obliged to be in contact with the mass of men who hold quite contrary views, only danger can result, for all they see and all they encounter goes against this principle, and unless one is sustained by faithful resistance, which is very difficult, it cannot avoid being shaken. What is pitiful is that the principle is sometimes preserved, and yet one acts as though it no longer prevailed and had been lost from feeling and memory.

I cannot get over what is happening in Ireland. All the hopes one had vanish; God hides himself, allows the evil cause to triumph and the good to be oppressed. One may say to God now what his prophet once said, why Lord do the ungodly prosper and everything succeed for those who live in violation of your law [Jr 12:1]? We must worship God's counsels, which are always full of justice, and it is not for men to enter into discussion over what he does or does not do. I pray God, Mgr, to increase more and more your feelings and enlightenment, for I can assure you that one cannot turn to him too much when one thinks that those who desire to please him are beset with traps on every side, and that men as well as devils will not cease to wage cruel war on them as long as they are capable of doing them harm, that is as long as they live. I beg you to believe that no one could be more respectfully and devotedly yours than I.'

James II had landed in Ireland in March in an attempt to regain his throne. The siege of Londonderry had lasted from 20 April to 1 August, when William of Orange's troops relieved the garrison. With French help, James continued the campaign in Ireland for another year.

890911 DOM JEAN MABILLON, OSB   11 September 1689
BN 17681,f.84: *Ami de la Religion*, 128, 1846, p. 522

R. thanks Mabillon for his recent treatise on the Mass and agrees with his interpretation. Would very much like to meet him.

This was an essay 'refuting recent interpretations of the words Mass *and* Communion *in the Rule' (Ch. 17). See Mabillon,* Ouvrages posthumes *(1724) vol 2, pp. 272–310.*

890914 JEAN FAVIER   14 September 1689
CF 344,f.87, orig.; Gonod 45

R. had written three weeks before [the letter is lost]. His *Explication do la Règle* has just appeared [second edition]. Recommends acceptance of proposals to turn abbey at Beauvais into a seminary.

890914a CLAUDE NICAISE   14 Sepember 1689
BN 9363,f.77 orig.; Gonod 100

R. has written to Tréville. Approves Mabillon's recent essay on meaning of Mass and Communion in the Rule [cf. 890911]. Opts for smaller measure for *hemina*. Does RP Boccone really want to shut himself up at la T.?

Boccone had been talking of coming to la T. ever since 1680 but nothing came of it.

890926 ACHILLE DE HARLAY   26 September 1689
BN 17423,f.71 orig.

Delighted to offer congratulations on appointment as Premier Président.

891000 DUCHESSE DE GUISE   [October 1689]
Mug II/104

Situation in Ireland. Promotion of Pope [Alexander VIII, elected to succeed Innocent XI on 6 October].

891002 JEAN FAVIER   2 October 1689
CF 344,f.89, orig.; Gonod 46

Favier had written on 23 September on proposal to make abbey at Beauvais into seminary. Glad he approves of *Explication*. Dismisses rumour that next Pope may make him a cardinal.

The timing of the rumour is strange; Innocent had died on 11 August and R. could not have heard of the new election for about a week after writing this.

891003 ACHILLE DE HARLAY   3 October 1689
BN 17423,f.82 orig.

Harlay is 'one of those who honour their office more than it honours them'.

891012 CLAUDE NICAISE   12 October 1689
BN 9363,f.89 orig.; Gonod 103

Let men say what they will about R's conversion.

*891013 RM MARIE-LOUISE [BOUTHILLIER]   13 October 1689
TA orig.

'I am very glad, my dear sister, that you sent the book to Father Tourné; he has written to me about it in the most obliging way.

Monsieur le Théologal seemed to have all the views you could wish on your subject. I will briefly say, about the silence which you speak of, that if you are asked your opinion on something, you must say what it is in your conscience and leave it at that; secondly, if you see that your advice might cure some ill or prevent it, you should give it; thirdly, should they want to make use of your silence to authorise what is not right, you should again explain yourself, but do so in every case with such moderation that it can be seen that necessity and truth together are what opens your mouth; above all never insist and avoid anything that gives the impression of obstinacy or stubbornness.

For the rest, my dear sister, you could not do better, seeing that you intend and are obliged to seek for perfection, than submit in all things to God's guidance and accept with total resignation any opposition that you may encounter, from whatever quarter. It is enough that you should know that providence controls everything, that there is nothing God does not do or permit for the sanctification of those who are his. You must believe that you belong to that number, and consequently embrace gladly anything which may make you worthy of receiving from his hand the reward he has destined for those who belong to him.

Believe, my dear sister, that trials are necessary, that souls languish when they do not have any, piety grows weaker, and that those troublesome events which nature avoids as much as possible because she finds them importunate and hostile, are those which excite our souls and pull them from that torpor and lethargy by which those who profess to belong to God are often taken unawares. It cannot be denied that it is painful always to have one's arms ready and fight without respite; yet what should console you, and all who are in a situation like yours, is to know that perseverance alone wins the crown, and that, as one is surrounded by enemies up to the moment of death, there is no instant when one is not obliged to defend oneself. Farewell, my dear sister, we do not fail to commend you to God, and will continue to do so as far as possible.

PS Please assure Monsieur le Théologal that I am extremely grateful for his friendship. Also assure the Mother Superior of my respect for her. Express also to M l'abbé Bruzeau my obligation at his kindness in thinking of me.'

Paul Bruzeau, priest of the community of Saint-Gervais, Paris, was mentioned several times with approval by Arnauld as an apologist. Between 1678 and 1684 he published several works against Protestant doctrine.

891014   J-B DE SANTEUIL, SAINT-VICTOR   14 October 1689
La Vie et les bons mots, II p. 81

R. was surprised to hear that Santeuil had thought of him in composing hymns of holy monks.

Santeuil composed a vast number of latin hymns for various liturgical occasions. The Feast of Holy Monks (13 November in the monastic breviary) prompted three such hymns, one of which Dubois quotes (II, p. 185) beginning 'Felices nemorum pangimus incolas'. The descrip-

tion *of the heroic life of solitaries was reputedly based on that led at la T.*, where Santuil had close contacts, including dom Le Nain, a former Victorine who also composed latin hymns.

* 891017   BISHOP OF LUÇON [HENRI BARILLON]   17 October 1689
P f.633

'I am most mortified, Mgr, that you, of whom I thought first on the distribution list of the *Explication de la Règle de Saint-Benoît*, should have been the last to receive and read it. You will have seen nothing in it, as I have already told you, but truths and principles which you have approved. The work has been appreciated by everyone who was not prejudiced against it. The Benedictines and Carthusians are almost the only ones who are not pleased with it and have tried to decry it. However, my consolation is to learn from many sources that people in the world as well as religious find edification in it.

I could hardly fail, Mgr, to be surprised by what you tell me and I think that surprise has been general. These are things which one can neither avert nor foresee, and they do not change once they have happened. Everyone is liable to such events; the absent always lose their cause, either because they lack defenders, or because they have only feeble ones. At the end there is profit to be gained from everything. I do not doubt that I shall make holy use of this circumstance.

You would have been very wrong, Mgr, to refuse Monsieur de Barillon what he asked you after such a long separation. As he very much wants to come to la Trappe, and has even planned to do so, I do not doubt that he will make the journey with you and will even be very glad to find an opportunity. I do not need to tell you that it is one of the greatest consolations I could have, to see you here together.

I am more sorry for you than I can say about the pain you are having from your usual trouble. Those are the sort of ills it is hard to cure; remedies sometimes bring relief, but I assure you that the true and only relief comes from patience and from looking to God, without whose providence not a hair of our heads can fall. I have had attacks of rheumatism for the past five or six months which often cause me acute pain, and although I have not neglected it, I see that I shall have to bear it as it grows worse up to the moment of my dissolution, which cannot be far off in view of my age and feeble constitution. As long as one lives and dies in the fear and love of God that is the main thing.

I am delighted that you are pleased with Monsieur de La Foucherie. I hope he will be a good churchman. God surely intended him for the church and not the cloister. I hope, Mgr, that nothing stops you passing by our desert, and that I may once more in my life receive your blessing. I am with all possible affection and respect yours' etc.

Carthusians were sure to disapprove of anything by R. but benedictine reaction was not so uniformly hostile. In the second paragraph R. probably refers to the Chancellor's ban on any further public dispute between him and the Carthusians. He had written a letter to Le Camus on 20 July, justifying himself against dom Le Masson, but this was suppressed and published only in 1710. M de La Foucherie seems to be the cleric mentioned in 890317 and 890414; he was a friend of Nicaise.

891019 NICOLAS CHARMOT   19 October 1689
Carp p. 618; Québec, B 161 du Séminaire, carton S, 19

On the point of shipwreck by the Cape of Good Hope Charmot had thought of la T., prayed and was saved. General advice on missions. God's mercy is essential, and one must be prepared to give up even life for Christ.

The MS at Carpentras alone gives the right name; all other sources either give no name or call him Chaumont.

891031 RP BOCCONE   31 October 1689
TC II/77

Thanks Boccone for remembering him. 'You know that all human knowledge is of scant use unless related to the end you have before your eyes.'

891100 DUCHESSE DE GUISE   [? November 1689]
Mug II/105
Bad weather. Report that new Pope has attended opera; if true, R. condemns it.

891103 CLAUDE NICAISE   3 November 1689
BN 9363,f.79, orig.; Gonod 101

Boccone will need permission to come to la T. Quesnel has written. Abbé de La Chambre did not come.

The question of La Chambre's visit came up in 1688. Quesnel's letter is unknown, but probably concerned the dispute with Mabillon.

891114 JEAN FAVIER   14 November 1689
CF 344,f.91, orig.; Gonod 47

R. repeats the proposal for Saint-Symphorien at Beauvais. Abbé Jacques de Forbin-Janson [Bp's nephew and a canon] has visited la T. and confirms situation. M Tristan is taking care of it.

* 891119 BISHOP OF LUÇON [HENRI BARILLON]   19 November 1689
P f.773

'I was on the point of writing to you, Mgr, when I had your letter telling me that you are in Paris and are thinking of coming to see us. According to the hope that you give us thereby, you can imagine how impatiently I shall await that pleasure, all the more so because, if I were deprived of it on the present occasion, I have no grounds for expecting it for the rest of my life. I am afraid that your brother's occupation will delay the moment. He tells me that he has completely made up his mind, and that it is only a question of taking his time. As you say nothing about your health, I am sure it is good, and praise God with all my heart. Mine is flagging; I am suffering from rheumatism which causes me continual pain, more or less acute according to the changes in the weather. The outer man must be destroyed, and if I am what I ought to be, I should see that destruction with pleasure. My professed claim to belong to the world no more demands no less a renunciation. I beg you, Mgr, to ask God to grant me as much renunciation as he bids me have, for fear that on the day when he is to undertake the final, exact examination of my works it may be said of me the terrible words *appensus es in statera et inventus es minus habens* [Dan 5:27]. Do me always the honour of your friendship, and please believe that no one could be with more fidelity, affection and respect than I yours' etc.

Barillon left for Paris on 23 October to see his brother Paul (after eighteen years) who was on the point of retiring and in failing health.

891126   CLAUDE NICAISE   26 November 1689
BN 9363,f.251, orig.; Gonod 104

Discusses Boccone; and Quesnel, whose criticism he scorns.

891200   DUCHESSE DE GUISE   [December 1689]
Mug II/110

The innocence of the canons of Beauvais recognised.

In revenge for an imagined slight, Raoul Foy, a canon of Beauvais, had falsely accused his colleagues of conspiracy against the King. Some were arrested, but released on 5 December 1689. Despite his victims' pleas, Foy was executed in 1691. R. was indirectly involved because of his close relations with several of the canons.

891200a   DUCHESSE DE GUISE   [December 1689]
Mug II/111

R. writes nothing in his letters which anyone is not welcome to read.

891200b   CLAUDE NICAISE   [? December 1689]
BN 9363,f.90, orig.; Gonod 105

R. sympathises with Nicaise in his troubles.

* 891206 BISHOP OF LIMOGES [LOUIS D'URFÉ] 6 December 1689
TC II/78

'I do not doubt, Mgr, that you are returning loaded with trophies and merit at the end of your campaign. You have been working for the glory of Christ, and I am sure that you give yourself up to this obligation with such wholehearted zeal that you establish his kingdom where it is not and confirm it everywhere that you find it already established. As I associate myself closely with all the labours which such continual and tiring functions may have caused you, it is quite right that I should also do so with the grace and blessings you have received. I expect that happiness if you ask it of Our Lord. The prayer of the righteous has great power with him, and I hope that if you offer him yours to that end, they will have all the effect I could wish.

You say, Mgr, that your health is weakening, and that you feel dangerous indispositions. But I cannot believe that God wishes to end a life which is so useful to his people. The number of chief shepherds attached to their duties is so small, so few make these duties their chief business, that rightminded people who love his Church are specially obliged to take an interest in their preservation.

I regard your idea that you are approaching the end of the road as an effect of God's mercy, wishing you to prepare for a remote event as if it were at hand, and it is certain that the sight of the last moments always makes a special impression, and anyone who thinks he has only a short time to live behaves differently from what he would do if he thought he had more. This final moment is more powerfully affecting when it is before one's eyes, and the great saints have always made their ways still stricter when the end seemed to them to be near. That is to say, according to the words of Scripture, that the righteous man must make new efforts to increase his righteousness and do all in his power to become more worthy of the compassion of the one who is to judge him. The way to become acceptable to him is to meditate on his judgements and consider them as the focal point to which one should relate all one's actions and all the details of one's conduct.

Prelates have a consolation peculiar to them, I mean those who in the Lord's house are faithful dispensers, and that is that, since their ministry is purely one of charity, their care and solicitude speak constantly for them. It is a voice which rises up to his throne, soliciting and urging him, but with an importunity incapable of displeasing him. You are of that number, Mgr, that is a belief that your humility should neither conceal nor weaken. That belief, strictly speaking, is your strength, and sustains your courage amid all the obstacles, temptations and different difficulties which are inseparable from the nature and greatness of your tasks.

It is true that the conscientiousness required of ecclesiastics, particularly those in the highest ranks, is greater than people think, and it is enough to know, in order to be convinced, that they are obliged to instruct by example even more than words, *forma facti gregis ex animo* [1 P 5:3]. It would not be possible to say more in fewer words. I wish you, Mgr, increase in all kinds of grace, and I can assure you that there is no one in the world who is with more sincere, inviolable and perfect respect than I yours' etc.

891208 MADEMOISELLE [? DE LA TREMOUILLE] 8 December 1689
TC II/291

She still wants to leave the world. 'It is true, as you say, that it is harder to commit oneself at your age because one listens to one's own arguments.'

CF 890829, which strongly suggests the same addressee.

*891228 RM MARIE-LOUISE [BOUTHILLIER] 28 December 1689
TA orig.

'Monsieur l'abbé Berrier did not bring me your letter, my dear sister, but he did talk about you and told me your news. You are right to esteem him, for he is a man of much merit, I mean the sort you and I should specially prize, and which is found only in those who belong to God and serve him; as for other merit, however great it may be, I do not see that it should be accounted of any value or given any importance.

Besides, my dear sister, you could do no better for your peace of mind than follow your feeling of giving yourself up entirely to God, and letting him dispose of all that concerns you. He knows your needs much better than you know them yourself, and there is no better way of making him take care of them than handing them over to him with perfect trust in his mercy, which has never failed any of those who hoped in him. To walk in any other ways is to want to get lost; those are the only ones indicated by Christ, and we must believe that he keeps away from all who are rash enough to stray from them; that is one misfortune into which I am sure you will not fall.

I am sorry, my dear sister, about your indisposition. I do not doubt that you receive it as coming from the hand of him who sends it, and make good use of it. I am indisposed with extremely painful rheumatism, which means that I can only walk and stand with difficulty. Pray God for me and ask him that I should not be so unfaithful to my calling as not to endure it gladly, or at least patiently, as much as I am obliged to.

I do not know what the paper is of which you speak. I do not remember showing any to M l'abbé Le Boulanger; it is a blessing to know someone so virtuous and to share in his friendship and in his prayers.

I do not deserve to be in the thoughts of M le Président Larcher. I feel with him for all the gifts of grace that God has given him; he responds, according to what I hear from all sides, with such fidelity that he cannot help making great progress. You can judge from that that it would give us great pleasure to see him in our desert. Farewell, my dear sister, I assure you that I remember you before Our Lord and that no one could have more affection for you than I.'

No identifiable letters survive from R. to Louis Berrier (1655–1739), but they certainly wrote to each other and Berrier was a frequent visitor. He had founded a convent in Bossuet's diocese of Meaux, and in 1687 became a conseiller in Parlement, but then suddenly in 1690 gave up all his benefices except the benedictine priory of Perrecy, near Autun, where in 1698 he became a regular. He was highly thought of by Bossuet. In June he had brought some relics to La Trappe as a gift, and had evidently just paid another visit.

The abbé Le Boulanger is most likely R's correspondent of 1685, at the time he was preparing for ordination. Pierre Larcher, of a distinguished family of magistrates, became president of the Chambre des comptes in 1651 and remained until 1700.

90/1   DUCHESSE DE GUISE [1689/90]
Mug II/87

R. prays for success of King's arms.

From 1688–97 Louis XIV was fighting a coalition of most European powers, including the Empire, Holland, and England.

90/2   DUCHESSE DE GUISE [1689/90]
Mug II/88

R. sure that Willaim of Orange will meet resistance.

90/3   MONSIEUR [1690]
Mug II/137

R. has sent books to M's wife. Mentions that abbé N. has resigned his canonry and archdeaconry to M de Janson. R. ought to have thought of M. and his wife first.

Louis Berrier, R's friend, has resigned all his benefices save that of Perrecy in 1690; his canonry of ND de Paris went to Bruno de Janson, nephew of the Bp of Beauvais (who died in 1692). The date is thus certain, but not the identity of the addressee, who may well have been one of Berrier's two brothers.

90/4 CLAUDE NICAISE 1690
BN 9363,f.91, orig.; Gonod 106

Thanks Nicaise for a game 'a holy and ingenious invention'. Asks for confidential information on dom Le Maréchal, monk of Bonport [dioc. Evreux] now at Cîteaux, who wants to come to la T.

Cf 830826.

*900102   MARÉCHAL DE BELLEFONDS 2 January 1690
BN na 12959,f.135, orig.; TC II 174

'I can wish you nothing better, Mgr, at the beginning of this year than that God should strengthen more and more the feelings which he gave you so long ago. I am not afraid that the world will assert itself, nor that you will find it more attractive or fair than it has so far seemed to you. But yet, as it happens only too often that one does not bother to avoid the evil one knows and do the good one knows oneself obliged to do, one must be always distrustful of one's fragility and weakness, and turn to God, who alone can provide our hearts with stability.

If men were as upright as they should be, and acted in accordance with true principles, the things of this world would be useful instead of harmful to them, they would recognise God in all his works, and these diverse events which estrange them from him would serve only to bring them closer, but wickedness is so great and so universal that it overcomes their conviction and their obligation to make such use of events as will contribute to God's glory and their own peace.

What things have not come to pass since the siege of Vienna? What could more enlighten us than what we have seen, and still see, throughout Europe over the past ten or twelve years? What could more fittingly teach us the uncertainty and vanity of men's thoughts and disabuse us for ever of the object of their devotion and ambition? Nevertheless it makes no impression, and each continues along his usual way. Examples have no effect, people follow the promptings of their greed and let themselves be consumed by worthless interests, as if they had neither experience nor understanding.

God will call for a strict account of our indifference towards his careful instructions, and of the fact that instead of applying to ourselves these extraordinary occurrences and seeing in them what one cannot fail to see, we look at them, each man for himself, as if they did not concern us all and as if these imaginary goods that we have, or want to have, had a consistency and reality for us that they do not have for others. That may well be called the greatest of all illusions, since it involves us in countless commitments, disturbs our conscience, filling it with anxiety and confusion, and deprives us of that tranquility without which one cannot serve God in a way pleasing to him. I am sure that I am telling you nothing that you do not know perfectly well and are ready to subscribe to.

I pray God, Mgr, to heap blessings on you, and continue to pour his grace on your person and your house. There is never a day when I do not ask that with all my might, and I will continue to do so until my last moment. I beseech you to be persuaded of this, as also of all the fidelity and respect with which I am yours etc.

PS Permit me to report to you on the remedies you kindly sent me. The brother with chest inflammation who was coughing blood is completely cured. The other who had scrofula is cured too, but for some months, since the powder he was taking as a purge was not available, his glands have swollen again, in other words the ailment has begun to attack him again, but he continues to use the plaster. If you were kind enough to send us something for him, we should be very pleased.

As for me, my rheumatism is much worse. I blame the season and my negligence'.

The Turks had unsuccessfully besieged Vienna in 1683.

*900102a BISHOP OF LUÇON [HENRI BARILLON] 2 January 1690
P f.634

'What you do me the honour of writing to me, Mgr, consoles me by giving me the hope of seeing you. My joy will be complete if your brother is also with us. He must however consider his health and not expose himself to relapses. The fact that he must still take quinine shows that his cure is not quite confirmed. It is true that my desire to see him once again in my life is greater than I can say. I am sure that he believes that, convinced, as I do not doubt that he is, that no one could have more affectionate and faithful respect for anyone than I have for him.

I praise God, Mgr, that you have not suffered your usual indispositions. That is what is most to be feared, because, as for rheumatism, the Paris air and usual reliefs will soon bring recovery; the air here is more trying and harsh, and as for me my indisposition increases instead of diminishing. I attribute that to the site of this place and the hard winter, which is as harmful in its damp as in its cold.

At the beginning of this year I wish you, Mgr, a long and happy life. Those who belong to God as you do and serve him as much as you do ought to live three times as long as other men. We should regard it simply as an effect of God's wrath when he takes back to himself before their time those who have been set up in the leading positions in his Church, when they are full of zeal and enlightenment, and the sanctification of their people is their main concern. I ask your blessing, and the continuation of all your kindness, and assure you that it would not be possible to add to my gratitude, anymore than to the profound respect with which I am yours' etc.

900108   DOM EDMOND MARTÈNE, OSB   8 January 1690
BN 25538,f.91, orig.

R. thanks Martène for gift of his commentary on Rule of St Benedict.

900118   MONSIEUR L'ABBÉ   18 January 1690
TC II/106

Prediction has often been made that la T. will run out of funds. If that happens there will have to be less almsgiving and fewer admissions. Hopes to see him.

*900121   BISHOP OF LUÇON [HENRI BARILLON]   21 January 1690
Carp p. 635; Dub II/211

'I have given much thought, Mgr, to the subject on which you did me the honour of writing, and I confess that I found it very difficult to decide between the different views which occurred to me. I considered the bad climate of the place in which you are, your uncertain health, the interest we have in prolonging your days, finally my special attachment to you personally. All that leads me to wish that you would change your residence and stay no longer in a region in which your life seems to be exposed.

However, when I look closely at what God desires of someone like you, whose virtue and reputation are so distinguished, at what the Church expects of you, at the edification which you owe the world, I cannot help changing my thoughts, and telling you that it seems to me that you should persevere where it has pleased divine providence to place you, and give an example which has never been more needed than at present, since we live in an age when translations have become so frequent and common that the Church may be said to be in a state of perpetual motion.

In the second place, you know, Mgr, that Christ is the gate by which we must enter his sheepfold; he himself said that the only lawful shepherds are those whom he calls. He it is who must form vocations, and I cannot see that the way now being offered and opened to you can be considered his. Thus it would not be he who would be sending you and giving you your mission, and it would be a matter for fear that far from finding the repose sought in such a new alliance, it would result only in regret and sorrow in having contracted it to the prejudice of the original alliance.

Thirdly, it is God who holds your fate in his hand; he decides as a sovereign about life and death, and he multiplies our years when he pleases, independently of our efforts. Our precautions are so unsure that we run into the dangers we try to avoid, and it happens only too often that all our care has no other effect than to draw on us the ills which we seek to prevent. In a word, it is God who has placed you and established your bonds, he has so far blessed your ministry, and it can hardly be that, if you were to move, a conscience as tender and pure as yours would not be exposed to much remorse: *Quod Deus conjunxit, homo non separet.*[Mt 19:6]

There, Mgr, you have my thoughts, since you bid me tell you. However, I do not fail to submit them to your own enlightenment, for I know that God is the master of rules, he speaks to his servants and lets them know what he does not declare to others'.

Barillon's friends had been pressing him to accept translation to a more salubrious region (Luçon is mostly swamp) but in the end he followed R's advice. For some reason this letter is not in the collection copied at Luçon.

900123   BISHOP OF COMMINGES   23 January 1690
         [LOUIS DE RECHIGNEVOISIN]

Carp p. 609; Sol. *ND de St Bernard de Comminges*

R. recommends having a priest available at chapel of Alan to hear confessions of pilgrims.

900203   RM PRIEURE   3 February 1690
TC II/217

How could she imagine that her [male] superior was not able to make the rule in question? 'Do you not know that it is by external contacts that the devil lays traps for those in retreat?' Nuns must not be alone with visitors in the parlor.

* 900212   BISHOP OF LUÇON [HENRI BARILLON]   12 February 1690
P f.774

'We shall continue to hope, Mgr, for the honour you promise us, and I confess that I should be most sorry if anything prevented you from taking the road to us, for I think that if we see each other in our desert it will be for the last time, since my health gives me no cause to think that I still have far to go. One indisposition follows another, and with a delicate constitution, what else can one expect but imminent deliverance? Above all, Mgr, if you do decide to come this way, make sure that your brother comes too. For the rest, I beg you to believe that I often consider your troubles, and all the difficulties which I know you encounter move me more than I can say. We are sorry for you, and pray God for you with all our might, for I fully understand the situation in which you are. God has so far sustained you with almighty protection, and we must hope that he will do so in the future. I do not doubt that you belong to the number of those of whom it is written that the eyes of his mercy are ceaselessly upon them. I am sure that your eyes never lose him from sight and that you consider him as the only one who can give you relief amid your tribulations. We shall offer him our continual prayers for that. I humbly beg you not to doubt that, and to believe that no one could be with deeper and more tender respect than I yours' etc.

900218   RELIGIEUSES, LES CLAIRETS   [? 18 February 1690]
A 3389,f.80 vo.

R's satisfaction at their attitude.

This letter was written immediately after his return from the visitation which ended on 17 February.

900220   CLAUDE NICAISE   20 February 1690
BN 9363,f.93, orig.; Gonod 107

Nicaise now free of benefices. His essay on the ancient monument (tomb).

900221   RP DE L'ORDRE   21 February 1690
TC I/153

He must not involve himself in ecclesiastical functions.

900221a DUKE OF PERTH   21 February 1690
TC I/152; TC II/72
Suffer persecution as God's order.

900300 DUCHESSE DE GUISE   [? March 1690]
Mug II/98
R. pleased at news from Ireland. Praying for Dauphine.
The Battle of the Boyne was on 11 July, so there was still room for hope for James' cause in Ireland. The Dauphine died on 20 April, so the letter is probably of March or April.

* 900326 BISHOP OF LUÇON [HENRI BARILLON]   26 March 1690
P f.775

'I am not surprised, Mgr, that you are staying longer in Paris than you had expected; it is hardly likely that having so much to do you would fail to finish it. Such journeys as those you make to Paris are rare and unusual, and so that should make you profit from them and make the most of every moment. My consolation is that you do not dash our hopes of having the honour of seeing you on your return. I confess that if I were deprived of it, it would be no ordinary mortification. I hope that your brother has both enough free time and health to come along too. I could hardly consider that as a matter of indifference, with all the attachment I have for him and what concerns him.

As for what concerns you, Mgr, I can say that there is never a day when I do not commend you several times to Our Lord. I am more keenly alive to your interests than I can say, and am attached to your person by bonds and commitments that I could not express. Please believe, I beg you, that no one could be with more tender and profound respect than I yours etc.

PS Kindly assure your brother, Mgr, that no one could honour him or think of him more than I do. If I do not tell him myself it is for fear of being importunate.'

* 900420 MARÉCHAL DE BELLEFONDS.   20 April 1690
BN na 12959,f.137, orig.; Mug I/62

'Although you are always very present in my mind, Mgr, and there is never a day when we do not think of you before God, and several times, our memory of you has been more urgent and vivid than usual for some little time, and we really joined in all your troubles and anxieties as soon as we heard the state in which Mme la D[auphine] was and still is. From the way they speak of her illness there are more grounds for fear than hope. We ask her recovery of God, and the preservation of her person, with all possible diligence, but we have not so far deserved to be heard; at least her illness, from what we hear, pursues its normal course.

We could not pay too much heed to her condition, Mgr. She is one of the greatest princesses in the world, amidst all the things and persons from whom she could expect help, and yet she is unable to receive from any quarter assistance which is any use to her, and whatever is done for her relief all must yield to the will of God and his intentions must be fulfilled.

Such occasions make us realise exactly that all men's thoughts are vain and all their diligence of little use. Strive and agitate as we may, it is all without effect if God's orders are to the contrary.

However, as they are unknown to us and we cannot penetrate his secrets, we must walk in our accustomed ways and do all that christian prudence requires us to do, but with the qualification and dependent attitude that we regard events as coming from his hand, and receive them without ever feeling either opposition or repugnance. Such a disposition is necessary for this world and the next, for unless we limit ourselves to these rules there is no certain peace or constant rest on this earth and the slightest mishaps will throw us into confusion and distress.

As regards eternity, what good can be expected by anyone who has refused due submission to God and has not shown the consideration and respect he is obliged to have for the workings of his providence? It seems to me, I do not know if I am mistaken, that God has never spoken more precisely and clearly by the situation in the world than he is doing at the present time, and yet I see almost no one profiting by it; everyone follows and holds to his path as if we had no ears to hear, nor docility to submit. None the less it is written that only he who hears the voice of God, that is, who follows it, belongs to him, and that not to follow it is a sign of not belonging to him. We have every interest in asking him for this understanding, since it is the feature which distinguishes true Christians from those who are not. God has furnished you, Mgr, with these principles and this enlightenment, we must ask him to strengthen them and give you the grace to express them in your works. You know that the most lofty and holy knowledge is sterile if it does not go over into action, and that is the only reason God has given it. I am with deep respect, I beg you to believe yours etc.

PS I have a request to make of you, Mgr. M le marquis de Bellefonds has a young man in his regiment called Favier, whom he took from the cadets of Strasbourg because he seemed to have good military qualities and gave him the rank of second lieutenant. He is the nephew of a most virtuous ecclesiastic who was my tutor more than thirty years ago. The good man has written to me and the favour he asks is that I should ask you to be kind enough to write to your son, so that he will recommend the young man to be sensible, to fear God, and not give way to the disorders and dissipation common to men of his profession. It would be a comfort to the uncle who is more than eighty.'

The Dauphine was Marie-Anne-Christine of Bavaria, who died on the very day this letter was written. The autopsy found that she had widespread internal cancer.

The marquis was Bellefonds' son, serving in Flanders. Favier had long since retired to Thiers, in Auvergne.

* 900427 MARÉCHAL DE BELLEFONDS. 27 April 1690
BN na 12959,f.140, orig.

'Finally, Mgr, what we feared has happened; God has taken Mme la Dauphine back to himself. The moment had arrived and men were not able to delay it with all their care and all their efforts. This is a loss which you must have felt keenly for many reasons. Yet I do not doubt that the detachment which God has given you for so long and the view he has given you of earthly things made you look upon this event, distressing as it is, in a spirit of perfect resignation. It is enough for a Christian to know that God disposes all events and his providence rules them for him to receive them from God's hand with all due submission. We have no right to examine his counsels, we are indispensably obliged to worship them and bow our heads when he is pleased to lay on us the weight of his arm. You know your duties in this respect, Mgr, and I hope that he will never permit on any occasion that you should fail in them. I humbly beg you to believe that no one could be more concerned than I in all that affects you. I have shown my concern before God on this occasion and will continue to do so as long as I am able, and in a manner worthy of the devotion I have for your person and the profound respect with which I am yours' etc.

Bellefonds had been closely associated with the household of the Dauphin, whose tutor he had once hoped to become.

* 900427a BISHOP OF LUÇON [HENRI BARILLON] 27 April 1690
P f.775

'It is no small mortification, Mgr, to be deprived of a joy to which I had been looking forward for so long, and I confess that my regret is all the greater because I have no more hope for the future. Your residence and my poor health are two unanswerable arguments. We must wish whatever is pleasing to God and be convinced, at whatever cost, that he does all things for the best. It is certain that I should have had a lot to tell you which will now be buried in perpetual silence, since letters are no good except for saying what one does not mind becoming public.

I shall follow you, Mgr, to your diocese in spirit and heart. I will share all your troubles, and cares, and can assure you that no one could be more aware of them than I am. If your brother does me the honour of coming to see me, as you say he still wants to, I shall be really delighted. In my present state there are few people whom I should like to have in our solitude, but you know that as far as I am concerned I make quite special distinctions and exceptions for him. I pray God, Mgr, to fill you with grace and blessings, to sustain your ministry, and make you a faithful steward in the ruling of his house, so that having all the merit, you may also have the reward. I am with all possible affection, attachment and respect yours' etc.

Barillon had gone back to Luçon on 11 March.

900521 RP, SUPÉRIEUR DE L'ORDRE   21 May 1690
BN na 12959,f.194, orig.

R. will send back 'D' when RP wishes, but he will be more useful to his house in a month or two.

900524 CLAUDE NICAISE   24 May 1690
BN 9363,f.94, orig.; Gonod 108

Hopes Nicaise will manage to come to la T.

900602 JEAN LE NAIN   2 June 1690
Tour. orig.

Sub-prior [Dom Pierre, son of M] has also written to console him for loss of sight, but cataract can be operated on later. R. thanks him for help in his sister's [Mme d'Albon's] lawsuit.

900700 RM SUPÉRIEURE   July 1690
TC II/79

She had done all she should not have done to secure election and should resign 'a superiority to which your greed alone committed you' or continue in it, doing penance. 'God will forget your sin if you are sorry for it.'

900702 J-B DE SANTEUIL, SAINT-VICTOR   2 July 1690
La Vie et les bons mots, II, p. 82

Praises poetic value of Santeuil's work. Dom Le Nain's hymns are unworthy to be seen by Santeuil, but Le Nain is most grateful.

R. did not think much of dom Le Nain's literary ability, and later apologised to Gerbais for Le Nain's prose.

* 900710 BISHOP OF LUÇON [HENRI BARILLON]   10 July 1690
P f.635

'Whenever I have news of you, Mgr, it never fails to fill me with joy. It is not that I am surprised that you should think of me, for I am sure that few people have the place in your heart that I do; it is a good fortune which I feel and appreciate as I ought, and I try to show you this before Our Lord. I praise God for the state in which you have found your diocese; your work there is so solid that an absence of a few months is unable to weaken what your solicitude and vigilance have established. As regards the new converts, the great success with which God has been pleased to support the arms of the King in Flanders will dash their hopes and give them very different ideas from those which they have fed upon for some time now.

The warnings given by the Bishop of Meaux, which you have doubtless seen, seem to me so powerful and likely to upset all their machinations that they could not subsist for a moment, short of prejudice, or rather fearful possession, by the devil. That shows clearly that men may speak but it is for God alone to change and break hearts.

Only two days ago I received your brother's letter, telling me that he still plans to come and see us, but that he has had some attacks of fever, from which he has been cured by quinine, which have prevented him. People in the world are to be pitied, I mean even those who are most upright. The world attaches and tethers them with bonds which will one day seem mere cobwebs, but what is terrible is that such enlightenment will come to them only after the event and will be of no use or benefit to them, *morituri vitae et mortis me, fine victuri.*

It still really grieves me that I was deprived of the honour of seeing you on your return road to your diocese. God did not permit it because I desire it too ardently. Wherever you may be, Mgr, you will always be very present to me. I keep a vivid memory of all the goodness with which you have honoured me, and nothing can equal my heartfelt affection and profound respect for you.

I learn from many quarters that the King has restored Cardinal Le Camus to favour; I admit that I am quite delighted.'

Between 1689 and 1691 Bossuet published his six Avertissements [Warnings] aux Protestants *directed against such leading divines as Gilbert Burnet in England and Pierre Jurieu in Holland.*

Ever since his promotion in 1686 Le Camus had been out ot favour with Louis.

The Latin quotation as copied does not make sense, nor can it be traced.

The Battle of the Boyne puts an end   11 July 1690
to King James' hopes of regaining his throne

900720   RP ABBÉ, VAL-RICHER [DOMINIQUE GEORGES]   20 July 1690
Maupeou *Vie*, I p. 534

Discusses Mège's Commentary.

900727   CLAUDE NICAISE   27 July 1690
BN 9363,f.96 orig.; Gonod 109

Approves of M Anisson's book [Anisson was about to become royal printer; the book is unidentified].

900800   RM [SADOT OR JADOT]   August 1690
TC II/292
Follow the rule scrupulously and she will become a great saint.

900800a   MARQUISE   August 1690
TC II/102
It is not enough to recognise, or even condemn, her previous state, she must now take action and do works.

900824   MONSIEUR   [24 August 1690]
Mug II/33
Fr Candide has arrived; 'his fathers will not be pleased, but he has a brief'.

This was Candide Chalype, a Recollect from Paris, who had obtained a brief to come to la T. partly through du Charmel's good offices. He had stayed at Chartres with Félibien on the way, and this letter is probably to either du Charmel or Félibien. He stayed only four days, and then went back to Paris, where he stirred up serious trouble with tales of heresy and sedition, involving Bossuet, among others. Some of the rumors were at first heeded, but he was eventually exposed, exiled to Verdun, and forced to recant.

900911 [CLAUDE NICAISE]   11 September 1690
BN 9363,f.243, orig.; Gonod 110
R. defends his instructions to Les Clairets against reading the Old Testament. Quotes St Teresa on simple nuns concerned only with sewing and spinning.

After much pressure from the abbess and nuns, R. had most reluctantly agreed to become visitor of les Clairets and paid his first visit in February 1690, returning for the benediction of the abbess in July. The Carte de visite was published, and R's strict limitation of the nuns' permitted reading matter came in for much criticism. In this he was simply being consistent with what he had said in Sainteté, but his strictures on the immorality of some Old Testament stories genuinely shocked some people.

*900920   BISHOP OF LUÇON [HENRI BARILLON]   20 September 1690
P f.793 and f.776 (last two paras. detached in error and copied as a separate letter).

'I have the honour of writing to you today, Mgr, to make a recommendation on behalf of one of my intimate friends, Monsieur l'abbé de La Chambre, who has two small priories in your diocese. One is called Saint-Pierre de Beauvezi and the other Saint-Martin de Saleizaine. The favour I ask of you for him is to see that they do not overcharge him in taxing him on the tithes. You can well imagine, Mgr, that when one asks something of you one keeps within the bounds of justice.

I have not yet sent you a little pamphlet which has been circulating for some days, consisting of an account of a visit I made to an abbey of nuns dependent on la Trappe, and the account of the death of one of our monks, because it is not I who had given it to the public, and I did not think it deserved your seeing it. However, since it has found almost general approval in the world, and has been read with edification by persons of all professions and callings, I am ashamed that you do not yet have it, or that you have had it from other hands than mine; I am arranging for it to be sent to you.

There is one thing in the *carte de visite* which has been censured by certain critics, whom I shall not name, and that is the passage where I said that reading the Old Testament was not suitable for nuns. I based myself on St Basil, St Nilus, and Cassian, who wrote that it was not proper for solitaries, and on that fact that I cannot understand how such a variety of stories, facts, and expressions, which even persons of solid virtue should only read with caution, might serve as reading matter for women living in retreat and obliged to live in angelic purity. The slightest things can excite and disturb the imagination; is there not reason to fear that stories told in a vivid manner might produce disagreeable impressions on minds nourished in solitude and consequently having more time and means for reflection than others? It is not, as St Basil and St Nilus say, that Scripture is anything but very holy, since it is dictated by God's Spirit, but all sorts of persons are not capable of making holy use of it. St Nilus said on the same subject *omnia licent sed non omnia expediunt* [1 Co 10:23].

I am sure, Mgr, that you will not be one of those who censure my ideas, and I confess that, informed as I am, by countless reports coming to me from every side, of the state of the majority of religious communities of women, I cannot believe, Mgr, that my opinion is not well founded, but I will believe I am wrong if you tell me so.

I have nothing to report from here, Mgr, except that you are honoured most specially, and that nothing could be added to the attachment and profound respect with which I am yours' etc.

'PS I cannot help telling you that it will soon be six weeks that I have been ill with an extraordinary temperature which is still going on, and has caused me almost three weeks insomnia. I am beginning to get a little better, but it is not a complete recovery. Pray God for me, I beg you, and ask above all from him that he gives me grace to finish my course better than I have done so far.'

La Chambre *was curé of Saint-Barthélemy in Paris, a friend of Nicaise and a visitor to la T. at least once in 1688. He died in 1693.*

'Saint-Pierre' *is Saint-Pierre-des-Champs, a small benedictine priory near Beauvoir-sur-Mer; the other place may be Sallertaine, not far away, both in Vendée. The pamphlet is the* Carte de Visite . . . à ND des Clairets, *published by Muguet in 1690 together with the* Instruction sur la mort de dom Muce *(the ex-grenadier who died in 1689). Both pieces aroused opposition, and R's prohibition to the nuns on reading the Old Testament, despite arguments from the Fathers, was much criticised. Just what St Nilus said, and where, cannot be identified.*

901022 ARCHBISHOP OF REIMS [LOUIS LE TELLIER]   22 October 1690
Carp p. 663
R. reaffirms his loyalty to the King in the light of fr Chalype's calumnies.

901026 MONSIEUR L'ABBÉ TÉTU   26 October 1690
TC I/70
R. claims that *Carte de visite* of les Clairets and *Instruction sur la mort de dom Muce*, though correct, were printed without his authority, as were the *Règlements*, published twenty years earlier from originals taken away by novices. He always regrets breaking silence by word or pen. Sorry not to have seen Tétu as he did last year.

The lurid life and edifying death of dom Muce Faure was the subject of a special pamphlet of some ninety pages. A former grenadier, he joined the Cluniacs and was ordained; then, shocked at his own sacrilege, he fled and took up arms again allegedly ready to serve even in the Turkish forces. Suddenly seized with remorse he walked vast distances to la T., arriving in 1689. R. was so impressed at his penitence that he dispensed him from the full year as a novice, professed him in February 1689, but had to bury him in May, aged 33. Incredulity greeted the account of his crimes, and R. secured a certificate from the authorities in Valence to the effect that Muce really had been as bad as he had said. A revised version of the 1671 pirated edition of the Règlements was published by Michallet in 1690, and was in fact R's work.

901114 CLAUDE NICAISE   14 November 1690
BN 9363,f.95, orig.; Gonod 111
Criticism of R's account of dom Muce.

An alleged old soldier had written on 30 September 1690 from the Invalides (the soldiers' home) a spirited defence of the grenadiers, and a refutation of R's contention that Muce had learned his evil ways in the army, and this pamphlet circulated widely.

901119 ARCHBISHOP OF PARIS [FRANÇOIS DE HARLAY]   19 November 1690
Carp p. 665
R. reaffirms his loyalty to the King in the light of Chalype's calumnies.

* 901129 MARÉCHAL DE BELLEFONDS   29 November 1690
BN na 12959,f.142, orig.

'I was most sorry, Mgr, that you left la Trappe without the chance of talking about the King of England. I did all I could, but could not find the time. I was dying to tell you my impressions of this prince who is so worthy of the respect and compassion of all men of good will. I confess, Mgr, that I saw in him a depth of piety and religion that surprised me, a detachment from all worldly things and a resignation to God's will which can only be the effect of his grace and the impression made by his Holy Spirit. He is fully aware of the degree and extent of his disgrace, when he looks at it with human eyes, but this realisation only causes him to offer to God a continual sacrifice and thus attract the protection he needs in so total and complete a misfortune.

One cannot fail to see that what consoles him is that he is convinced that what he is losing he had only for a few moments, that he was bound sooner or later to be deprived of it, but what he awaits is eternal and Jesus Christ is preparing a crown for him which knows no change, and cannot be taken from him either by the wickedness of devils or the conspiracy of men. I was struck by the restraint and moderation with which he spoke of his enemies; he does not utter a word in that respect which is not in accordance with the strictest rules. Nature has no part in what he says about them, all its reactions are halted. This is assuredly something that is not within the power of man, and there is no room for doubt that in such moments God is entirely master of his heart. The vigour of his faith and the ardour of his zeal for the interests of the Church and the service of Christ are without equal, and he deems himself happy in his misfortune to have been judged worthy to suffer for the glory of his name. He knows and feels that persecution is the mark of those who belong to Christ.

We saw him, you remember, Mgr, approach the holy table with a quite unusual piety. He prayed God during the office and throughout High Mass, without a moment's interruption. He left the carpet on which he was, placed himself on the bottom step of the altar and rejected the cushion offered to him. At the same time took place a detail worthy of note: as he was being given the sacred host, the choir sang what is called the communion of the mass, which could not have been more appropriate and explicit if it had been done deliberately: *Confundantur superbi quia injuste iniquitatem fecerunt in me; ego autem exercebor in mandatis tuis* [Ps 118:78]. May the proud be confounded with the injustice with which they have treated me; as for me, Lord, my consolation will be to submit to your commands.

The main thing is that all his behavior is visibly based on true principles. I mean on his trust in God's goodness and firm conviction that all passing things are unworthy of being desired by those who live in hope of goods that will never pass away.

It must be admitted, Mgr, that the state in which we see this unfortunate prince gives a good idea of the vanity of what is most splendid on earth, and at the same time of the immensity of God's mercy. We see the former in the audacity of the usurper and the fall of this great king, in the revolt of his people and the perfidy of his servants, and the latter in the firmness with which he bears the weight of a disgrace which would have overwhelmed him a hundredfold if the almighty hand of God had not saved him from that misfortune. Happy he who knows the uncertainty of human things, but happier still is he who is not content with mere speculation and takes care to regulate his ways by this knowledge, good use of which is so rare and so necessary.

I can assure you, Mgr, that if he found some consolation amongst us, as he indicated, he has left us an edifying memory which we shall never lose. After the King whom God has engraved in our innermost hearts, and all that concerns his sacred person, he will occupy the first place in our hearts. I owe that to the many great qualities he has received from God, to his persecution, his inflexible attachment to the defence of the faith, and I owe it also to all the signs he gave me of a goodness which I did not deserve.

There, Mgr, is a part of what I had to say to you and could not stop myself writing for my own satisfaction. It only remains for me to ask you for the continuation of the honour of your good graces, and to protest that it is with all possible respect and sincerity that I am yours' etc.

James paid his first visit to La T. on 24 November, after his final defeat at the Battle of the Boyne (12 July). Bellefonds was in his entourage.

901213   RP, CONFESSEUR DE RELIGIEUSES   13 December 1690
TC II/55

Christmas blessings on RP's house [This is probably dom Jacques de Lanchal, confessor at les Clairets from 1688 until his death in 1692].

901218   TRM [? GIF]   18 December 1690
TC II/201

'Your chagrin comes from the devil alone.' She thinks her abbess is hostile. R. speaks of her contribution to the state of the house.

This is most probably the ex-abbess, then prioress of Gif, Anne de Montglat.

901221   JAMES II   21 December 1690
W orig.; SP p. 59

God permits external trappings, but kings must not become attached to them and must always have God's designs in mind.

James first visited la T. on 24 November 1690 and initiated the correspondence by writing to R. on 8 December. Copies of thirty eight of his letters survive in the Tournouer collection. Admitting that he paid his first visit out of curiosity, James says a year later (2 December 1691) that he then began to think more seriously about his salvation. In 1696 he confirmed that he had visited la T. every year since 1690, and on 15 March 1698 he wrote: 'it took that visit [to la T.] to give me knowledge of myself and make me despise all that seems great in the world'. James' letters are far from banal and show unmistakable affection and respect for R., as well as genuine concern for his own spiritual state.

901224 RP PRIEUR, BARBEAUX 24 December 1690
Autographes Troussures, p. 547

This letter was sent via the College des Bernardins in Paris. R. would like to help, but the two monks asked for are too uncertain in health, and transplanting monks is often dangerous in itself.

Simply because this collection includes so many letters to Robin Couturier, a monk of Barbeaux, during his term of office as prior at Perseigne, this letter too may be to him; a new prior had gone to Perseigne in 1687, and dom Robin, if alive, presumably went back to Barbeaux.

901224a CLAUDE NICAISE 24 December 1690
BN 9363,f.97, orig.; Gonod 112

Praises Santeuil. Bellefonds has given away copies of R's letter to him on James II [901129].

91/1 MONSIEUR [?1691]
TC I/122

R. defends his attitude to James II, whose visit he had not sought. 'SS Antony and Arsenius would have spoken out from the depths of their desert' for so righteous a cause, as he did.

When French policy aimed to restore James, R's approval of his resignation looked like defeatism.

910104 CLAUDE NICAISE 4 January 1691
BN 9363,f.99 orig.; Gonod 113

R. asks for a copy of his letter to Nicaise about the Old Testament 'for I can hardly recall it'.

910104a RM ABBESSE, LES CLAIRETS 4 January 1691
[FRANÇOISE-ANGÉLIQUE D'ETAMPES DE VALENÇAY]
TA orig.

R. has had a bad fall. Wishes her a blessed year.

* 910110 MARÉCHAL DE BELLEFONDS 10 January 1691
BN na 12959,f.144, orig.

'I wish you, Mgr, a year full of prosperity, and pray God to cause you to grow more and more in knowledge, fear, and love of him. Those are solid and genuine goods, it is to those that we should attach ourselves and to which all other goods should either yield or relate. That is something the world will not agree with and will one day be obliged to acknowledge to its confusion and shame.

I had already been informed, Mgr, that copies had been seen of a letter which I wrote you on the subject of the King of England, and I did not doubt for a moment that it would have the fate it has had, I mean that it would find people to approve and to criticise, and that men would speak of it differently, according to the different reactions of their charity or their passions. Essentially everything I said was sincere; I will go further, it was true, for I not only said what I believed, but what actually is. If I could have foreseen that the world would take that as it did, and as has appeared, I would have explained myself much more strongly and fully, not for the conviction of the censors, because I know that men are not willing to change their minds, but for the consolation of men of good will who are and will be edified to see in our time so violent and complete a persecution borne with so much faith, constancy, and piety.

People claim that I was wrong to write on such a subject. If I had given the letter to the public, or had spoken of worldly affairs, they might have been right, but by God's grace I fell into neither of those misfortunes, for I wrote only to you, Mgr, and said nothing that a man of my profession may not, and even should not, say, since this letter which is making such a stir contains only some reflections on the goodness of God and his extreme mercies in according protection to a Catholic king, whose firmness has been such that he preferred to risk losing three great kingdoms rather than acquiesce in what he regarded as contrary to his plans for preserving or spreading the religion to which he was invincibly attached. Who better should publish God's greatness abroad than those engaged more closely than others in his service, like religious and solitaries?

In the end, Mgr, men must be allowed to say what they will, and when one is convinced that there is nothing blameworthy in what men are pleased to criticise and condemn, the only course to follow is to remain in peace. One would be either very weak or very unhappy to make one's peace depend on the fantasy of those who have arrogated to themselves the right to judge things and persons without equity or understanding.

That, Mgr, is the situation in which I am. I do not believe you would advise me to change it. You know too well how God makes himself heard in respect of those who try to please men at the expense of what they owe to truth. Keep your accustomed kindness towards me, and please believe that no one is more sincerely and respectfully than I yours' etc.

R. refers to 901127. He must have known that it would be copied but always claimed that this happened without his knowledge or consent. James had in fact annoyed his French allies by an intemperate display of his Catholic plans in the first place, and then by his reported resignation to defeat just when they were engaged in naval and military operations to restore him.

* 910120   BISHOP OF LUÇON [HENRI BARILLON]   20 January 1691
P f.636

'When I received your honoured letter, Mgr, I was on the point of anticipating you and telling you that we do not fail to ask God to give you renewed strength and fidelity in the continued discharge of your ministry, with all the vigilance and conscientiousness with which you began it. As the difficulties do not grow less, and people do not take all the care they should to profit by the diligence of those who lead them, great patience is needed, and if one did not look to God in being so painstaking, and console oneself in him for the fact that it is not as successful as it should be, one would spend one's life in dejection. God, Mgr, whom you have had before your eyes up to now, has supported you and will support you, and you will find in the witness of your conscience what you are unable to find in the attitude of those whom he has committed to your charge.

The visit of the King of England did not cause us so very much trouble. He came alone and spent a single day in our monastery. I confess that he filled us with edification, and that I have never seen piety more sincere, firm, and enlightened than his. With that he has an incredible fund of goodness, and a submission to all God's wishes which can only be the effect of quite extraordinary grace and protection.

I ask, Mgr, for your holy blessing and the help of your prayers, and beg you to believe that I shall all my life have all the consideration for your person that it merits, nothing could equal the affection and respect with which I am yours' etc.

910121   RP ABBÉ, VAL-RICHER [DOMINIQUE GEORGES]   21 January 1691
Maupeou, *Vie* I p. 531

R. denies writing against Mège, who has written two letters against him on Old Testament reading.

910124   JAMES II   24 January 1691
W orig.; *SP* p. 61

On 17 January James had sent an account of his brother, Charles II's, conversion. R. comments on unique authority of Catholicism. Sends a work on Gospel truth for Lord Dumbarton.

George Douglas, Earl of Dumbarton, had accompanied James on his visit to la T. He died in 1692

910206   J-B DE SANTEUIL, SAINT-VICTOR   6 February 1691
La Vie et les bons mots, II p. 83

Praise for Santeuil's hymns.

910214   CLAUDE NICAISE   14 February 1691
BN 9363,f.100, orig.; Gonod 114; TC II/97
Confirms authenticity of copy of his letter sent by Nicaise. 'A man of war can become a great saint . . . if he considers God in the person of his king . . . if he risks his life in the service of his prince as he would in the service of Christ.'

910222   RP ABBÉ, val-richer [dominique georges]   22 February 1691
Maupeou, *Vie* I. p. 532
Sends pamphlet attacking *Carte de visite* at les Clairets.

910307   CLAUDE NICAISE   7 March 1691
BN 9363,f.102, orig.; Gonod 115
The only reason monks take up study is 'to try to regain distinction for knowledge, having lost it for strictness of discipline, regularity and holiness of life'.

910403   JAMES II   3 April 1691
W orig.; *SP* p. 64
R. has almost been killed in a fall. James mortified by refusal of Louis to let him come to Mons, but R. sees in this a sign of Louis' sense of responsibility for James' safety.

910404   PAUL BARILLON   4 April 1691
TC II/138
R. has nothing to say to someone so enlightened. Use sickness to prepare for the end.

*910405   BISHOP OF LUÇON [henri barillon]   5 April 1691
P f.777
'I cannot prevent myself writing to you, Mgr, not only to ask for news of you, but also to speak of your brother's indisposition. I hear from several sources that it is much more serious than he thinks. The curé of Saint-Jacques wrote recently that he had seen him, and found him so enlightened on all the obligations of a Christian that he had nothing to be told, or taught, on the subject, but you know, Mgr, that the kingdom of God does not consist of talk but of deeds, and what is called probity in this world, however much one has of it, is of little help for the next, where God will judge us on how we have practised chrisitian truths.

Your brother has had intentions for a long time now, but I find it difficult to believe that he has so far taken the necessary trouble to make them effective. As God has not allowed me the pleasure of seeing him after hoping for it for so long, I have written to him according to the promptings of my heart and the feelings of lively affection which God gave me for him so long ago. Life is something so uncertain and we see so many people from whom it is snatched when they are in robust health that one cannot help fearing for those in whom it is attacked by real illness. I do not doubt, Mgr, that you are fully informed about his condition, and tell him what you better than anyone know to be of use to him. We must ask God to give him in any case the attitude one must wish him to have, and which alone deserves to be desired. That is something we do not fail to do. His consolation and salvation move me more than I can say.

Monsieur du Charmel has been here, Mgr, for some days, and we have already talked a lot about you; you can imagine in what terms and in what way. You could certainly not fall into the hands of anyone who honoured you more. I am writing from the infirmary, where I have been for nearly four months as a result of so violent and serious a fall that I went nearly fifty days without once closing my eyes or being able to lie on a bed. I spent all that time on a chair in great pain and discomfort, and it is only twelve or fifteen days since I have begun to stand and walk with a stick. God has preserved me from fever and many other ills which, to all appearances, I should not have escaped. I hope with Our Lord's grace that the spring will make me well again. I ask for your holy blessing and beg you to believe that nothing could be added to the affection and respect with which I am yours' etc.

In 1686 an official report (by Colbert de Croissy) described Paul Barillon as irreligious, but his great friend, Mme de Sévigné, took a more favourable view. Illness and the loss of his embassy naturally prompted more serious thoughts, and Marcel, the curé of Saint-Jacques, not one to gloss over spiritual defects.

910405a   CLAUDE NICAISE   5 April 1691
BN 9363,f.104, orig.; Gonod 116

Praises Santeuil's hymns. Wishes religious were convinced of their duty of silence and solitude.

910421   DUCHESSE DE GUISE   21 April 1691
Mabillon, *Ouvrages* I p. 402

R's disagreement with Mabillon.

*910513   BISHOP OF LUÇON [HENRI BARILLON]   13 May 1691
P f.778

'I do not doubt, Mgr, that your brother was extremely pleased to see you. I confess that I am pleased also to learn, while his continuing and uncertain illness causes me such distress, that God has so moved his heart. You know, Mgr, what the worldly spirit is like, how it takes hold of people's hearts, or rather poisons them, and one can say that the people who live most by the rules of probity and honour are often those whose conversions are most rare and difficult, and that because they see nothing in their lives to make them afraid. However, there is an infinite distance between this probity with which they are satisfied and the virtue which makes Christians.

Your brother has always been fully enlightened. His understanding went further than is usual among people who are in the world. God was most merciful in adding feelings in his heart, for it would be quite useless to have the true light of understanding if that was as far as one went, since God judges men not by speculations but by their emotions and works. I hope that he will restore your brother to health and that we shall see him recover like a new man. I desire that personally more than I can say, but should Providence dispose otherwise, there would be some comfort to be derived from the situation in which it has pleased God to put him, and his complete and serene resignation to all God's wishes.

So long as God reigns, is served, and sees his orders accepted in men's souls as they ought to be, those who love his glory above all else should be content, whatever happens, and they are not permitted to desire more. I am sure, Mgr, that that is your situation, and none could be more worthy of you. I pray Our Lord to confirm all the detachment and submission he has put into your brother, and that he should remain so completely in God's hand that no temptation can draw him away. Do me the justice of believing that no one in the world could be with more affection, fidelity and respect than I yours' etc.

Barillon had arrived in Paris on 5 May to be at his brother's side.

* 910519   RM MARIE-LOUISE [BOUTHILLIER]   19 May 1691
TA orig.

'It is true, my dear sister, that my illness did not have all the results it might have had, but I am still not cured, since I can walk only with support.

I see on your side that you have not been without trials, and that God has visited on you a very dangerous indisposition. God, as you say, warns us by the ills with which we are attacked, and we should find comfort in knowing that they only come upon us by the order of his providence. The main thing is to profit by them, and be fully convinced that there is no moment when he may not call us to give exact account of a life that belongs to him and should be employed solely in serving and pleasing him. The best thing we can do, my dear sister, is to look on the past as lost, and make urgent and lively resolutions for the future, or rather the present, to avoid most carefully everything which we know he forbids to us, and embrace what we know to be in conformity with his holy will, and ask him with firm confidence to be not only our light but our strength, not to be content with showing us the way, but to guide us on it himself and prevent us straying from it. In a word, my dear sister, our hope and our faith must save us, and ensure that God forgives us the countless miseries and infidelities which make our works so unworthy of him and of the sanctity of our calling. It is above all important to preserve our peace of mind, so that it should not, if possible, be affected by anxiety, or weakening, or confusion. Farewell, my dearest sister, pray God for me and believe me to be yours without reservation.'

*910527   MARÉCHAL DE BELLEFONDS   27 May 1691
BN na 12959,f.146, orig.; TC II/137

'It is so long, Mgr, since we had news of you that it is impossible, being as interested as I am in all that concerns you, that I should not be really impatient to hear some, particularly as I have known for some days that you have been indisposed. It is true that those who told me so assured me at the same time that your health was better, which somewhat calmed my fears.

I do not doubt that you profit from everything and use as you should the different events that may befall. God has given you too much awareness and enlightenment for them to be useless to you, and you know too well the obligation of those who are his to study his will and support all his intentions to fail to do so. All piety, as you know, Mgr, comes down to knowing and following his will, and our peace of mind is so closely attached to the fidelity with which we discharge this duty that once we depart from it we deserve to be anxious and confused. To wish what God wishes is the only way to preserve one's peace in this world, and those who want something else will fail to have it, because they are in a situation of violence.

It is much to be wished that men knew this truth, and were more affected by it than they are. For if that were so they would not be devoured by their passions and would not expose themselves, as one sees every day, to end a life full of grief and bitterness by still more disagreeable and unhappy extremities.

When one comes down to it, everything passes with prodigious speed, and as there is nothing here on earth whose movement we can arrest by all our efforts, the uselessness of our trouble and precautions should be combined with the conviction, given us already by faith, that there is nothing better to do so long as we are alive than blindly to abandon ourselves to God's guidance and to regard with pleasure the fact that he ordains as he pleases what concerns us. To love him and depend on him is the way to win him, and to ensure that all his dispositions towards us are favourable. If it should be goods that we receive from his goodness, we deem ourselves unworthy; if evils, of whatever kind, we think that he is sparing us and that we deserve infinitely greater ones. Thus we perceive his mercy everywhere, according to the word of his Holy Spirit, who tells us, through our own mouth, that everything contributes to comfort and favour those who fear him. I pray Our Lord to strengthen all the grace he has given you, to increase unceasingly the gratitude which I am sure you feel, and make you proof against anything capable of injuring it at all. I am with inviolable devotion and respect yours' etc.

*910528   BISHOP OF LUÇON [HENRI BARILLON]   28 May 1691
P f.637

'I confess, Mgr, that one of the greatest joys I could have would be to hear that your brother's health has been restored, for I am sure that the grace that God has given him in his illness is not of such a kind as to be forgotten once the danger is past. From what I hear from many quarters, it has made so deep an impression that all hopes are possible. When a man as fundamentally good as he turns towards God, the change is solid and consistent and not subject to the reversals and backsliding to be observed in souls which lack all natural probity, firmness, and rectitude. All such qualities are, as you know, Mgr, gifts of God, which he often uses to bring about in those he favours his eternal decrees. Your brother has always been so faithful in his dealings with men, and has always behaved so irreproachably, that he would be both sorry and ashamed, having received so much from God, to be lacking in the gratitude he owes to him. I do not doubt that the consolation he will experience in loyally following God's orders and wishes will smoothe his ways and raise him above any temptations which may be encountered on a quite new road of which he will have had no experience.

God is full of goodness; he has given him evidence of that by taking trouble to go and look for him at the ends of the earth, so to speak, and one may well think that he has not reached out his hand only to withdraw it. Your brother can abandon himself into God's arms without fear; trust, if sincere, has never been confounded. We shall go on praying God for him. We take too keen an interest in what concerns him, and with too much affection, to fail to do so, please assure him. I am, Mgr, with all possible fidelity and respect yours' etc.

910603   CLAUDE NICAISE   3 June 1691
BN 9363,f.105,orig.; Gonod 117

Praises 'easy, pure vein' of Santeuil's style. Awaits Mabillon's work on monastic study. Sends to Boccone via Nicaise his *Explication*.

*910604   [PAUL BARILLON]   4 June 1691
P f.779

'God knows, Monsieur, how delighted I should have been if you had been able to come along with Monsieur Courtin and Monsieur de Fieubet. It is only a pleasure deferred, for I hope that God will give you back your health and once it is fully restored there will be nothing to prevent you carrying out the intention you have had for so long of coming to see us. We shall tell you then, Monsieur, much that cannot be written down. For now it suffices that I should assure you (and I believe you are fully convinced) that I could not have felt more keenly all the different reports I have had of your illness, and particularly the many signs you have received of God's goodness, regarding which I am sure you will keep your appreciation and memory for ever. I shall constantly ask that of God in my prayers. I beg you, Monsieur, to have no doubts on that score, and to believe that nothing could equal the affection, tenderness and respect with which I am yours' etc.

This was probably the last time R. wrote to Paul Barillon, who died at the end of July. Courtin and Fieubet were, as fellow diplomats, old friends of Barillon.

910605   RP ABBÉ, VAL-RICHER [DOMINIQUE GEORGES]   5 June 1691
Maupeou, *Vie* p. 534

R. not surprised that Georges reacts to Mège's letters against R. as he does.

* 910618   BISHOP OF LUÇON [HENRI BARILLON]   18 June 1691
P f.779

'I see, Mgr, since you do me the honour of writing to me, that there is much cause to fear for your brother in the state in which he is. I am told, however, that he still has enough strength to resist his illness, and that there is still cause for hope. Such conjectures do not satisfy those who are concerned as I for his recovery. We must ask God to sustain him and give him back to the world, all the more because all appearances lead one to believe that if God saves him from his present danger, he will keep the pious and religious sentiments which God has given him, and that would be most edifying for the public. I confess, Mgr, that the greatest joy I could have would be to learn that he is out of danger. We shall not fail to offer our prayers to God, that he may decide his fate for his glory and the consolation of his friends. I beg you to believe that no one could be more moved by the worry such a long and uncertain illness causes you. I am sure, Mgr, that you do not doubt my sentiments on that score, and are convinced of all the affection and respect with which I am yours' etc.

* 910625   BISHOP OF LUÇON [HENRI BARILLON]   25 June 1691
P f.780

'I see from your last letter, Mgr, that there are grounds for hoping that your brother's illness may be cured. God grant that we are not mistaken and that he will finish with the good health we wish him; although we ask that for him most earnestly, we regard as a matter for real consolation the peace and resignation which he maintains in the state of uncertainty in which he is, between life and death, which of all situations is that most likely to cause agitation and upset. That, Mgr, is evidence that God is the master of his heart and prevents anything arising there contrary to the total dependence in which he must be before God's will, which is always just and holy. We shall continue to offer to God his person and sufferings, and to pray him as much as we are able not to cease looking on him in his mercy. You do not doubt, Mgr, that I share as much as I should all the pain that your affection for him may cause, convinced, as I am sure you are, of the sincere and profound respect with which I am yours etc.

PS I beg you, Mgr, to tell your brother that the care with which we commend him to God is as great as it could be, and nothing is more dear to us than his person.'

* 910627   RM MARIE-LOUISE [BOUTHILLIER]   27 June 1691
TA orig.

'I am most obliged to you, my dear sister, for thinking of me and my health. It is gradually coming back, but I am still very weak. The coming warm weather may finish the cure, if such is God's will.

Monsieur de Fieubet is most kind; I am sure that he commended your interests with the greatest pleasure. I shall not fail to write to him and express the gratitude felt by your house, and my own personal gratitude.

As for you, my dear sister, since you have been charged with business, do it as best you can, since it is a disposition of divine providence. In that you are doing God's will and you must believe that any distractions caused by this unusual employment will not be imputed to you. He knows that it is not possible not to keep the ideas and impressions of the things one has to deal with.

I cannot tell you exactly what would be the most convenient time for Monsieur M's intended visit, for every day people come here whom we are not expecting, and even more at the time you indicate than many others, but we will gladly receive him, whenever it pleases him to come and see us.

Poor Monsieur Lasnier was very old; I think he was hardly less than eighty. We must worship God's designs on Madame Chabot for leaving the bosom of heresy to enter that of the Church and for finishing her days in the frame of mind you tell me. I am, alas, obliged to pray God for her, for she was really a friend of mine.

God is doing you a special favour in making you wish for death, for all one does here on earth is to offend God and displease him. As the holiest people are those who fall most seldom and whose faults are lightest, so we cannot do better than ask him to transfer us to that new earth which is the abode of his justice and where it is never offended or altered. Farewell, my dearest sister, pray God for me, and believe me with all possible affection yours etc.

PS I am sending you the reply to the letter you addressed to me. Please assure the Mother Superior of all my respect. The misfortune that happened to you alarms me; be careful that it does not have any effects and do not neglect it.'

The favour done by Fieubet is unknown, but it must have been one of his last official acts, since he went into retreat at Grosbois on 4 August.

Mme Chabot was the daughter of the distinguished Huguenot comte de Jarnac; converted, she became a Carmelite in 1639 under the name of Claire du Saint-Sacrament and died aged seventy, having been reelected prioress for the third time in 1690.

* 910629   BISHOP OF LUÇON [HENRI BARILLON]   29 [June] 1691
P f.780 (dated July)

'I could not have heard, Mgr, better news than that which you tell me; I confess that it would be an enormous joy to see your brother at la Trappe in as good health as we wish him, and full of gratitude, as I believe he will be, for God's mercies towards him. One must agree, Mgr, that they are extraordinary, for however great his probity, and whatever loyalty he has shown to his friends, all that has counted for nothing in God's judgement. That is a coinage which does not bear his mark, and we may say that God has bestowed on him that ample grace observed in him, independently of his works, which had won him the approval and esteem of men. For my part I do not doubt that he will continue to harbour all the gratitude he owes to God, and that giving proof of it will be his whole pleasure. That is something we shall constantly ask for him; we have it too much at heart to fail to do so. I am with inexpressible affection and respect yours' etc.

* 910709   BISHOP OF LUÇON [HENRI BARILLON]   9 July 1691
P f.781

'I see, Mgr, from your last letter and from one I have just received from the curé of Saint-Jacques, that there is more reason than ever to fear for your brother, and at the same time I learn that he is in so Christian a frame of mind that it cannot but be a consolation to those who are really concerned about him. For my part, I confess, if anything could ease the grief I should have at losing him, it would be having no room for doubt that God had concluded his life with a blessed end, something which one must desire above all for those with whom one has ties of friendship, or rather charity, when it follows the true rules prescribed by God. We shall, Mgr, redouble our prayers that God's will may be done, whether it pleases him that your brother should remain here on earth for his sanctification or whether he has resolved to show him the final mercy. I cannot tell you, Mgr, how much I feel for you, but I am sure that you are fully convinced of all the fidelity and respect I have for you.'

* 910709a   RM MARIE-LOUISE [BOUTHILLIER]   9 July 1691
TA orig.

'I have received your two letters, my dearest sister. I had already written to Monsieur le Théologal as you requested, and I praise God that the Archbishop left him with you. I will have the novena said as you ask, and will not fail to send you a cross for Madame la Chanceli6ere. Please tell her if you see her that I do not deserve the honour she does me, however profoundly I respect her person and her virtue. We will pray God for her as she desires. Farewell, my dearest sister, pray for me and believe me all yours.'

The wife of the Chancellor at the time, Louis Boucherat, was Anne-Françoise de Loménie, but the widow of Le Tellier, the former Chancellor, was also called Mme la Chancelière, and since she had close links with the Annonciades, it is probably she to whom this reference applies.

*910718   BISHOP OF LUÇON [HENRI BARILLON]   18 July 1691
P f.781

'I am still impatiently waiting, Mgr, for news of your brother's health. Your last letters did not leave much hope, so our consolation is purely in the grace God has shown by taking over mastery of his heart. Ultimately there is no one who would not wish to be in the situation in which he is, for there is no room for doubt that God will receive him into the arms of his mercy, having given him so many marks of his goodness. He will go before us by only a few moments, if God calls him, and we can count on not being long in following him. I am sure, Mgr, that you regard his present situation, between life and death, with a detachment worthy of your piety and virtue, knowing full well, as you do, that we must cling to God alone, that one day we shall find again in him everything and everyone we have lost on earth and that there is not one of them worthy of our attachment. Please believe, Mgr, I beg you, that no one could feel for you more than I do, and that nothing equals the tender and profound respect with which I am yours' etc.

910718a   CLAUDE NICAISE   18 July 1691
BN 9363,f.107, orig.; Gonod 118

Awaits Mabillon's book. Surprised that satire against Grenadier still circulates.

*910726   BISHOP OF LUÇON [HENRI BARILLON]   26 July 1691
P f.782

'I am impatiently waiting, Mgr, for news of your brother, for from what I learned in the latest letters his state must be regarded as critical. My consolation is to know that he is persevering in those christian sentiments which God had given him, and that there is no doubt, if God takes him back, it will be to grant him the mercy for which he hopes. I am sure that, however great your affection for him and however much you wish God to prolong his days, all such feelings will give way to the joy you will have at being as certain as one can be that God has given him eternal happiness. It is certain, looking at things with living faith, that is, a faith which gives us true ideas and compelling insights into time and eternity, that we can wish nothing better to those of our family and friends than a happy death. I wish you, Mgr, all grace and blessings and am with all the affection and respect you know yours etc.

PS I cannot help saying that the situation of Monsieur de B[arillon] throughout his illness and God's conduct towards him should be a sanctification for your whole house, however God disposes of him.'

*910730   BISHOP OF LUÇON [HENRI BARILLON]   30 July 1691
P f.782

'At last, Mgr, God has been pleased to call your brother to him. We may use such a term, since it is written that the righteous are in God's hand [Wis 3:1], and since he finished his days in the christian frame of mind in which you saw him. he died the death of the righteous, and consequently he will forever rest in the arms of God. Your consolation must be to have contributed so much by your presence, your care, and all the words of life you spoke to him during the course of his illness to excite his faith and maintain his patience.

I do not need to tell you, Mgr, how I feel for you in the state in which you must be, for I am sure that you expected as much from so tender and faithful an attachment as that which I have long had towards you. You know, Mgr, what I lose in losing your brother and the friendship he had for me. Yet our feelings must go back to God, as their principle and end, and we must receive the orders of his providence with a resignation worthy of the blessing we enjoy of belonging to him.

I hope, Mgr, that after giving the necessary time to console an afflicted family, when you think about returning to your diocese, you will remember that you promised to travel by way of our desert. I can assure you that one of the greatest joys I could have is that of seeing you here and at the same time receiving your blessing, which, in all likelihood will be for the last time in my life. I await that moment with extreme impatience. I am with profound respect yours' etc.

Paul Barillon died on 23 July.

910730a   MARQUIS DE POMPONNE   30 July 1691
A 6039,f.20, orig.
Congratulates him on royal favour.

Pomponne had just been brought back as minister on the death of his enemy, Louvois.

910800   ARCHBISHOP OF PARIS [FRANÇOIS DE HARLAY]   [August 1691]
Mug I/110

R. visited les Clairets a month ago [late June] and twenty-seven out of thirty-four religious asked to join the Reform; what should R. do?

910830 CLAUDE NICAISE   30 August 1691
BN 9363,f.109, orig.; Gonod 119

Retreat of Fieubet. Conversion of Santena. No comment to make on Mabillon.

Fieubet had visited in June and planned to live in retreat (as a layman) with the Camaldolese at Grosbois near Paris. He died there in 1694. Santena, son of the governor of Turin, was on active service in the north of France when he became converted. Through du Charmel he came to see la T., and on the second occasion, in July 1691, heard how fr Palémon des Arcis, a former infantry captain, had just died. He immediately asked to enter la T., and a few days later received the habit and the name of Palémon. He was professed in July 1692, and died in November 1694, aged forty-two, an object of interest for King James, Bellefonds, and other distinguished visitors.

910903 JEAN FAVIER   3 September 1691
CF 344,f.93, orig.; Gonod 48

R. has heard from his niece [great-niece] 'de Tours' of her intention; she must think about it. Complains of flood of visitors taking up his time, 'on the other hand they are men of rank and piety who only come to us in search of edification'.

For three or four years 'Mlle de Tours', daughter of Mme de La Barge, had been hesitating over a monastic vocation, and details of her worldly and rebellious nature are vividly depicted in extant letters to Favier from her aunt, Louise-Henriette (who died in December 1688).

*910905 MARÉCHAL DE BELLEFONDS   5 September 1691
BN na 12959,f.148, orig.

'I learn, Mgr, from M le comte de Saint-Vallier that you believe you wrote me a letter which I did not answer. If that is so, it must be one which was not given to me. I should never fail in the punctiliousness I owe you. I know too well how much to appreciate all that comes to me from you. M. de Saint-Vallier will have been able to tell you our news, and that everything goes on here as usual. We have indeed too many reasons for loving retreat as soon as we take note of what is happening in the world. Everything tells us that nothing is worthy of our attachment, since there is nothing constant and what seem to be the greatest and firmest fortunes have no more consistency and duration than a vapour. Such events speak louder and clearer than all the sermons of preachers, and if we lived more attentively than we do, we should enjoy an almost unknown peace and tranquility, because we should not place our affections on things whose deprivation always causes extraordinary reactions; one loses painlessly what one possesses detachedly.

No one could be more apprised of all these truths than you, Mgr, you see things from close at hand, and as you put them in their natural light, they cannot get the better of you. God has given you discernment and you do not judge or believe them other than they really are. That is a very special, and very rare, grace, for all one sees is people who are blind and deluded, or behave as though they were.

We have had for the past two months, as you have no doubt heard, a most unexpected conversion, that of M de Santena. What is most surprising is to see in him the docility and simplicity of a sixteen-year old novice. Such effects of God's mercy are past understanding. I see no difference between that and seeing a century-old oak bend like a reed. It must be admitted that God is great in his works, but chiefly when he gives us signs of the power he has over the hearts of those who have had the misfortune, or rather the temerity, to rise up against him.

M de Fieubet's retreat has been accompanied by more moderation, but if, as there is reason to believe, it perseveres, it cannot fail to provide much edification, for hitherto people of that kind have hardly ever been seen to take such a step. These are different ways leading to the same end, and showing in God a diversity of conduct which makes men inexcusable and at the same time offers consolation to sinners. I wish you, Mgr, every blessing. I do not need to tell you that I regard that as a duty. I am sure that you are convinced of it, as of all the respect and devotion with which I am yours' etc.

Pierre-Félix de la Croix de Chevrières, comte de Saint-Vallier (1614–99), was a distinguished soldier and courtier, related by marriage to Saint-Simon. On Santena and Fieubert, see 910830.

910905a JAMES II   5 September 1691
W orig.; *SP* p.64

In his letter of 30 August James had spoken of morally virtuous Protestants. R. accounts for this 'the devil is an imitator of Christ . . . with his martyrs and confessors', but only to mislead people.

*910920 MARÉCHAL DE BELLEFONDS   20 September 1691
BN na 12959,f.150, orig.

'I did not fail as soon as I learned of the death of M de N. to think of your person and your interests from every point of view. I thought that times were more favourable, but at the same time I thought that in the steps you would be obliged to take you would not depart from the very christian disposition in which God has been pleased to put you, which means awaiting all things from his providence without haste or anxiety.

The state of your affairs and the care you must have for your family demand that you should give way to some reactions; it would be driving indifference too far not to do so. It is true, as you say, Mgr, that providence controls everything, and often independently of men's efforts. We see some who succeed in ill-conceived enterprises and others, acting in the wisest way and neglecting nothing that might be necessary for a favourable outcome, have results quite the opposite to what they expect. That is a good reason for keeping humble those who have most merit and reputation in the world. That is to say that God wishes all men to depend on him, to look to him in all things, to think and say with all their heart, when they have forgotten nothing attaching to their care and diligence in the affairs with which they are charged, that they are just useless servants [Mt 25:30]. It is a fortune to have such feelings, since there is nothing that could contribute more to keep one in peace and serenity, and a contrary situation is fit only to bring confusion and disturbance.

God has given you too much grace up to now, Mgr, to refuse you what you need in order to remain within the bounds you have prescribed yourself. As you have so far kept him the fidelity you owe him, you may hope for everything from him. You know that faithful friends obtain everything, and that what most excites and moves his mercy is the use we have made of the proof of it we have received.

However delighted we would have been, Mgr, to see you this year in our desert, we prefer to know that you are where I believe you are at present. It would not be right to put our consolation above your interests; your friends and relations would have cause for complaint.

You will be no less present to us, Mgr, I humbly beg you to believe, and we shall not fail to recommend to Our Lord all that concerns you for this world and the next. I am sure that you are convinced of this, as of all the respect and devotion with which I am yours' etc.

The death referred to is mysterious; the most likely candidate would seem to be Louvois, the powerful minister and longstanding enemy of Bellefonds, who died on 6 July.

*911001   MARÉCHAL DE BELLEFONDS   1 October 1691
BN na 12959,f.152, orig.

'I do not doubt, Mgr, that you have felt keenly the death of Mother Agnès, though her age and her delicate constitution were two good reasons for you to be prepared for it. It is however so considerable a loss that it must inevitably have caused you real grief. Indeed her virtue and her example sanctified not only all her house, but it can be said that the whole Church was edified by it. Countless people were aware of the ample wisdom and charity she had received from God, and whenever she had an opportunity to help those who needed her either for advice or the esteem she enjoyed in the world she always took it with joy. In a word, any good that a person of her kind and condition can do, she did, and her memory will always be held in blessing.

It must be admitted that the world is full of lessons; God never ceases to speak by all the events that occur; all these different deaths tell us one thing, that those whom God takes to himself precede us by only a few moments. One must try to become worthy of the fate of some, and do everything to avoid that of others.

One of our religious died yesterday after seven years of most painful illness, and one thing I can say is that during all that time I never saw him impatient for a moment.

I do not doubt, Mgr, that you find nothing to criticise in Mother Agnès. For my part I feel a particular loss, for it would be hard to express the goodness with which she honoured us. I wish you, Mgr, all possible blessings. I am with the deepest respect and devotion yours' etc.

RM Agnès died on 24 September, aged eighty, after a long period of bad health. The monk who had died was fr Bruno Ledigne, professed 1675, and subject of a Relation.

911004   CLAUDE NICAISE   4 October 1691
BN 9363,f.110, orig.; Gonod 120

SS Benedict and Bernard understood the sense of Scripture perfectly well without studying oriental languages. Comments on Nicaise's new book on Sirens of antiquity. [*Dissertation sur les Syrènes*, Paris, 1691].

911007   MARQUISE D'HUXELLES   7 October 1691
Tour. orig.

General sense of loss at death of RM Agnès de Bellefonds. A good sign that she too feels this. R. owes RM Agnès so much. M de Saint-Vallier has delivered message. R. can only see certain person when Mme de Guise visits.

Saint-Vallier was a friend of Bellefonds and the brother of the Bp of Quebec. The intending visitor was probably R's niece, Mme de Belin, who was attached to Mme de Guise and could come with her into the monastery.

911013   GUILLAUME DE LA FAGE,   13 October 1691
         VICAR-GENERAL [COMMINGES]
Sol, *ND de Saint-Bernard de Comminges*

General approval of developments at Alan.

[See 900123].

*911018   BISHOP OF LUÇON [HENRI BARILLON]   18 October 1691
P f.783

'I confess, Mgr, that I am too alive to the interests of your house not to be touched with real joy at the news you give me of your niece's marriage. All that I hear of the Procureur-Général, of his ability, probity, piety, integrity, convinces me that it is a union which God had devised for the consolation of you and your family. What is remarkable is that everyone speaks with one voice about him, and is united in giving him the same testimonial. I am sure that you are convinced of my interest; my attachment for your person, and that which I had for your brother, does not allow me to feel in any ordinary way about it.

I see, Mgr, that you are going to resume your usual labours and that your love of residence takes you away from your friends, that is, that your duty outweighs all other considerations. We do not fail to commend you to Our Lord. You know how dear you are to me, and in truth you fill as much place in my heart as you could. What you said of the P[rocureur]-G[énéral] is worthy of his virtue and feelings, and will mark him out favourably from those who do not act like him. Monsieur l'abbé T. tells me what you told him, and is resolved to execute it. He also writes that the sale of his house is complete and he seems very pleased. Monsieur de Saint-Louis is most grateful for your kindness to him. I should find it hard to express the respect he feels for you. I would say the same thing of our house. Always love me, Mgr, and I beg you to believe that no one could be with more heartfelt affection and respect than I yours etc.

PS We shall commend to God with all possible care the persons of the Procureur-Général and his wife, and pray him to bless an alliance which is his work rather than that of men.'

The niece is Paul's daughter Bonne, second wife of Pierre-Arnauld de la Briffe (1649–1700) who in 1689 succeeded Achille de Harlay as Procureur-Général (the senior legal office after Premier Président). Barillon had last visited la T. in September, when he had seen M de Saint-Louis. Abbé 'T' is probably Tétu, a mutual friend of R. and Barillon.

911029 [ANTOINE BARILLON]   29 October 1691
BN 22222,f.127, orig.

Has heard from Pr[ocureur]-Général, Monsieur's brother-in-law, of Monsieur's kindly disposition. Hopes to see him at la T., where he, as a loyal subject, will appreciate the community's devotion to the royal cause.

Paul Barillon's daughter, Bonne, had just married Pierre-Arnaud de la Briffe, Procureur-Général since 1689, and this letter is thus presumably to her brother, Antoine, marquis de Branges, who became a conseiller au parlement early in 1692.

911105   RP ABBÉ, VAL-RICHER [DOMINIQUE GEORGES]   5 November 1691
Maupeou, *Vie* I p. 536

R. is sure they agree on Mabillons' book [*Traité des Etudes monastiques,* just published].

*911108   BISHOP OF LUÇON [HENRI BARILLON]   8 November 1691
P f.784

'This means, Mgr, that you are going to take up again the fatigues of your diocese after satisfying what God asked of you for the good of your house. You have the consolation of having contributed greatly to your brother's salvation, which had to be a matter of the highest importance to you, and of establishing in a most christian manner someone dear to you, in whom you could not dispense yourself from taking an interest.

I do not need to tell you how concerned I am in all that affects you; on that score you have no doubts as to my feelings. In truth, they could not go further and could not possibly be stronger or more extensive. We shall not fail to offer your person to Our Lord with all the care of which we are capable, and ask him to be at the head of whatever you undertake for his glory and service, so that you may find your sanctification in your devotion to that of the people he has committed to your charge and guidance. Remember me, Mgr, in your prayers, and please believe that it is with inviolable affection, respect and attachment that I am yours etc.

PS I am much obliged to you for speaking on my behalf to the Procureur-Général. It is a benefit for me that he should know my longstanding attachment to your house and my special esteem for his person. I avoid legal affairs with the greatest care, but they could happen despite me.'

Barillon left for Luçon on 15 November, after delays caused by his brother's death and niece's wedding.

911111   BISHOP OF COMMINGES   11 November 1691
         [LOUIS DE RECHIGNEVOISIN]
Sol, *ND, de St Bernard de Comminges*
Everything is most edifying.

911112   JAMES II   12 November 1691
W orig.; *SP* p. 65

Encloses Association, signed by R. and thirty-four monks, and time-table of daily life at la T. 'God's hand steers the vessel, and despite all the reefs, all the storms on the way will not fail to make the voyage successful.'

911125   JEAN FAVIER   25 November 1691
CF 344,f.95, orig.; Gonod 49

Discusses *Sainteté* and, arising from that, proper conditions of religious profession. 'I agree that my sisters were not canonically received at the Annonciades . . . especially my younger sister, who joined after my father's death.'

R's point seems to be that their acceptance was decided by the money he and his father paid out. His elder sister, Claude (RM Marie-Dorothée) joined as a child, and was professed at fifteen, while Marie-Louise entered at sixteen, but it is hard to see how they were canonically irregular except on the technical point of their financial contribution.

911126   CLAUDE NICAISE   26 November 1691
BN 9363,f.111, orig.; Gonod 121

R. denies criticising Mabillon as he is said to have done.

*911210 MARÉCHAL DE BELLEFONDS   10 December 1691
BN na 12959,f.154, orig.

'You will see, Mgr, by the letter which I have the honour to write to you that the person giving it to you did not turn out to have the disposition for embracing the life of a lay-brother. After spending some days with us he indicated that his inclination was towards being a choir monk, but as he knows no Latin at all, he has resolved to apply himself for a certain time to acquiring the essentials, that is, for understanding the breviary, in order to avoid the distraction which those who have no knowledge of Latin find it hard to resist. I hope he will succeed. You can easily imagine, Mgr, that it is a joy for me to have someone in our monastery who comes through you. I do not need to assure you that you are present to us before Our Lord, for I do not doubt that in that respect you do me full justice. Your person and all your interests affect me so closely that I think about them before God as much as I can. We hoped in vain for the honour and consolation of seeing you this year. God has put it off to another time. I will not cease to pray him to meet you in all your ways and shower you with blessings. I am with deep respect yours' etc.

911213 GUILLAUME DE LA FAGE   13 December 1691
         VICAR-GENERAL, COMMINGES
Sol, ND de St Bernard de Comminges

Approves his cautious conduct on subject of supposed miracles.

911219 MONSIEUR   19 December 1691
Tour. orig.

Thanks him for support.

92/1 MONSIEUR   [? 1692]
Mug I/109

On Mlle de X who is delaying her entry to les Clairets because of her pension. Abbé Le B. might bring M with him when he comes to la T.

On 11 September 1692 R. was writing to Marie-Louise about the difficulty of a young woman in gaining entry at les Clairets, and since abbé Le Boulanger was a mutual friend this letter seems to date from that time.

*920107 MARÉCHAL DE BELLEFONDS   7 January 1692
BN na 12959,f.155, orig.

'After assuring you, Mgr, of the care we took to recommend you and all your interests to God at the beginning of this new year, allow me to ask you to continue your goodness towards me. Time advances, and as health and strength do not increase with age, the best thing to do is to think of the moment which will end it. That alone, it seems to me, can enable us to find peace in this world, for if we are overtaken by disgrace or any kind of ills, looking at the moment which is to deliver us diminishes them and makes them bearable. If we are made anxious by the deprivation, or rather by the desire for a good we do not have, that same instant which would rob us of it if we had it easily consoles us for not having it. In fact those who accustom themselves to look at the end of life and become familiar with it, never form any attachment for earthly things, and thus live in a liberty which means that their peace of mind is never interrupted or disturbed.

It is quite amazing, Mgr, to see that everything that happens in the world constantly sets this truth before our eyes, that everything warns us and, so to speak, preaches to us that everything passes like a flash of lightening, that lives are cut short, fortunes overturned when they seem most assured, and yet that people try to enjoy them as if they were immutable and were never liable to be lost. If our souls were less hard, these sorts of events, which make only superficial impressions, would make deep ones. We should live completely in expectation of the future, and the present would be for us as if it were no longer. Christ's prohibition on loving the world or anything pertaining to the world would be implemented more faithfully than it is, the Church would be more edified and no longer would one see those blatant disorders which grieve all those who truly love his honour and glory. I pray God, Mgr, never to cease strengthening the detachment he has given you, so worthy of your virtue and of all the grace he has granted you, and to allow nothing in the diverse events of which life is so full to arise and impair it in any way. I am with all possible respect and devotion yours' etc.

* 920108   BISHOP OF LUÇON [HENRI BARILLON]   8 January 1692
P f.785

'Allow me, Mgr, to begin this year by asking for your blessing, and assuring you that one of our first concerns was to offer you to God in our prayers. I am too keenly interested in everything that affects your person not to keep my memory of you very much alive; and if I were a better man than I am you would realise that more.

I cannot help saying, Mgr, that whenever I see you in the place where you are I am touched by the troubles you have there, especially when I note the scant help that you receive from men. Yet God who has supported you up to now will continue to do so, and your fidelity will be all the more pleasing to him for the fact that it is accompanied by nothing from human beings. In short, Mgr, you work on the firmness of your faith and the trust God has given you in his mercy. Keep for me your usual kindness, and please believe, I beg you, that no one could add to the devotion, affection and respect with which I am yours' etc.

*920114 BISHOP OF LUÇON [HENRI BARILLON]   14 January 1692
P f.785

'It is four or five days, Mgr, since I had the honour of writing to you before your last letter reached me. I am infinitely obliged for all the evidence you give me of your kindness. I can only say that my gratitude could not be greater. It is before God, Mgr, that we try to show that with our feeble prayers. Your fidelity and attachment to your ministry is more powerful before God than any help you may receive through the intermediary of men.

I knew a good part of what was said about the person you mention, but at the same time I knew, through well informed people, that he was innocent of the things imputed to him. His silence and moderation on such an occasion have edified everybody. Alas, one is exposed, wherever one is. God does not allow any situation in this world to be tranquil, and the reeds are battered by the winds as much as the cedar trees. God alone is the place of our rest, and it is in his arms that we must seek it. I pray God, Mgr, to keep you on the earth for many long years, for your own sanctification, as for the glory of his Church. I am with inexpressible devotion, affection and respect yours etc.

PS All those here whom you honour with your remembrance thank you most profusely. They one and all respect you deeply and remember you before Our Lord.'

920121 DUCHESSE DE GUISE   21 January 1692
BN 15172,1, orig.; Gonod 172

On M de Ch[?armois]; do not rely on men.

920122 RP ABBÉ, VAL-RICHER [DOMINIQUE GEORGES]   22 January 1692
Maupeou, Vie I p. 505; A 3389,f.94vo.

Unexpected decision of Abbess of les Clairets to join the Reform.

*920124 BISHOP OF LUÇON [HENRI BARILLON]   24 January 1692
P f.785

'I wrote to you, Mgr, only two days ago. I do so again today to beg you to be good enough to tell the Procureur-Général that I have told you of his kindness in writing to the judges at Mortagne, because he had learned that they were not treating us justly in a case we had before them. I did not fail to thank him in a letter to which he replied in the most obliging way. I beg you, Mgr, to thank him again on your behalf, so that he can see from the trouble I have taken to inform you how much I appreciate the favour he did us. I am with the most tender and profound respect yours' etc.

Mortagne was the nearest seat of justice to la T.

920125 CLAUDE NICAISE 25 January 1692
BN 9363,f.112, orig.; Gonod 122

Death of Abbot of Cîteaux [Jean Petit, on 15 January, aged sixty-five]. He did not leave the Order any better than he found it: 'he had good intentions but little enlightenment'. R. would be mad to accept the post even if offered.

920204 DUCHESSE DE GUISE 4 February 1692
BN 15172,2, orig.; Gonod 173

Prevalence of hypocrisy. The King's piety should convert his whole realm.

920204a JEAN FAVIER 4 February 1692
CF 344,f.97, orig.; Gonod 50

Continuing problems at Beauvais, R., though younger, expects to die first.

920224 DUCHESSE DE GUISE 24 February 1692
BN 15172,3, orig.; Gonod 174

M. de Nocey died that day. [The ex-Oratorian had lived as a hermit in the woods since 1679].

920303 DUCHESSE DE GUISE 3 March 1692
BN 15172,4, orig.; Gonod 175

Calm and peaceful death of Nocey, who was brought from his hut to the former abbot's lodgings a few days before he died.

*920303a BISHOP OF LUÇON [HENRI BARILLON] 3 [March] 1692
P f. 640 (Wrongly dated October)

'At last, Mgr, my *Réponse* to dom Mabillon, parts of which I read to you when you came here, is printed. I have arranged for it to be sent to you. I have observed all possible restraint towards him, and avoided saying anything which would be inconsistent with the esteem and consideration I have for him personally. I hope, Mgr, that you will find nothing in it with which you do not agree and judge worthy of your approval. I confess that I thought that my conscience prevented from keeping silent on such an occasion and that I ought to bear witness to an important truth of which I am completely convinced.

A very extraordinary ceremony took place here recently. The Bishop of Lescar came and was present at the profession of his son, moved to the bottom of his heart by regret at losing him, and perhaps at the same time by joy that he was consecrating himself to Christ in a state which seemed quite certain to him. He had intended to employ him in his diocese, using him to relieve him, and could have done so with profit, but he preferred to deprive himself and sacrifice his own consolation to the salvation of his son.

I have nothing new to tell you, Mgr, from these parts, except that there is nowhere where you are more present, that in our inmost heart you occupy the place due to you and that it would be impossible to have more affection, devotion and respect than I have as yours' etc.

The Réponse *came out in March, and the October dating of this letter is certainly wrong. The Bp of Lescar, Dominique d'Esclaux de Mesplez, had been a lawyer in Paris, but on being widowed took orders and was made a bp in 1681. One of his numerous children was professed at la T. in his presence as fr Euthyme in February 1692, but left later and went to the CO house of Sauvelade in the diocese of Lescar.*

*920310   MARÉCHAL DE BELLEFONDS   10 March 1692
BN na 12959,f.157, orig.

'I learned of your illness and recovery, Mgr, at the same time. I praised God for saving you from a peril, which, at least as I have heard, was considerable. He preserved you in order to accomplish your sanctification, and you will not fail to use this prolongation of your days according to his will and designs. This incident has simply confirmed you in the dispositions in which you have long been, I mean of forming no attachment to what may be taken away at any moment. Those who belong to God and profess to serve him profit from everything, since there is nothing in which they do not see his providence. They worship all his ways and their consolation is to accept and submit to them. They look at life and death with the same eyes and in the same spirit of dependence, and if God gave them the choice they would prefer the latter and would say like the prophet *melius est mihi mori quam vivere*. [Jon 4:8]

It is certain, Mgr, that the things of this world are so mixed and God has taken such care to put bitter things among those in which we might find some pleasure or sweetness that the only course one can adopt is to live in total detachment from everything here on earth, since it could never provide us with any solid or genuine consolation. Yet, although God omits nothing that could detach us, and tells us incessantly that deprivation is necessary and since the Fall man must live with renunciation, that is what people avoid as much as they can, and there is almost no one who does not put earthly goods in his heart, perishable as they are, as if their enjoyment were to be immortal. Blessed are those whom God preserves from so general an error, and who according to the precept of Jesus Christ know no other riches and fortune save those that cannot be torn from them.

We will not cease asking God to increase the feelings he has given you on this, Mgr, and to add constant fidelity. I beg you to believe that I consider as one of my chief duties to recommend to him all that concerns you, and that it is with deep respect that I am yours' etc.

920312   RP ABBÉ, val-richer [dominique georges]   12 March 1692
Maupeou, *Vie* I p. 536

R. has arranged for his *Réponse* [to Mabillon] to be sent.

920317   DUCHESSE DE GUISE   17 March 1692
BN 15172,5, orig.; Gonod 176

The sermons of the Capuchin RP Séraphim are likely to produce a spiritual renewal at court.

RP Séraphim (1636–1713) was one of the most celebrated preachers of the day, much favoured by Louis XIV.

920322   CLAUDE NICAISE   22 March 1692
BN 9363,f.113, orig.; Gonod 123

R. has replied to Mabillon, trying to avoid giving offence.

920330   CLAUDE NICAISE   30 March 1692
BN 9363,f.114, orig.; Gonod 124
R's *Réponse.*

920401   ETIENNE BALUZE   1 April 1692
BN fonds Baluze 361,f.95, orig.

R. glad to have been able to make public acknowledgement of his esteem for Baluze.

920402   PIERRE MAUPEOU   2 April 1692
Maupeou, *Vie* II p. 68

Glad that Maupeou approves of book sent [*Réponse*].

920407   LOUIS MARCEL, curé saint-jacques-du-haut-pas   7 April 1692
BN 19656,f.197; Mabillon, *Ouvrages,* 1 p. 400; Gonod 213

R's esteem for Mabillon.

920407a   DUCHESSE DE GUISE   7 April 1692
BN 15172,6, orig.; Gonod 177

Regarding Mme de Mornay: 'God wishes to be heeded when he has spoken', but if bad health is the reason she will not be blamed for leaving where she is. Mme de Guise must regulate her communions according to how she feels at any given time.

Françoise-Renée de Coetquen-Combourg lost her husband, comte de Mornay, at the siege of Mannheim in 1688 and withdrew in 1692 to les Clairets. Her brother, a close friend of Saint-Simon, also died on active service in 1693.

920416   CLAUDE NICAISE   16 April 1692
BN 9363,f.116, orig.; Gonod 125

The *Réponse*. Praises Abbess of Puits d'Orbe and her house. Refers to his youthful Anacreon: 'I liked and enjoyed literature, and that is all'. Praises Régnier and his writings.

Puits d'Orbe at Châtillon-sur-Seine, diocese of Langres, was a benedictine house of the Val-de-Grâce reform; the abbess was then Nicole Philippe. Régnier had just translated Anacreon into Italian.

920421   DUCHESSE DE GUISE   21 April 1692
Mabillon, *Ouvrages* I p. 402; Gonod 214

R. defends his position in dispute with Mabillon. He is ready to do anything except 'harm the truth'.

920423   DUCHESSE DE GUISE   23 April 1692
BN 15172,7, orig.; Gonod 178

Bellefonds delivered her letter [he had come with James II]. Her footman finds life at la T. too hard and is writing to Monsieur de Charmois.

Cf 920121. Possibly la Charmoye, a Reformed house in the diocese of Châlons-sur-Marne.

920428   DUCHESSE DE GUISE   28 April 1692
BN 15172,8, orig.; Gonod 179

R. has seen M Chevalier after his mission at Moulins-la-Marche [near la T.] R. very willing to accept a conference with Mabillon, as proposed by Mme de Guise.

Enguerrand Chevalier (or Le Chevalier) was superior of the seminary at Séez and had been curé at Alençon 1678-80 after vainly trying to come to la T. (1631-97).

920500   DUCHESSE DE GUISE   [April/May 1692]
BN 15172,9, orig.; Gonod 180

Mme de Mornay has suddenly changed her mind, but from physical weakness rather than from choice. R. maintains his position in dispute with Mabillon. Believes abbé Jannon in Paris to be his friend.

Hugues Jannon (1631-98) was also a friend of Bossuet.

920506   COMTE DE SAINT-VALLIER   6 May 1692
BN na 12959

R. had hoped to see the comte's brother before he left to become Bp of Quebec. Glad that Pope has at last given bulls to the French bishops; all must hope for true reconciliation between Rome and France.

Delay in granting bulls arose from the long quarrel over the régale *(royal rights over certain vacant sees) and the Gallican dispute in general. In July 1691 Innocent XII had succeeded Alexander VIII, which had helped.*

*920519   RM MARIE-LOUISE [BOUTHILLIER]   19 May 1692
TA orig.

'I have had confirmation from many quarters of what you tell me, my dear sister. It is certain that people are flocking to answer the book of which you speak. If the reply deserves a further answer, and God wants it to be given, he will give us the means to do so.

It is true that the book has the approval of many people. I have seen the verses composed against me; they are not correct on all points. I shall try with the grace of God not to fall into the misfortunes with which I am reproached. Ultimately there is nothing from which one cannot profit, and if we have not committed the errors of which we are accused, there are others of which we are guilty and of which no word is said. Those verses are not by dom Mabillon; he is a man of too much equity and piety to occupy himself with trifles of that kind. I admire you, my dear sister, for the way you behave amid all those who are condemning me; you let them fire into silence and then confound them. One is fortunate, as you say, to be mistreated by men. The son of God suffered countless injustices and outrages, and after that, whatever men may do, we have no cause for complaint. We must ask him for his spirit at this holy season, so that he gives us strength to suffer in peace all the most offensive and insulting assaults that may come from the world. Remember me before him, my dear sister, and pray him to have mercy on me. I shall not fail to commend all your needs to him. I am with all my heart yours, I beg you not to doubt it.'

The book is R's Réponse *to* Mabillon. *The praise of the latter is interesting, and undoubtedly sincere, as the two were to meet only in 1693.*

920523   CLAUDE NICAISE   23 May 1692
BN 9363,f.118, orig.; Gonod 126

Sends Association to Puits d'Orbe.

920524   JEAN FAVIER   24 May 1692
CF 344,f.99, orig.; Gonod 51

Beauvais is about to be settled. Discusses Mabillon's book [*Réflexions sur la Réponse*...];

'I have never been able to understand how monks, solitaries by their profession, could be intended to preach and teach.'

920528   MADAME DE LA SABLIÈRE   28 May 1692
TC II/223; U 723

Her views on society quite right. Always some waste of time when spent with social people. 'Nothing is more pointless than prescribing hard rules to people who do not like keeping them.'

920530   DUCHESSE DE GUISE   30 May 1692
BN 15172,10, orig.; Gonod 181

The attack on Namur [which began on 26 May].

920609   DUCHESSE DE GUISE   9 June 1692
BN 15172,11, orig.; Gonod 182

On the campaign in Flanders. 'The English lack both fidelity and good faith.'

*920609a   MARÉCHAL DE BELLEFONDS   9 June 1692
BN na 12959,f.159, orig.

'At the very moment that I received your honoured letter, Mgr, I learned that the news of the naval forces are not as we had hoped and that the state in which M de Tourville arrived in Cherbourg shows that the battle was not successful and the advantage went to the enemy.

I confess that this event caused me great sorrow; for unless God does great things to redress the losses suffered in this action, it is a great obstacle to the plans made for landing in England. God's counsels are impenetrable, but is it possible that the most unjust cause that ever was could triumph over the best, and that the impiety of a usurper should prevail over a legitimate king distinguished by his religion and piety? We must be tireless in asking God with continual prayers to protect him, to look with merciful eyes on the firmness of his faith and his total and far-reaching submission to all the dispositions of God's providence.

Concerning him I agree, Mgr, with all that you tell me about him; I have always thought that his actions could not be judged more favourably, that his reasons were right, that he saw all that one could see, and that all he lacked was a facility for expressing himself. I find it hard to pardon those who stop at the surface and are unwilling either to go further or to amend their prejudices.

I do not doubt, Mgr, that the present state of affairs is afflicting for you; if it is as I hear, you are too concerned in it not to be much affected.

The King of England does me infinitely more honour than I deserve. I beg you,

Mgr, to testify as occasion offers that my devotion to his person and all his interests could not be greater or more inviolable, and that no day passes without my offering him to Our Lord with all possible fervour. His goodness towards me puts me infinitely in his debt. Do me also the favour of saying a word of gratitude from my part to the Confessor and Lord Melfort. I found in him a goodness, gentleness, and desire to belong to God that enchanted me.

I wish you, Mgr, all kinds of blessing, and beg you most humbly to believe that you are present to me before God, and that nothing could increase the deep respect with which I am yours' etc.

Anne de Cotentin, comte de Tourville (1642–1701), the best French naval commander of the age, had been defeated by the English off Cap de la Hougue (east of Cherbourg) on 29 May. James' confessor was Fr Sanders, SJ, who, together with John Drummond, Earl of Melfort, accompanied him to la T. in 1690 and again in April 1692.

Following the failure of the Roussillon campaign of 1684, Bellefonds had once more fallen out of royal favour, but was recalled to service in 1692 and put in command of the army in the Cotentin with which James proposed to invade England. The destruction of the fleet, which James and Bellefonds watched together from the top of a church tower nearby, ended all hope of invading England but raised fears of English raids on the French coast.

* 920619   BISHOP OF LUÇON [HENRI BARILLON]   19 [June] 1692
P f.638 (wrongly dated January).

'I confess, Mgr, that I am most mortified by the fact that although you were one of the first persons I had in mind when I gave orders for distributing my *Réponse* to dom Mabillon, you should turn out to have had to wait nearly three months to have it. Cardinal Le Camus tells me that I have fully proved that the monks of old did not include study among the exercises which were suitable for monks and solitaries, although some of them were scholars, as I agreed myself, but he says that they can now be given such an occupation, since it is no longer possible to make them go back to their original sanctity, but he maintains that it must be the sort of study which cannot distract them from the piety in which they are obliged to live, and that they must spend their lives in study and prayer; that is something it would be hard to combine, if by study is meant deep learning.

He also tells me that having learned that the religious of Saint-Maur were complaining, he read with care all the passages which might concern them and did not find one which was not written with all necessary moderation and discretion.

The view of all those who are not prejudiced is that what I have said is decisive. Dom M[abillon] is still going to reply, and no one doubts that it is at the urging of his fathers; as for me, I have resolved to keep silent.

It is true that the son of the Bishop of Lescar has made his profession. The time for that of Monsieur de Santena is approaching. So far no one could have a better spiri-

tual attitude than he has, and I hope that God will give him grace to complete the work he has begun.
You have heard the fate of the fleet. It is clear that the counsels of men are not those of God. We must adore them just as they are; he is master, he decides everything in absolute fashion. However, it is a consolation for us to know that the vessels of the King all together make up a considerable fleet, which prevents the enemy from undertaking anything. His Majesty is victorious in Flanders, and he captures towns under the eyes of the Prince of Orange, who can do nothing to stop him. The fire that took place in the citadel of Turin, which burned all the bombs and grenades that the Duke of Savoy had been able to collect for his enterprise, nullifies all his plans. You will be surprised, Mgr, that I talk to you of the news. I confess that current events impress me so strongly that that is what I most think about before God. The truth is that when God has restored peace to all of Europe, and when the King's arms are, as I hope, triumphant from the protection given by God, then I shall gladly return to the state of ignorance in which I was before the recent upheavals.

I pray God, Mgr, to go on supporting you in the functions of your ministry, to give you the health you need, and to bless your resolution to make a general retreat. I am with a devotion and respect too tender and profound to be expressed yours' etc.

The three month delay in sending the Réponse *dates this letter in June. On Lescar see 920303. Santena was professed in July as fr Palémon. The French fleet had been defeated off Cap de la Hougue on 29 May. Duke Victor-Amadeus II of Savoy had joined the Grand Alliance with Spain against France in 1690. The fire in the arsenal in his capital, Turin, was disastrous and apparently accidental. In the Low Countries the French were doing well; the siege of Namur was a good augury.*

* 920619a MARÉCHAL DE BELLEFONDS   19 June 1692
BN na 12959,f.161, orig.

'You will not doubt, Mgr, my extreme distress when I learned the fate of the naval forces. We must both adore and wonder at the counsels of God, so different from those of men, and there can surely be nothing more unpleasant, looking at things with human eyes, than to see the frustration of so well planned an undertaking, in a cause which has right on its side. That teaches us that there is only one course to follow in this world, if one wishes to live in peace, and that is to have God's will before one's eyes and submit to it as soon as it is known, for to reason about his intentions and conduct leads to a welter of trouble and worry from which it is not possible to extricate oneself.

I can easily imagine that the King of England has been deeply affected by this event, but as he lives in a state of dependence on all the orders and dispositions that come from above, he will have received this like many others, with all the faith and religion that God asked of him. It must be admitted that these are sore trials.

For the rest, Mgr, it can be said with all that that God does not cease to protect the King's designs. We learn that there are still more than sixty vessels left, and that once assembled together they will form a body capable of frustrating any plans the enemy may have made. The King is the master in Flanders, and the Prince of Orange is present to see his conquests, without being able to oppose them. The fire which occurred in the citadel of Turin reduces to smoke all the plans of the Duke of Savoy and makes all of Dauphiné safe. I tell you what you know much better than I, but I confess that it is impossible to take as much interest as we do in current affairs and keep silent when one has occasion to speak.

We live in a time, Mgr, which obliges us to lift our hands constantly to heaven; that is the sole duty of those who are no longer in the world, soliciting God's mercy in the public need. He wishes to be pressed, as you know, and is pleased when men, so to speak, wrest from him by their fervour and the assiduity of their prayers what he desires to grant them.

I do not doubt that you have received the answer to the letter which you did me the honour of writing by M du Praël. I wish you all kinds of blessings, and am with all possible devotion and respect yours' etc.

William of Orange was personally conducting the campaign in Flanders, and getting the worst of it. Dauphiné, as the province marching with Savoy, had had most to fear from the Duke's operations.

920619b   CLAUSE NICAISE   19 June 1692
BN 9363,f.121, orig.; Gonod 128

Discusses Mabillon. Nicaise is going home to Dijon and will not see R. again.

920626   DUCHESSE DE GUISE   26 June 1692
BN 15172,12, orig.; Gonod 183

The capture of Namur [the town], explosion at citadel of Turin. Devotion of Mme de Saint-Loup to Mme de Guise.

920630   ETIENNE BALUZE   30 June 1692
BN fonds Baluze 361,f.84, orig.

Asks him to send Casanata a letter with R's *Réponse*.

Baluze reported having done so on 7 July. Cardinal Casanata became Vatican librarian in 1693 (1620–1700) and was a friend of Nicaise.

* 920705   MARÉCHAL DE BELLEFONDS   5 July 1692
BN na 12959,f.163, orig.; TC II/136

'The letter which you did me the honour of writing, Mgr, affected me as deeply as it possibly could. I am touched by your situation beyond anything I can express, and it could hardly be otherwise, seeing how much interest I take in all that concerns you.

I confess however that I cannot sufficiently praise God for the dispositions he gives you and the way in which you receive the orders of his providence. Indeed, without extraordinary protection, you would not have the peace of mind, which you tell me you enjoy, in a situation so likely to disturb and confuse someone with only ordinary virtue. Your feelings about the future must be very intense for you to consider present things as you do, and to suffer deprivation in a spirit of such complete detachment. God, who sees everything from the heights of heaven, and whom nothing can escape, will put to your account your perfect submission to all his wishes, and will take pleasure in filling these empty places, for which you show such christian indifference, not only by the rewards he is preparing in heaven, for those who for his sake despise earthly goods, but also by solid consolations, exceeding anything for which we could wish or hope from men, and which he has never refused to those who are ready to sacrifice every time he desires it what they would prefer above all to keep, if they followed natural inclinations. It can be said, Mgr, that you have no ears to hear the voice of nature, and that it is that of God which you heed. That is exactly the mark which distinguishes those who are his from those who are not. You have every reason to preserve continual peace, assured as you must be that you belong to the number of those who are according to his heart, provided you keep the faith he asks of you and no consideration separates you from him.

I wish more than I can say, Mgr, that nothing happens to prevent your intention of coming to see us. I do not doubt that you will find in solitude what you will not meet with elsewhere. One's reflections in solitude are always more pure and lively. I beg you to believe that we shall await that moment with extreme impatience, and will not fail to recommend to Our Lord your person and your house with all possible care. I am with a sincerity and respect I cannot express yours' etc.

While the naval defeat of la Hougue could hardly be blamed on the land commander, the subsequent attack by fireships, which caused immense damage to the stranded vessels, was specifically blamed by some, though not by Tourville himself, on Bellefonds. Pending new orders, he found himself charged with the defence of the whole coast from le Havre to Saint-Malo, and between 11 and 30 July made a tour of inspection as far as le Tréport (the extreme limit of Normandy in the North), constantly harried by imperious ministerial orders about coast defence, cannon, ship repair and so on. As if this were not bad enough, he fell foul of Louis at his autocratic worst, after appointing his cousin, the marquis de Saint-Pierre, to an official defence post, and was cruelly snubbed. All this seems to lie behind R's references to a painful situation, and can be traced in detail in the surviving correspondence with the navy minister, Pontchartrain, extending from April to September 1692, and showing Bellefonds in a remarkably good light. (See Société de l'Histoire de Normandie, Mélanges, 7e série, [Rouen, 1907], pp. 133–194).

920708 DUCHESSE DE GUISE   8 July 1692
BN 15192,13, orig.; Gonod 184

About to sing *Te Deum* for capture of Namur [citadel, on 1 July]. Sorry for the Irish. *The defeat of James II had left the Irish Catholics under Protestant rule with no hope of rescue. The consequences have never been forgotten in Ireland.*

*920709 BISHOP OF LUÇON [HENRI BARILLON]   9 July 1692
P f.781

'Allow me, Mgr, from time to time to ask for news of you. I take too much interest, as you know, not to wish to know what is new. I do not think, in the weather we are having, that you have been able to get about in your diocese. Rain has been continual in these parts and as it seems that your region has been no more fortunate, the roads will not have been passable. As long as your health is preserved, that is the main thing and what I wish more ardently than I can say.

Dom M[abillon], whom you mentioned in your last letter, has replied to my *Réponse*. His reply was read in manuscript by competent persons, and they did not take too high a view of it. It would take something quite extraordinary to make me write a second time, for my best course is to keep quiet, unless forced by urgent reasons, which I do not think will happen. The Benedictines are very annoyed with me, but if I said anything regarding them, I did so with such moderation that they should be pleased. I do not doubt that you have heard of writings and verses being circulated abroad against me and my conduct; that does me no great harm. Words pass away, whether they are good or bad, and the best thing to do is to profit from anything men say about us, whether they are right or not. Today we are singing a *Te Deum* in thanksgiving to God for the taking of the citadel of Namur. We asked God for it most insistently. It is a resounding victory, with the King present and the enemy nearby, but not daring to strike a blow to prevent him. The action has been so great that it makes one forget what happened at sea.

I wish you, Mgr, all kinds of blessing and am with profound respect and unshakable attachment yours' etc.

Mabillon had just published Réflexions sur la Réponse de M l'Abbé de la T.... *The citadel of Namur surrendered to the King's forces on 1 July.*

*920712 RM MARIE-LOUISE [BOUTHILLIER]   12 July 1692
TA orig.

'You must believe, my dear sister, that what Monsieur Masson told you results from his charity and his good opinion of our house. It is, however, an advantage to us to share as much as we do in the friendship of someone of his virtue, for I do not doubt that he offers us to Our Lord and prays for us.

It is true that Monsieur Pinette left la Trappe recently in much better health than when he came. The only reason for that that I know is that he enjoys being here. It is certain that no one could have a better or more tender heart than he, and there is no equal to his loyalty to his friends.

My rheumatism continues. The weather here, which is continually foggy and unpleasant, is just right for making it worse. Ask God, my dear sister, to make me as submissive as I ought to be to the dispositions of his providence, so that at no time should I entertain a single thought which is contrary to his orders. I am more than I can say yours' etc.

*920718   BISHOP OF LUÇON [HENRI BARILLON]   18 July 1692
P f.786

'I wrote to you only a few days ago, Mgr, and I should not waste your time as I am doing were I not obliged by an urgent matter. A good man whose interests I have much at heart has a case in the Parlement in which your nephew, Monsieur de Barillon, is judge. I did not want to interfere by writing to him on my own account, but in God's name I beg you to send me a letter for him. The man you will be commending is called Monsieur Sabain. I shall be particularly obliged to you for the service you do me. I have nothing to report, Mgr, from these parts. I beg you to believe that you enjoy the greatest honours here, and no one could with more affection, gratitude and respect be yours etc.

PS I thought, Mgr, that it would be better and take less time if you were kind enough to address the letter you write to your nephew to Monsieur Sabain himself, at Paris, *chez* Monsieur Marchand, cloître Saint-Médéric'.

Paul Barillon's son, Antoine, had become a conseiller au Parlement in January 1692. Sabain is unidentified.

*920810   MARÉCHAL DE BELLEFONDS   10 August 1692
BN na 12959,f.165, orig.

'For so long, Mgr, you have looked on things of this world as true Christians must, and know that there is nothing over which providence does not extend and that it rules our lives up to the last moment, that one cannot doubt that you have accepted as from the hand of God the loss you have just suffered of your son, that is, with perfect submission to his will. He puts men into this world and takes them out of it without inviting us to partake of his counsels. He is the sovereign master who disposes all things, and no one has the right to ask him to give reasons for his conduct.

I am sure, Mgr, that what touches you most is the fact of an unexpected death, but in that God's secrets are incomprehensible. In a moment he can show mercy to anyone he pleases. The blow is admittedly hard, and so exceptional a trial needs a virtue as strong as yours. However, whatever you may find in your own heart, and whatever everyone else may tell you on this occasion, your enlightenment and knowledge will avail you little unless God takes a hand, applies them himself and speaks to your heart as well as to your mind; he alone can give you the consolation you need. That is what we ask of him with much prayer. I beg you to believe, Mgr, that no one in the world cares more for your interests than I, that one of our chief cares is to recommend your person and your house to God, and that nothing can equal the devotion, gratitude and respect with which I am yours etc.

PS I have written to you two or three times, but I doubt whether you have received my letters. So many extraordinary things have happened that I feel impelled to say something to you, having so much cause to do so.'

Bellefonds' only son, Louis-Christophe, had died of wounds received at Steenkerke, near Soignies, on 3 August, aged 30.

*920812   BISHOP OF LUÇON [HENRI BARILLON]   12 August 1692
P f.786

'One of my intimate friends, Mgr, is pressing me to ask you to be good enough to give a preaching appointment in your diocese to a Dominican father who is prior of Pons, in Saintonge. He assures me that the man would be able to do the task very well. I should be most obliged if nothing prevented you granting my request and acceding to my humble prayer. As I wrote to you only a short time ago, there is nothing to tell you from here. The Carthusians recently produced a very vehement and sharp paper against me. Their occasion for doing so is a letter which, they say, I am circulating against their observance. I never even thought of doing so. There is indeed one which I wrote five or six years ago, but after writing it I held it back and did not publish it. Those who tell the truth always have to pay for it. I pray God, Mgr, to be in all your ways; may his spirit be the master and director of all your conduct, as it has been up to now. I am with more gratitude, affection and respect than I can express yours' etc.

Despite the discrepancy of date, R. seems to be referring to his letter of 1689 to Le Camus, withheld from publication but circulated in MS. Dom Le Masson was so annoyed by it that he composed a reply, a copy of which he sent to the minister Le Peletier, among others, but he also obeyed the order to keep the quarrel out of print.

920824   JEAN FAVIER   24 August 1692
CF 344,f.101, orig., Gonod 52

Abbé de Forbin-Janson dead, trouble at Beauvais continues. Mabillon said to be preparing a further reply. 'Men will not let go of their opinions.'

*920826   MARÉCHAL DE BELLEFONDS   26 August 1692
BN na 12959,f.167, orig.

'This is the fourth letter I have had the honour of writing to you, Mgr, since the affair of la Hougue. They must have been lost. The last was entirely about the loss of your son. I felt it more keenly than I can possibly say. The circumstance of his death touched me deeply. What you told me about him the last time you were here came back to me at once, and I perfectly understood how grieved you would be. I wrote to you that God's secrets were unknown, that sometimes he showed mercy to those for whom it seemed he should have only rigour and severity. Finally there are occasions when God wants us to hope, although there is little reason to hope, *in spem contra spem*.

I do not doubt that God, from whom you have received so many graces, will have given you that of adoring his judgement on this occasion and submitting to it. There could hardly be an occasion when you more needed his protection than this. We have not failed to offer our prayers to God for his eternal rest and your consolation. We have in the end that of knowing that his goodness is immense, and the words *miserebor cujus misereor* [Rm 9:15] prevent us from pronouncing and oblige us to remain in a state of suspension regarding those whom he takes away by unexpected deaths.

As you live attentively and profit from everything, this event is more likely than any other to complete your detachment from earthly things. For what can we count on in such great uncertainty? God alone cannot be lost when we wish to keep him, and to him we must attach ourselves. All the rest should be considered as merely transitory, and liable to be taken away at any minute. We will not cease recommending to God your person and everything concerning you. I am sure, Mgr, that you do not doubt this, and are perfectly convinced of all the devotion and respect with which I am yours' etc.

In fact, none of the four letters was lost and Bellefonds preserved them all.

920901   ETIENNE BALUZE   1 September 1692
BN fonds Baluze, 361,f. 87 orig.

Deep gratitude. Delighted at letter Baluze received from Casanata about him.

Casanata also wrote direct to R. on 5 August in Latin, warmly commending Sainteté.

920903   CLAUDE NICAISE   3 September 1692
BN 9363,f.122, orig.; Gonod 129

Had written to Nicaise a letter for Cardinal Barbarigo about *Réponse*. Does not expect to see Nicaise again.

Cardinal Gregorio Barbarigo (1626–97) had been Bp of Padua since 1660 and a close friend of Alexander VII. A nephew and a cousin, also Barbarigo, were also cardinals at this time.

920908   LOUIS MARCEL   8 September 1692
         CURÉ SAINT-JACQUES-DU-HAUT-PAS
BN 19656,f.199; Mabillon, *Ouvrages* I p. 405

R. has received several letters about Mabillon's *Réplique* [the *Réflexions*].

*920911   RM MARIE-LOUISE [BOUTHILLIER]   11 September 1692
TA orig.

'It is true that the person of whom you speak has written to me several times about the trouble she was having, not only with regard to my sister, but in general in relation to a number of people whom she did not name, and as this was a detail I did not know, I told her in general the things one says to people experiencing the difficulties and distress which come to us from the world. She could turn that to good or bad use as she chose.

As for my sister, as I know that she caused her pleasure on some important occasion, it occurred to me that there was wrong on both sides. It is not just that Madame de R. is very excitable and temperamental, the other also has tiresome moods. All that teaches me, my dear sister, to leave people in the world for what they are and not get mixed up in their affairs. It is all over with Madame de R., for she will never have news of me again.

I cannot tell you anything about the young woman of whom you speak. So many people have presented themselves, and still do so, at les Clairets that at the present time the house is quite full, and when it was seen that they were quite disinterested, people flocked there, and these are people who have nothing. However they cannot take on such a great number of persons, there must be a limit. I do not think they are in a position to listen to the person of whom you write.

I do not know who the boy is of whom you speak; you must give me his name. What your Mother Superior wrote to me is something that will never be repeated to anyone at all; it will be as secret as if she had never said anything. Farewell, my dearest sister, pray God for me, and believe that no one could be more yours than I.'

920928   CLAUDE NICAISE   28 September 1692
BN 9363,f.124, orig.; Gonod 130

Muguet [the publisher] will send book to Nicaise. Approves of what Nicaise sent from Boccone.

*921015   MARÉCHAL DE BELLEFONDS   15 October 1692
BN na 12959,f.168, orig.

'M. de Belzai gave me the letter you did me the honour of writing, Mgr. I found him as you said, full of zeal and with the intention of attaching himself solely to God and his service and of bringing to him all the gifts and talents he has received from his providence. There is no room for doubt that he is a true pastor. As he needed recommendations for the Parlement at Rouen, where he has an important affair, I gave him letters for Madame de Guise, who has many friends there.

We do not fail, Mgr, to pray God to keep you in the situation in which he has put you, in complete dependence on all his wishes. Apart from that there is only trouble and confusion. A Christian should know no other happiness but that of being attached to his God, to regard all his orders and inclinations as sovereign laws, which it is not permitted to challenge. I am with all possible devotion and respect, I beg you to believe yours' etc.

The Parlement at Rouen was the supreme court for the whole of Normandy.

921030   CLAUDE NICAISE   30 October 1692
BN 9363,f.125, orig.; Gonod 131

Muguet has sent the packages. Continued satire circulating against R.

921105   J-B DE SANTEUIL, SAINT-VICTOR   5 November 1692
La Vie et les bons mots, II p. 70
Praises Santeuil's Hymns to St Bernard.

*921119   MARÉCHAL DE BELLEFONDS   19 November 1692
BN na 12959,f.171, orig.

'I share your feelings of consolation, Mgr, at the death of M le marquis d'Amfreville. It is certainly a most extraordinary thing that a man of his profession, brought up in a trade in which God is so little known, should finish his course with so much edification. That shows clearly that God has his elect everywhere, that he does not lose them from sight, and that they find him in their normal needs and in time of urgency. I remember, Mgr, that he came here with you seven or eight years ago, and that I heard him say things indicating a depth of religion and faith that surprised me. It must not be doubted that he kept these dispositions and that God revived them at the moment that he wanted to grant him final mercy.

Such examples instruct us, and teach us to hope for everything from God's goodness, but not to neglect to behave according to his orders on the pretext that there is no situation or time in which he does not give evidence of his compassion. His charity, which is immense, must not make us worse and our conscience, to be what it must be, should be accompanied with exact and faithful behaviour on our part. You are fortunate, Mgr, in knowing these truths, but still more so for practising them, and doing what you know a Christian should do, who wants to be ready, uncertain as he is of the moment when it will please God to break his bonds and summon him.

The Son of God himself has spoken to us of the happiness to be enjoyed by the servant whom his master finds watching over his conduct and the duties with which he charged him. I pray God, Mgr, never to cease increasing what he has put in your heart, to make you persevere in the ways he has shown you, and to allow nothing likely to separate you from what you know he asks of you. You know that there will be a great accounting for grace, when he has given it abundantly. I am with all possible devotion and respect yours etc.

PS Allow me, Mgr, to send you a note of an affair concerning a lady, widow of a gentleman who was my personal friend. I beg you to consider this note with your habitual enlightenment and justice. I do not know the full facts of the case, but she is said to be involved with people who are trying to cheat her out of funds. If she were to lose, a large part of her property would be at stake. I consider her fortunate to have you for judge.'

Charles-François Davy, marquis d'Amfreville, Bellefonds' son-in-law, died on 3 November aged fifty-two, from wounds received at la Hougue. He had married Bellefonds' daughter Jeanne-Louise only in January 1691, after a lifetime spent at sea. R. had many military friends, and received several remarkable ex-soldiers into the monastery, so that his habitual view of a career of arms as leading to impiety was not just instinctive prejudice.

921120   RELIGIEUSES, LES CLAIRETS   20 November 169[2]
A 3989,f.89 (dated 1693)

Expresses his delight at request, signed by abbess and forty-two religious, to join the Strict Observance, and accompanies letter with formal deed of approval as Visitor.

The MS is very unreliable about dates, but the chronology seems to be as follows:
on 4 October 1691 a number of nuns, including the abbess, began to practise abstinence from meat under the direction of the confessor;
nearly a year later, on 14 September 1692, those who had previously hesitated for health or other reasons joined their sisters in a formal capitular resolution to seek authority to extend abstinence to the whole community;
they then addressed the request mentioned above to R.
Unfortunately the copy is undecided as between 13 and 18 November for the date of the request (both dates appear within a few pages), and 1693 seems to leave an improbably long gap between resolution and request. At all events Les Clairets did eventually join the Strict Observance.

921200   DR HECQUET   [November / December 1692]
Dubois II/ pp. 342–348 (from lost orig).

R. is consoled at manner of Mademoiselle de Vertus' death [21 November 1692].

*921229 RM MARIE-LOUISE [BOUTHILLIER]   29 December 1692
TA orig.

'I see, my dear sister, that your friendship for me causes you to be moved by what you hear said of me at the present juncture, and I think that if there is anything in that connexion which might add to your peace of mind, it is to assure you that I am aware of everything that is going around in the world, and far from feeling in any way hurt by it, I praise God that things are happening as they are, and that he is giving me cause to exercise towards those who do not love us that charity so often recommended and so little known, and is obliging us to wish them no less good than they wish us evil. That is how I feel towards them, and I should be really delighted to give them effective proof of it. I do not doubt that you are pleased to see me in such a situation. As far as friends go, I know that there are few sincere ones, I realise that every day, but that does not stop one getting on well with the world, although with some reserve and restraint. I wish that you would indicate who you want to talk to me about; it would do to put in your next letter and as a detached note 'I meant to talk to you of so and so'. The world is a strange place, we have to live there as long as it pleases God that we should be there, but we are fortunate indeed when we leave it, and leave behind almost nothing that deserves to be regretted.

It is true that people in Rome are saying what you tell me, although there is no truth in it. Pray God for me, my dear sister, as I do for you, and believe that it is not possible to be more yours than I am.'

930101 DUCHESSE DE GUISE   1 January 1693
BN 15172,14, orig.; Gonod 185

There is one Gospel only for princes as for others.

930103 DUCHESSE DE GUISE   3 January 1693
BN 15172,15,orig.; Gonod 186

A St Augustine has been sent on to her.

*930103a BISHOP OF LUÇON [HENRI BARILLON]   3 January 1693
P f. 787

'It is, Mgr, a matter neither of habit nor of formality that I ask for your blessing and renew the assurance of my service at the beginning of this new year, but [done] to satisfy the feeling in my heart. I am so convinced of all I owe to the sincere friendship with which you honour me that I could never repeat it too often to my liking, although I do not doubt that in that you do me all the justice I deserve. I pray God to strengthen your health and to continue to pour his blessings on the efforts you make to make him known and loved by all those whose souls he has put in your hands. Your fidelity, Mgr, will attract all the protection from him which you need. You know that it is that fidelity that solicits and urges his mercy, and can obtain anything from him. Keep your usual kindness for me, I beg you, and believe that no one could be with more sincere devotion and inviolable respect than I yours' etc.

*930108   MARÉCHAL DE BELLEFONDS   8 January 1693
BN na 12959,f.173, orig.

'I wish you, Mgr, a renewal both of grace and health, and pray God that in multiplying your days, he will multiply those christian dispositions which he has up to now given you so generously. You know that those who are his must be always going forward, and that the use they make of the marks of his goodness received by them attract the protection which they need to persevere in his service. Once one does not strive to advance one may be said to be looking back, because one has stopped doing what he wants us to do. You see too clearly the things to come and know too well those you have before your eyes for anything to divert you from the way in which I am sure you are. All that strikes your senses and all you see here on earth is unable to produce in you those harmful impressions which catch unawares all those who do not set them in their true light, that is, who attach to them an importance of which they are not worthy. In fact, to attach oneself to them results from great passion or great ignorance.

We have learned, Mgr, of the death of the comte de Grammont. Everyone knows how he lived. Someone wrote to me that God touched him in his illness and that he had resolved, if God restored his health, to repair the past by behaving quite differently. If God took him when he felt thus, he granted him much grace, for those wishes which come from him are effective and thus count for merit and reward. It is taking things very far and waiting until it is very late, and shows the infinite resources of God's goodness. The libertines abuse this goodness, others profit by it, and such examples only serve to increase their fidelity and regularity. It takes a strange reversal of values to find cause for becoming worse in experiencing the immensity of God's charity. I will continue to offer him my prayers for your person and all that concerns you, as I do every day of my life. I humbly beg you not to doubt this and to believe that no one in the world is more devotedly, sincerely and respectfully than I yours' etc.

Philibert, comte de Gramont (or Grammont), (1621–1707), is best known for his entertaining and scandalous Mémoires, *edited by his brother-in-law, Hamilton, in 1713. He was a popular but notorious rogue and libertine, whose wife, having been brought up at Port-Royal, remained pious and tried to reform him. He fell dangerously ill in 1692, and in December was persuaded by his wife to take the sacraments, whence his rumoured conversion; but he recovered, and on his deathbed in 1707 showed no sign of serious penitence. Saint-Simon gives a spirited account of his death, but since he claims that Gramont had never been ill before, his word is not too reliable. R. could have heard the rumour from almost anyone,* but in 1693 Gramont's friend, Saint-Evremond, who was also a friend of Paul Barillon, actually published a comic epitaph of Gramont, which may have circulated in MS before its publication. It is most likely that R. had this in mind. On Gramont and the whole episode see Charles de Saint-Evremond, Lettres, vol. II, pp. 302–309, ed. R. Ternois, (Paris, 1968). I owe this reference to my friend Dr. D. C. Potts of Keble College, Oxford.

930112 DUCHESSE DE GUISE   12 January 1693
BN 15172,16, orig.; Gonod 187
Siege of Rheinfelden raised [6 January].

*930120 RM MARIE-LOUISE [BOUTHILLIER]   20 January 1693
TA orig.

'I did not doubt, my dear sister, that you would agree with all my ideas, and rightly judge that all these rumours and writings spread abroad make no unpleasant impression on me. That is a grace from God, for by nature I am very liable to feel any wrong done to me. As for my justification, that is in God's hands; you know that men do not do all the harm they would like to.

I did not understand the person you meant to indicate by the two M. M. G. It would have been shorter to name the person simply without saying why.

My indisposition continues, and even gets worse, because the season is so damp; there is no remedy I can take, because the trouble is almost universal. God, who presides over everything, will deliver us from it when he pleases; it is he who sends down ills, it is for him to deliver us. Pray for me, my dearest sister, and believe that no one could be more cordially yours than I.

PS What you tell me about the Pre[monstratensian] father is pointless; the Pope does not grant briefs for translation at present.'

In 1684, after R. had admitted two Premonstratensians to la Trappe, the General of the Order complained to the Chapter of the Reformed abbots then sitting, and though they upheld R. on that occasion he never again considered admitting religious of that Order.

*930123 RM MARIE-LOUISE [BOUTHILLIER]   23 January 1693
TA orig.

'You have cleared up a problem, my dear sister, by naming the person of whom you had spoken obscurely, but I should be very glad to know what she said so that I can take appropriate measures. It is true, as you say, that there is no friendship or loyalty in the world. Those who know it for what it is, and no longer belong to it, should consider themselves very fortunate, and such a separation is a reward already in this world. One must go further, though, and see that the separation is of use to us for eternity as well as for time. It is very much to be wished that poor Monsieur

Pinette were younger than he is for his friends' consolation; a man who does nothing but good here on earth will be a real loss when he has gone. We must ask God to prolong his days. Pray for me, my dear sister, and believe me unreservedly yours.'

930128   CLAUDE NICAISE   28 January 1693
BN 9363,f.126, orig.; Gonod 132

Nicaise can accept a post at Sainte-Chapelle [at Dijon]. If Barbarigo were pope he would call Nicaise to Rome.

930207   CLAUDE NICAISE   7 February 1693
BN 9363,f.127, orig.; Gonod 133

Discusses Mabillon. Will send Association requested by nuns of Notre-Dame du Tard.

Tard was a cistercian house reformed by Saint-Cyran and transferred in 1623 to Dijon from the country outside.

930208   DUCHESSE DE GUISE   8 February 1693
BN 15172,17, orig.; Gonod 188

Death of Pellisson, without a chance to make confession. R's rheumatism is painful and prevents him standing in choir as he should.

Paul Pellisson (1624–93) was converted from Protestantism in 1666 and had a distinguished career as historian and member of the Academy. He had been in contact with R. for a long time.

930223   DUCHESSE DE GUISE   23 February 1693
BN 15172,18, orig.; Gonod 189

R. dismayed that the Catholic Duke of Savoy encourages Protestants. R. forced to enter infirmary.

930306   CLAUDE NICAISE   6 March 1693
BN 9363,f.129, orig.; Gonod 134

Continuing criticism of R. Better that Thiers should not write in his defence.

The attack in question was that of Denys de Sainte-Marthe, a Maurist, and later general of the Maurist Congregation, who had written an intemperate defence of Mabillon's position against R. in the form of Quatre Lettres, *published in 1692. Thiers, ever impetuous, replied with* Apologie de M. l'abbé de la Trappe, *published and immediately suppressed in 1694. Sainte-Marthe had to make* amende honorable *to R., but the harm he had done remained.*

930316   DUCHESSE DE GUISE   16 March 1693
BN 15172,19, orig.; Gonod 190
Peaceful and edifying death of a monk the day before [dom Dorothée, former J-B Vitry, canon of Meaux, professed April 1691].

930316a   CLAUDE NICAISE   16 March 1693
BN 9363,f.131, orig.; Gonod 135
Sends letter to a religious of Maizières [a Reformed house in diocese of Chalon-sur-Saône] who wants to come to la T. but it must be handed directly to him, not to his prior. Comments on recent earthquake in Catania: 'God exercises his judgement on men, but they behave no better for it'.

930316b   BISHOP OF MEAUX [J-B-BOSSUET]   16 March 1693
A 5346,f.239; Bossuet, *Correspondance*, V p. 322
Death of dom Dorothée.

*930326   RM MARIE-LOUISE [BOUTHILLIER]   26 March 1693
TA orig.

'I am overjoyed, my dearest sister, to learn that you are cured. Father du Buc and Monsieur Pinette assured me that it was so two days ago. God has spoken to you in the illness he sent you, and I do not doubt that you responded as you should by making good use of it. Your illness was more acute and serious than mine, but it did not last so long. I pray Our Lord to strengthen you more and more in his grace and in what I am sure you feel for all transitory things, and those one can lose at any moment, I mean health and life. Eternity alone is worthy of our attachment, and the rest should be considered as though it were no longer in being, and is only worthy, whatever it may be, of being sacrificed to him who destines us for better things. It is in that direction, my dear sister, that you must turn the eyes of your spirit and all the impulses of your heart. That is the real way in which we are obliged to use them if we want to follow God's orders and regard his will as the only rule of our conduct. Pray God for me, and believe that no one could be more fully yours than I.'

Alexis du Buc (1638–1709) was superior of the Theatines in Paris, and a noted preacher, who claimed to have converted numerous Protestants. He was a supporter of Fénelon but so well thought of in Rome that he was called there by the Pope as theologian and in fact died there.

930328   MONSIEUR   28 March 1693
Landévennec Abbey, ? orig.
Detailed account of death of dom Dorothée.

930412 DUCHESSE DE GUISE   12 April 1693
BN 15172,20, orig.; Gonod 191

Death of Mademoiselle de Montpensier (la Grande Mademoiselle). 'Her patience, resignation and forgiveness of her enemies a good indication of God's mercy.' Praises Mme de Guise's disinterestedness.

This princess, daughter of Gaston d'Orléans and half-sister of Mme de Guise, was born in 1627 and died on 5 April 1693. She was reputedly the richest heiress in Europe, and on bad terms with Mme de Guise, to whom she left nothing, whence the comment on disinterestedness.

*930413 BISHOP OF LUÇON [HENRI BARILLON]   13 April 1693
P f.641

'I would like, Mgr, to be able to help in bringing into effect the good intentions of these unreformed Benedictines about whom Father Le Balleur writes to you. Their life has so little to do with the Rule they embraced that many changes would have to be made in order for them to be put into a fit state to effect their salvation and serve God in a manner agreeable to him, and that is not possible unless they live, as St Bernard says, speaking of the obligations of those who do not keep the rule exactly, *pie juste et sobrie* [Pre 16].

I will tell you briefly, Mgr, that they may well dispense themselves from the abstinence and fasts prescribed by the Rule, since the Church permits it, but as regards interior practices, they must devote and apply themselves to these and find the secret of filling their days so that they have no occasion to go looking for extraneous occupations or remaining idle, and that is what they will never achieve except through reading holy books and work. If they were willing to reduce themselves to such subjection, they might put themselves on a sure path and compensate by their piety what might be wanting in penitence and external mortification.

Their whole life must consist in singing in church, reading, manual labour, and some spiritual conferences, but unless all that is inspired with a real spirit, and combined with much piety, they will find it hard to rise, to subsist and reach the state in which they want to establish themselves, especially if they have no one at their head to be their leader and guide. Nothing is more rare than to see religious succeed in this sort of situation. If zeal is slight, nothing much is done; if it is ardent and alive, it leads on to higher aspirations and is not satisfied with a mediocrity which retains almost nothing of the Rule. However, it seems that that is what these religious are proposing. In the end they are monks of St Benedict, and they will not be acquitted before God for living as ecclesiastics. I am sure, Mgr, that you will agree with what I think, if you think about it for a moment.

For the rest, Mgr, you delight me by saying that your health is better than it was. I pray God to strengthen it, and to give his blessing to the visits you are about to make, that is that you waste none of your time and that every one has its particular intention.

I have nothing new to report from here. You are more honoured here than anywhere in the world, I beg you to believe that, as well as the inviolable attachment and tender and profound respect with which I am yours' etc.

On Le Balleur see 890117. The 'anciens' Benedictines were those who belonged to none of the congregations [Cluny, St-Maur, St-Vanne) but remained under episcopal jurisdiction. Most of their houses were very rundown. The community in question is very likely the rump of the former cathedral-abbey of Maillezais (a very rare arrangement in France), which had been more or less secularised when the see was transferred to La Rochelle in 1666. Le Balleur's interest is easily explained; Maillezais is only a few miles from les Robinières. The only similar community in the diocese of Luçon was Orbestier, but there would have been no reason for Le Balleur rather than Barillon himself to act in that case. Yet again the reforming zeal of Le Balleur, and his connexion with R., can be seen to go well beyond his own Order. It is not without irony that Rabelais, tiring of the strictness of the Franciscan Observant house at Fontenay-le-Comte, had transferred (c. 1523) the few miles to Maillezais to enjoy the easy going life of the Benedictines there.

*930420   BISHOP OF LUÇON [HENRI BARILLON]   20 April 1693
P f.787

'If the weather is as bad in your parts as it is here, I am sorry for you, Mgr, as I believe you are on your visitations and I know how the roads you have to take are broken up and potholed by this continual rain. Although God has given you back health, I cannot help fearing for the fatigue and hardships to which you must be exposed. We shall commend the course of your journey to God with all possible diligence for the success of your labours, with regard to the sactification of your diocese, and for the preservation of your person, which could not be more dear and precious to me than it is.

I am still troubled by very painful rheumatism. I can only walk with difficulty and always with the risk of falling. That means, Mgr, that God is warning me to pay more attention than hitherto to my rule of life. He wants me to have its end constantly before my eyes, through the consequences of an indisposition which is gradually bringing me there, and by the weakness it causes me. It seems to me that I could not do better than apply to myself those words of the Holy Spirit: *partibus judicans das locum poenitentiae.* [Ws 12:19] That means that he does not want to take me by surprise, and is giving me time to work at my conversion in a manner worthy of my calling and my duties. For that I ask you, Mgr, for the aid of your prayers, in which I have the greatest confidence, and I ask it with all possible insistence. You owe them to my wretchedness, as well as to the inviolable attachment and faithful, tender respect with which I am yours etc.

PS Allow me, Mgr, to remind you of Father du Vernay, OP, for a preaching post at

Beauvoir-sur-Mer or Noirmoutier. He is recommended to me by one of my best friends, who assures me of his ability and piety.'
Father du Vernay is the prior of Pons in 920812. The two places referred to are in the northwest corner of Vendée.

930500   DUCHESSE DE GUISE   [? May] 1693
BN 15172,21, orig. (unfinished); Gonod 192
General advice.

*930511   MARÉCHAL DE BELLEFONDS   11 May 1693
BN na 12959,f.175, orig.

'As soon as I showed M de Saint-Louis, Mgr, what you did me the honour of telling me about M de Villeneuve, he replied that he was delighted to accept anything coming in your name, and that it was enough that you indicated your desire. As he lives in great calm, there is nothing he would fear more than finding someone whose character did not suit him, but your reference on M de Villeneuve removes all fear, and it will be a consolation for M de Saint-Louis to have him.

Allow me, Mgr, to tell you something that occurs to me. As we have been told from a number of sources that you are coming to command in Normandy, we thought that you would not mind, if that were so, if I made a request of you, which is to write to M de Saint-Louis, as you may deem appropriate, that he should hold himself in readiness to report to you at a time to be stated later. Apart from the fact that he will do so with the greatest pleasure, whenever you order him, that will protect him from any orders which may come to him from M de Matignon or M de Beuvron. This is a special favour for which he hopes from your kindness, and in which all of us are extremely concerned. If the news turns out to be true, as nobody doubts, I am sure we shall have the consolation of seeing you as you pass by, since la Trappe is not far from your route.

I see, Mgr, that you continue to live in the state of detachment from passing things in which God has long since put you, and though this inner separation in which a Christian should live is not as complete as you would wish, it is a disposition which has still driven deep roots into your heart, and it will increase. You want it too much for God to leave it as it is. You know that the ardent desire for a true good is regarded by God as an ardent prayer and cry from the heart; that is his word and it does not fail to be heard, according to the prophet's expression, *desiderium cordis audivit auris tua.* [Ps 10:17]

We continue as usual to recommend to Our Lord all that affects you in this world. It is one of our principal cares, I humbly beg you not to doubt it, any more than the deep respect with which I am yours' etc.

Villeneuve was mentioned earlier (820608) as having been granted retreat at Vincennes.

M de Saint-Louis, a former cavalry officer, had been living in the former commendatory abbot's lodgings since 1684, in relative seclusion, but under no vow, which suggests that Villeneuve also had a military background. Bellefonds in fact never took up any command again.

Jacques Goyon, comte de Matignon (1644–1725), who was the brother-in-law of abbé Luthumière at Valognes, had just become Lieutenant-General, and was Governor of Cherbourg and the Cotentin; François d'Harcourt, marquis de Beuvron (died 1705), was Lieutenant-General in Upper Normandy. As such they had local authority over Saint-Louis, but their orders could apparently be trumped by those of Bellefonds, senior marshal of France.

*930527   BISHOP OF LUÇON [HENRI BARILLON]   27 May 1693
P f.642

'I was sure, Mgr, that you would approve all my views on the subject of the unreformed Benedictines. A religious cannot be saved without keeping his Rule, and although he may not observe it in every detail, since the Church has granted some dispensations, he must discharge the main points; that is something on which everyone must agree if they judge according to genuine principles.

I praise God, Mgr, that your visits have gone off successfully and that your health did not suffer; God, who presides over all things, has preserved it for you.

I will say nothing of Father du Vernay, except that he was commended to me by a religious who is one of my close friends, who assures me both regarding his virtue and ability and takes the responsibility of saying that he will give satisfaction. It is with that reference that I took the liberty of commending him to you.

I do not doubt, Mgr, that you are moved by the misery of the people, so great and universal that people are reduced to the most extreme need. I do not know what will happen unless God has pity on the world.

As for Cardinal Le Camus, I do not at present have any news about him. He is left where he is and it is most unlikely that he will move. As for me, Mgr, I am still afflicted with my usual trouble, and have much difficulty walking. As for hoping to see me improve, my age and the climate of this place prevent me having such hopes. The main thing is to worship God's designs, and accept all that happens to us on earth as coming from his hand. Sickness, health, death, and life are equal so long as one is perfectly submissive to the orders of his providence, and can say a heartfelt *non contradicam sermonibus Sancti* [Jb 6:10]. I ask you, Mgr, for your blessing and the aid of your prayers, assuring you that no one in the world could be with more attachment, affection and respect than I yours etc.

PS For the rest, Mgr, I have some news for you: dom Mabillon has been to see me; I embraced him very cordially, and for his part he acted towards me in the most charitable way possible. Thus we feel towards one another as God wants us to feel. He is a religious of certainly great merit, who combines profound humility with great learning.'

On the unreformed (anciens) Benedictines, see 930413. Mabillon's visit had been that *very day (27 May), and as R. spoke of him in the same terms to everyone there is no reason to doubt his sincerity.*

930604   CLAUDE NICAISE   4 June 1693
BN 9363,f.132, orig.; Gonod 136

Letter handed over at Maizières. Mabillon has been [27 May] 'with all possible signs of friendship and charity on all sides.... It is undeniable that one could hardly find more humility and erudition together than in this good father.'

930607   DOM JEAN MABILLON, OSB   7 June 1693
BN 19656,f.189, orig.; Mabillon, *Ouvrages*, I p. 416

R. deeply touched by meeting with Mabillon.

930610   CLAUDE NICAISE   10 June 1693
BN 9363,f.133, orig.; Gonod 137

Mabillon came with only one companion; 'his deep humility and great learning'.

*930613   RM MARIE-LOUISE [BOUTHILLIER]   13 June 1693
TA orig.

'This note, my dearest sister, is just to remind you of me and ask you to go on praying for me. Brother Chanvier will tell you our news; my rheumatism will not go away. The warm weather has not yet reduced it, I do not know if it will have more effect later. God is master of sickness, of health, of life, and of death; anyone who has enough faith to abandon himself entirely to his hands has no more fear or anxiety. The number of those is small; ask him, my dear sister, to give me grace to join them. I am all yours, I beg you to believe, and with all my heart.'

Chanvier was a donné (oblate) *who acted as messenger and geneial man of affairs for la T He accompanied the monks who went to establish the house at Buonsolazzo, near Florence, in 1705, at the request of the Grand Duke of Tuscany. This was the only colony founded by la T.*

930615   DUCHESSE DE GUISE   15 June 1693
BN 15172,22, orig.; Gonod 193

Advises her to communicate on St John's Day [24 June] and not wait till following Sunday. Praises progress of Mme d'Auvergne.

Mme d'Auvergne is Elisabeth-Eléonore de la Tour d'Auvergne, niece of Cardinal Bouillon, who on R's advice had recently left her house of Canonesses in Paris for Les Clairets, where she became prioress almost immediately after her profession. She went on to earn warm praise as Abbess of Thorigny, 1702–31, and died in 1746.

930629   CLAUDE NICAISE   29 June 1693
BN 9363,f.134, orig.; Gonod 138
R. is ignoring criticism from Maurists.

930725   CLAUDE NICAISE   25 July 1693
BN 9363,f.185, orig.; Gonod 139
Despite rumours to the contrary, the meeting with Mabillon was completely courteous and cordial. Gerbais has paid his first visit; 'an entirely good man'.

*930726   BISHOP OF LUÇON [HENRI BARILLON]   26 July 1693
P f.643 (possibly January)

'I have delayed a long time, Mgr, in replying to the letter from Father Le Balleur which you took the trouble to send me. There was a long memorandum which I had to read carefully, and I was obliged to visit les Clairets during an interval when my health was a little better than usual; all that as well as what little time remains to me, after the essential obligations which I cannot avoid, has prevented me answering.

My opinion, Mgr, about what Father Le Balleur writes is that the religious in question should embrace a mitigation of St Benedict's Rule authorised by the Holy See. That of Cîteaux, authorised some twenty-seven or twenty-eight years ago by Alexander VII, is of that kind; it includes considerable relaxations, and nothing too severe, but a religious who has professed in the Rule of St Benedict can effect his salvation and even live with edification, so long as he faithfully observes it and does not add new exemptions to those granted by the Church.

I am telling Father Le Balleur where he will find the Brief containing the mitigation I mention, but as these religious are accustomed to living a very soft and easygoing life, it is to be feared that any subjection, however moderate, will seem like an iron yoke to them. As you say, Mgr, the time must come when God looks with merciful eyes upon those who have stayed away from him for so long. What one can say, which is only too true, is that we no longer see nowadays those great changes of life which were seen in earlier times, and indeed the world is no longer worthy of them.

I will say nothing of my health. It is, as usual neither good nor really bad. My indispositions do not prevent me from discharging all my exercises. I pray God, Mgr, to preserve yours. It is dear and precious to the Church, you make such holy use of it that all must ask God to preserve it for the benefit and edification of the public. Believe, Mgr, that no one takes more interest in it than I, and nothing could be added to the profound and tender respect with which I am yours' etc.

This letter is almost certainly wrongly dated, and should probably come before that of 13 April. R. paid his last visit to les Clairets in March 1692. The long memorandum is probably Mabillon's Réflexions of that year, and the reference to the dating of Alexander VII's brief In suprema of 1666 suggests some time in 1693, perhaps January, for this letter. These are still the same Benedictines as in 930413 and 930527. Nothing came of Le Balleur's efforts or R's advice.

930802   MADEMOISELLE DE COURCELLES,   2 August 1693
VAL-DE-GRÂCE
BN 19656,f.191, orig.; Mabillon, *Ouvrages* I p. 416

Confirms Mabillon's visit, 'not a mere ceremony on either side, but a thoroughly sincere and cordial interview.' Sorry at her continued ill health.

930802a   JEAN GERBAIS   2 August 1693
BN Fichiers Charavay (no further trace)

This letter has disappeared and there is no record of its contents.

930807   DOM JEAN MABILLON, OSB   7 August 1693
BN 19656,f.193, orig.

R. is always glad to receive anyone or anything from Mabillon. A person he sent has had to abandon the novitiate against his own and R's inclinations.

930813   MONSIEUR JOLLIN, CHANOINE DE SAINT-MARCEL   13 August 1693
A 5172,f.60, orig.

Legal proceedings against M Béchamel and Mlle Guignard.

The Filles de Ste-Agathe were first (1697–1700) lodged in the property of a Mlle Guignard, who may be this same person (see 970330).

*930820   MARÉCHAL DE BELLEFONDS   20 August 1693
BN na 12959,f.177, orig.

'We shall expect the King of England, Mgr, for the time that you indicate he will visit our desert. We hoped to have the honour of seeing you in these past days, but as I saw that you had put off coming here, where you had ordered your horses to be brought, I thought that the occasion of the battle which we had just won in Flanders was the reason for delaying your journey. The groom waited three or four days and went off before we received the letter telling us to send him back to Vincennes. Our consolation, Mgr, is that you have not changed your plans, only deferred the moment.

I confess that I have often thought about your son's death, and that one can see circumstances in it which may be considered evidence of the mercy God granted him. Nothing is more hidden than his judgements. He needs only an instant to make a man eternally happy, and that instant in your son may have been the result of your piety and that of your wife. I do not doubt, Mgr, that you are reflecting deeply on the present state of affairs. How many marks of God's protection there are over France! He never tires of favouring the King's arms, they prosper on sea and land. That should be a good reason for obliging all right-thinking people to solicit his goodness, so that he may complete what he has begun, and crown all these advantageous events with a still more advantageous peace. That is the chief duty of those who lead a life of retreat, for God has surely only separated them from the world so that they should incessantly address prayers to him for those with whom they no longer have contact. We do not fail, Mgr, to recommend to God your person with all possible diligence. I beg you to believe that I regard that as one of my principal obligations, and that nothing could equal the gratitude and respect with which I am yours etc.

PS M de Villeneuve has gone back. He will tell you his reasons. I saw him only once, because the day after he arrived here I was struck with such a violent attack of erisypelas on the face that I looked quite frightening, and was in no state to be seen by anyone. I am still not quite better although it has gone down a lot.'

James came on 14 September. William of Orange had suffered a major defeat at Neerwinden on 29 July. Thoughts about Bellefonds' son were no doubt prompted by the occasion of the anniversary of his death (3 August). On Villeneuve see 930511.

930823   DUCHESSE DE GUISE   23 August 1693
BN 15172,23, orig.; Gonod 194

Monsieur [Philippe, duc d'Orléans] was most impressed by his visit to la T. Thanks her for kindness to Mme de Belin [R's niece]. Perhaps best that Mme de Mornay's sister should leave the cloister if she has no vocation. Cardinal de Bouillon has been three days at la T. and leaves next day.

The future Regent had visited la T. on 11 July and took back to Versailles a piece of their black bread, which was inspected at court with amazed horror. Mme de Mornay's sister was a Fille de Calvaire.

930826   JEAN GERBAIS   26 August 1693
A 5172,f.63, orig. (PS to a letter from dom Le Nain)

R. thinks dom Le Nain has taken Gerbais too literally in sending him a MS of his history of Cîteaux.

*930831   JEAN GERBAIS   31 August 1693
BN na 12959,f.202, orig.

Has sent RP Majeur to see Fieubet and du Charmel to dissuade him from his plan.

He must remain with his congregation and give public edification. Praises 'simplicity and humility' of the Abbot of Cîteaux [since 1692, Nicolas Larcher].

It was just two years since Fieubet had withdrawn to Grosbois, to a small community of Camaldolese, where du Charmel often visited him. The superior (entitled Père Majeur) appears from other letters to Gerbais to have become discouraged by defections and accusations of Jansenism. It seems that he did stay.

930831a BISHOP OF LUÇON [HENRI BARILLON]   31 August 1693
P f.788

'Here, Mgr, is the religious for whom I had the honour of writing to you, who will receive your blessing. If, as I do not doubt, he matches the testimony given to me of his virtue and ability, you will be thoroughly pleased with him. I shall be most obliged for all the signs he receives of your kindness and protection. I am, Mgr, with the deep respect you know, yours' etc.

This is presumably Fr du Vernay, OP, first brought to the bishop's attention the previous year. (See 920812.)

930913 DOM DU VERGER, COLLÈGE DE NARBONNE   13 September 1693
BN 25557,f.1, orig.

Letters from Narbonne have been either lost or heavily delayed. The visions [at Alan] need careful investigation, but it does not seem likely that the devil would encourage a Marian cult. 'The youth and simplicity of the girl, the consistency of her story and patience in the face of criticism are all in her favour.' Praises fr Dosithée.

Du Verger was chaplain of the cistercian convent of Fabas, where the girl, Madeleine Serre, was lay sister. She continued to see visions, and R. strongly recommended that she should not be allowed outside the cloister, where she died in 1739. Bp de Rechignevoisin had died in May 1693, but the Vicar General, La Fage, remained in touch with R. regarding events at Alan.

930914 LOUIS MARCEL,   14 September 1693
           CURÉ SAINT-JACQUES-DU-HAUT-PAS
BN 19656,f.200, orig.

Mabillon's friendship now 'sincere and constant'.

930914a MADAME [? DE SAINT-LOUP]   14 September 1693
U 723

R. is used to calumny. Case of a novice of 19 sent away by R. although novice-master wanted to keep him.

From the date the novice may well be the poet Antoine Houdar de La Motte (1672-1731) who spent two months in the novitiate in 1693.

*930914b MARÉCHAL DE BELLEFONDS   14 September 1693
BN na 12959,f.179, orig.

'We are infinitely obliged to you, Mgr, for your kindness in speaking to the [? principal] surgeon about our indisposition. The note which you have done us the honour of sending on his behalf is so exact and correct that even if he had seen the affliction with his own eyes he would not have explained himself more clearly. We shall follow as exactly as possible all that he tells us. The wound is not too bad; we shall stop it closing up again too soon, although it does not look at all as if a new abscess is forming. We began today to use the healing waters. I cannot tell you, Mgr, now much we appreciate your kindness towards us. We shall try to show you before God how much. I am with all possible devotion and repsect yours etc.

PS You can assure your wife and your daughters that we shall take particular care to ask Our Lord Jesus Christ not to cease from strengthening their piety and increasing more and more their contempt for transitory things, as well as the feeling he has given them for that which is the sole object of their hopes. I forgot to tell you that the King of England spent the feast here in a way which filled us all with edification.'

The surgeon is presumably Guy Fagon (1638-1718), who had just become the King's chief doctor. 14 September is the feast of the Holy Cross.

930929   DUCHESSE DE GUISE   29 September 1693
BN 15172,24, orig.; Gonod 195

She was right to defer her devotions for reasons of health. Mme de Belin coming from Averton [her home] to join Mme at Alençon.

931007   CLAUDE NICAISE   7 October 1693
BN 9363,f.186, orig.; Gonod 140

Discussion of rice as food. Death of M Ouvrard 'a man of solid piety'.

Ouvrard was the canon of Tours who had accompanied Nicaise on his only visit to la T. in 1687.

931008   JEAN GERBAIS   8 October 1693
BN Fichiers Charavay, orig.

Refers to dom Le Nain's MS.

931026   DUCHESSE DE GUISE   26 October 1693
BN 15172,25, orig.; Gonod 196
Disavows book of *Maximes* circulating under his name.

This refers to the unauthorised publication (by Maupeou, probably) of what later came out as Instructions morales.

931026a   CLAUDE NICAISE   26 October 1693
BN 9363,f.187, orig.; Gonod 141
No wish to answer Carthusians; 'I will keep eternal silence on their subject'.

His bitter dispute with dom Le Masson had in fact been ended on royal orders in 1689, and R's letter of that year was only published in 1710, when both men were dead.

931102   DUCHESSE DE GUISE   2 November 1693
BN 15172,26, orig.; Gonod 197
Reflections on All Saints' Day.

931110   MONSIEUR   [after 8 November 1693]
Buffier, *Vie de . . . Val-Richer*, p. 209
Praise of Abbot of Val-Richer, who died 8 November.

*931114   RM MARIE-LOUISE [BOUTHILLIER]   14 November 1693
TA orig.

'I have read your letter, my dear sister, and after much thought I can tell you that you should forget all memory of the past, cast yourself into God's arms, and hope that your fidelity in satisfying the demands of your profession more exactly than you have done hitherto will make up for whatever may be defective in your previous conduct.

Although your situation is painful, and there is nothing more distressing than the aridity and dryness of which you complain, it can still be most useful. Such are the ways in which God shows his mercy on those who serve him; they test their faith, and provided that they maintain their trust and submissively accept whatever state he is pleased to set them in, that they offer him the difficulties that go with it, that they believe and confess themselves unworthy of the gifts of grace and consolations he grants or refuses when it pleases him, then they will work at their salvation and obtain from God, by submitting to his will, the help they need to rise to the perfection to which he destines them; these are ways which nature finds disagreeable and adjusts to with difficulty, but they none the less contain infinite blessings.

Thus, my dear sister, one must be neither distressed nor alarmed by such a state of mind. Tell God that you are in his hand, that he should do to you whatever he chooses, that you are content to suffer anything as much and in whatever way he wishes, so long as he supports you in the temptations which come upon you and does not allow them to be strong or violent enough to remove you for one moment from his order and the obedience you owe him. Above all ask him to preserve you from those thoughts of despair and discouragement which the devil normally uses to catch unawares those who are in the frame of mind in which you are.

We will not fail to pray him to give you all the protection you need to love and worship his will.

The religious of whom you speak is, by all the rules, under a delusion, and the one who is supporting her no less so. Every person consecrated to Christ by religious vows, acting by their own spirit, following their own will, is on a path quite the opposite of that on which they should be, quite obviously going astray and following a road which is leading them straight to their ruin. The nuns who claim that her opinions should be accepted and that she should be granted what she wants to prevent her destroying herself are mistaken. They are doing just what is needed to set her on the way to inevitable ruin. You should pity her, my dear sister, you should pray God for her, but to give in to her wishes and desires would be false charity, misplaced kindness. Not only does God not demand it of you, but you would be offending him if you let yourself do it. Farewell, my dear sister, pray God for me and believe that I am yours, I beg you.'

931128   JEAN GERBAIS   28 November 1693
Tour. orig.
Gerbais has received the book of *Maximes* issued without R's agreement. Printer circumvented ban by publishing it as *Instructions*. Asks Gerbais to prevent similar unauthorised publications by showing no one the latest *Relations* [of lives and deaths of monks].

Refers to Muguet's publication of Instructions sur les principaux sujets de la piété et de la morale, *due probably to Maupeou, who had had the* MS *for some years. Cf 931026.*

931130   [JEAN GERBAIS]   30 November 1693
Tour. orig.
Note of thanks for package brought by fr Chanvier [the abbey's factotum].

931207   DUCHESSE DE GUISE   7 December 1693
BN 15172,27, orig.; Gonod 198
In her present ill health she need not hesitate to give up saying the breviary. Mark of a true Christian is to forgive and forget. Suicide of M de Vauguyon.

On the death of his wife, twenty years older than he, in October, Vauguyon shot himself at Versailles on 29 November, after a life of scandal yet protected by royal favour.

931223   JEAN GERBAIS   23 December 1693
A 5172,f.76, orig.
Gerbais is a good friend, but R. does not need apologists.

*940107   BISHOP OF LUÇON [HENRI BARILLON]   7 January 1694
L orig.; P f.788
'Allow me, Mgr, to ask for your holy blessing at the beginning of this year. I have asked Our Lord to renew your zeal and solicitude for the government of the souls committed to your charge, and that he will at the same time give them the necessary docility to profit from the care you take to control their behaviour and make them live like real Christians. We shall also continue to pray God to preserve your health for the edification of the Church and the consolation of those whom you honour with your friendship. I ask you to continue it, and to believe that it is not possible to be with more devotion, affection and respect than I yours' etc.

940108   PIERRE MAUPEOU   8 January 1694
Maupeou, *Vie*, I p. 523
R. 'Quite scandalised' by appearance of *Instructions morales* which he had done everything to prevent.

940128   JEAN GERBAIS   28 January 1694
A 5172,f.86, orig.
Thanks Gerbais for kindness to dom Le Nain.

940211   CLAUDE NICAISE   11 February 1694
BN 9363,f.188, orig.; Gonod 143
R. has heard of a scurrilous pamphlet against him circulating in Dijon, *Gulielmus a Sancta Amore heresiarcha redivivus* . . . and asks for details. Thiers' book in R's defence has been seized at Lyon.

Guillaume de Saint-Amour was a thirteenth century opponent of the Mendicants, condemned for heresy. Thiers published his Apologie de M l'abbé de la T. *at Grenoble in answer to the* Quatre Lettres *of 1692, of Denys de Sainte-Marthe.*

*940222   RM MARIE-LOUISE [BOUTHILLIER]   22 February 1694
TA orig.
'It is true, my dearest sister, that I was much upset by Monsieur Pinette's death, but two things made it less painful for me: first, his great age, which made one look

on him since a long time ago as a dying man; and then the way he prepared to end his days, which leaves no room for doubt that God has granted him the rest enjoyed by his saints.

As for you, my dear sister, let me say that there is nothing which God's law obliges us more strictly to do than to say and do good to those who do us only harm. Christ expressed himself so precisely on that point, by his example, his words, and by that of the apostles, that there is no clearer obligation or one less open to doubt. What should lead us to fulfil it still more is that it is said everywhere in Holy Scripture that God will literally treat us as we have treated others, so that if we want him to show compassion to us who offend him, and have offended him, all the days of our life, we must forgive, and from the heart, those about whom we have cause to complain. Thus there is no excuse, no explanation to be given to a duty as clear as that to reduce its force and extent. We must excite our faith, invoke God's protection, and obtain at any price the grace to discharge it with all necessary fidelity. You must above all be convinced that your profession requires you to obey this precept with a perfection worthy of your calling. We will ask God to give you all the grace you need to that end. I do not doubt that you are profiting by the heavy mortality of which you speak. It should cause two deep impressions on your heart: the first to detach yourself from a life which one may lose at any moment; the other to prepare yourself for eternity by a holy death. Farewell, my dearest sister, remember me before God, and believe that no one could be more yours than I.

I had not heard that Madame de Belin was ill, only that she was indisposed.'

Pinette had died on 29 January. Mme Belin was Mme d'Albon's daughter by her first marriage.

940308   CLAUDE NICAISE   8 March 1694
BN 9363,f.190, orig.

Regrets that Thiers was unable to publish. R. does not lack opportunities for self-denial.

*940324   BISHOP OF LUÇON [HENRI BARILLON]   24 March 1694
L orig., P f,788

'I have received the letter, Mgr, which you did me the honour of writing, and which you are worried about, but as I wrote you one at the same time, I did not want to reply for fear of being importunate, knowing that all your moments are precious and that you have none to lose. I praise God for giving you health amid all your occupations and in the bad climate in which you live, and regard that as the result of quite special protection. You have been busy all winter, Mgr, and spring has hardly appeared when you go back to your usual labours. God is fond of your people to have given them such a shepherd, and one might say that the shepherd is well favoured to have received from his goodness such apostolic sentiments. I do not doubt that you have encountered many difficulties in the arrangements you have made for the subsistence of the poor; whatever efforts have been made in these parts, the poverty has been, and still is, beyond anything one could imagine. If God does not take a hand for the future I do not know what will become of us. We must not tire of hoping from his mercy and entreating his divine providence.

I do not need to tell you, Mgr, how much your person is present to us before him, and there is nothing I commend to him more than your interests. I am with inexpressible fidelity and respect yours etc.

PS My health is a little better than it was, but I still experience much discomfort.

You have Father Thouron in your diocese, preaching in your church. I am sure you will be very pleased with him. He is a man of much merit, who has always enjoyed much esteem and been highly recommended wherever he has been. His principles are very holy, and although he speaks the truth, he is very prudent and sensible, and so does not upset things.'

Jean-Baptiste Touron (or Thouron) became an Oratorian in 1663. A noted preacher, he died in 1725.

940505   CLAUDE NICAISE   5 May 1694
BN 9363,f.192 orig.

R. has received a certificate from lieutenant general in Montélimar attesting truth of facts in R's account of dom Muce's crimes. A second Grenadier in the novitiate.

The second 'Grenadier' was fr Zénon de Montbel, a former captain of Musketeers, who died in 1695 after two years at la T.

940509   JEAN GERBAIS   9 May 1694
A 5172,f.88, orig.

Thanks Gerbais for helping dom Le Nain, whose book [history of the Order] may be of some use despite imperfections.

It was published in nine 12° volumes 1696-97.

*940516   BISHOP OF LUÇON [HENRI BARILLON]   16 May 1694
L orig.; P f.644

'The letter with which your nephew honoured me, Mgr, confirms what you tell me of his feelings towards me. I may certainly feel entitled to claim some share in his friendship, seeing that you have for so long honoured me with yours, and that your brother was disposed, as you know he was, up to his dying moment towards me.

I see, Mgr, that your people have been most fortunate in having you during the time of great need in which the whole of France finds itself. Your charity and solicitude have prevented them succumbing like many others beneath the weight of public poverty. The dispositions for next year promise nothing good; the drought is extraordinary. Two days ago we had five or six hours of rain here which cheered the countryside a little, but that is nothing unless it goes on. God makes it only too plain that he is angry, but the people become no better. We need someone to come between God and men and say like the prophet: *O! mucro Domini usque quo non quiesces* [Jr 47:6]. Righteous people must not cease from raising hearts and hands in the hope that God will allow himself to be touched by the assiduity of prayers and will not be inexorable.

We shall not fail to commend to Our Lord the continuation of your visits, and we shall pray him to bless your labours and preserve your health. I beg you to believe that my attachment to your person is without equal, like the affection and respect with which I am yours etc.

PS I was sure, Mgr, that you would be pleased with Father Touron; he is a man of most christian principles and irreproachable life.'

The nephew must be Paul's son Antoine. On Touron see 940324.

940528   MONSIEUR BLAMPIGNON   28 May 1694
Carp p. 758

R. approves of book by dom Lamy, which has been sent to him [*De la connaissance de soi-même*].

940606   CLAUDE NICAISE   6 June 1694
BN 9363,f.194, orig.

Dom Lamy's new book. Dom Soyrot 'a good fellow but of irregular habits—does not stay long in one place.' Further references to dom Muce and Thiers.

Dom François Lamy had met R. at Mme de Guise's request as a preliminary to R's meeting with his fellow Maurist Mabillon; his book is a vast treatise on monastic life. Soyrot was the former Carmelite of Dijon, who came to la T. in 1679, left after profession to become novice-master at Cîteaux for a while, and was also at Hautefontaine, but eventually came back to la T. where he died in 1720.

*940613   RM MARIE-LOUISE [BOUTHILLIER]   13 June [1694]
TA orig.

'Monsieur Masson, my dearest sister, will tell you our news. I wish he could carry away as much edification from our house as he brought to it. You will learn from him that I am indisposed with rheumatism, which has been more pressing than usual for some days; I hope it will not come to anything. Pray God for me, I beg you, as I do for you all the days of my life. I am yours with all my heart, yours' etc.

*940618   BISHOP OF LUÇON [HENRI BARILLON]   18 June 1694
P f.789

'I have to make you a very humble request, Mgr, for someone who is one of my intimate friends and has a case in the Parlement in your nephew's court, and although you did me the honour of telling me that I had only to address myself to him, I could not bring myself to do so, since I was sure that your recommendation, Mgr, would be much stronger than mine. I should be particularly obliged if you would grant me that favour on this occasion. It is a question of a man being persecuted by powerful people who are treating him unjustly. His name is Monsieur Sabain; be kind enough to send me the letter.

I have nothing new to report from these parts. The poverty is extreme, and the people are suffering to the point of dying; we see some at our gates who are dying and others on the point of expiring. The poor receive little help. I have no doubt that you have given full orders about it in your diocese. I ask you, Mgr, for your holy blessing, and assure you that nothing can equal my attachment and respect for you, or the affection with which I am yours' etc.

On Sabain see 920718.

940622   JEAN GERBAIS   22 June 1694
A 5172,f.90, orig.

General thanks. M Le Nain gives R. hope of seeing Gerbais.

940628   CLAUDE NICAISE   28 June 1694
BN 9363,f.196, orig.

Lamy only speaks in passing of study.

To avoid further controversy on this sensitive issue, the censors (in the person of Blampignon) had sent Lamy's book to R., who disagreed with some of it but fully approved publication.

940718   CLAUDE NICAISE   18 July 1694
BN 9363,f.198, orig.

Thanks to R's intervention Lamy was able to publish his book, and admits as much, despite false rumours. Nicaise has sent R. a hostile epigram: 'Nothing is so profitable to me as the evil said about me'.

R's estimate of his part in ensuring publication for Lamy may be sincere, but does not correspond with the known facts.

*940829 MARÉCHAL DE BELLEFONDS   29 August 1694
BN na 12959,f.181 (copy made by Lévêque from orig. in private hands).
TC II/193

'I am deeply sorry, Mgr, to be deprived of the honour of seeing you this year, but I know only too well from all you are good enough to write to me that inability alone prevents you from making the journey. However, the solitude in which you would have been in this place would have contributed not a little to confirm you in the feelings you have.

God visits you in many ways, Mgr, and it may be that he is leading you in the way of privation. To that he joins, in truth, very special grace, namely, your complete resignation to his will. It is clear that if the outward man in you is growing weaker, the inner man is recovering a quite new force and vigour, and whatever you may think, God's protection must be very great for you to keep as much peace of mind as you seem to have in a situation so likely to take it away. But however faithfully you try to conform to his designs, you will inevitably find cause for self-reproach arising, for whatever one does, one never gives full measure and always does less than one should. Indeed, if it ever happened that one felt guilty of nothing, one would have to say like the apostle, I see nothing to criticise in myself, but that does not mean that I am righteous; *Nihil mihi conscius sed non in hoc justificatus sum* [1 Co 4:4].

Your comfort, Mgr, in the reasons which you might think you have to afflict yourself is to consider and tell yourself often, as you no doubt do, that none of the things which you might desire for the relief of your woes has any certain consistency. Nothing is so fragile as health, and the other things which the world is able to give us are not any more reliable. Those on which one counts most escape when one is least thinking of them; everything, looking at it properly, is in continual decay. The only happiness one can enjoy here on earth is knowing that better things await us, hoping for them from God's goodness and striving to become worthy of it by constantly sacrificing to him all those things which pass away and attaching no more importance to them than if they had already passed away.

There is nothing under the sun, Mgr, which does not preach these truths to us which the spirit of God teaches and which does not say to us in the prophet's words: Children of men, how long will you love vain things and seek those whose beauty is only false and apparent? *Ut quid diligistis vanitates et quaeritis mendacium* [Ps 4:3]? Life, affairs, fortune, situation in the world confirms this great lesson, and it is an inexpressible misfortune to know it at a time when it is generally not known and not to make holy use of it.

You must be persuaded, Mgr, that God will not withdraw the hand he stretched out to you, that he will not refuse you the protection which he has given you up till now when you most need it, that he will cover you against this crowd of enemies surrounding you, and that he will make you superior to all their efforts and ensure that their wickedness, however lively, will be unable to harm you.

The course that you are taking of wishing for nothing, asking for nothing, and submitting entirely to the dispositions of divine providence, will bring on you countless blessings, for nothing more excites and powerfully presses God's mercy than to abandon oneself to it without qualification and reservation. In a word, Mgr, follow the feelings and lights that God has given you and you cannot go wrong.

We shall not fail to recommend to Our Lord as much as we can your person and all that concerns you in time and in eternity. I beg you most humbly to believe that no one could be more inviolably devoted or more deeply respectful than I, yours' etc.

940830 MONSIEUR BAZIN, CURÉ SAINT-HILAIRE, PARIS   30 August 1694
A 5172,f.98, orig.

Note of thanks for his visit.

940830a MONSIEUR JOLL[A]IN,   30 August 1694
SUPÉRIEUR DU RÉFUGE, PARIS
A 5172,f.100, orig.

Regards to him and his brother. PS about Mlle Guignard, who should stay where she is [cf 930812].

940830b [JEAN GERBAIS]   30 August 1694
A 5172,f.62, orig.

Asks Gerbais to tell the Abbot of Cîteaux that R. allows meat broth to the sick when required, as dom Arsène can confirm. 'I would not want our brothers to live softly or impenitently, but I would also not wish to withold relief they may need'. Confirms sending a monk to help Berrier at Perrecy.

Dom Arsène de La Croix was the brother of the Abbot of Cîteaux's secretary. Berrier had resigned all his benefices except the benedictine priory of Perrecy (dioc. Autun)in 1690, and he began to reform this small independent house with the aid of dom Jacques de La Cour (later Abbot of la T.), the monk referred to here. It remains wholly mysterious why a Cistercian was sent to a house of another order.

*940830c BISHOP OF LUÇON [HENRI BARILLON]   30 August 1694
P f.790

'My respect for your occupations, Mgr, prevents me from writing as often as I should wish. It is an honour and consolation of which I deprive myself against my inclinations, and I content myself with thinking about you before Our Lord as often as possible.

As for my health, Mgr, since you are kind enough to want to know news of it, I can say that it is sometimes good and sometimes bad, and that at best I am never fully well. The incision made last year in my left arm has still not closed up, and although it does not cause me great pain, I still feel it. At my age, and with the life we lead, it would be deceiving oneself to hope that my strength will come back. It suffices that I should retain enough to discharge my exercises and maintain the calling in which God has been pleased to put me.

I sympathise more than I can say, Mgr, in your loss of poor Monsieur Louis; he was so attached to your person that he could hardly have failed to be a help to you. He was very able. There are few people like that; from the way he seemed to me to take everything that affected you, I do not doubt that you were able to have every confidence in him. God disposes of all things as he pleases, and the only way to remain in serenity and peace is to love being dependent on him and live in continual resignation. I am sure that such sentiments are prominent in your heart. We shall not fail to commend to Our Lord your health and your occupations. I hope that your part of the world is not attacked by the contagious illnesses which are prevalent here, so that you should not be exposed to them in the course of your visits. Keep for me, Mgr, all the friendship with which you have so long honoured me, and rest assured, I beg you, that nothing can equal the affection and respect with which I am yours' etc.

Louis died on 11 August. He had from the start been one of Barillon's closest collaborators and had edited the diocesan conferences for publication.

940900   MADAME LA MARÉCHALE D'HUMIÈRES   [September 1694]
TC II/212

Condolences on death of her husband.

Louis de Crevant, duc and (1668)maréchal d'Humières, born in 1628, had died on 31 August. He had accompanied the duc d'Orléans on his visit to la T. just a year earlier.

940902   CLAUDE NICAISE   2 September 1694
BN 9363,f.200, orig.; Gonod 145

'So there at last M. Arnauld is dead. When he had run his course as far as he could, it had to come to an end. Whatever may be said about it, that means the end of a lot of questions; his erudition and authority carried much weight for his party. Happy he who has no other than that of Christ.'

This comment, eleven lines out of three pages on other matters, aroused the Jansenists to fury, above all because of the reference to 'party' and what they took to be R's studied dismissive attitude to their hero, who had died in exile in Brussels on 8 August. Quesnel in particular wrote vehement letters, one of twenty pages, expressing his outrage. Nicaise took it on himself to show the letter to equally indiscreet friends, and must be held responsible for betraying R's confidence.

940912   JEAN GERBAIS   12 September 1694
A 5172,f.103 orig.

Edifying death of Fieubet. Calumnies continue against R. but the King ordered Père de la Chaise [his Jesuit confessor] to send R. a warm letter. He is always available to his monks, and in urgent cases gives appointments. Use of Maisne as secretary justified. R. dictates only during hours of manual labour and is constantly interrupted by monks wanting to talk to him. True that Maisne went with him to les Clairets, as well as another monk, but only to advise the abbess on buildings, and did not enter the enclosure. R. wishes that Abbot of Cîteaux would himself come on a visit to scotch such rumours.

Fieubet had just died at Grosbois a few weeks after a final visit to la T. Growing resentment of Maisne's power is evident in the charge that, like any other secretary, he tried to protect R. from what he judged to be importunate callers, mostly, of course, monks. The choice of a secular in such a key post was widely criticised, and his company at les Clairets was evidently open to misinterpretation. This letter was, as usual, in Maisne's hand (See 890113a).

*941011   BISHOP OF LUÇON [HENRI BARILLON]   11 October 1694
P f.648

'I saw Father Thouron two days ago, Mgr, and he told me all your news in detail and at length. I confess that it gave me inexpressible joy to hear him confirm the ideas I had conceived of your conduct, and what he saw with his own eyes. Such a thing is encountered only in pastors sent out by God's hand into the field of his Church and in whom he has put all the qualities necessary to discharge with success and blessing the chief and most exalted of all functions. This good father never ends when he goes into the detail of what you are doing for the sanctification of your people; your vigilance, your wisdom, your charity, your gentleness and firmness all together can only be combined to the degree that they are in you through a quite special protection of God. I have praised him and will praise him all my life for all the signs of his mercy that he has given you, and I shall pray him as much as I am able to increase more and more the gifts of grace he has bestowed on you and poured into your heart as on to ground of infinite fertility and abundance. To all that he added that God gave you health to discharge all your duties, and that it held up despite your continual cares and solicitude. Would to God that la Trappe were near Luçon, but he has disposed otherwise. For the rest, Mgr, Father Thouron did not forget to tell me all your kind feelings towards me and the pleasure you took in expressing them. I was fully convinced, and indeed have too many pieces of clear evidence to be able to doubt it. I can assure you that my response is the most real gratitude possible, and on that score God has given me feelings to which nothing could be added. I have no words, Mgr, to tell you how much I honour you, but I beg you to believe that there is no equal to the attachment, affection, and respect with which I am yours etc.

PS Allow me to tell you that there is a young boy in these parts of only eight or nine who expounds Scripture, and the *Imitation of Christ* and has all the look and manners of an ecclesiastic, whom one cannot see without edification. They would like, if possible, to put him in your seminary, because they are convinced that he would have an education there which would fully match all the grace Our Lord has given him. I do not know whether the proposal I am making is reasonable or not; he is the nephew of a curé who gives all he has to the poor of the parish, so the affair would be one of pure charity.'

On Thouron, see 940324. Unfortunately no more is known of the pious child.

941014   RP CHARTONNET, SAINTE-GENEVIÈVE   14 October 1694
Reims, Archives municipales, Tarbé, XV,f.139, orig.

Delighted to hear of successful outcome of recent General Chapter of Sainte-Geneviève. Warm praise of dom Dorothée.

Dorothée de l'Epine was a former Canon Regular from Paris, professed in April 1694, died 1704, whom Chartonnet, as Visitor of his congregation, would have known. This seems to be the last extant signature of R., who lost the use of his hand through acute rheumatism at this time (according to Quesnel, after penning unworthy words on Arnauld; a good story, but not quite true.)

*941025   BISHOP OF LUÇON [HENRI BARILLON]   25 October 1694
L orig.; P f.790

'I cannot dispense myself, Mgr, from expressing my sympathy in the grief which I am sure you feel at your recent loss of poor Madame de Barillon. I know how you have spoken to me about her; and I know too that a heart made like yours loves as it should love. Attached as she was to her family, her preservation can only have been most useful and necessary to them. God has disposed of her as it pleased him, he is the master and our only wish is to adore his will and submit to it.

I have learned the news this moment. The curé of Saint-Jacques told me. We shall not fail to pray God for her. There is every reason to believe from the life she led that he has judged her with mercy. I do not need to tell you what I feel on this occasion, for I am sure that you do me justice, Mgr, and are fully convinced of my attachment to your person and all that affects you. I am with all possible fidelity and respect yours etc.

PS I ask your pardon, Mgr, for not signing this letter. I have an inflammation of the right hand which prevents me.'

Mme de Barillon was Paul's widow; she died on 16 October. Marcel, curé of Saint-Jacques, was the confidant of the whole family.

941110   COMTE DU CHARMEL   10 November 1694
TD E
Death of fr Palémon de Santena [9 November].

*941117   RM MARIE-LOUISE [BOUTHILLIER]   17 November [1694]
TA orig.

'I have received your letter, my dear sister, through Monsieur de Virville, but I did not see him, being obliged by the worsening of my usual ailments to withdraw to the infirmary. I have had a new inflammation on my right hand which prevents me from using it; I hope it will not come to anything.

Monsieur l'abbé Le Boulanger is most kind and friendly, and gives evidence of it at every occasion. I confess that no one could appreciate it more than I do. You can use the way he gave you to give me news of yourself, and I will use the same channel to answer.

I do not doubt, my dear sister, that your intention of belonging to God increases day by day. When you have attained it as much as you desire, all your troubles will fade away like smoke, and as he will be absolute master of your heart, he will inspire in it the impulses he chooses and strengthen you in that holy peace which is the consolation of those who belong to him and who, by a special grace, know him alone and have taken him for their sole portion. Farewell, my dear sister, pray for me and believe that I am with all possible affection yours.

PS We will not fail to offer our prayers to God for all the persons whom you commend to us.'

*941125   MARÉCHAL DE BELLEFONDS   25 November 16[94]
BN na 12959,f.184, (copy made from orig. in private hands by Lévêque); TC I/91

'It would have been a great consolation to us, Mgr, if your engagements had allowed you to pass by our desert as you had intended, but I see that you do not do all you would like and that God does not consult your inclinations in the way he treats you. The main thing is that you remember solitude in the midst of the world and that your occupations there, which are so opposed to solitude, do not efface it from either your memory or your heart. Those who have tasted the benefits and advantages of retreat and have been obliged to leave it though the events of life, should constantly have on their lips Job's words: *Quis mihi tribuat sim juxta menses pristinos* . . . [Jb 29:2], for whatever one does to preserve that innocence and prevent it being impaired by the impurity of the world, so many things escape which one can almost not refuse to prescribed occasions and the necessity of contact, that one has only too much cause to regret times past and reproach oneself severely; especially when one is convinced, as you doubtless are, that one owes everything to God, and that he cannot fail to judge what contributes neither to his glory nor to the sanctification of souls. Although one must follow and give in to orders and remain in the situation in which he appears to want us, yet when it is accompanied by honour, glory, distinction, and other attractions of fortune, that is, when it is surrounded with snares and dangers, one is scarcely mistaken in desiring and seeking ways out, in order to serve God in the leisure and holy security found only away from the movement and agitation of creatures. Such a feeling, Mgr, should put us on our guard and make us observe every step with special care, so that in the various things and affairs one is obliged to deal with one never, if possible, loses from sight the one whom one would never for anything in the world wish to displease, for in truth our ways are only straight so long as we have him before our eyes, and once one goes off it there is nothing left but disorder and confusion. I am sure that you acquit yourself of all the cares and obligations with which you are charged with such purity and detachment, and keep the scales so balanced and even that while giving to men what you cannot dispense yourself from giving them, you make yourself worthy of obtaining from God the grace for which you hope, that is, to finish your course in his peace and charity, whatever the place and station in which it may please the disposition of his providence to place you. His mercy knows no limits, and in every place his almighty hand sustains and protects those who have the good fortune to be his. You are so present to us before God, Mgr, that we do not fail to offer him your person, and to ask him insistently not to tire of pouring his blessings upon you and making your house as regular and Christian as you wish it to be. That, Mgr, is the only means I have of showing you with how much devotion and respect I am yours' etc.

Bellefonds died on 5 December 1694.

941202   JEAN GERBAIS   2 December 1694
A 5172,f.108, orig.

Death of M Talon. R. is not well.

Jean Talon, born 1625, had been an able administrator in Canada.

941216   CLAUDE NICAISE   16 December 1694
BN 9363,f.204, orig.; Gonod 146

Quesnel would do well to take a rest: 'he is a man of merit who combines great wisdom and great learning'.

Quesnel had begun a protest campaign against R's supposed disrespect at Arnauld's death. (See 940902).

941218   CLAUDE NICAISE   18 December 1694
BN 9363,f.202, orig.; Gonod 147

R. has received anonymous threats for what he allegedly said about Arnauld. Asks Nicaise to divulge just what he wrote.

941220 JEAN GERBAIS   20 December 1694
A 5172,f.110, orig.

Rumours of dissension at la T. prompted R. to send a renewal of vows of the whole community to the Abbot of Cîteaux, who replied kindly and with expressions of confidence in R.

Mary II of England dies.   28 December 1694

950103 JEAN GERBAIS   3 January 1695
A 5172,f.116, orig.

Thanks Gerbais for his good offices at Cîteaux. Du Charmel has been. All is peaceful at la T.

*950103a BISHOP OF LUÇON [HENRI BARILLON]   3 January 1695
L orig.; P f.791

'I pray God, Mgr, to give you a happy year and to add many more like it. That is no compliment I am paying, but I beg you to believe that I am speaking with all my heart. I do not doubt that your virtue increases with your days, and that your chief care is to progress in the ways traced out for you by God. I do not doubt, I say, that he will increase your zeal and vigilance for the sanctification of the people whom he has given into your charge. I shall continue to pray him, and all my brethren with me, that he heaps blessings on you and gives you grace to discharge your ministry in so holy and faithful a manner that you can say like the Apostle *fidem servavi, cursum consommavi* [2 Tm 4:7]. Allow me too to ask for the help of your prayers and blessing, while I assure you that nothing could be added to the attachment, affection and respect with which I am yours etc.

PS Excuse me for not signing. The inflammation of the hand whch I told you about still prevents me.'

950112 CLAUDE NICAISE   12 January 1695
BN 9363,f.205, orig.; Gonod 148

Quesnel has written a twenty-page letter about R's alleged condemnation of Arnauld. R. sad and amazed.

950120 JEAN GERBAIS   20 January 1695
Reims, Archives municipales, Tarbé, XV,f.140, orig.

Association signed by Zozime, prior, Pierre [Le Nain], sub-prior, and seven others. Sent on 31 March [See 950331].

950130 CLAUDE NICAISE   30 January 1695
BN 9363,f.207, orig.; Gonod 149

R. finds the general excitement about Arnauld incredible: 'I know that he lived and died in the communion of the Church; I believe God has shown him mercy.'

*950200 RM MARIE-LOUISE [BOUTHILLIER]   [February 1695?]
TA orig.

'I am moved more than I can say, my dear sister, by your concern for me in my illness. The troublesome cough which I had for nearly five months is at present a little less, but the pain in my hand, which is the main one and affects me continually, is getting worse instead of better. So I can tell you frankly that I have need of your prayers much more for the comfort and support of my soul than for my cure and restoration to health, which seems most unlikely. Ask God, my dear sister, to destroy in me all will but his, to give me a patience worthy of my calling and of all the signs I constantly receive of his mercy, for you know that there is nothing on which he looks with more indignation than ungrateful souls. I pray God, my dear sister, to strengthen you more and more in the frame of mind in which he wants you to be, and not to allow temptations or troubles to arise in your heart, to give you at the same time the grace you need to make holy use of it, that is, it must contribute to your sanctification, bring you forward in his ways, and make you better and holier.

One of our religious has just died, after spending five years with us in what one might call a blameless manner. He ended his race with an end as happy as could be, since he retained to his last gasp the most unfavourable opinion of himself possible, and at the same time entire confidence in Christ's mercy. I commend him to your prayers and those of all your holy community.

I am with all possible affection and esteem yours etc.

PS I find it difficult, my dear sister, to let you write to me on behalf of the ecclesiastic of whom you speak, because I hardly see anyone and sometimes spend days without being able to speak to anyone at all.'

Although this letter is undated, it must have been written before R's resignation in May 1695, because the signature (in Maisne's hand) refers to him as 'abbot' and the religious whose death is mentioned can only be Basile Anzoux, who died in February 1695, having been professed in September 1689.

*950216 BISHOP OF LUÇON [HENRI BARILLON]   16 February 1695
L orig.; P f.649

'I am delighted, Mgr, that you have arrived in Paris in perfect health. I hope that the business that brought you there will have a successful conclusion and turn out to your consolation. I am sure you believe that no one takes more interest in what concerns you than I, for indeed I am almost infinitely sensitive on that score.

You give me, Mgr, a hope which will occupy all my feelings until I see its effect and fulfilment, and I pray God that nothing prevents the execution of what you are kind enough to promise me. That joy is all the more dear to me because it is most likely it will be the last time, for although my health is not as desperate as has been made out, and believed, in the world, yet I am advanced in years and with a delicate constitution, and obliged moreover to live without many of the things which might contribute to preserving life. I assure you, Mgr, that when I consider the world as it is I feel joy at the thought that I shall soon be in a position to leave it. Among men there is no friendship, no sincerity. Even those on whom one thought one had some reason to rely fail us as much as others, and if one withheld some outer signs, once the veil covering them is drawn aside, instead of the reality one imagined, one would see only illusions. I will wait until I have the honour of seeing you to tell you many things. Meanwhile continue your usual kindness towards me and rest assured, I beg you, that nothing can equal the tender affection, respect and longstanding fidelity with which I am and will remain to my last breath yours' etc.

Barillon had arrived in Paris on 29 January to attend to family business.

950310   JEAN GERBAIS   10 March 1695
A 5172,f.118, orig.

M. Lefranc, an advocate in Parlement and friend of R., is bringing *Relation* of fr Palémon [de Santena] for Gerbais' approval.

*950317   BISHOP OF LUÇON [HENRI BARILLON]   17 March 1695
L orig.; P f.791

'Permit me, Mgr, a humble request, in case you should know the Bishop of Boulogne, who is at present in Paris. An ecclesiastic of his diocese who was curé at a big parish in a place called Saint-Pol has come to our monastery to retire and consecrate his life to the service of Christ. He told us that people had stirred up a lot of trouble for him, and that a sentence had even been passed against him which banished and drove him from his home and obliged him to give up his benefice. He claims that all these accusations were fabricated by people stirred up by his very judges, and that he is completely innocent. He has shown us a declaration from an unmarried woman, clearing him on her deathbed of a crime which he was said to have committed with her, and of which she had herself accused him. He shows a great desire to do penance, although he is not guilty, from what he maintains, of the things of which he was accused. He has an *exeat* from the Bishop of Boulogne from which it seems that he has incurred every kind of censure. If nothing prevents you, Mgr, from informing yourself of the truth of the matter, and you were good enough to do so, I should be extremely obliged. I ask for pardon for taking the liberty, but I am sure you will forgive me. I still hope to have the honour and joy of seeing you and assuring you once more in my life tht it is not possible to be with more inviolable attachment or more tender and profound respect yours' etc.

The priest in question was Nicolas Beugnet, professed as dom Abraham in April 1696. Ordained at about 22, he was involved in scandal at St-Pol and dismissed. In Paris he met a charitable lady who sent him to la T. According to the Relation *of his death, he tried at first to justify himself, but was then converted to penitence and practised austerities which frightened even the other monks. He became reconciled with his bishop, and died an edifying death in 1698, aged about sixty. Claude Le Tonnelier de Bréteuil was Bp of Boulogne 1681-98.*

950320 CLAUDE NICAISE 20 March 1695
BN 9363,f.209, orig.; Gonod 150
Nicaise is in poor health.

950331 JEAN GERBAIS 31 March 1695
A 5172,f.124, orig.
Sends Association, but could not sign it.

See 950120. The delay was presumably due to his hope that he might be able to sign it later.

950411 JEAN GERBAIS 11 April 1695
A 5172,f.126, orig.
Calumnies still abroad.

950411a CLAUDE NICAISE 11 April 1695
BN 9363,f.211, orig.; Gonod 151
R. can no longer sign.

950430 JEAN GERBAIS 30 April 1695
A 5172,f.128, orig.
Thanks him for looking after *Relation* of Santena. Dom Le Nain nearly died following a haemorrhage but is recovering.

950512 JEAN GERBAIS 12 May 1695
A 5172,f.130, orig.
Dom Le Nain's book received; he will correct it when well enough.

Rancé offers his resignation to the King, and requests 30 May 1695
the appointment of dom Zozime Foisil as successor.

950530 LOUIS XIV 30 May 1695
Dubois II/450

Letter of resignation, requesting permission to propose a successor.

When the King originally granted R. permission to become regular instead of commendatory abbot, it was clearly understood that on R's death or resignation la T. would return to commend, hence the unusual procedure for ensuring succession. In 1677 R. had already obtained a papal brief authorising the religious of la T. to elect their own prior when the abbey returned to commend (usually the Strict Observance nominated priors at meetings of superiors) but not even the Pope could prevent the commend system operating in France and only R's personal prestige and direct appeal to the King could alter the usual course of events.

950600 DOM JEAN MABILLON, OSB [after May 1695]
BN 19656,f.155, orig.

R. has resigned. Compliments.

*950605 BISHOP OF LUÇON [HENRI BARILLON] 5 June 1695
L orig.; P f.792

'I shall await, Mgr, as one of the greatest consolations that could come to me the honour you plan to do us, and if God preserves me until then, it will be the most extreme joy to receive your blessing, and to be able once more to assure you that of all the people in the world you are the one I have most tenderly honoured, and for whom I have the most inviolable attachment and respect. I confess that it has been no small satisfaction to have found in you, Mgr, such faithful and constant friendship. God alone knows how much I am and have always been yours' etc.

950612 LOUIS XIV [12] June 1695
Dubois II/452

Respectful thanks to King for allowing R. to choose a successor as regular abbot.

950612 JEAN GERBAIS 12 June 1695
A 5172,f.132, orig.

First copies of *Relation* of Santena received. Five incisions in right hand have neither cured it nor relieved pain.

The King approves Rancé's resignation and choice of successor   20 June 1695

950630   JEAN GERBAIS   30 June 1695
A 5172,f.136, orig.
The King's approval of R's resignation and choice of successor shows how wrong people were to imagine that la T. would go to the grave with R.

950705   PIERRE MAUPEOU   5 July 1695
Maupeou, *Vie*, II p. 216
The King's kindness in accepting nomination of Zozime.

950711   CLAUDE NICAISE   11 July 1695
BN 9363,f.213, orig.; Gonod 152
R. a little better. King has granted his choice of successor.

950714   JEAN GERBAIS   14 July 1695
A 5172,f.140, orig.
R. looks forward to seeing Gerbais.

950725   JAMES II   [25 July] 1695
W orig.; *SP* p. 104
PS only survives. Encloses papers requested.

950812   JEAN GERBAIS   12 August 1695
A 5172,f.142, orig.
Delighted at Gerbais' visit [22 July]. Death of Abp of Paris [Harlay]. Tillemont [dom Le Nain's brother] has written to dissociate himself from Quesnel's attack.

*950818   BISHOP OF LUÇON [HENRI BARILLON]   18 August 1695
L orig.; P f.792

'It is for us, Mgr, to express our gratitude for all the kindness shown to us on your last visit to our desert. I very humbly beg you to believe that I keep a memory of it which will never be erased. As for my health, it is still the same, I am no worse than when you saw me, but as to genuine recovery, I do not yet see any. I still feel the same pain and am still unable to use my hand.
    The death of the Archbishop of Paris has caused me much sorrow. Ours, as you

know, Mgr, was a friendship going back more than fifty years. God acts when he pleases as sovereign master, and whatever he does, we must worship his conduct and submit. You know what obligations I had to him. Do not cease loving me, Mgr, however unworthy I may be. I beg you very humbly to believe that no one in the world could be with more gratitude, attachment and respect than I yours etc.

PS Monsieur de Saint-Louis and Monsieur Maisne assure you of their profound respects.'

François Harlay, Abp of Paris, died on 6 August. He was a close friend of R's youth. Barillon had called at la T. in June or July on his way to Paris.

*951005   BISHOP OF LUÇON [HENRI BARILLON]   5 October 1695
L orig.; P f.792

'I am most sorry, Mgr, that you should be going back without concluding the affair for which your charity [made] you go away. Is it possible that someone who ought to have [? no interests but] yours has had his own on such an occasion as this. [? God], Mgr, will take account of the trouble you have taken and the efforts you have made; all things in the world are uncertain, and often fail just where we think they should succeed. There you are, Mgr, in your diocese, and for a long time, unless I am mistaken, continuing as you have so happily begun to establish and confirm your people in the service and fear of God, that is, to procure their sanctification, and here I am at la Trappe, awaiting the day and the hour, which cannot be far off, when I hope that God will judge me, not in the wrath which I have so justly drawn on my head by my bad conduct, but in his mercy, in which my realisation of my own unworthiness does not prevent me from having absolute confidence. I have great hopes in the aid of your prayers, and ask for them, Mgr, with all my heart. I have some right to expect them, knowing as I do that you are good enough to count for something my inviolable attachment to your person, and the profound respect with which I am yours' etc.

Barillon finally left Paris on 13 October. His brother-in-law, the comte de Chastellux, had died in July and it may be that disputes over the inheritance lay behind R's opening remarks.

951018   JEAN GERBAIS   18 October 1695
A 5172,f.148, orig.

Denies telling Berrier to accept RP Benoît, already rejected by R. on grounds of age. At present no vacancy among lay brothers, but the young man would learn stocking-weaving while waiting and would then be useful.

Benoît had apparently left the Camaldolese at Grosbois to try a vocation elsewhere; several of his confrères were doing the same, as other correspondents of Gerbais reveal.

951103   JEAN GERBAIS   3 November 1695
A 5172,f.153, orig.

Several people, including a converted Protestant, have pressed R. to publish *Relations*, and he now sends twenty. [i.e. *Relations* of twenty monks]

This must be the edition of 1696.

951121   JEAN GERBAIS   21 November 1695
A 5172,f.157, orig.

R. sends copy of letter from M de Laquerre of ND-des-Anges in Provence, reporting the edifying effect of hearing the *Relations* of Santena and pressing him to publish more.

Laquerre's letter is A 5172,f.152.

951126   JEAN GERBAIS   26 November 1695
A 5172,f.159, orig.

Proposes ten *Relations* for each of two volumes. Benoît has now been professed at Perrecy.

951127   JAMES II   27 November 1695
W orig; *SP* p. 109

R. would write more often but for his respect for James, who enjoys peace despite all.

951203   DOM ANDRÉ JANNEL, osb   3 December 1695
U 6094 orig.

Had hoped to see him. Details of M Lyon, who will spend the rest of his life in a hermitage two or three hundred yards from la T., and will attend Mass daily. He has found reliable people to look after his children.

On Jannel see 750900. Lyon, a rich Parisian tradesman, decided on losing his wife to embark on a religious life. Gourdan was mainly responsible for sending him to la T., where he took the name Théonas, but lived without vows, as described, for thirty-six years.

951214   JEAN GERBAIS   14 December 1695
A 5172,f.155, orig.

If Gerbais agrees, R. will ask the Chancellor [Boucherat] to send *Relations* to him for approval. [Gerbais was a censor.]

The Bulls approving Rancé's resignation 16 December 1695
and dom Zozime as abbot arrive

951218   JEAN GERBAIS   18 December 1695
A 5172,f.161, orig.
Gerbais ill with rheumatism. R. accepts his suggestion of changing *Relations* into *Instructions* [as had already been done in the case of dom Muce].

Dom Zozime Foisil takes possession   28 December1695
as abbot of La Trappe

*960103   BISHOP OF LUÇON [HENRI BARILLON]   3 January 1696
L orig.; P f.654

'I had already learned, Mgr, of the death of poor abbé Pic[quet]. At the same time I had felt sorry about the fate of the benefice which falls vacant by his death, since I can well imagine that it will fall into the hands of men who will not resemble him. You took all possible steps to prevent that happening; we must have every hope, Mgr, in God's goodness and the King's piety. It is true that I should be most distressed if, having been preserved for so long from the ill fortune to which benefices are exposed which are in the possession of worldly-minded people, it were to be abandoned by God like so many others.

My successor's Bulls have arrived. The Pope granted them free of charge. Cardinal de Janson has taken every possible care of them and through his diligence has succeeded. What you have been told is not true; the 200 *livres* mentioned are not for him, it is a due established long ago, called *propina*. However the rumour has still been spread without any grounds.

What you do me the honour of saying about my resignation absolutely strengthens my resolve. My successor has taken possession, but will only be blessed in a month's time, as the Bishop of Séez is not in these parts. I am no more involved in the government of the house, and have handed over its conduct entirely to him. However, I am not yet as withdrawn as I should like, because monks come to see me and so far I have not been able to refuse to see them, but I hope that God will make mercy complete and give me time to think about myself after thinking about others, although I did so in a most unworthy manner, far short of my duties.

I wish you, Mgr, a renewal of grace in this new year and pray God to heap blessings on you, including the prolongation of your days, of which you make such holy use. I beg you to believe that you are and will be very much present before him until my last breath, and I regard that as one of the chief duties of my life. I hope also that you will be good enough to remember me before him. I humbly beg you to believe that no one could be with more tender devotion and respect than I yours etc.

PS There is nowhere in the world, Mgr, where you are more honoured than here. Monsieur de Saint-Louis and Monsieur Maisne appreciate your kindness in remembering them. They will not fail to do as you wish, although they think they are most unworthy to be heeded by God. As for the Abbot, he has the honour of writing to you himself and assuring you of his profound respect for you.'

Picquet had been Barillon's successor at R's former priory of Boulogne. Zozime Foisil was appointed to succeed R. in May 1695 and took possession on 28 December. Cardinal de Forbin-Janson, Bp of Beauvais, was French ambassador to Rome 1690–97. Zozime wrote a respectful letter to Barillon on 5 January and the original is at Luçon.

960105 JEAN GERBAIS 5 January 1696
A 5172,f.165, orig.

R. will do what he can with *Relations*; 'people are asking if la T. has become dumb.' Reports edifying effect of *Relation* of dom Muce on monk who after reading it gave up idea of asking to be secularised.

960119 CLAUDE NICAISE 19 January 1696
BN 9363,f.214, orig.; Gonod 153

The new abbot [Zozime] has taken possession. Thiers very ill at Vibraie. [He recovered and lived on till 1703.]

960124 MONSIEUR BOSQUILLON 24 January 1696
Le Nain, *Vie* (1719) II p. 602

Warm thanks for Bosquillon's account of la T.

960313 CLAUDE NICAISE 13 March 1696
BN 9363,f.215, orig. Gonod 154

Death of Zozime [aged 46]. 'So long as God is satisfied with me, the approval of men is a matter of total indifference to me.'

Dom Zozime died suddenly on 3 March and was succeeded by dom Armand-François Gervaise; the former Carmelite.

960317 JEAN GERBAIS 17 March 1696
A 5172,f.167, orig.

'God still leaves me in the world because I have not done penance and he wants to give me time to do so.' Death of Zozime and nomination of successor.

*960404 BISHOP OF LUÇON [HENRI BARILLON]   4 April [1696]
P f.659

'It is true, Mgr, that the loss of the man I had chosen as my successor affected me more than I can say. God had given him great spiritual gifts to acquit himself of his task most successfully. One badly needs to turn to God on such occasions, for there alone can one find consolation. The King has been good enough to grant me a second time the religious I nominated to succeed the one who has died. The indisposition of which you speak, Mgr, causes me sorrow and anxiety. I thought you had completely got rid of it. We shall not fail, each and every one of us, to ask God to give you relief in the troubles which he allows to befall you, and to maintain your health, which you use in so holy and edifying a manner. So exemplary a life as yours, Mgr, ought not to end. I cannot say how much I honour you, but it is indeed not possible to add to the sincere, tender and profound respect with which I am yours' etc.,

The nomination of dom Armand-Françoise Gervaise was approved on 29 March.

960512   CLAUDE NICAISE   12 May 1696
BN 9363,f.216, orig.; Gonod 155

The new abbot [Gervaise] is 'a man with all the necessary good qualities and who, from what it seems, will worthily acquit himself'.

960522   MONSIEUR DE LAQUERRE   22 May 1696
Marseille, Bibliothèque Municipale, 1276

On Arnauld's death; some lines extracted from R's letter have been quoted as false evidence of his intention to give offence.

960614   JEAN GERBAIS   14 June 1696
A 5172,f.171, orig.

R. wanted to follow Gerbais' advice about *Relations*, but people will not leave him alone.

960700   RELIGIEUSE   [after June 1696]
TC II/15

King and Queen of England have visited. James detached from worldly things; 'nature has given way to peace'.

Queen Mary of Modena first visited in June 1696.

960715 CLAUDE NICAISE   15 July 1696
BN 9363,f.218, orig.; Gonod 156
Barbarigo has spoken well of R. to Nicaise.

960922 JEAN GERBAIS   22 September 1696
A 5172,f.175, orig.
R. will accept Gerbais' advice and give no preface to *Relations*. People keep pressing him to publish them to help others prepare for death.

961004 JAMES II   4 October 1696
W orig.; *SP* p. 120
James must abandon himself to God.

*961011 BISHOP OF LUÇON [HENRI BARILLON]   11 October 1696
L orig.; P f.656
'If you have been so long, Mgr, without news of us, it is because I am afraid of interrupting your occupations, for as regards the retreat in which I am, I have never had the intention of extending it to you, and it will always be a great comfort to keep up some contact with you. Besides, allow me to tell you, Mgr, that Monsieur de Barillon, your nephew, has paid me the honour of a visit. No one could be more pleased with him than I. He is not as lively as his father, but as regards intelligence, wisdom, and sense, he has all that one could have. All he says is correct, precise, and agreeably expressed. I found in him moreover moral principles which surprised me, in a word, I observed in him all the qualities of a complete *honnête homme*. We revived all my old friendship with his father. There, Mgr, you have a sincere declaration of my views concerning your nephew. I pray God to pour all kinds of blessing upon him. I have promised to write to him at least every three months, if God still keeps me alive.

I have heard, Mgr, of the accident which occurred in your house. I praised God that you were not there, for surely someone would have been bound to be hurt by such a sudden and rapid collapse. Providence is wonderful; it must be agreed that God takes care to protect men and keep them from countless ills which would befall them if he did not take care to save them. I offer you to him, Mgr, all the days of my life, I pray him not to cease strengthening the zeal he has given you for his glory, the edification of his church, and the salvation of the people committed to your charge and leadership.

Never tire of loving me, Mgr, however unworthy I may be, and rest assured, I beg you, that no one could add to the sincerity, affection and respect with which I am yours etc.

PS Allow me to tell you that the Bulls for our new abbot have arrived, and that His

Holiness has for a second time granted us complete *Gratis* [exemption from fee]. I owe that to the offices of Cardinal de Janson and Cardinal Colloredo.'

The nephew is Paul's son Antoine. The nearest equivalent to 'honnête homme' would be 'perfect gentleman'. Gervaise was blessed as abbot by the Bp of Séez on 18 October.

961018   CLAUDE NICAISE   18 October 1696
BN 9363,f.219, orig.; Gonod 157

Has only just had Nicaise's letter of 4 August. There can be no question of accepting a Carthusian nor of replying to dom Le Masson. Gervaise has taken possession. A M Boivin making trouble over land he has bought which belongs to la T.

961109   CLAUDE NICAISE   6 November 1696
BN 9363,f.220, orig.; Gonod 158

Nicaise should not go to Paris. R's health is bad.

961112   CLAUDE NICAISE   12 November 1696
BN 9363,f.221, orig.; Gonod 159

Trouble with Boivin. Regrets impossibility of receiving Carthusian; the Carthusian general would only get a brief from Rome ordering him back. Quesnel is too sensitive, and wants everyone to think like him. R's confidence in Abbot Gervaise.

961231   BISHOP OF AVRANCHES [P-D HUET]   31 December 1696
Florence, MS Ashburnham, Papiers Huet, f.105, orig.

Regrets he is unable to accept person sent by Huet for lack of true vocation.

97/1   JEAN GERBAIS   [? 1697]
A 5172,f.196, orig.

Prevented by illness from seeing two gentlemen sent by Gerbais; regrets.

*97/2   RM MARIE-LOUISE [BOUTHILLIER]   [1697/8]
Tour. orig.

'I am very glad, my dear sister, that you have seen Brother Chanvier and are satisfied with him. Yet my ills are still the same, and there is no hope of cure. As for patience, I ask God for it every day of my life, for our duties in that respect are greater than people think. It is something to suffer, but it must be with perfect submission to God's will. It is through such a christian frame of mind that we turn to holy use the misfortunes which he allows to befall us, whether of body or of spirit.

At last poor Madame la Chancelière has ended her race, and in a way which leaves no room for doubt that God showed her great mercy. She well deserved it through her piety and her attention to following his will, and she may be said to have regarded that as her principal obligation and omitted no means of discharging it. We prayed God for her as she wished, and will continue to do so with all possible care. Farewell, my dear sister, do not forget me before Our Lord, I beg you, and believe that no one could be more affectionately yours than I.'

The wife of the Chancellor, Louis Boucherat, was Anne-Françoise de Loménie, to whom R. had earlier referred in a letter to his sister (910809). Her death in 1697 is the only way of dating this letter, which could, however, also refer to Elisabeth Turpin, widow of Chancellor Le Tellier, a great benefactress of the Annonciades who died in 1698.

*97/3   RM MARIE-LOUISE [BOUTHILLIER]   [1697/8]
Facsimile of orig. in *La Trappe mieux connue*, 1834

'I am delighted, my dearest sister, that you have received the book that was sent to you and are pleased with it. I tried in it to express the feelings and insights given me by God, and I am much comforted to know that they have impressed you as you say. They are great truths which I wrote down very simply. As your heart is perfectly sensitive to everything concerning salvation, that is all you need to make you appreciate anything which you think might contribute to it. Pray God for the author, and ask him to fill him with the understanding and enlightenment which he needs so much and which are so necessary for a man of his profession and calling. That, my dear sister, is a favour which I hope for from your charity, as well as that of believing that no one could be with more esteem, affection and attachment than I yours' etc.

The letter is signed 'former abbot' and is thus later than May 1695. R. published books in 1697 and 1698, one of which must be referred to here, most probably his Conduite chrétienne *of 1697, possibly the* Maximes *or the* Conférences ou Instructions *of 1698.*

970110   JAMES II   10 January 1697
W orig.; *SP* p. 121

R. pleased that James enjoyed *Relations*. Thanks him for kindness to his brother [Henri]. Will send explanation requested of passage of Scripture.

970129   MADAME DE SAINT-LOUP   29 January 1697
Le Nain, *Vie* (1719) I p. 40

Comments on his relations with the late Bp Pavillon of Alet. Disagreed with him about the Signature [against Jansenism] but otherwise followed his lead.

970200 MONSIEUR DE SAINT-ANDRÉ, curé bannost   February 1697
BN na 16316, orig.

Thanks him for book received. Praises Bossuet's zealous opposition to Fénelon's 'pernicious errors'.

This refers to the Quietist controversy and Bossuet's ultimately successful attempt to get Fénelon's Maximes des Saints *banned in Rome [1699].*

970300 BISHOP OF MEAUX [J-B BOSSUET]   March 1697
Bossuet *Correspondance*, VIII p. 201

R's indignation at Fénelon's teaching; 'illusions so contrary to the Gospels'.

970314 JAMES II   14 March 1697
W orig. (3 pieces); *SP* p. 122

Sends correct version of passage wrongly copied in James' MS of *Instructions pour la conduite d'une dame*.

This is the Conduite chrétienne *addressed to Mme de Guise, (who had died in March 1696), and published in October 1697. James' version had read 'he came only for those who would walk after him in his ways' which R. corrected to 'he came only to inspire and teach those who came after him to walk in his ways'. The different theological implications need no underlining.*

970330 MONSIEUR BOILEAU   30 March 1697
BN na 16316, p.116

S[ainte] A[gathe] lucky to have Boileau as director. Approves Boileau's rules and moderating influence on Sr Eu[?génie]. No outside contacts, reasonable silence. Charity essential in a superior. Use of humiliations must be discreet. 'You are right to recommend gentleness. That is how to insinuate oneself, persuade and get people to accept rules.'

A foundation for fallen women (sixty of them) had been set up in 1696, partly on R's suggestion, called Filles de Sainte-Agathe *in Paris, and Boileau (who did much work of the kind) had been appointed by the Abp to supervise. The only full details are in the Carp.* MS *pp. 814–18. They were also known as 'Filles de la T.' and 'Filles du silence.'*

970414 BISHOP OF MEAUX [J-B BOSSUET]   14 April 1697
BN na 12959,f.206, orig.; Bossuet *Correspondance*, VIII p. 228

R. has just received the book [*Instructions sur les états d'oraison*]. 'The chimaeras of these fanatics. It is absolutely impiety, concealed in quite new language, conceived only to seduce souls.' ['It' is Quietism].

970500   BISHOP OF MEAUX [J-B BOSSUET]   May 1697
Bossuet *Correspondance*, VIII, p. 259

R. asks for a copy of what he wrote about Quietism, as he has forgotten precise terms.

970509   MONSIEUR INNES, CHAPLAIN TO THE QUEEN OF ENGLAND   9 May 1697
Scottish Catholic Archives, Edinburgh, Blair Papers, orig.

R. has received the Queen's letter and looks forward to seeing her, but does not write for fear of importuning her.

She had already come in 1696.

970703   BISHOP OF MEAUX [J-B BOSSUET]   3 July 1697
Bossuet *Correspondance*, VIII, p. 293

R. has now received copies of his two letters, which he does not regret writing, since Bossuet approves.

970707   BISHOP OF NOYON [FRANÇOIS DE CLERMONT-TONNERRE]   7 July 1697
BN 24123,f.65

Approves Bp's pastoral letter against Quietism.

970803   CLAUDE NICAISE   3 August 1697
BN 9363,f.224, orig.; Gonod 161

Santeuil has visited. Quietism being checked. *Maximes chrétiennes* published without R's authority; his health bad and he no longer sleeps.

971003   PIERRE MAUPEOU   3 October 1697
Maupeou, *Vie*, I p. 507

R. expresses confidence in Maupeou as his future biographer.

971003a   CLAUDE NICAISE   3 October 1697
BN 9363,f.226, orig.; Gonod 162

Death of Santeuil who 'would have done better to stay at Saint-Victor following the advice and example of Gourdan'. Rome's decision about Fénelon 'will determine the feelings of all rightminded people'.

Santeuil died at Dijon on 5 August after a visit of several weeks to la T. At Bossuet's instigation, the Pope had agreed on 10 September to judge Fénelon's Maximes des Saints, *allegedly Quietist.*

98/1 CLAUDE NICAISE [1694 or 1698]
BN 9363,f.85, orig.; Gonod 144 (date quite uncertain)
References to Boivin lawsuit and Arnauld dispute.

980108   CLAUDE NICAISE   8 January 1698
BN 9363,f.229, orig.; Gonod 163
Praises Bosquillon's translation of St Ephrem. Sometimes sees Thiers 'a very close friend'. Let Rome put an end to Quietist affair. Not possible to receive a Carthusian. Benedictines wholly opposed to R.
Bosquillon had translated Ephrem's treatise on compunction as IV Discours de la Componction (*Coignard, Paris, 1697*).

*980115   BISHOP OF LUÇON [HENRI BARILLON]   15 January 1698
L orig.; P f.658
'The kindness you show me, Mgr, is great, but does not surprise me, for one should expect anything from a heart made like yours. If I have not written to you for a long time it is because I have nothing worth telling you from here and I respect every moment of time which I know you turn to such holy use. I praise God, Mgr, for his blessings on your labours. There is not a day in my life when I do not commend to him your person and all that concerns you. In a word, the friendship with which you have honoured me for so many years is always present to me, and I have no words to show you how grateful I am for it. As for my health, since you wish me to give you news of it, it is worse than ever, my indispositions grow worse, I can no longer use one arm and this incapacity is accompanied by acute and almost continual pain. I often spend nights without sleep. I have been in the infirmary for three years without being able to perform any part of the Rule. I cannot take a step without a monk at my side. In a word, Mgr, *ingredior viam universae carnis* [1 K 2:2]. The outer man is almost destroyed, and that causes me no sorrow since it is the will of God, to which I submit, but what afflicts me is that the inner man is very far from what it should be. A Christian in the state in which I am must regard each day of his life as his last, and prepare himself in the morning as though he were to die in the evening, and that is what I do not do. I beg you, Mgr, to have pity on my wretchedness and ask God to make me for what little time remains what my profession requires me to be in order to go and appear before him.
In a word, Mgr, I expect everything from your charity. On my side I shall pray God to fill you with the grace you need and make you worthy of the sanctity of your calling. I beg you to believe, Mgr, that nothing could be added to the attachment and inviolable fidelity, as well as the profound respect with which I am yours etc.
PS Some works I have composed have been printed, Mgr: two volumes of *Maximes chrétiennes*, and another of a *Conduite* [*chrétienne*] addressed to Madame de Guise. I

had ordered them to be sent to you, but I see that that has not yet been done since you do not mention them. As for the *Instructions*, I think they will appear very shortly.'

Maximes chrétiennes *appeared in 1698*, Conduite chrétienne *in 1697. The* Conférences ou Instructions sur les épîtres et les évangiles . . . *came out later in 1698.*

980417   CLAUDE NICAISE   17 April 1698
BN 9363,f.238, orig.; Gonod 164

R. waiting impatiently for Rome to condemn Quietism. He knew about seizure of Thiers' book.

Presumably Thiers' Apologie seized in 1696 by order of the Chancellor.

980605   CLAUDE NICAISE   5 June 1698
BN 9363,f.239, orig.; Gonod 165

Regrets that Fénelon has 'found protectors where he ought to have found only severe judges'. Surprised at Nicaise's report of the *Religieuse portugaise*; 'disorder, or rather the desire to establish it, finds protection everywhere'.

The papal commission felt unable to condemn Fénelon in May 1698. The Lettres d'une religieuse portugaise *of Guilleragues were first published in 1668, and subsequently expanded and frequently republished. They describe in passionate language the love affair between a Portuguese nun and a French officer, and are based on an actual affair.*

980714   JAMES II   14 July 1698
W orig.; *SP* p. 132.

James had seen Maisne, who had gone to Versailles on business, but the abbot [Gervaise] asks him to take no action with the King for the moment.

James had been at la T. early in July. Gervaise was encountering so much opposition that he was thinking of resigning.

980800   ARCHBISHOP OF PARIS [LOUIS DE NOAILLES]   [August 1698]
Gonod 219

Encloses Gervaise's resignation. Has not yet proposed a successor but asks Noailles to assure King, if asked, that worthy candidates exist.

In his letter of resignation to the King, Gervaise recognises that he has caused royal displeasure, and in a later letter to Noailles says that in the interests of his salvation as well as of la T. he feels he must go elsewhere.

980818 CLAUDE NICAISE   18 August 1698
BN 9363,f.241, orig.; Gonod 166

Bossuet's book on Quietism 'decisive' [*Relation sur le quiétisme*, a personal attack on Fénelon]. The pastoral instruction on the subject by Bp of Chartres 'convincing'. The Carthusian will never succeed in coming to la T.

980900 ARCHBISHOP OF PARIS [LOUIS DE NOAILLES]   [September 1698]
Gonod 220; orig. (reportedly initialled by R.) offered for sale in Paris, June 1983, but I have been unable to extract details of document.

R. had originally approved Gervaise's resignation, but it has caused so much public talk and scandal that he suggests that it might be better to defer accepting it for a time.

R's letter was accompanied by a petition signed by all the monks asking that Gervaise remain as abbot.

980900a JAMES II   September 1698
W orig.; *SP* p. 133

The King has quashed the affair [of Estrées] and had never given permission.

Gervaise had wanted to take over a house at Estrées (dioc. Evreux) as a sort of extension to la T., though it had been earmarked for a mission centre. This and his quarrel with the Abbess of les Clairets had done him no good, as James' letter to R. of 26 September makes clear, though James had tried to defend Gervaise for excessive zeal.

980909 ARCHBISHOP OF PARIS [LOUIS DE NOAILLES]   9 September 1698
Tour. orig.

R. asks him to keep proposed successor's name secret until King's return.

981123 ARCHBISHOP OF PARIS [LOUIS DE NOAILLES]   23 November 1698
Sainte-Geneviève,1175,Suppl ZZ f in fo 316,f.112, orig.; Gonod 221

R. feels obliged to give some explanation of Gervaise's conduct; he finds office of abbot incompatible with his need for peace, and will shortly take action. Recommends dom Malachie Garneyrin as successor, and totally refutes charge of Jansenism against him, but will accept whoever the King wishes.

This pathetic document, written by the faithful dom Maur, witnessed by dom Robert and dom Pierre Le Nain, was initialled by R's hand guided by them, and shows a desperate attempt at authenticity in a crisis clouded by suspicion and abuse of R's authority, above all by Maisne. Dom Malachie was refused by the King, on the ostensible grounds that he was a

Savoyard (*and not a French subject therefore*), *but he ended up as Abbot of Buonsolazzo, in Tuscany.*

981203   ARCHBISHOP OF PARIS [LOUIS DE NOAILLES]   3 December 1698
Gonod 222

R. again supports candidature of dom Malachie but does not want anyone to know that the proposal comes from him.

See *981123 on Malachie. The fact that R. could not write in his own hand makes all these letters to Noailles, except 981123, suspect, and there is no doubt that he was being manipulated and confused by the different parties to the intrigue, notably Maisne, who had made common cause with the enemies of dom Gervaise, especially Saint-Simon.*

981226   RELIGIEUSE   [? 26 December 1698]
BN 12804,f.240, orig. (Date and part of text heavily erased, but reading of date is fairly reliable).

Her deep distress at recent injustice does her credit, but R. is glad at the humiliation. Asks her to forget all that has happened. Maisne is away on business (but adds PS in his own hand).

This cryptic letter seems to refer to the final stages of the disgrace of Gervaise, and is perhaps addressed to RM Harlay, in any case not to R's sister.

990114   CLAUDE NICAISE   14 January 1699
BN 9363,f.245, orig.; Gonod 167

Praises Bossuet's works. Dom Jacques de La Cour nominated as abbot [his confirming bulls arrived on 16 January].

990115   JAMES II   15 January 1699
W orig.; *SP* p. 135

R. Claims that dissension at la T. had affected only two or three, but that community life remains unaffected. Louis has approved R's nominee [his second choice, after dom Malachie].

Two or three supporters of Gervaise protested at his replacement by dom Jacques de La Cour on the occasion of the formal reading of the latter's bulls of appointment on 16 January. They, and Gervaise himself, all left la T. in the course of the next few months for other monasteries. Gervaise went first to Clairvaux, but stayed nowhere for long. He died more or less under arrest at the monastery of le Reclus in Champagne in 1751.

990200   MONSIEUR D'ALBERGOTTI [February 1699]
BN 24123,f.73
Details of death of Monsieur's nephew, fr Achille Albergotti.

He died 13 February, aged 27, professed 1697; a colonel, converted in 1696 by reading Relation of fr Palémon de Santena, a soldier and Italian like himself.

*990225   RM MARIE-LOUISE BOUTHILLIER 25 February 1699
Arch. dioc. Séez, orig.

'We shall not fail, my dearest sister, to pray for the person whom you commend to us, and if our prayers were such as you believe them to be, and as they ought to be, she would soon feel some effect, but, alas, we are in a state of languor and bear an infinite weight of wretchedness when people imagine that we are in the clouds. It is true that our will is intact, but our works bear no resemblance. I have every confidence in your prayers, and ask for them with all possible insistence, as also for the favour of believing that no one else could have more affection and esteem for you than I.'

990312   CLAUDE NICAISE 12 March 1699
BN 9363,f.242, orig.; Gonod 168

R. praises Abbess of ND du Tard. Still waits for condemnation of Fénelon.

990323   BISHOP OF ALET [CHARLES TAFOUREAU] 23 March 1699
TC II/9

At Bp's request, R. outlines the sacred duties of a bp, who must be above reproach.

Dom Jacques de La Cour takes possession as abbot 5 April 1699

990600   JAMES II [received 25 June 1699]
W orig.; *SP* p. 138

Hoping for James' visit.

990630   CLAUDE NICAISE 30 June 1699
BN 9303,f.247, orig.; Gonod 169

R. is pleased with outcome of General Chapter at Cîteaux [commenced 18 May] and kindness of Abbot [Nicolas Larcher]. Glad that affair of Quietism is over. Comments on Casanata's prominent part in it.

The condemnation of Fénelon's Maximes des Saints *had at last been published on 12 March, in a decree largely inspired by Casanata.*

990709   ARCHBISHOP OF PARIS [LOUIS DE NOAILLES]   9 July 1699
Tour. orig.
Dom Gervaise has at his own request gone to Clairvaux two days ago; R. encloses a note of explanation. Thanks Abp for writing to Cîteaux.

Dom Jacques de La Cour had been confirmed as abbot of la T. on 16 January, and Gervaise, clearly in the throes of a nervous breakdown, found it impossible to stay, as the enclosed document makes clear. As mentioned earlier, the prior, dom Jean-Baptiste de La Tour, and the procurator left at the same time, almost certainly taking with them the precious documents collected for Gervaise's projected biography of R.

990809   CLAUDE NICAISE   9 August 1699
BN 9363,f.240, orig.; Gonod 170
'One should not neglect one's health, but should not make an idol of it.' Pernicious opinions of Quietists. Dispute between abbé Ber[rier] and Abbess of Saint-Julien referred to R. for arbitration.

Catherine d'Aumont had been Abbess of the benedictine house of Saint-Julien du Pré, Le Mans, since 1678; the dispute is not known.

990826   JAMES II   26 August 1699
W orig.; *SP* p. 140
Asks for continuation of James' friendship.

990915   DOM JEAN MABILLON, OSB   15 September 1699
BN 17681,f.86; *Ami de la Religion*, 128, 1846; p. 522
Thanks Mabillon for kindness shown to a religious who had challenged character of superior chosen by R. and had left.

This seems to be the ex-Vannist Colomban Plouvier, professed in August 1698, who went back to the Benedictines, presumably after objecting to dom Jacques' appointment.

990923   JAMES II   23 September 1699
W orig.; *SP* p. 142
R. is sorry to hear so rarely from James [who answered letter of 26 August only on 22 September].

991010   JAMES II   10 October 1699
W orig.; *SP* p. 142

About abbé de Saint-Jacques, whom James had met at la T. and would like to spend the rest of his life there, after having had to leave religious life once to pay off family debts.

This probably refers to François d'Aligre (1620–1712), a Canon Regular who became Abbot of Saint-Jacques de Provins in 1643. He was offered a bishopric, but declined, and in 1672 left his monastery to help his father, Chancellor in 1674. On his father's death in 1677 he went back to his monastery.

991112   JAMES II   12 November 1699
W orig.; *SP* p. 144

Health of James and the Queen restored. Discussion of abbey at Montmartre, given to James by Louis for English benedictine nuns. R. recommends a worthy couple ready to help the Abbess in temporal matters.

000304   CLAUDE NICAISE   4 March 1700
BN 9363,f.246, orig.; Gonod 161

Thanks Nicaise for book and letter from Mme Joly. 'My infirmities and the pain I have been attacked by for many years enable me to look on every day of my life as that of my death.'

The book was the biography of R's kinsman, Bénigne Joly, 'father of the poor', who had died in Dijon in 1694 after a life devoted to charitable work among the poor.

000620   BISHOP OF MEAUX [J-B BOSSUET]   20 June 1700
Bossuet *Correspondance*, XII, p. 266

R. wants to remind Bossuet of him once more. Visit of a Danish gentleman, known to Bossuet [the convert Winslow, or Vinslov 1669 1760, who settled in Paris and became profess of anatomy].

About noon, Rancé dies, attended by the Bishop of Séez,   27 October 1700
Louis d'Acquin.

UNDATED LETTERS

These are letters, mostly from Muguet and TC, which not only bear no date, and usually no addressee, but are too vague in content to permit even tentative dating. They are given in the order in which they appear in their respective series, none of which is chronological.

Undated Letters

UD 1 RELIGIEUX Mug I/15
'The whole rule can be reduced to two points . . . interior and exterior things.'

UD 2 CURÉ OF PARIS Mug I/77
'Your spiritual direction, free of the false principles used at present as a basis for ruling the consciences of all.'

UD 3 CURÉ OF PARIS Mug I/78
'We have already done what you asked for the person . . .'

UD 4 RM SUPÉRIEURE Mug I/82
Has received Association.

UD 5 RM SUPÉRIEURE Mug I/83
Thanks her again for Association.

UD 6 FRIEND (MAN) Mug I/84
'I see that it would have been better to be patient.'

UD 7 RM [? AT GIF] Mug I/85
'God has finally submitted your heart to his will' and she has accepted the charge [possibly of abbess, in 1674].

UD 8 MADAME Mug I/89
Regrets being unable to speak to her in the outside chapel.

UD 9 SUPÉRIEUR Mug I/90
'. . . it does not wholly consist in singing in choir, attending divine office, observing some aspects of the Rule.'

UD 10   RELIGIEUX   Mug I/92
The misdeeds of others do not justify our own.

UD 11   RELIGIEUSE   Mug I/97
'As I know your inclination towards solitude and silence . . . it is no good trying to suppress my thoughts. . . .'

UD 12   'A LADY WISHING TO GO INTO RETREAT'   Mug I/98
'Nothing is more agreeable than to imagine a fearful solitude, a dark forest, a cave. . . .'
   Cf 720600, probably to Mme de Saint-Loup.

UD 13   RM SUPÉRIEURE   Mug I/99
Thoughts on the Rule of St Benedict.

UD 14   SUPÉRIEUR   Mug I/101
Would like to accept him. He can see countless examples around him of cloisters which are not refuges.

UD 15   RELIGIEUX [OF ANOTHER OBSERVANCE]   Mug I/104
'You did absolutely right to confide in the duc de X . . . I do not doubt that if you return here after preaching your octave it will be for eternity.'

UD 16   SUPÉRIEUR   Mug I/105
'I have indeed read the *Livre de la mort des justes* with the greatest pleasure.'
   This could be the Maurist Acta Sanctorum.

UD 17   MADEMOISELLE   Mug I/108
'Your uncertainty as between the world and religion.'

UD 18   A LADY IN AFFLICTION   Mug II/1
R. wrote only two days earlier: she must make up for her fault.

UD 19   MADAME   Mug II/3
'You owe much to Our Lord for giving you a love of retreat.' She should observe Lent as strictly as her health permits.

UD 20 MADAME   Mug II/5
'I knew that you had been unwell, but I did not think that your illness was what you tell me.'

UD 21 PRINCESS   Mug II/6
Death of another princess and succession of her pupil (as head of religious house).

UD 22 RM ABBESSE DE LA COMMUNE   Mug II/7
       OBSERVANCE [? LEYME]
Do not begin reform by joining Strict Observance. She is infirm and may not be able to stand abstinence.

UD 23 MADAME   Mug II/9
'I am very sorry at the continuation of your illness.'

UD 24 BISHOP   Mug II/10
New Year greetings, follow same path despite criticism.

UD 25 MADAME   Mug II/12
'Your deep awareness of your wretchedness is a sure and short way for obtaining great mercies from God.'

UD 26 RM   Mug II/13
'One so rarely finds more peace and comfort in a new observance . . . that one cannot be too wary of oneself. . . .'

UD 27 MADAME   Mug II/14
She is infirm; he assures her of his prayers.

UD 28 BISHOP   Mug II/15
R. sends close friend to remember him to bp. Sorry for bp in his troubles.

UD 29 BISHOP   Mug II/17
'You combine the solicitude of a bishop with the austerity of a solitary.' [Possibly Le Camus].

UD 30   CURÉ   Mug II/24

'What you tell me about M. [a bp] consoles me . . . I thought indeed . . . that his apostolic firmness would be protected.'

UD 31   BISHOP   Mug II/28

'I can assure you that I am deeply touched by your troubles and difficulties. . . .'
Cf UD 28 and 30. Le Camus is a likely identification.

UD 32   ECCLÉSIASTIQUE   Mug II/29

Had not answered letter, while leaving it to God to give him fidelity to carry out plan.

UD 33   'ILLUSTRIOUS PRELATE'   Mug II/34

'You sigh for a life of retreat and you are right.'
Bossuet or Le Camus is the most likely candidate.

UD 34   MADEMOISELLE   Mug II/38

'You should not be troubled at leaving your father's house to give yourself to Christ . . . your father is too christian to lay on you the curse with which he threatens you.'

UD 35   MADAME   Mug II/39

'I shall not fail . . . to devote all my prayers and those of our brothers . . . for the return of this soul' and will pray also for her husband.

UD 36   RELIGIEUSE (NOVICE)   Mug II/41

'I was too fond of your father not to keep his memory alive.'

UD 37   RP SUPÉRIEUR   Mug II/45

'I shall not make any difficulties over the brief you have obtained . . . I have accepted fourteen or fifteen members of different orders.'

UD 38   MONSIEUR   Mug II/47

'Your letter both surprised and delighted me . . . it would never have occurred to me that you might think of coming a second time to la T.'

UD 39   MADEMOISELLE [? DE VERTUS]   Mug II/55
'I see your ills recurring as God prolongs your days. . . .'

UD 40   RM SUPÉRIEURE   Mug II/56
'I cannot fail to share all your troubles . . . brusque and haughty, you act autocratically' according to her, but with so many women in her charge, that is usual.

UD 41   RM SUPÉRIEURE   Mug II/57
She must not resign. Has been twenty years in office. Wait five or six months to look for a successor.

This and the preceding letter seem to be to the same person, and among R's correspondents the superiors with twenty years service are the Abbess of Leyme (elected 1654) and of Maubuisson (elected 1664). The former is the more likely addressee.

UD 42   MONSIEUR   Mug II/58
Speaks of an ecclesiastic of great merit.

UD 43   RP SUPÉRIEUR   Mug II/61
R. defers to RP's feelings, but if one of his religious wants to come he must seek the General's permission and then come and see.

UD 44   MONSIEUR   Mug II/63
'Your brother RP N. came here three or four years ago' and was clothed six months ago.

UD 45   RELIGIEUX   Mug II/64 (really 60a)
Replies to six doubts on superior, employment, translation, masses, benefices, and reading.

UD 46   MONSIEUR   Mug II/67
R. deeply touched by letter about a priest affected by 'a series of corrupt and iniquitous practices passing belief'. The man should give up his benefice, retire to Paris near Saint-Victor and overcome his passions.

UD 47   RP DE L'ORDRE   Mug II/71
He must not come without permission.

UD 48   RM   Mug II/76
Her state 'usual enough in people who have come back to God after a worldly life'.

UD 49   RP SUPÉRIEUR   Mug II/82
'A religious may not retain a small or large sum of money for any reason' whatever they do in the Common Observance.

UD 50   MONSIEUR   Mug II/84
Thanks him for remembering him. Danger of insomnia after fasting.

UD 51   MADAME   Mug II/90
'It is in God's order that someone charged with a family takes the necessary care of them . . . but it is never permitted to take such cares as far as anxiety and confusion . . . God wants nothing less of you than complete and sincere detachment from all that is transitory.'

U 52   BISHOP   Mug II/91
Reports on one of bp's household sent five or six months ago, but who lacked a vocation and has gone, perhaps on to Rome.

UD 53   MADAME   Mug II/95
Does not doubt she will have a happy year. 'I confess quite simply that I am easy to deceive . . . men are generally wickeder than I think.'

UD 54   RM   Mug II/101
'I praise God for giving you peace in your present state. . . .'

UD 55   RP ABBÉ [? FOUCARMONT]   Mug II/106
'I should like to do what you ask [send money] . . . This region is so wretched . . . that every week we have to give bread to 3,500 poor folk.'
   This sounds like an appeal for contributions to the Strict Observance expenses of the mission to Rome of 1677, which attempted to win concessions from the Pope.

UD 56   FRÈRE   Mug II/107
'You ask for my prayers but not my advice'; he left la T. to study after being professed, but R. will pray for his conversion.

UD 57 MADAME [? DE SAINT-LOUP]   U 723

'I should prefer you to be in retreat and in a house of penitence than anywhere else
... Paris would not suit you.'

UD 58 MADAME [? DE SAINT-LOUP]   U 723

'If I have the honour of seeing you again before you leave these parts, we shall give
up everything else to talk solely about yourself.'

UD 59 MONSIEUR   BN 24123,f.66, orig.

'I have read your letter ... I am not the director of the person in question and hardly
ever involve myself in giving advice when asked.'

UD 60 BISHOP OF PAMIERS [ETIENNE CAULET]   PR 91 bis

Pensions payable to former monks of la T. paid to cellarers of monasteries where
they are. They own nothing directly.

UD 61 MONSIEUR   TC I/3

Has been planning retreat for three years: 'when he [God] has spoken and knocked
in vain a long time, he stops talking and remains perpetually silent'.

UD 62 RELIGIEUSE   TC I/13

Despite her promises she has relapsed. She must follow her superior's advice and not
change her house.

UD 63 RELIGIEUSE   TC I/43

Eleven pages of rules for benedictine nuns: no keys to cell or chest, no gifts, no contracts with parents, never male workmen in cloister. Condemns abbesses who want
to be called Madame.

UD 64 MADEMOISELLE   TC I/52

She must not be upset at her slow progress but persevere.

UD 65 RELIGIEUSE   TC I/56

She is free to keep silence and retreat without telling even her confessor.

UD 66   TWO BROTHERS, HUGUENOT GENTLEMEN   TC I/58
'Not only would you risk nothing [by conversion], but you lose all by remaining [in error]' and R. pledges his word before the eternal judge.

UD 67   RELIGIEUSE   TC I/59
She has separated herself from God through pride and must find her way back.

UD 68   RM SUPÉRIEURE   TC I/65
At her request gives nine rules for her monastery, including ban on private conversations, 'the plague of monasteries'. Even visitors should practice abstinence and visits be restricted to a minimum.

UD 69   RELIGIEUSE, 'UNKNOWN SR PÉLAGIE'   TC I/69
She entered religion without a vocation, but must now make reparation.

UD 70   BISHOP   TC I/89
R. writes on behalf of an abbot who is sick to ask for the return of two monks of that abbey employed on parochial duties in bp's diocese, one of whom supports his father in this way.

UD 71   RP DE L'ORDRE   TC I/90
Let him come to la T. as he plans; transgressions of Common Observance.

UD 72   RM ABBESSE [? LEYME]   TC I/92
R. has already told her that those who speak of him do not know him. Best wishes to her and prioress.

UD 73   RP   TC I/111
R. striving to be forgotten by the world. He awaits death in his solitude.

UD 74   RP   TC I/112
'One of my friends . . . who has an archdeaconry of four hundred parishes and a simple priory is about to give up the latter benefice.' R. approves.

UD 75   MONSIEUR   TC I/113
Advises him not to accept diocese, having a benefice already.

UD 76   MONSIEUR   TC I/116
Our duties to our friends must not stop there and we must offer everything to God.

UD 77   RP ABBÉ   TC I/124
'We must not reject from holy houses those who are burdened with crimes.'

UD 78   MONSIEUR   TC I/171
'I assure you that however badly I am treated, I shall never lose an opportunity of serving those who wish me ill.'

UD 79   RM SUPÉRIEURE   TC II/4
'If you derive any vanity from your birth, humble yourself.' An abbé has betrayed R's confidence; she should discuss it with her brother.

UD 80   MADEMOISELLE DE VERTUS   TC II/5
She wants to improve her way of life and should just follow the practice of the well-ordered house (Port-Royal) where she is.

UD 81   MADAME   TC II/6
Will always appreciate her kindly interest. Reference to a letter of R. where error and heresy are allegedly to be found.

UD 82   MONSIEUR   TC II/7
After much thought and prayer R. advises him to spend the rest of his life in retreat from the world.

UD 83   PRINCE DE HARCOURT   TC II/10
God has given him an ecclesiastical vocation which he must now examine.

The Harcourt who married Brancas' daughter in 1665 must be excluded, and the most likely candidate seems to be Alphonse-Louis (1644–89) who became (commendatory) abbot of Royaumont in 1649.

UD 84   RP SUPÉRIEUR   TC II/14
Discusses the Rule of St Benedict. One should undergo any suffering for Christ's sake.

UD 85   MONSIEUR ECCLÉSIASTIQUE   TC II/16
'It remains true that one may not wish for a benefice involving care of souls . . . without offending conscience' [presumably as an absentee].

UD 86   MONSIEUR ECCLÉSIASTIQUE   TC II/18
Condemns pluralism. Thinks the burden of ecclesiastical benefices is heavy in obligations.

The letter between these two is to Favier, 600510, and it is quite likely that these two are also to him.

UD 87   MONSIEUR   TC II/22 and
                                                       TC II/61 (longer)
'You are very fortunate in being able to dispose of yourself as you will . . . you feel no special inclination for any calling, either for the law, the army, or the cloister. . . .' He should leave Paris 'that Babylon'. Sends a rule of life: prayer, Mass, work in the garden.

UD 88   RP   TC II/27
'I should like to think that my letters are of some use to you.' He should avoid hearing confessions.

UD 89   CANON OF X   TC II/28
'I do not doubt that the promise to keep God's commandments involves a new and enhanced obligation to observe them.'

UD 90   RM ABBESSE   TC II/29
R. knew of her last illness from which she has now recovered.

UD 91   RM   TC II/30
'I wonder at divine providence towards Monsieur N. . . . extraordinary that he should have been taken from his own country and brought to a strange land.'

UD 92 RELIGIEUSE   TC II/33
She needs humility; he had hoped for better and more religious conduct from her.

UD 93 RM   TC II/36
R. would like to comfort her mother, prays daily for her.

UD 94 RM [? LOUISE ROGIER]   TC II/44
R. believes her self-reproach is sincere; he will never forget her concern for his conversion. 'Had I been less wicked, and not continually put obstacles in the way of your prayers, I should have taken thought about my salvation sooner.'

UD 95 RM ABBESSE   TC II/49
R. has done all he can to achieve reconciliation with abbot of X for her sake more than his. People are trying to stop her living according to the Rule; silence essential.

*UD 96 RM SUPÉRIEURE [MADAME DE BELLEFONDS]   TC II/59
'You know in advance my opinions on the problems you propose. It is true that it seems tiresome to refuse a nun permission to go to the waters when there is some likelihood that that will be useful to her health. Yet when one considers the drawbacks attached to this kind of journey, and how many bad things may happen to her in the outside world, away from the company of her sisters and the sight of those appointed to guide her, there is no doubt that it is much better for her to suffer patiently her infirmities in the cloister than to leave in search of a cure that is not certain and may bring upon her worse ills than those she is enduring. Apart from that the bad example she gives to the whole community is so considerable and may have such consequences that everything should be done to avoid them; for once the doors have been opened it will be difficult to close them again, and there will be no lack of reasons and medical advice to support the desire to leave the monastery; and when a community is numerous, that can only cause great disturbance and introduce endless irregularities. Thus, Reverend Mother, I would think it appropriate for you to point out to your sisters the advantage of constant and uninterrupted stability, and how, by making themselves faithful and abandoning themselves to God, they will receive from him all necessary help and blessings. They must be persuaded that if he is not pleased to relieve their bodies, at least he will not fail to sanctify their souls, which should be the only object of all their desires. I hope that God gives you all the guidance you need, that he increases your piety and makes all your sisters respond to the care and zeal which I am sure you take over their salvation. I am with more esteem and respect than I can express, yours' etc.

Though it was to RM Agnès de Bellefonds that R. wrote most regularly, it is not impossible that this letter is to her sister, Laurence, Abbess of Rouen. Apart from anything else, RM Agnès must have known him far too well to put the question. The copyist leaves it uncertain.

UD 97   COMTESSE [? DE BELIN]   TC II/63

'She had made him hope for a conversation which ill health eventually made impossible.'

This can only have been one of Mme de Guise's entourage, since he saw no other women. If not his niece, perhaps her mother, comtesse d'Albon, R's sister.

UD 98   RELIGIEUSE   TC II/91

'Allow me to ask your news . . . I do not doubt that you are at last obtaining from God what you asked him for.'

UD 99   RP   TC II/92

'We have no other occupation than to offer prayers for . . . the Church . . . the King . . . and the State.'

UD 100   MONSIEUR   TC II/93

'Your complaints about aridity are common to all those who return to God from the dissipations of the world.'

UD 101   MONSIEUR L'ABBÉ   TC II/94

Only M's kindness makes him appreciate R's letters. Vanity of worldly values.

UD 102   DIRECTOR OF A SEMINARY   TC II/96

'No one should leave his ecclesiastical place . . . for a cloister without extraordinary reasons.'

UD 103   RP FROM FLANDERS   TC II/108

God's mercies are infinite; R. is willing to take him back a third time.

Cf letter 80/9 to Albert of Liège, the Guillemin.

UD 104 RM   TC II/114

She must not give way to melancholy, but read *Acts of the Martyrs* and *History of the Saints*, do manual work and stop brooding.

UD 105 RELIGIEUSE   TC II/122

She is a faithful friend. R. not surprised at her concern in his illness.

UD 106 MADAME   TC II/123

Her husband has died, and though R. did not write, he commended her to God.

UD 107 RELIGIEUSE   TC II/ 124

Faithful as she is, he does not doubt that God will grant her fresh grace.

UD 108 MARQUISE   TC II/125

Glad that her attitude is so christian. 'I am careful not to count myself among the cedars since I am a very fragile reed.'

UD 109 MADAME   TC II/126

'It would help you to participate often in the holy mysteries, and I see no reason to prevent you communicating on Sundays and feast days.' She should confess a few days beforehand, exercise self-control, and mistrust her impulsiveness.

UD 110 RM ABBESSE, OSA [? ESSAI]   TC II/127

She fasts on Wednesday and Friday; would her health allow more? Perhaps abstinence on Monday and Wednesday for her nuns.

UD 111 RM ABBESSE   TC II/128

'It seems to me that whole years are not enough for thinking about the end of our lives.' She does not know who is opposing moves to improve her nuns.

UD 112 MADAME   TC II/129

'God grants you much grace in letting you have such a poor opinion of yourself.'

UD 113 MADAME   TC II/135
'I see that your love of retreat and penitence grows stronger.' She should please God where she is instead of trying to change what does not depend on her.

UD 114 RM   TC II/139
'There is no doubt that a religious must keep silent when accused of things she has not done and reported to her superior' unless the report distresses the superior.

UD 115 MONSIEUR   TC II/184
'I confess that the excesses you have committed are extreme', but God will be merciful.

UD 116 RM SUPÉRIEURE   TC II/221
'There is nothing about which men know less than God's particular treatment of souls.'

UD 117 MONSIEUR   TC II/222
M. would do well to go into retreat, but must avoid visits in a place where his birth and career have won him so much respect.

UD 118 MADAME DE SAINT-LOUP   TC II/224
All who care for her will be glad that she is at last going to do what God inspired her to do so long ago. Her doctor is joking when he says it will kill her.

UD 119 COMTESSE   TC II/227
Her deplorable state is forcing her into action, and R. is glad. She must make the break without delay.

UD 120 RELIGIEUSE   TC II/228
'It is a sign of your friendship that you take the trouble to ask after me . . . It is better to await eternity, since that is an event we cannot escape.'

UD 121 MADAME   TC II/232
Pleased at her letter; thought she would come out all right.

UD 122 MONSIEUR TC II/233

'The curé you are worried about . . . is not here and never came', and R. would be reluctant to accept anyone usefully carrying out the cure of souls.

UD 123 MADAME TC II/237

Always glad to hear from her. Detach herself from the world.

UD 124 MONSIEUR ECCLÉSIASTIQUE TC II/238

'I am not surprised that you find few people who think like you.'

UD 125 RM TC II/239

'The devil who cannot prevent you wanting to serve Christ . . . is trying to fill your spirit with empty fears.'

UD 126 MONSIEUR L'ABBÉ TC II/240

R. and he think differently about R's illness; R. sees himself as a useless servant.

UD 127 RM TC II/241

'You must not doubt that Our Lord who has given you signs of his mercy from your tenderest childhood . . . will continue to sustain you'.

UD 128 RELIGIEUSE TC II/242

Glad to have news of her.

UD 129 RP ABBÉ TC II/243

'There is nothing we deserve less than the opinion you hold about us and our brothers.'

UD 130 RELIGIEUSE TC II/244

'If we want to belong to God we must simply abandon ourselves to his providence.'

UD 131 RELIGIEUSE TC II/247

Wishes her a happy year and blessed life.

UD 132   RELIGIEUSE   TC II/249
'Keep on knocking at the door.'

UD 133   MONSIEUR   TC II/256
Has not had news for a long time and M's uncertain health is always a cause for anxiety.

UD 134   MONSIEUR   TC II/257
Death of M.X. 'a cedar brought crashing down in a moment... A fortune overturned... a life spent uselessly, to say the least'. The devil tries to hinder those engaged in work of sanctification, whence M's languor.

UD 135   RM   TC II/272
'God shows you great mercies in making you envisage the end of your life before it arrives.' God will be compassionate, despite her past life.

UD 136   RP ABBÉ [? CHÂTILLON]   TC II/331
The religious arrived two days ago; he must not resign, and would regret choosing an unworthy successor. 'Be wary of the postulant who is given to prayers of quietude [mystic peace of soul]. In many people that is a real illusion.'

Despite countless checks and cross checks it remains virtually certain that some of the above are duplicates, at least in part, of dated letters to known addressees.

COLLECTIONS OF *EXTRACTS* FROM LETTERS

There are a number of such anthologies, both printed and MS, but two deserve special mention:

BN 12804   'Lettres de Bénédictins'; letters from Rancé, the only Cistercian represented in the two volumes of this very miscellaneous collection, are extracted in a very cramped hand from f.240–f.276. The letter on f.240 is original, but heavily erased, all the others are extracts ranging from two to about twelve lines, some roughly dated (from about 1686–98), some to a nun ('ma soeur'), but none with either a specific name or date. The following extracts, which do not seem to be known anywhere else, are worth quoting:

    f.245   'Dom M[abillon] has been here . . . He spent a day and a half . . . and it can be said that he is a man of great humility and great learning at the same time.' [1693]

    f.265   'I was born, since you wish to know, on the 9 January 1626.'

    f.268   'Those of our religious who are not priests communicate on Sundays and feast-days.'

    f.269   'Some of our religious who are not priests have my permission to communicate three or four times a week at private Masses. They are very simple and innocent souls.' [1690]

BN 19324   An anthology arranged by spiritual themes of mostly short extracts from undated letters, some of which can, however, be identified because a hand other than that of the copyist has written in the name of the addressee, thus providing identification for many otherwise unknown letters.

INDEX OF ADDRESSEES

This index contains all named addressees and, wherever possible, information about them. Those addressed by title (e.g. prior, abbess) have generally been identifiable, but a small number of names elude precise identification. Only certain, or highly probable, identifications have been given (and where doubt exists this has been indicated by ? before the entry); no attempt has been made to list the numerous unnamed 'canons regular', 'ecclesiastics', 'religious' and so on, though it is quite certain that many of these could be the same as those named. Forms of proper names in the seventeenth century were anything but fixed, especially when they included the definite article (e.g. Bouthillier and Le Bouthillier both exist) and extensive cross referencing has been resorted to. Apart from standard abbreviations, co has been used for Cistercian Common Observance, CR for Canon Regular and so for Cistercian Strict Observance. Normally all religious of the same house have been listed together under the name of the house. Personal surnames appear as SMALL CAPITALS. Cities and geographical locations appear in roman typeface. Institutions appear in **bold typeface**.

ALAIN, dom *See* MORONY
ALBERGOTTI, M., uncle of fr Achille, 990200
ALBERT, RP, Guillemin at Liège, 80/9, 800730, ?UD 103
ALBON, Charlotte Bouthillier, comtesse d' (1625–16 April 1697). R's sister. Married c. 1639 to René Faudoas d'Averton, comte de Belin, by whom she had a son who died in infancy, and a daughter, Antoinette, who married a cousin and became comtesse de Belin (q.v.). In 1642 Belin was murdered by his brother-in-law, and about three years later she married the comte d'Albon, by whom she had three daughters. They had an estate near Vichy, were friends of Mme de Sévigné, and combined personal piety with the life of courtiers. There is no

evidence that she saw R. after his final visit to Paris in 1675. ?730907, 790203,791220a, 800100,820730a
ALBON, Gilbert-Antoine de Chazeul, comte d' (died December 1679). His family came from the Lyonnais. Married Charlotte Bouthillier c.1644. A well known *dévot*, member of Compagnie du Saint-Sacrement, and friend of the ducs de Luynes, Mazarin, and Roannez. At one time (c.1650) moved in circles favourable to Port-Royal, but was not a Jansenist. 781022,?790201
ALBON, Louise Henriette *See* **Visitation**
ALÈGRE, Jeanne-Françoise de Garande, marquise d' (1658–1723). Married in 1679 to Yves, marquis, later maréchal,

275

d'Alègre. A niece of the Bps of Pamiers (Caulet) and Orléans. After an early life of dissipation she was converted and became the friend of both Bossuet and Fénelon. Mme de Sévigné tells the story of how, in a fit of religious zeal, she ran away (in July 1684) to take ship for the Indies, where she felt called to a life of penitence; her family brought her back (from Rouen). (Sévigné, *Lettres*, III: 132–34: letter of 5 August 1684). 820720, 820906b,821115,830707,830909, 831116,851115

Alençon *See* **Clarisses**

Alet *See* Pavillon, Tafoureau

AMELINE, Claude (1633–1706). In 1660 member of Oratory at Saumur, a friend of Malebranche. By 1663 precentor, then senior archdeacon, of Notre-Dame de Paris and visitor to several religious communities, including Gif. In 1699 he wrote book against Quietism. 820400a

Amiens *See* Lefèvre

ANDILLY, Robert Arnauld d' (1588–1674). Prominent lawyer and intendant to Gaston d'Orléans, 1625. Withdrew to Port-Royal in 1646 and was allowed to remain there during the persecution until 1664. He published editions and translations of St John Climacus (R's first introduction to that master of monastic spirituality), St Augustine, and St Teresa. 580104, 580303,580404,580626,580710, 580718,580730,580820,580824, 580910,580920,581006,581024, 581109,581126,581214,581227, 590126,590302,590319,590409, 590616,590712,590804,590822, 590917,591026,591108,591122, 591225,591228,600208,600222, 600303,600310,600405,600730, 600822,600908,601017,601208, 610120,610328,681024,711013, 711227,720125,730607a,730619, 730702 (P. Varin, *La Vérité sur les Arnauld* [Paris, 1847] quotes extensively from these letters but is otherwise unreliable).

ANDRÉ DE LA CROIX, RP, Theatine, 81/9

ANDRÉ, dom *See* Ferrand, Jannel

Angers *See* Arnauld, Henri

ANJUBAULT, M., Principal of the Collège de Mayenne from 1676 (1649–97). A fervent Jansenist and zealous pedagogue. 860220

Annonciades, an order founded in 1604 at Genoa by Vittoria Fornari and B. Zannoni, SJ. The first house in Paris was established 1621, on the rue de la Couture Sainte-Catherine. (Source of information is surviving archives of the last remaining French house, at Langres, which include MS obituaries of all religious of the Paris house and some printed *Lettres circulaires* as well.)

RM PRIORESS (Marie-Christine Leprestre, 1614–81, prioress 1669), 691227

BOUTHILLIER, RM Marie-Louise-Isabelle, (1630–14 May 1705). Entered the convent in 1646, and despite poor health insisted on being professed the next year (though not at first as a full member). For some twenty years her health gave her constant trouble, but then improved. She spent much time on the gate as *tourière*, but never held the office of superior. The obituary is silent on the details, but it seems

Index of Addressees 277

that she only became a full choir religious after her father's death, to judge from a letter of R. 601116,620214, 66/1,670910,691218,70/2, 700728,710426,730607, 740123,741008,750410a 751100h,821012b,830211, 830400a,830501,830914, ?831112,831226,840216, 840323,?841014,841220, 850214,850317,850617, 850821,860121,860304, 860613,870202,?870206, 880202,880228,881129, 890422,890623,891013, 891228,910519,910627, 910709a,920519,920712, 920911,921229,930120, 930123,930326,930613, 931114,940222,940613, 941117,950200,97/2,97/3, 990225
Picot, RM Marie-Luce (1609–89) professed c.1626, prioress 1685–89, subprioress at her death on 13 June 1689. 820523a, 821012a,850617a,?860215a, 880229
Arnauld, Antoine (1612–94). Youngest brother of Arnauld d'Andilly, disciple of Saint-Cyran, doctor of the Sorbonne. Ordained 1641, he withdrew to Port-Royal (of which two of his sisters were abbesses). His *De la fréquente communion* provoked fury from the Jesuits, and he became leader of what opponents called the Jansenists. Censured and disgraced in 1656, he was rehabilitated in 1669, but when the Peace of the Church ended in 1679 he went into exile in Brussels, never to return. His integrity, intellectual stature, and persecution made him the real moulder and leader of the Jansenist party for nearly half a century. He admired what R. had done at la T., but contact lapsed after 1679. 720419,741023, 761014,790110
Arnauld, Henri, Bp of Angers (1597–1692). Ordained after beginning a legal career in 1624, he became Bp of Angers in 1649. A devoted pastor and convinced Jansenist, like his brother Antoine, he was known as a consummate politician. 73/4, ?731025
Avranches *See* Huet

Baluze, Etienne (1630–1718). Appointed by Colbert in 1667 as librarian of what is now the BN. Professor of Canon Law at Collège Royal 1670. Author of learned works on history and law. 920401,920630,920901
Barbeaux, abbey of SO, diocese of Sens;
RP Prior, 681030,780222, 820713,901244
dom Paul, 820906,830207b
See also Couturier
Barillon, Antoine, son of Paul (q.v.), 911029
Barillon, Henri, (1639–99) Bp of Luçon, 1671–99. A childhood friend of R. he was brought up after his father's early death by his pious uncle, Morangis, and was educated by Oratorians. He was ordained in 1660 and accepted R's priory of Boulogne after going to consult Bp Pavillon at Alet. Marcel, curé of Saint-Jacques, was his director and Le Camus his close friend. Appointed to Luçon in 1671 on Le Camus'

recommendation, he devoted himself to pastoral pursuits, especially seminaries, clergy conferences and the large Protestant population. Attacked in 1684 by nephritis, he was never robust again, and died after an unsuccessful operation. He made much use of Oratorians in his diocese. 650904,711026, 711120,720217,720411,720602, 721025,730719,741029,760522a, 780113,780922,781217,790723, 801126,820507,820921a, 821222a,821225,821231,830117, 830131,810311,830401,830613, 830817,831023,831231,840910, 841009,850104,850409,850611, 851129a,860131,860523,860812, 860913,861102,861207,861229, 871122,880115b,880424,880607, 881013,881016,881229a,890117, 890317,890414,891017,891119, 900102,900121,900212,900326, 900427a,900710,900920,910120, 910405,910513,910528,910618, 910625,910629,910709,910718, 910726,910730,911018,911108, 920108,920114,920124,920303a, 920619,920709,920718,920812, 930103a,930413,930420,930527, 930831,940107,940324,940516, 940618,940830,941011,941025, 950103,950216,950317,950605, 950818,951005,960103,960404, 961011,980115

BARILLON d'Amoncourt, Paul (died 23 July 1691). Maître des requêtes 1657, conseiller d'état 1672. Accompanied Courtin as Ambassador to Cologne 1673. Ambassador to London 1677–88, returned to Paris after expulsion in January 1689, after James II's deposition. Friend of La Fontaine, Mme de Sévigné, and Mme de La Fayette, with a reputation for some lack of piety. Brother of Henri. 780615,820507,820706f, 830501,910404,910604

Bassenville *See* GUÉRIN

BAUDUY *See* **Celestines**

BAZIN, M., curé of Saint-Hilaire, Paris. Involved in publication of Le Nain's life of R. 940830

Beauvais *See* **Saint-Symphorien**

BEAUVILLIER, Paul, duc de, comte de Saint-Aignan (1648–1714). Created duc 1679. Tutor to the duc de Bourgogne (Louis XIV's grandson) from 1689, and from then on one of the most influential men at court, with a reputation for solid piety. 810123,810825

BELIN, Antoinette de Faudoas-Averton, comtesse de, (c.1641– after 1694). R's niece. Orphaned by the murder of her father in 1642, she married her first cousin, Emmanuel, in 1655 and was widowed in 1667. She lived at Averton (Mayenne) and was one of Mme de Guise's entourage, apparently visiting la T. in that capacity, but, according to dom Le Nain, always refused an interview by R. 770114a,771202, ? UD 97

BELLEFONDS, Agnès de *See* **Carmelites**

BELLEFONDS, Bernardin Gigault, maréchal de (1630–94). Son of Governor of Valognes. Orphaned at 12, and largely brought up by aunt, Laurence, Abbess of Rouen. After military service in Catalonia, Italy, and Flanders, he was promoted maréchal in 1668, and was entrusted with embassies to Spain, England, and Rome. He was a great personal favourite of Louis XIV, who allowed him more latitude than most of his subjects. In 1672 he spent Holy Week at la T. and was then disgraced and dismissed from court for refusing to serve under Turenne. By 1673 he was back on active service in the Low Countries, quarrelling with the commander, Condé, but by 1679 he was 'grand écuyer' (equerry) to the Dauphin's wife. In the intervals of campaigning he transformed his house at l'Isle-Marie (not far from Valognes) into a retreat centre staffed by Eudists, built a chapel and also a hospital for infirm soldiers. In 1684 he took command in Roussillon and once more fell into disgrace. When James II fled to France he accompanied him to Normandy (and to la T. in 1690) and in 1692 was in command of the land forces preparing operations against William of Orange. He took some blame for the naval disaster at la Hougue, and withdrew finally to Vincennes, of which he had been Governor until 1692, when he handed over the title to his grandson (aged 7). There he died, and was buried, on 5 December 1694, but his heart was interred separately, like that of his son, at l'Isle-Marie. Like his parents he was a considerable patron of the Jesuits, but this did not prevent him cultivating the friendship of Jansenists. He was a close friend of Bossuet, and between them they enabled Mme de La Vallière to flee from court and enter the Carmel. Bellefonds remained closely linked with her, almost as spiritual director. All evidence shows him to be an independent, pious, and scrupulously honest man. 720501,720825,730209, 730920,731113,740328,740702, 740704,740825,740909,750227, 750410,750922,760106,760314, 760415,760507,760611,760812, 760928,761106,770420,770702, 770829,771223,780804,781006, 781130,781130a,790214,800103, 800914,810123a,820423,820608, 820911,820921,830415,831024, 840311,841230,850802,851125, 851129,860225,870211,870309, 870329,881001,881017,890105, 890507,890627,890704,890709, 890718,890728,890815,890903, 900102,900420,900427,901129, 910110,910527,910905,910920, 911001,911210,920107,920310, 920609a,920619,920705,920810, 920826,921015,921119,930108, 930511,930820,930914,940829 941125

Bellérophon, Jean de, R's tutor, an Auvergnat like Favier 581031

Bernardines du Précieux Sang *See* **Henriette**

Bernardins, Collège des *See* **L'Étoile**

Berziau, RP André de, Cong. Orat. (1620–96). Professed at Oratory in 1652, helped Pinette run Institution de l'Oratoire, 810602

Besançon *See* **Carmelites** (men)

Béthune *See* **Capuchin**

Béthune d'Orval, RM Marie-Angélique de, sister of Abbess of Gif, at Port-Royal de Paris (CO), 830227

Blampignon, Nicolas, curé of Saint-Merri, Paris from 1668 (1640–1710). Fashionable preacher and controversialist, doctor of the Sorbonne and censor. 940528

Boccone, RP Paul, CO. Born Palermo 1633, at Cistercian house

in Florence. Scholar, botanist, and correspondent of Nicaise. 891031
BOCQUILLOT, Lazare (1649-1728). Successively soldier and lawyer, then ordained 1675. At Port-Royal for a time, then returned to Avallon, his birthplace, in 1686. Publisher of homilies and learned articles approved by R. and Mabillon. A friend of Nicole, he later had contacts with Orval. (See *Vie de L. Bocquillot*, [1745]) 881125,881200
BODEAU,M. 820524a
BOILEAU, Jacques (1649-1735). Tutor to sons of ducs de Luynes and Noailles. Became theological advisor to Abp Noailles of Paris and acted as superior to many religious houses in the diocese. 970330
BONA, Jean, Cardinal (1609-74). Of Dauphinois origin. A Feuillant of the Italian (Bernardine) Congregation he became General in 1654 and was reappointed, against normal practice, in 1657 and 1660, through the direct intervention of Pope Alexander VII, whose close friend and counsellor be became. Created cardinal by Clement IX in 1669. Against all forms of laxity, he was of similar temperament to R. but no more a Jansenist than he. He was very learned and on close terms with Maurists. His death deprived R. personally and the SO in general of a good and powerful friend. (See L. Ceyssens, OFM, 'Le Cardinal Jean Bona et le Jansénisme' in *Benedictina* 10 [1956] pp. 79-119 and 267-327). 700105,730409
BONNEJOIE, M. de 800516,800530
BOSQUILLON, Noël (1665-1734).

Friend of Santeuil: (the translator of St. Ephrem's *De compunctione* was Jean Bosquillon.) 961024
BOSSUET, Jacques-Bénigne (1627-1704), Bp of Meaux. Graduated in theology in same list as R. in 1652, ordained the same year and worked in Metz, but returned to Paris in 1659 and was soon favoured as a court preacher. Converted Turenne in 1668, was appointed Bp of Condom 1669, but resigned the next year on appointment as tutor to the Dauphin. His task completed in 1681, he was appointed Bp of Meaux, and the next year persuaded the Assembly of Clergy to adopt the Gallican articles which he himself had drawn up. He strongly supported the Revocation of the Edict of Nantes in 1685, and wrote numerous polemical works against Protestants, but also discussed possibilities of reunion in a lengthy correspondence with Leibnitz. His protégé, Fénelon, became an enemy over the Quietist affair in 1695 and Bossuet secured Fénelon's condemnation in Rome in 1699 by quite unscrupulous means. Bossuet wrote extensively: instructional works on history, politics, and philosophy for his royal pupil; many polemical works; and some remarkable devotional works, written in the last decade of his life for nuns and published posthumously, but he was best known as a preacher, especially on such formal occasions as the death of the great. He was violently opposed to casuists, but while sympathetic to augustinian theology was totally intolerant of

any challenge to authority, and thus no friend of the Jansenists. A close friend of Bellefonds, he probably became close to R. about the time of the spectacular conversion of Anne de Gonzague in 1672, in which he invited R. to play a part. 720220,750900, 810424,820627,821005,871123, 930316b,970300,970414,970500, 970703,000620

BOUILLON, Émilie de *See* **Carmelites**
BOULANGER *See* LE BOULANGER
BOUTHILLIER, Henri *See* RANCÉ
BOUTHILLIER, Marie de Bragelogne, Mme de, died 1673. Married R's uncle Claude (died 1652) and was the mother of Léon, comte de Chavigny, Gaston d'Orléans' favourite (died 1652 also). Her cousin, Anne de Bragelogne, was dom Le Nain's grandmother. A woman of great piety and a friend of RM Louise Rogier and Arnauld d'Andilly. 640430
BOUTHILLIER, Marie-Louise *See* **Annonciades**
BOUTHILLIER, Thérèse *See* **Les Clairets**
BOUTHILLIER, Victor (1595–1670), 01Abp of Tours. At Paris Oratory 1617–21, but never professed. Bp of Boulogne 1626, coadjutor to Abp of Tours 1630, succeeded as Abp 1640. He wanted to make his nephew, R., coadjutor but was frustrated by Mazarin 1657. An energetic prelate, but R. strongly disapproved of his attitude. 58/5
BRANCAS, Charles, comte de (1618–81). Son of duc de Villars and close friend of Gaston d'Orléans. He supported Mme de La Vallière against the Queen Mother. After a dissolute life he turned to piety, and was a frequent visitor to the Carmelites of the rue Saint-Jacques, in whose church he was buried. 760813,761028,761121, 770920
BRAQUITI, dom Bernard, Carthusian at Avignon. 800208
BRETAGNE, Premier Président de (born 1628), became Président of the Parlement at Dijon. 881229
BRIE, RP Nicolas de, CR, Saint-Jean-des-Vignes, Soissons, ? 83/1
BRUSCOLY, RP François, Cong. Orat. (died 1678); born in Paris, entered Lyon Oratory 1655, ordained 1657. Back to Paris, rue Saint-Honoré, in 1659, where he stayed until his death. 770324,780213, 780224,780324,780410, 780501

Capuchin, RP Jean, Béthune, 80/1, 800124
Carmelites (men), sub-prior, Besançon, 800613
Carmelites (women), convent in the rue Saint-Jacques, between the Sorbonne and Port-Royal de Paris, founded 1604. (*See* V. Cousin, *La Jeunesse de Mme de Longueville*, vol. 2 (1853), still invaluable on the community).
BELLEFONDS, RM Agnès de (1611–24 September 1691). Aunt of the maréchal. Born Judith, she left court to enter Carmel in 1629. After first becoming sub-prioress in 1645 and then prioress in 1649 she was repeatedly reelected to these offices with a break in tenure imposed only by canonical requirement. Universally revered and loved, she was an outstanding figure in a convent full of women of exalted birth and exemplary piety. Always very close to

her nephew, she passed on letters between him and R. 74/2,750604,751100,76/1 761102,77/1,770912,770914, 78/5,? UD 96 (or possibly to her sister Laurence, Abbess of Rouen).

BOUILLON, Sr Émilie de (1639–96). Daughter of duc de Bouillon, niece of maréchal de Turenne, she was professed in 1660, and her sister Hippolyte in 1663. The pattern of identifiable letters makes it certain that R. wrote to her regularly. Her brother, Emmanuel-Théodose, Cardinal and Ambassador to Rome, visited la T. more than once, and wrote extant letters to R., but none from R. survive. 750800,760200,770400, 770903,770918,770925, 780611,820706g,830530

ÉPERNON, Sr Anne-Marie de Jésus d' (1624–1701). Illegitimate granddaughter of Henri IV. Destined for a royal marriage, she defied her family by entering the Carmel at Bourges in 1648, was professed in 1649, and moved to Paris, where she spent the rest of her life. R. seems to have met her first in 1674, and regularly wrote. Her saintly reputation inspired abbé de Montis to write a hagiographical *Vie* (1774). 741200,750500,760824 761129,770214

LA VALLIÈRE, Sr Louise de la Miséricorde. Louise-Françoise le Blanc de la Baume, duchesse de (1644–1710). Became Louis XIV's mistress in 1661 and bore four children, of whom two daughters survived and were legitimised. In 1671 she ran away to a convent at Chaillot, but was forcibly brought back. Bellefonds and Bossuet together ensured that when she tried again, at the Carmelites in 1674, she was successful. Clothed in June 1674, professed a year later, she became a model of penitential piety. Her letters to Bellefonds have been published several times, and her *Réflexions sur la Miséricorde de Dieu* (1680) were first published on the suggestion of Bossuet and paid for by the Queen, and went through numerous editions, including an almost immediate English translation, *The Penitent Lady*, London, 1684. R. certainly wrote her more than the only two letters that can be identified. 740319,810100a

CASTELLAIN *See* Vaucelles

CAULET, Étienne (1597–1680) Bp of Pamiers. Appointed to Pamiers in 1644 from Saint-Sulpice. Like his neighbour at Alet, Pavillon, he was a staunch supporter of Port-Royal and became involved also in the long wrangle between Louis XIV and Rome over the *Régale* (royal rights in their and other dioceses). One of those from whom R. early sought advice, he wanted R. later to make a foundation in his diocese. He visited la T. in 1675. 690326, 710607,720307,720723a,73/5, UD 60

CAUMARTIN, Louis-François Le

Fèvre de (1624-87). Friend and
agent of Retz, conseiller d'état
1672, Intendant in Lyonnais,
then in Champagne (with
jurisdiction over Clairvaux). His
son, Jean-François Paul, was given
the abbey of Buzay in 1675 (at
the age of 7) which no doubt
explains R's correspondence about
dom Garreau. 800829,801124,
801200,820725,850819
Celestines, order founded in Italy
in 1250. The General remained in
Italy, but by the seventeenth
century the French Provincial was
effectively autonomous, and it is
almost certain that letters
addressed to the General were in
fact to the Provincial. From
1667-March 1670 this was Louis
Tertorin, from March-October
1670 François Gervaise (who died
after being reelected for a third
triennate), and from October
1674-80 Louis Tertorin again
(who also served three triennates).
The Order was not in a happy
state, and Jansenist influences made
things worse, so that defections to
la T. and elsewhere (e.g. Septfons)
were numerous. (See MS history of
the Order, A 5145).
 RP 'GENERAL', 680819,681027,
  690817,700615,700817a
 BAUDUY, RP Bonaventure (died
  1693) prior of Marcoussis,
  author of a life of Celestine
  Blessed Pierre de Luxembourg
  (1681). Extracts from
  undatable and unidentified
  letters in BN 19324.
 RONAT, RP Joseph, prior of
  Sens. ? 711004,? 711204,
  720600,721104
Chaise-Dieu *See* La Chaise-Dieu
Châlons-sur-Marne *See* VIALART

Champagne, abbey of SO, diocese
of Le Mans, 'RP' ? 80/2,801231a
CHAMPAGNY, (or CHAMPIGNY),
 RP de, possibly RP Cosme
 (1648-1726), a Barnabite preacher
 in Paris and head of college at
 Passy 800701
CHARMOT, Nicolas (c.1655-1714).
 Leading China missionary 1685-
 91, became director of Missions
 Étrangères (Foreign Missions) in
 Paris and Procurator in Rome,
 where he was a vigorous opponent
 of Jesuit policy in China. 891019
CHARTONNET, RP Antoine-François,
 CR of Saint-Vincent, Senlis (died
 1729). Elected Visitor of
 Congregation of Sainte-Geneviève
 1694. 941014
Châtillon, abbey of SO in diocese
of Verdun
 CLAUDE LE MAÎTRE, abbot (1669-
  7 August 1693). Born c.1633,
  professed Châtillon 1650, then
  at Foucarmont and Collège
  des Bernardins, before
  returning to Châtillon 1659.
  Then prior at Hautefontaine,
  and elected abbot at Châtillon
  when Abbot Jacques Minguet
  resigned and entered la T.
  Driven out by war, monks
  returned 1678. Related to
  Arnauld, a friend of Le Roy,
  and in close touch with Orval
  he sheltered Nicole and other
  Jansenists. Some original
  letters from Le Maître to Le
  Roy survive (U 745). See
  especially E. Jacques, 'Charles
  de Benzeradt et les influences
  Port-Royalistes in *Aurea-Vallis,
  Mélanges*, (Liège: Soledi, 1975)
  pp 157-96. 730723,? 751000,
  79/1,790710,790817,800113,
  800131,800616,800918,

810911,820627,830112,
830508,? UD 136
CHÉNEVIÈRES, M. de 800100c
CHEVREUSE, Charles-Honoré
d'Albert, duc de (1646–1712)
770122
CHOISEUL, Duplessis-Praslin, Gilbert
de (1613–89), Bp of Comminges,
then Tournai. Doctor of the
Sorbonne 1640. Bp of Comminges
1644. Apparently the first to
suggest, about 1659, that R.
should go to Alet for advice and
also to mention a monastic
vocation. Translated to Tournai
1671. Published books of Catholic
apologetics against atheists and
heretics in 1680 and 1689, and
showed himself in both his
dioceses a devoted pastor. He was
fond of R. but deplored his
extremism. 750200,750500a,
770815,820620
Cîteaux,
Jean Petit, Abbot of, (1670–92).
Born 1628. Professed at
Cîteaux, ordained 1653,
doctor of Canon Law. Prior
at La Bussière and Bonport.
Vaussin's successor, Louis
Loppin, having died only
weeks after his election in
June 1670, Petit was elected
abbot almost unanimously,
and with the warm and public
approval of SO leaders,
including R. Intellectually very
able, and an ascetic, but
authoritarian and legalistic, he
finished by antagonising those
he should have reconciled.
(See L.J. Lekai, *The Rise of the
Cistercian Strict Observance*,
Washington, 1968) pp 144–
57. 700713,710225,710407,
? 710826a,720505,720529

Clairets, See Les Clairets
Clairvaux,
PIERRE HENRY, Abbot of
(1654–76) 730104
PIERRE BOUCHU, Abbot of
(1676–1718). Nephew of
Abbot Vaussin of Cîteaux,
professed at Cîteaux c.1643,
then Abbot of Septfons 1649,
and of La Ferté 1655. Elected
to Clairvaux February 1676,
but did not actually move
until May 1677. He had been
expected to succeed Vaussin in
1670 and became one of
Petit's bitterest enemies
thereafter. 790526,810221
Clarisses, Alençon, RM Luce de
Saint-Pierre 810519
CLERMONT-TONNERRE, François de,
Bp of Noyon (1629–1701, bp
from 1661). 970707
Cluny, 'Abbé Général de la
Congrégation de', presumably the
superior and vicar general (not an
abbot), Pierre Simon from
1676–85 810829
'RP de la Congrégation de'
880723
Colombe See LA COLOMBE
Comminges, Bp of See CHOISEUL,
RECHIGNEVOISIN
COMPAGNON, Mme 740500
CORNUTY See Tamié
CORVILLY, M. l'abbé de 841211
COURCIER, Pierre, Théologal of
Paris c.1680 (died 1713) 870504a
COURSELLES, M de 801219
COURSELLES, Mlle de, Val-de-Grâce,
Paris 930802
COURTIN, Honoré (1622–1703). A
friend of R. from boyhood.
Diplomatic colleague of Paul
Barillon, conseiller d'état 1673.
Suffered from cataracts. Visited la
T. with Fieubet in 1686, and

thought of retiring there as a layman, but R. dissuaded him. Despite increasing blindness he stayed on as one of Louis XIV's most trusted diplomatic advisers. 871030a

COUTURIER, dom Robert (or Robin), SO.
Perseigne. Professed at Barbeaux, prior of Preuilly 1664 (?–1670), prior of Perseigne 1678–81 (and probably longer), possibly returned to Barbeaux as prior addressed from 1687. 711212, 790610,790904,790906, 791205,791213,801120b, 801122,801224,810206, 810923,811005,811022, 811123,811208
See also **Barbeaux**

DAGUESSEAU, Mme 881008
DAURAT, RP, Cong. Orat., extracts from undated and unidentified letters in BN 19324
DAURAT, M., conseiller de la grande chambre, 80/7
DES CHASSAY (? D'ESCHASSÉ), M. 820706
DESLIONS, Jean (1615–1700), dean of Senlis 1638–92 760309
DIROIS, François, 1620–93, personal theologian to Cardinal d'Estrées, ambassador in Rome. Doctor of the Sorbonne 810825b
DORIVAL, dom François, OSB, Luxueil (Cong. de Saint-Vanne) 781208
DRUEL, Nicolas, succeeded R. as commendatory abbot of Abbaye du Val (CR, diocese of Bayeux) 1662–76, when he resigned and became a regular. 761115
DU CHARMEL, François de Ligny, comte (1646–1714). Converted after a worldly life and lived at Institution de l'Oratoire. From c.1684 usually spent Lent at la T. 941110

DUHAMEL, Henri (1610–13 November 1682). Ordained 1641, curé of Saint-Maurice, Sens, 1642, and quoted with approval by Arnauld in *De la fréquente communion* for his rigorist sacramental practice there. Curé of Saint-Merri, Paris, 1644. Exiled for refusing to sign Formulary in 1654. Persuaded to sign in 1664, he returned briefly to Saint-Merri, then became a canon of Notre-Dame. In 1671 returned to Saint-Maurice, in succession to Cordon, who had entered la T. Thenceforth, after a visit to la T., lived a quasi-monastic life, and abandoned his former instransigence including Jansenism (see *Vie de M. Du Hamel*, n.p.n.d. [by S. Treuvé]) 800127,801120,811211,820309, 820524,820806,821107

DUHAMEL, M., nephew and successor of Henri 821222
DUPLESSIS-GUÉNÉGAUD, Elisabeth de Choiseul, marquise de (died 1677). Cousin of Gilbert de Choiseul, Bp, and of the Barillons. Wife of Henri (died 1676), Colbert's predecessor as minister. Her salon, a meeting place for high society, was frequented by R. before his conversion. 760400
DU SUEL, François (died 1686). A doctor of theology, first tried the Oratory, then curé of Châtres (now Arpajon) near Versailles 1661–76. Spent three weeks at la T. in 1673, but was dissuaded by R. from staying. Canon penitentiary of Arras from 1676.

Books on St Philip Neri, and a translation of a life of Cardinal Bona (1682), also some essays on conversion and indifference to worldly goods. His stay at la T. inspired the *Entretiens de l'abbé Jean et du prêtre Eusèbe*, (Paris, 1674, several reeditions), a quite fictitious and even implausible account of R's alleged spiritual teaching. 780315,800100a, ? 820115,? 830830a,? 840814
Du VERGER, dom, Proviseur Collège de Narbonne, CO 930913

ENTRAGUES, Mme d', probably Catherine de Courtavel de Saint-Rémy, widow of Camille, marquis d'Entragues (died 1679) 880118
ÉPERNON *See* Carmelites
Essai, abbey OSA, diocese of Séez
  Marie-Françoise Trotti de La Chétardie, abbess 1638-76 ?1672
  Françoise Trotti de la Chétardie, coadjutrix to above (her aunt) from 1652, abbess 1676-10 June 1687. Born 1629, at Jouarre 1636, professed Essai 1646, consecrated by Bossuet 1684. Succeeded by her sister Marie. A very pious woman, but a poor administrator, she introduced abstinence on Mondays. The abbey was in the patronage of Mme de Guise, as lord of Alençon. Her uncle became curé of Saint-Sulpice, Paris, and briefly Mme de Maintenon's director. (See MS chronicle, printed in *Archives de l'Orne*, Alençon, 1894, H 3976, H 3 pp. 132-41.) 790200, 81/5,81/6,820308, 820822,820910,830114

Étoile *See* L'Étoile
ÉTRECHY, M. d', 'chez Procureur-Général' 820112
EUGÉNIE, RM, Brussels 730225a
Évreux *See* MAUPAS DU TOUR

FAVIER, M. (father of following) 420904
FAVIER, Jean (1609-1703). A native of Thiers, in the Auvergne. Ordained c.1634. With his fellow Auvergnat Bellérophon, he became R's tutor c.1631 and remained with the family until 1642. He remained in close contact not only with R. but also with his sister, the comtesse d'Albon, and her children. Some correspondence with Grammontine monks (a local Order) survives, also some original letters from Mme de La Barge, Louise-Henriette d'Albon, Maisne, and Félibien, all, with R's letters, at Clermont-Ferrand. (See E. Jaloustre, *Un Précepteur auvergnat de l'abbé de Rancé* [1887]). 420926, 421011,421200,430325,430900, 431100,440213,440317,441019, 451125,461000,461016,470516, 470730,481222,500219,510212, 580514,580727,600510,? 610408, 620818a,630903,640704,650925, 661022,670903,690611,700124, 701101,710708,710803,711019, 711215,720401,720507,720608, ? 720829,721028,721207,730203, 730209a,730503,730508,730611, 730802,730914,731229,740424, 740707,740722,751003,760806, 760829,770223,770720,780303, 780705,780807,790515,790729, 791203a,800201,800828,800930, 810213a,810525,810622,810831, 810908,820430,820806a,830513, 830530b,841015,850708,850920, 860228,870227b,870703,871028, 880415a,880727,881107,890914,

Index of Addressees

891002,891114,910903,911125,
920204a,920524,920824
FAVORITI, Mgr Agostino, assistant
secretary of state to Pope Innocent
XI (1624–82) 780123
FÉLIBIEN, Pierre, canon of Chartres
from 1677 (died 22 April 1691)
(*not* the brother of André Félibien
des Avaux, also of Chartres, who
published the first description of
la T. in 1671). R's companion on
the journey to Rome in 1664,
and author of a chronicle of that
experience, now lost. 820301,
820730b
FERRAND DE GRANDMAISON, dom
Bruno (originally a
Premonstratensian), professed at la
T. in 1684, died 1686, aged 65;
name at la T. Paul. Apparently a
friend of R's worldly days.
780711,780717,781011,781126,
801116
FERRAND, dom André, OSB (unless
this is a confusion with above,
there is no known Benedictine of
that name, and it may well be a
misreading for Jannel, *q.v.*) 820906c
FERRAND, M., maître des requêtes
801115
Ferté *See* La Ferté
Feuillants, RP Général; from
1681–87 this was Jean-Baptiste
Pradillon, who died in 1689.
851000
Flandre, RP de, apparently a
geographical, not a family
designation, UD 103
FLORIOT, Jean, 1604–91, Jansenist
author of *Morale chrétienne* . . .
du Pater (1673) 73/7
FONSAL, M., maître des requêtes
801205
Fontfroide, abbey of CO, diocese
of Narbonne;
GARREAU, dom Joseph, doctor
of the Sorbonne, prior of
Buzay (CO, diocese of
Nantes), disgraced and sent to
Fontfroide, professed at la T.
in 1684, aged 40, died 1690.
He had been syndic of
Brittany, but the cause of his
fall is unknown. 801031,
811214
MONTAIGNAC, dom Joseph de
870213
FORCOAL, Jean, Bp of Séez, from
1671 to his death 25 February
1682, 741000b, 810521
Foucarmont, abbey of SO, diocese
of Rouen
JACQUES FLEUR DE MONTAGNE,
Abbot 1674–78, ? 741000
JEAN-EDMOND DE LA TEULLE,
Abbot 1678–97, ? 800131a
See also CORNUTY
FOUCHIÈRES, dom Henri de, OSB
(Saint-Vanne), professed Saint-
Vincent de Besançon 1651, died
Luxueuil 1702. 790104
Foy, M., conseiller du Roi,
Beauvais. 510312

GARREAU *See* Fontfroide
GERBAIS, Jean (1629–99). Doctor of
Canon Law, fervent Gallican,
opposed to the theatre and a
moral rigorist. A book on the
ordination of religious in 1665
was followed by one in 1679 on
'major cases' which he thought
should be judged by bishops, a
view much resented in Rome. His
extant correspondence includes
letters from Abbot Beaufort of
Septfons, as well as from other
friends of R. 930802a,930826,
930831,931008,931128,931130,
931223,940128,940509,940622,
940830b,940912,941202,941220,
950103,950120,950310,950331,
950411,950430,950512,950612,
950630,950714,950812,951018,

951103,951121,951126,951214,
951218,960105,960317,960614,
960922,97/1
Gif, abbey OSB, diocese of Paris; RM ANNE-VICTOIRE de Montglat, c.1647–1701. Brought up at Port-Royal until the schools were disbanded in 1659. Professed at Gif in 1667, she became novice-mistress and sub-prioress before reluctantly accepting election as abbess in 1675, and took over in May 1676. The death of a dozen or so nuns in her first year enabled her more easily to establish reform with the help of Ameline, Archdeacon of Paris and the visitor. In 1686 she resigned after much heart-searching in favor of Anne-Eléonore de Béthune d'Orval, brought in from Reims, but in February 1687 was prevailed upon to become prioress. She was excessively scrupulous about her own shortcomings, but the reputation of Gif under the rule of herself and her successor stood very high. 74/1,75/1,790600,800718, ? 850422,? 880115,? 890105a, ? 901218

GOËLLO, Anne d'Avaugour de Bretagne, Mlle de (1626–1707). Younger sister of Mme de Montbazon and Mlle de Vertus, she lived at the mansion of her nephew, the prince de Soubise, in Paris. She seems to have spent her later life in a sedately sociable, rather than reclusive, manner, after a period of worldliness. 751100,810421a,820723,841130

GOISDAN, M., curé 801010

GOURDAN See **Saint-Victor**

Grandselve, abbey of CO, diocese of Toulouse: fr Jean-Philippe Loume 780229

GRAVE, Pierre, curé of Saint-Louis-en-l'Isle, Paris (1662–93), 821217

Grenoble See LE CAMUS

GRILLIÈRE See LA GRILLIÈRE

GUÉRIN, dom Simon, Carthusian at Bassenville, near Clamecy, diocese of Nevers 720120

GUISE, Elisabeth d'Orléans, duchesse de (1646–96). Daughter of Gaston d'Orléans by his second marriage; she married Louis-Joseph de Lorraine, duc de Joyeuse, later duc de Guise (1650–71) in 1667. Their only child died (aged 4) in 1675. She divided her time between Alençon, the fief she had inherited, and Luxembourg Palace in Paris, which she had to share with her half-sister, Mme de Montpensier. Her sister had married the Grand Duke of Tuscany, but left him and the children for life in a convent, making regular visits to Alençon and often from there to la T. She was extremely devout, but very conscious of her royal dignity and treated most people with some hauteur. Her court (and the entourage in whose company she visited la T.) included Mmes de Belin, d'Huxelles, de Vibraye and other correspondents of R. 790815,790821,821119,830914, 840210a,840519,840929a, 841004a,850224,850715,860101, 860214,860216,860406,860605, 860611,860813,860825,860912, 860919,861003,861121,861128, 861205,861216,861219a,861225, 861230a,87/2,870116,870125, 870213a,870227,870227a,

870304,870306,870316,870327,
870504b,870509,870526,870610,
870814,870823,870831,870924,
870930,871009,871015,871200,
88/1,88/2,88/3,88/4,880100,
880101,880200,880226,880300,
880900,881100,881118,89/1,
89/2,89/3,890208,890300,
890400a,891000,891100,891200,
891200a,90/1,90/2,900300,
910421,920121,920204,920224,
920303,920317,920407a,920421,
920423,920428,920500,920530,
920609,920626,920708,930101,
930103,930112,930208,930223,
930316,930412,930500,930615,
930823,930929,931026,931102,
931207
GUY *See* **La Colombe**

HAMON, Jean (1618-87) solitary and physician at Port-Royal. He had been one of Racine's teachers. 750700
HARCOURT, prince d', reference to ecclesiastical career excludes Alphonse-Henri Charles de Lorraine, who married Brancas' daughter; perhaps Alphonse-Louis (1644-89) who became commendatory abbot of Royaumont in infancy. UD 83
HARCOURT, princesse d', presumably Brancas' daughter Françoise, who became princesse on marriage in 1667 and died in 1715. 820613
HARDY, dom Robert, OSB, Visitor of Saint-Maur 820400
HARLAY, Achille de, comte de Beaumont (1639-1712). Procureur-Général in 1667, Premier Président in 1689, resigned 1707. 830402,840124, 850722,890428,890703,890926, 891003
HARLAY DE CHAMPVALLON, François

de (1625-95), Abp of Paris. Appointed Abp of Rouen 1651, of Paris 1671, member of the French Academy. A boyhood friend of R., a very politically minded prelate, distantly related to the above. 740800a,820413, 820512,820706d,901119,910800
HARLAY, RM Marie-Françoise de, Vis. (c.1644–1714). Brought up at les Clairets, where her aunt was abbess, she made her First Communion at the Visitation at Melun in 1656, and then went back to les Clairets with a view to succeeding her aunt. In 1662 for family reasons she had to return to the world, but after a conversion in 1665 she entered the Visitation at Melun, where she stayed and occupied all posts except that of superior. Her mother, Charlotte-Françoise de Thou, had married her cousin (and Achille's brother) Christophe-Auguste de Harlay, and after he died in 1670 she too entered the Visitation at Melun in 1678, taking the habit in 1700 (aged 77) and dying in 1704. ? 841110, 850400,? 851113,? 860103, 860221,870407,? 89/4,? 890400
HECQUET, Philippe (1661-1737). Religious controversialist and distinguished physician, who attended Mlle de Vertus and also the Carmelites of the rue Saint-Jacques, where he retired in 1727. 921200
Heisterbach, abbey of CO, diocese of Cologne: dom Richard Lapp, dom Théodore Bourlez, dom François Weber 720514,720514a
HENRIETTE DU SAINT-SAUVEUR, RM, Bernardines du Précieux Sang, rue de Vaugirard, Paris 880210a

HERMANT, Godefroi (1617–91) native of Beauvais, Rector of the University of Paris 1646–48, later canon of Beauvais. In 1656 expelled from the Sorbonne for supporting Arnauld. Author of memoirs invaluable for history of Jansenism, and editor of patristic authors including Athanasius, Basil, Chrysostom, and Gregory Nazianzen from 1658. Close friend of dom Le Nain's brother, Tillemont. 720922,73/1,730128, 740903,741227

Hospitalières *See* VIERGE
HOUSSAYE *See* LA HOUSSAYE
HUET, Pierre-Daniel (1630–1721) Bp of Avranches. A member of the French Academy and a leading scholar, bp from 1692 until 1699. 961231

'HUGUENOTS', MM (brothers) UD 66

HUMIÈRES, Louise-Antoinette de La Chastre, duchesse d', (1635–1723) wife of Louis de Crevant, duc and maréchal d'Humières (died 1694), and dame d'honneur to the Queen. 940900

HUXELLES, Marie Le Bailleul, marquise d' (1626–1712). Married first the marquis de Nangis (died 1644) then Louis Chalon du Blé, marquis d'Huxelles (died 1658). She was one of Mme de Guise's entourage, and a correspondent of several religious, including a Carmelite friend of Abbot Beaufort of Septfons who spread rumours about R. Saint-Simon describes her as arrogant and flirtatious but a notable hostess. 721202a,911007

INNES, Lewis (1651–1738). Principal of Scots College, Paris, 1682, chaplain to Queen of England and member of James II's council after 1689. 970509

INNOCENT XI, Pope (Benedetto Odelschalchi) (1611–89), Pope 1676. 771010

JADOT (or SADOT), RM, 900800
JAMES II, King of England (1633–1701). Second son of Charles I. Fought against Cromwell as Duke of York, then fled to France. Returned at the restoration of his brother Charles II (1660) and became Lord High Admiral. He converted to Catholicism in 1670, and despite opposition on that score from Parliament succeeded his brother in 1685. His initial policy of accommodation with the Church of England soon gave way to open preference for Catholics in public office and provoked revolt among the Anglican bishops and general public resentment. His son-in-law, William of Orange, was invited to the throne by leading men in Church and State, and landed unopposed in 1688 ('the Glorious Revolution'). James fought a rearguard action in Ireland but his defeat at the Boyne marked the end of his hopes. He seems to have been genuinely pious but endowed with very poor judgement. 901221,910124, 910403,910905a,91112 ,950725, 951127,961004,970110,970314, 980900,990115,990600,990826, 990923,991010,991112

JANNEL, dom André, OSB, Bossuet's cousin. Professed at Saint-Faron, Meaux, 1679, died Saint-Denis 1726. ? 820906c,951203

JOLLAIN, Jean ('au Réfuge'), syndic of the Sorbonne 1695–96. 940830a

Index of Addressees 291

JOLLAIN, Jacques ('Saint-Marcel'), brother of above. 930813
JOLY, Mme 820718

LA BARGE, Catherine d'Albon, comtesse de. R's niece, born c. 1645, married François, comte de La Barge, and lived near Thiers, Auvergne. They had three daughters, but no sons. Letters to Favier exist. 800100,? 820816, 861201,870118,890726
LA BARGE, Mlle de (unnamed daughter of above) ? 880810
LA BROSSE, Pierre de, Bp of Léon (1671-1701) 801218
La Chaise-Dieu-du-Theil, Fontevrist priory, diocese of Evreux, RM prioress 810511
La Colombe, abbey of SO, diocese of Bourges;
  PIERRE DE LA SALLE, Abbot 1667-1711. Professed at Clairvaux in 1683. Visitor and Vicar-General for SO in the province of Poitou. ? 730607c 790919,810831,820627
  DOM GUY 800129b,? 810831a
LA COUR, RP, CR at Saint-Jean-des-Vignes, Soissons; brother of dom Jacques, later Abbot of la T. 820306,821019
LA FAGE, Guillaume de (1637-1722). Vicar General of Commingues charged with affair of visions at Alan. 911013,911213
LA FAYETTE, Marie-Madeleine de La Vergne, comtesse de, (1634-93). Married François, comte de La Fayette, in 1655. He was much older than she, and she left him in 1658 to live in Paris. A leading light of salon society, intimate friend of La Rochefoucauld and Mme de Sévigné, also friendly with Bossuet and Têtu. Increasingly lonely in later years, she became very pious. Her masterpiece, the novel *Princesse de Clèves* (published 1678) shows exceptional sensibility and talent for psychological analysis, and she was a literary figure of real stature. 861022, 861227
La Ferté, abbey of CO, diocese of Chalon-sur-Saône; Pierre Bouchu, Abbot 1655-76 720707
LA GRANGE *See* Saint-Victor
LA GRILLIÈRE (also LA GRÉLIÈRE), Jeanne de Remefort de, died 23 July 1690. Mother of Mme de Tourouvre. Her husband was avocat- général at Metz and they lived in Paris and Poitou. She slowly went blind in later years and spent much time with her daughter. 830211b,860814
LA HOUSSAYE, Mme de 821001
LA MADELEINE, M. l'abbé de. Probably Érard-Anne Ragny de La Madeleine, dean of Autun 1677-82 (and nephew of the bp), and commendatory abbot of Tironneau 1669-1705, when he died. (A M. Camus, 'abbé de La Madeleine', was canon and théologal of Tours in 1667, but seems a less likely candidate.) 730101,830211,840430,840605a
LANCHAL, M. de, an official at Alençon and father of dom Jacques, a former Oratorian professed at Perseigne in 1681. 82/1
LAQUERRE, M. de, Marseille 960522
LA ROCHE *See* Visitation
LA SABLIÈRE, Marguerite Hessein, Mme de (1640-93). Born a Protestant, she married her cousin, also a Protestant, and had three children, when, in 1668, the marriage broke up. She started a

salon, attended by Paul Barillon among others, and in 1673 La Fontaine came to stay with her. After her husband's death in 1679 she was converted to Catholicism, but suffered much distress at the persecution of those members of her close family who refused conversion. By about 1685 she was incurably ill, and after losing her director, the Jesuit Rapin, in 1687 wrote to R., who, as always refused to become her director. She also wrote to Maisne direct, and copies of some sixty letters or fragments to R., and several to Maisne, survive, though only one from R. can be identified with certainty. She bore her affliction (breast cancer) with great courage, and seems to have found R's letters a real help. (See Vicomte Menjot d'Elbenne, *Mme de La Sablière* [1923]). 88/6,880730, 920528

LASSAY, Armand de Madaillan, marquis de (1652–1738) aide-de-camp to Louis XIV 1690–92. 830324

LA TRÉMOUILLE, Mlle [? Marie-Sylvie] de (1662–92). Daughter of Henri-Charles, prince de Tarente (who had been converted in 1670 from Protestantism after a visit to la T.). As the only unmarried daughter recorded, Marie-Sylvie seems the most likely candidate. 890829,? 891208

LAVAL, Commandeur de (Knight of Malta). He lived near la T. and was a friend of M. de Saint-Louis. 881202

LA VALLIÈRE *See* **Carmelites**

LE BOULANGER (or BOULANGER), M. l'abbé 850705,? 850830, 851225

LE CAMUS, Etienne (1632–1707), Bp of Grenoble. A boyhood friend of R. Doctor of theology 1650, then appointed royal chaplain. Appointed to Grenoble in 1671, made cardinal 1686. A close friend of Quesnel, whom he tried to bring to Grenoble as his Vicar-General, but after Quesnel went into exile (in 1684) their intimacy waned. He remained closely linked with the Oratory, and had many Jansenist friends and Jesuit enemies, but his orthodoxy is not in question. He became a benedictine oblate, and impaired his health through austerity and pastoral cares. He paid special attention to the moral instruction of his clergy, organised synods and seminaries, and in every way gave himself to his pastoral charge. He successfully maintained good relations both with R. and with the Grande Chartreuse (in his diocese) and was a thoroughly eirenic character. 721223,750420, 760317,760400a,771222,781105a, 791109,801027,801231,810615, 810800a,820104,820520,820700, 820704,820706e,820810,821207, 83/2,830101,861014,890720

LE CAMUS, Nicolas, 1625–1715. Brother of Etienne. Premier Président de la cour des aides 1672. 800129a

LEFÈVRE at Amiens. 801120a

LE NAIN, Jean (1609–98). Father of dom Pierre. Conseiller au Parlement 1632, adviser to Mme de Longueville, closely linked with Port-Royal, then maître des requêtes. Enjoyed a reputation for absolute integrity. 790607,900602

LE NAIN DE TILLEMONT *See* **TILLEMONT**

Léon *See* LA BROSSE

LE ROY, Guillaume (1610–84). A boy canon of Notre-Dame, Paris, he exchanged the canonry in 1653 for the abbey of Hautefontaine, where he took up residence in 1661. He made his abbey a centre and refuge for Jansenists. Until the quarrel over humiliations he had been one of R's closest friends. His secretary, Germain Willart (or Vuillart), kept all his correspondence (now at Utrecht). 69/1,72/6,720706, 720718,721202,730518,730712, 730819,731002,731129,740206, 751100a,770414,770625,781105b

Les Clairets, abbey of CO (then SO), diocese of Chartres.

RM THÉRÈSE BOUTHILLIER, R's sister (1622/3–February/March 1684). First documentary evidence of her presence at les Clairets is from 1647, but she had certainly been there much earlier. Her health was poor enough for her to apply for permission (refused) to take the waters in 1679, but allowed her to travel with her abbess, because R is known to have refused to meet them when they passed nearby. The tone of the few letters identifiably addressed to her suggests an intimacy which makes it likely that other, unidentified, letters are in fact to her. She remains almost wholly elusive. 621104,640430,710930, 730104a,800122,820523, 830121a,830220,? 840214

RM (friend of Thérèse) 840400a

FRANÇOISE-ANGÉLIQUE D'ETAMPES DE VALENÇAY (abbess 1687–1709). Brought up at the Visitation at Moulins, a member of a family highly distinguished in Church and State. Elected abbess in 1687, she amazed everyone by setting out at once to reform the house, never before having shown any signs of religious vocation (according to Mme de Sévigné). Her abbey was under the direction of Val-Richer, but she was determined to put it under Rancé, and finally overcame his resistance. In 1688 he sent her a confessor, and in 1690 conducted his first visitation (his first sortie from la T. since 1675). On R's resignation she soon quarrelled with Abbot Gervaise, whom she found insufficiently respectful, and contributed in large measure to his downfall through her use of family influence. Her zeal and piety seem proven, but she clearly lacked sense and moderation. (See *Vie de Mme de Valençay*, two slightly different MS versions in A 3389 and A 3989 attributed to the Oratorian, J-B Thouron). 870921,880609, 880818,880924,910404a

RRMM (collective letters): 880621,880924,900218, 921120

LE TELLIER, Charles-Maurice (1642–1710) Abp of Reims from 1671, younger brother of the minister Louvois 901022

L'Etoile, abbey of SO, diocese of Poitiers;

BERNARD DE CERISAY DU TEILLÉ, Abbot 1676–1702. Professed at Perseigne in 1657, he became prior of Tironneau in 1664, sub-prior of the Collège des Bernardins in 1671 and proviseur in 1672. On Abbot Jouaud's death he was nominated, but not accepted, as Visitor of the SO, but on election to l'Etoile in 1676 he was accepted as Visitor. He was a very able man, enjoying confidence and respect from all, and letters from him to Le Roy show him doing his best to reconcile Le Roy and R. (in U 749). 710121,? 730900a 751018,800120,830627

FR THÉODORE 820613a

Leyme, abbey of CO, diocese of Cahors:

ANNE D'ORVILLIERS de La Vieuville, Abbess 1654–85. From a leading Picard family, related through her mother to the Noailles. Professed at Abbaye-aux-Bois (originally at Noyon, but forced to move and by 1655 fixed in Paris) she was elected to Leyme in 1654 and went there with her sister Marguerite, also at Abbaye-aux-Bois, who became prioress. A zealous reformer, she had as much trouble from hostile Visitors as from recalcitrant nuns, but did some solid building in the church and established better discipline in the community. R's letters are much the fullest source of information about her, but see also E. Albe, 'L'abbaye cistercienne de Leyme' in *Revue Mabillon*, 2e série, 23 (1926) pp. 192–217. 73/8,730510,760100c, 760500,760827,770404, 780206,780307,781112a, 790202,790300,790511, 790817a,800314a,800609, 800730,801130,810100, 810312,810820,811214, 820125,820300a,820704, 820831,821014,821119a, 830121,850608,850806

Liège, RP from, 800730: *See also* ALBERT

Limoges *See* URFÉ

L'ISLE, dom Paulin de, OSB (1642–98). Professed c.1662 in Vannist Congregation. After a visit to la T. (c.1679) he began to press his superiors to allow him to transfer. Finally allowed to enter, he was professed in 1687. Novice-master 1696, he wrote to former Vannist colleagues inviting them to send postulants. See Lambert, *L'Idée d'un vrai religieux* (Châlons-sur-Marne, 1723). 860926,861007

L'ISLE, François de, canon of Châlons, brother of dom Paulin. 861106,870604,870629

LOGERIE, M de, Superior of seminary, Périgueux. 880502

LONGUEVILLE, Anne-Geneviève de Bourbon, duchesse de, 1619–79. Louis XIV's cousin, sister of the prince de Condé. Involved in constant intrigues, amorous and political, culminating in the civil war of the Fronde (1648–52), when Cardinal de Retz and La Rochefoucauld were rivals for her favours. After hostilities were over, she went to stay with her aunt, superior of the Visitation at Moulins, and by 1654 had converted. Singlin, of Port-Royal, was her director, and was succeeded by Sacy. Her husband died in 1663, her eldest son, Dunois, was ordained in 1669, despite mental instability so serious that he spent most of his life confined to an abbey near Rouen, and her younger son was killed in action in 1672. Later that year she withdrew to apartments in the Carmelite house of the rue Saint-Jacques, under the direction of Marcel, the parish priest. Mlle de Vertus and Mme de Sablé were close friends, she knew R. well, and was a staunch protector of Port-Royal. 720700,720920, 751100k,751200,770920c

LOUIS XIV, born 1638, King of France 1643-1715. 730807, 950530,950612

LOUISE-FRANÇOISE, RM See Visitation, ROGIER

LOUISE-HENRIETTE, RM See Visitation, ALBON

LOUME See Grandselve

LUCE, RM Marie See Annonciades, PICOT

Luçon See BARILLON

Luxueil See DORIVAL

LUYNES, Louis-Charles d'Albert, duc de (1620-90). Son of duchesse de Chevreuse, grandson of duc de Montbazon. Three times married. Several of his daughters were religious at Jouarre (diocese of Meaux) and correspondents of Bossuet and R. An admirer of Descartes, he was a neighbour and powerful supporter of Port-Royal. 790124

LUYNES, Anne de Rohan, duchesse de (1640-80). Second wife of Louis-Charles. She was the daughter of the duchesse de Montbazon, and her husband was the son of her own half-sister. ? 770801,770915,780303,780324, 790825,820906a

LUYNES, Mlle de, daughter (unidentified) of above. 790810, 810427

MABILLON, dom Jean, OSB (1632-1707). Professed in the Maurist Congregation at Saint-Rémy, Reims in 1653; from 1664 mostly at Saint-Germain-des-Prés, Paris. His edition of St Bernard (1667) was the one used by R. His work in benedictine history includes the *Acta Sanctorum O.S.B.* (1668-1701) and *Annales, O.S.B.* (1703-7). A scholar of the greatest distinction, he could hardly avoid answering R's attack on monastic study, but his innate modesty and courtesy stand out in the regrettable and long-running dispute. 820830,890911,930607, 930807,950600,900915

MADELEINE See LA MADELEINE

MALEBRANCHE, RP Nicolas, Cong. Orat. (1638-1715). Entered the Oratory in 1660. Probably the most distinguished French philosopher of the century after Descartes. He disagreed with the latter's dualism and metaphysics, and became involved in controversy with Bossuet and Arnauld, among others. He started to visit Perseigne from about 1674, and composed some of his work there. He best known books are *Recherche de la Vérité* (1674) and *Traité de la Nature et la Grâce* (1680). Contact with R. was a natural consequence of so many mutual friends at the Oratory and at Perseigne, but only two letters can be certainly identified. See J. Wehrle, 'Malebranche et l'abbaye de Perseigne' in *Province du Maine* 36 (1928) pp. 10-22 (though very thin). 720409,890829a

Malta, Knights of 88/5,890716.
See also LAVAL, MAREUIL
MARCEL, Louis, curé of Saint-Jacques-du-Haut-Pas 1667–1704. Confessor and confidant of numerous Jansenist sympathisers, and others, including the Barillons, Nicole, and Mme de Longueville. One of the most influential parish priests of the period, and on intimate terms with R. 770104, 800424,920407,920908,930914
MAREUIL, Commandeur de, Knight of Malta. Quesnel wrote to someone of the same name in 1681 at Marseille, and he may well be the same man. 890307
MARIE-LOUISE, RM See **Annonciades**, BOUTHILLIER
MARIE-LUCE, RM See **Annonciades**, PICOT
MARILLAC, Louis de (c.1648–96). He came of a family highly distinguished in public affairs, and his aunt Louise (died 1660, canonised 1934) was co-founder with Vincent de Paul of Sisters of Charity. He was a Doctor of the Sorbonne, curé of Saint-Germain-l'Auxerrois in 1670 and then of Saint-Jacques-de-la-Boucherie, almost next door. R. is known to have been in regular contact, and some of the unidentified letters are most likely to him. 731029
MARTÈNE, dom Edmond, OSB (1654–1739). Professed at Saint Rémy, Reims, 1672, then at Saint-Germain with Mabillon. A noted liturgist and historian. 900108
MATIGNON, Charlotte, comtesse de (1657–1721). Married her uncle Jacques Goyon, comte de Matignon, attached to the Dauphin in 1680. 830211a

Maubuisson, abbey of SO, diocese of Rouen
LOUISE-HOLLANDINE (1622–1709) abbess 1664–1709. She was born Princess Palatine of Bavaria. Converted from Protestantism, she was brought up at Port-Royal. Professed at Maubuisson 1660, she became abbess in 1664, after a succession of scandalous royal nominees. She remained in close touch with Arnauld and Nicole, and did her best effectively to undo the work of her disgraceful predecessors. She was sister-in-law of Anne de Gonzague. Some of R's letters to another nun, prioress or sub-prioress, are sometimes wrongly assigned to the abbess. She always signed 'Louise Palatine, Abbesse'. (See Bibliothèque municipale, Pontoise, MS 23. *Registre des religieuses professes de . . . Maubisson, 1627–1753*, in which Morony's signature can be seen as confessor. The same MS shows that there were five Madeleines at the abbey simultaneously, and it is therefore not possible to identify the prioress or sub-prioress.) 801111,801212, 810913,811102,820300, 820706,821215
RM **MADELEINE** (prioress or sub-prioress), 801114,801212c, 810913,820300b,820706a, 821214,830812
See also MORONY (who was confessor for a time)
MAUPAS DU TOUR, Henri Cauchon, Bp of ÉVREUX 1661–80, 681227

MAUPEOU, Pierre (died 1713). At la T. for about nine months before health obliged him to leave (c.1681). Already planning an eventual life of R. with Maisne. Defended R. against Larroque in 1685. By 1691 curé of Nonancourt, not far from la T., he was involved in the intrigues leading up to Gervaise's resignation, and his elder brother (dom Grégoire, a former Dominican, professed at la T. in 1688) who was cellarer by then was an useful ally. Published his *Vie de . . . Rancé* in 1702, but apart from some original letters (often misdated) it is an unreliable source. 860317,920402,940108,950705, 971003

MAZARIN, Armand-Charles, duc de, (1631–1713). Succeeded his father as duc de La Meilleraye, but took the title Mazarin on marrying the Cardinal's niece Hortense in 1661. He and his uncle, abbé d'Effiat, bought Vérets from R. He became Governor of Alsace and of the fortress of Vincennes. His wife left him in 1666 to live in London, one daughter married Bellefonds' son, and another eloped with the marquis de Richelieu. He was the object of much derision, but was very pious, and associated with R's brother-in-law Albon in devout works. 751100d,791220,800602, ? 801230a,820913a,840312

Meaux *See* BOSSUET

MESMES, Jean-Jacques de (1630–88). Maître des requêtes 1657, *Président du Parlement* 1671, member of the French Academy. One of a long line of distinguished magistrates. 830204

MONCHY, RP Pierre de, Cong.

Orat. (1610–8 November 1686). Of a noble Picard family, he was ordained 1635. A notable preacher, often at Saint-Jacques-du-Haut-Pas, and a friend of Marcel's circle. Attended Gaston d'Orléans (with R.) on his deathbed in 1660. Always refused to be R's confessor, but acted as adviser. Close friend of Le Camus. Wanted to retire to la T., but R. would not hear of it. One of the best known and most respected directors of the day. 80/10, 800130,800700,810629,810917, 811009,820500a,821214,840100, 850826,851108 (often given as MOUCHY).

MONTAIGNAC *See* **Fontfroide**
MONTGLAT *See* **Gif**
MONTHOLON, François de 821229
MONTIGNY, abbé S. de 880810a
MONTPENSIER, Anne-Marie-Louise d'Orléans, duchesse de (1627–93). Only child of Gaston d'Orléans' first marriage, reputedly the richest heiress in Europe, known as la Grande Mademoiselle. An inveterate intriguer, and even military leader in the Fronde, she never married. She detested Mme de Guise, her half-sister. 760917
MORONY, dom Alain, SO. An Irishman, born c.1630, professed at Perseigne 1657, prior 1664–66, then moved to la T. Sent to start reform at Tamié in 1677, and acted as prior. On his own urgent request was recalled, briefly, to Perseigne, and then became chaplain to Maubuisson, about July 1682, where he is last heard of about 1684. ? 800100c, 800900c,81/1,820500,830106, ? 840722

NICAISE, Claude (1623-1701). A canon of the Sainte-Chapelle in Dijon, he met R. in Italy in May 1666, but did not follow up the acquaintance until much later. He was a scholar in his own right (archaeology) and conducted extensive correspondence with scholars throughout Europe, much of which has been published. He was a person of monumental indiscretion and probably did R. far more harm than good.
800325,800626,801212a,810120 811128,820215,830114,830530a 830826,831209,840124a,840802, 850112,850422a,850512,851028, 860130,860328,860515,860923, 861024,861111,870206a,870324, 870601,870717,870814a,871109, 871214,880115a,880228a,880408, 880427,880603,880628,880712, 880905,881102,881122,881213, 890113a,890217,890303,890630a 890914a,891012,891103,891126, 891200b,90/4,900220,900524, 900911,901114,901224a,910404, 910214,910307,910405a,910603, 910718a,910830,911004,911126, 920125,920322,920330,920416, 920523,920619a,920903,920928, 921030,930128,930207,930306, 930316a,930604,930610,930629, 930725,931007,931026a,940211, 940308,940505,940606,940902, 940628,940718,941216,941218, 950112,950130,950320,950411a, 960313,960512,960715,961018, 961109,961112,970803,971003a, 98/1,980108,980417,980605, 980818,990114,990312,990630, 990809,000304

NICOLE, Pierre (1625-95). Arnauld's closest collaborator, but one of the most moderate Jansenists. A theologian, he never proceeded to priestly orders. He was engaged in much polemic writing against both Jesuits and Protestants, but his chief work is the *Essais de morale* (1671-78). He shared Arnauld's exile in 1679, and stayed for a time at Châtillon and Orval. In 1681 he returned to Chartres, his birthplace, and submitted to the Abp of Paris. He was opposed to R. on many issues (notably in the dispute with Mabillon) but remained on good terms with him.
? 720125,730927,751202, ? 780315a,871016,871228, 880422,890826

NOAILLES, Louis-Antoine (1651Q 1729) Abp of Paris 1695. Bp of Cahors in 1679, translated to Châlons the next year, to Paris in 1695, he was made cardinal in 1700. 980800,980900,980909, 981123,981203,990709

NOCEY, M. de, ex-Cong. Orat. (died 1692). 790909

Noyon *See* CLERMONT-TONNERRE

O, Marie-Anne de la Vergne de Guilleragues, marquise d' (1657-1737) *or* possibly Antoinette du Prat. 840929

Orval, abbey of SO, diocese of Trier;

CHARLES DE BENZERADT (1635-1707) Abbot 1668 1703. A Luxemburger of noble birth, he was professed at Orval in 1656, and became coadjutor in 1666. In 1669, at his own request, he met R. at Châtillon to discuss reform, visited la T., and sent one or two monks there for training, but reform only really began in 1672. Opposition from the 'anciens', who were numerous, delayed progress, but organ music was suppressed in 1684 and manual labour introduced in 1688. Contacts with Jansenists were close; Nicole, Quesnel, and Pontchâteau all visited for a while, and the abbey later suffered for this, though it had a good reputation for discipline. From 1681-97 it lay in territory annexed by France from the Empire, and Benzeradt made the point at the SO Chapter of 1684 that he had done homage to Louis XIV. He was the senior SO abbot at that chapter, and records show that he enjoyed the respect of his colleagues and of the Abbot of Cîteaux, who presided. He resigned in 1703. See essential articles by T. Réjalot, 'Le Jansénisme à L'abbaye d'Orval' in *Annales de l'Institut Archéologique du Luxembourg*, 63 (1932) pp. 59-82, and 65 (1934) pp. 133-49. Also *Aurea-Vallis, Mélanges* (Liège, 1975) pp. 155-96. 690324,720419a, 730125,75/2,790527, 790803,84/1,840512

Pairis, abbey of CO, diocese of Basle, devastated by Swedish occupation in Thirty Years War; Abbot 810202
Pamiers *See* CAULET
Paris, Abp *See* HARLAY, NOAILLES, PÉRÉFIXE
PAVILLON, Nicolas (1597-1677) Bp of Alet 1637-77. An associate of Vincent de Paul in Paris, Pavillon devoted all his life after arriving in Alet to the pastoral care of his very poor, scattered, rural diocese. His commitment to a life of evangelical simplicity made him an early supporter of Jansenism, and he remained loyal to his friends to the end. Henri Barillon and Tréville (who had a house at nearby Foix) consulted him among others. Relations with R. became rather strained when Paul Hardy, théologal of Alet, unexpectedly arrived at la T. and was accepted by R., but he always professed the deepest respect for his most decisive adviser. 610928,620419, 630530a,640527,700216,700405, 720723,750415,751200b
PELLISSON, Paul (1624-93). Distinguished scholar and historian, converted from Protestantism. 780510
PÉRÉFIXE, Hardouin de Beaumont de (1605-70) Abp of Paris 1662. He was responsible for the first persecution of Port-Royal. 681119
Perseigne, abbey of SO, diocese of Le Mans.
Philippe-Jean Guêtre de PRÉVAL (1652-1708) commendatory abbot 1673-1708. He was a canon of Le Mans, took his duties seriously and bequeathed his large library to the monastery. 80/3
RP PRIOR (1678-81) *See* COUTURIER
RP PRIOR 851003 (possibly still Couturier)
PERTH, John Drummond, Duke of (1648-1716). Lord Chancellor of Scotland 1684, converted to Catholicism through Bossuet 1688, accompanied James II into exile and became chamberlain to his queen and tutor to his son. 900221

PINETTE, Nicolas (1613–29 January 1694). Treasurer to Gaston d'Orléans in 1643. After some early stirrings, converted by an Oratorian friend while campaigning in Northern France. Thenceforth closely associated with the Oratory, and from 1652 involved in the creation of Institution de l'Oratoire (a retreat centre) which was fully functioning by 1657, and to which R. and many after him went for retreat and advice. He used his own money for it and lived there until his death. R. always stayed there on his visits to Paris. Pinette was a regular visitor to la T. He is known to have had a natural son, legitimised in 1654, and perhaps for that reason never took orders. 760100b,800108,801104,811230, 820302,830104,830207a,831206

POMMEREAU, Auguste-Robert, conseiller d'état (1630–1702). 81/2

POMPONNE, Simon Arnauld, marquis de (1618–99). Son of Arnauld d'Andilly. Secretary of State for foreign affairs 1671, disgraced 1679, reinstated on the death of his enemy Louvois in 1691. 620218,711115,? 730808, 741000a,791203,910730a

PONTCHÂTEAU, Sébastien-Joseph du Cambout, abbé de (1634–90). Connected with many noble and influential families. Orphaned by 1648, he retired under the influence of Singlin, to Port-Royal in 1669, always entertaining the idea of a monastic vocation. On diplomatic mission in Rome 1677–80, he joined Arnauld in Holland. He was at Hautefontaine in 1684, then Châtillon; retired to Orval in 1685, and avoided all outside contacts. Returned to Paris in 1690 and died some months later. Constantly disguised and using pseudonyms he spent much of his life running away from his noble relatives. He knew R. as early as 1656. A key Jansenist figure. See B. Neveu, *Sébastien-Joseph du Cambout de Pontchâteau* (Paris, 1969). 671106,680200,680305,680828

Port-Royal-des-Champs, independent abbey, diocese of Paris;
    RM MARIE DU FARGIS, Abbess 1669–78. 76/3

Port-Royal-de-Paris, abbey of CO, RM Abbess 830227a *See also* BÉTHUNE D'ORVAL

Prépotin, (a village very near la T.) curé of 810800b

PRÉVAL *See* **Perseigne**

Prières, abbey of SO, diocese of Vannes, RP procurator 801230

Provins, Saint-Jacques, abbey of CR; RP (unknown) 820913

QUÉRAS, Mathurin (1614–95). Doctor of the Sorbonne 1647, expelled 1658 for approving Arnauld. Superior of seminary and Vicar-General at Sens 1658–74. On death of Abp Gondrin he was obliged to move to Troyes, and became prior of Saint-Quentin. An austere but moderate Jansenist. 851206,870614

QUESNEL, RP Pasquier, Cong. Orat. (1634–1719). Entered the Oratory 1657, and stayed at Institution after ordination. Then at Saint-Magloire 1666–69, where he came to know Arnauld. At rue Saint-Honoré 1669–78, but then sent to Orléans, having annoyed

Abp Harlay. Forced into exile with Arnauld, he was in Brussels 1684. Escaped from arrest 1703 and fled finally to Holland. His edition of St Leo (1675) was put on the Index for its Gallican tone, but his main work was the frequently expanded and reedited *Réflexions morales* (first edition, 1672), defended later by Abp Noailles of Paris, and the eventual cause of the Bull *Unigenitus* in 1713. A very able man, he took over as leader of the Jansenists on Arnauld's death, and was made progressively more intransigent by condemnation and persecution. 691230,700115,700224a,700805, 700817,700917,701000,701019, 701122,710117,710302,711006, 711010,711103,711125,711209, 720819,721009,730118,730301, 730405,730624,730725,730729, 740521,750319,750704,750715, 751005,760130,760611a,761220, 770207,770207a,770218,770321, 780827,790104a,790119,790822, 800411,810722

RANCÉ, Henri [le] Bouthillier, chevalier de (1633-1726). R's younger brother. Became a Knight of Malta, took part in campaign in Flanders and was wounded in 1658. Then he was in the sea and land operation in Algeria, 1663. By 1701 was *chef d'escadre* and commander of the port of Marseilles after forty-six years unbroken service. Uniquely created supernumerary Lieutenant-General in 1718 in recognition of his seniority. Finally he retired 1720, and died at the home of his nephew, Vernassal, in Auvergne. His signature on documents from 1671 (and perhaps earlier) is 'Le Bouthillier'. His age, much misrepresented, is attested by official documents in the French naval archives (Archives de France, Marine C^7 268) 690523, 830207,860215

RANUZZI, Cardinal Angelo-Maria (died 1689). Nuncio in Paris 1683, Cardinal 1686, Abp of Bologna 1688. 871027

RECHIGNEVOISIN DE GURON, Louis de (1617-93) Bp of Comminges 1671-93. Doctor of the Sorbonne, Bp of Tulle 1653, translated to Comminges 1671, from 1688 involved with R. over the visions at Alan, he behaved with great tact and prudence. See Sol, *Notre-Dame de Saint-Bernard de Comminges* (1923). 880809, 881111,890719,900123,911111

Reims *See* LE TELLIER

RETZ, Jean-François-Paul de Gondi, Cardinal de (1613-79). Forced into an ecclesiastical career, he became coadjutor to his uncle, the Abp of Paris, in 1643. A leading figure in the Fronde 1648-52, largely because he detested Cardinal Mazarin. Created cardinal 1652. Arrested and imprisoned 1652-54, he escaped. His uncle's death in March 1654 was followed by his immediate installation as successor, supported by most of the Paris clergy, but he had to remain in hiding. He led a vagabond life, mostly abroad, until in 1662 he formally resigned his see and was allowed back to live at Commercy. He took an active part in conclaves in 1655, 1667, and 1669, but mostly lived in seclusion, with frequent retreats at the Vannist abbey of Saint-Mihiel nearby. The Pope in 1675 refused him permission to give up his cardinal's hat and become a monk, but after attending the conclave of 1676 he was at last allowed by Louis XIV to retire to his abbey of Saint-Denis (1678). He died the next year. Retz conferred minor orders on R. in 1648, supported him in Rome in 1664 and became ever more intimately linked, discussing his projected retreat. His sexual extravagances and vast debts made it hard for Retz to efface the past, but he did his best. Correspondence was certainly more frequent than the few extant letters suggest. 62/1,73/6,771001

RIOM *See* Visitation
ROBINÉ, RP, OSA, Doctor of the Sorbonne, extracts of undated and unidentifiable letters in BN 19324
ROGIER *See* Visitation
RONAT *See* Celestines

SABLÉ, Madeleine de Souvré, marquise de (1599-1678). Close friend of Mme de Longueville and La Rochefoucauld, loyal supporter of Port-Royal. 750805, 770803
SACY, Isaac Lemaître de (1613-84). Nephew of Arnauld, and apparently related to Abbot Claude Le Maître of Châtillon. Ordained 1649, he was one of the original solitaries of Port-Royal and later spiritual director of the nuns (and of Pascal 1656). His translation of the Bible (1667, known as the Mons Bible) aroused much controversy. He also published editions of the Fathers. He was imprisoned in the Bastille, 1666-68, and after 1679 had to flee. 72/5,730214

SADOT (or JADOT), RM 900800
SAINT-ANDRÉ, André Chapperon, abbé de (1654-1740). A Doctor of Law of Bourges, canon of Arras 1668-88. He spent some sixteen months at la T. without taking the habit. Curé of Bannost 1688, of Vareddes 1698, archdeacon of Brie (all in diocese of Meaux) 1706. He enjoyed Bossuet's confidence and supervised the disposal and safeguarding of papers on R's death. An anti-Jansenist, reputedly a cousin of Maisne, certainly much closer to R. than the single identifiable letter suggests. (See Bossuet, *Correspondance* II: 330, and V: 221). 970200
Saint-Antoine, Order of. Originally an Order of hospitallers founded in Dauphiné by the seventeenth century its members had the status of Augustinian Canons, with the mother house abbey of Saint-Antoine, Vienne. Dom Malachie Garneyrin, later Abbot of Buonsolazzo, was a member of the order.
RP General, 'Lyon' (presumably for Vienne); Payin Lajasse was Abbot of Saint-Antoine 1678-87. 810800
RP Superior, Paris 81/3
Saint-Antoine, abbey of CO, Paris. R's aunt, Marie Bouthillier, was abbess 1636-52, and both his sisters spent time there before becoming Annonciades.
MADELEINE MOLÉ, abbess 1652-81. 71/1
RRMM (about three nuns collectively addressed) 700100, 700224,710226,710813, 711013,740730
SAINT-COSME, Joachim Trotti de La Chétardie, abbé de (1636-1714).

Index of Addressees

J. Garin, *Histoire de l'Abbaye de Tamié* (1927). 78/3, 780206,781105,810920
CORNUTY, dom Jean-François (1641–1707). Professed at Tamié c.1660, where his brother was prior. Accompanied Abbot Somont to the Collège des Bernardins in 1662, but without warning arrived at la T. 1665 and was re-professed there conditionally 1666, with the understanding that he would return to Tamié if the house were ever reformed. Sent to Foucarmont and ordained there in 1672, he was novice-master there for about six years, despite constant entreaties to R. to have him back. On Somont's submission, he returned to Tamié in 1677, came back in 1682 with the two monks of la T. for a last visit to R., and on his return was made prior. In 1702 he became abbot of Tamié. 660119, 73/2,73/3,730207,770914a, 771000,80/11,820715, 831008
TAMIN (or FAMIN), M. l'abbé 841009
TÊTU, Jacques, abbé de Belval (1626–1706). Briefly shared R's retreat at Véretz 1658. Elected to the French Academy 1665. An erudite, fashionable, and sociable man, friendly with Mme de Montespan (Louis XIV's mistress) and Mme de Maintenon (whom Louis married), close friend of Mme de Sévigné, and royal preacher. 901026
Theatines *See* ANDRÉ
THÉRÈSE [Bouthillier] *See* **Les Clairets**

THÉRÈSE DE JÉSUS, RM, abbaye de Grâce (probably Val-de-Grâce) 81/11
TILLEMONT, Sébastien Le Nain de (1631–98), dom Pierre's brother. A noted ecclesiastical historian and leading Jansenist, a regular visitor to la T. In 1696 Tillemont's former teacher, the elderly Jansenist Wallon de Beaupuis, was refused entry when he arrived on a visit to la T., and this prompted Tillemont to write R. a highly critical letter, which R. answered briefly, though he retained a much longer draft which was never sent. These letters, and a number of other documents concerning R's relations with Jansenists, were published in 1702 and more fully (167 pages) in 1705 as *Lettre de Tillemont*. 840220,840304
Tironneau, abbey of SO, diocese of Le Mans; RP Prior 700100a
Tournai *See* CHOISEUL
TOUROUVRE, Marie de Remefort, marquise de (c.1633–1710). Married Antoine de La Vove, marquis de Tourouvre, 1664, five sons, four daughters. R's nearest neighbours, and as such inevitably called on by his visitors, including Mme de Guise and Bellefonds. 770308
Tours *See* BOUTHILLIER, Victor
TRÉVILLE (or TROISVILLE), Henri-Joseph de Peyre, comte de (1641–1708). Initial conversion from a very worldly life 1666, definitive conversion followed the death of the duchesse d'Orléans, 1670, to whom he was devoted. He was at the Institution de l'Oratoire 1674–79, and finally abandoned office of Governor of

Foix 1677, after a visit to Bp
Pavillon at Alet (near Foix) in
1675. Knew nearly all R's
friends, and frequented the
Carmelites. Introduced several
correspondents to R., including
Mme de La Sablière. 730225,
750303,751200,78/1,780803,
821029

URFÉ, Louis de Lascaris d' (1634–
95), Bp of Limoges 1676–95.
Godson of Louis XIII and very
aristocratically connected, he
abandoned a promising career at
court for Saint-Sulpice. Between
appointment in 1676 and
consecration in 1677 he made a
retreat at la T. He took up
residence in the diocesan
seminary and lived the kind of
quasi-monastic life that Le Camus
did. 870903,871005,871030,
871214,880128,880513,880613,
880719,890126,891206

VAILLANT, M., Doctor of the
Sorbonne. 830829

Val, abbey du *See* DRUEL

Val-de-Grâce *See* Mlle de
COURSELLES, THÉRÈSE DE JÉSUS

Val-Dieu, Chartreuse near la T.;
RP Vicaire 70/1

Val-Richer, abbey of SO, diocese
of Bayeux;
Dominique GEORGES, 1613–93,
Abbot 1651. After parish
work in his native Lorraine,
he came to Paris, to Saint-
Nicolas du Chardonnet, a
seminary which he helped to
direct for more than twelve
years. A friend was
commendatory abbot of Val-
Richer and resigned after
persuading Georges to take
over, which, after a novitiate
at Barbéry, he did, but as
regular abbot. He
accompanied R. on the
mission to Rome 1664–66,
became Visitor in 1669, and
played a prominent part in
affairs of the Order. A friend
of the Jesuits, he was strongly
anti-Jansenist, and his abbey
became a retreat centre for
like-minded clergy and
laymen. R. found him
narrowminded and not really
monastic in his attitudes. He
was superior of les Clairets
until R. took over. Maupeou
somehow obtained R's letters
to Georges and published
some of them. See C. Buffier,
sj, *Vie de M. l'abbé de Val-
Richer* (1696). 880118a,
880914,890113,890502,
890630,900720,910121,
910222,910605,911105,
920122,920312

Vaucelles, abbey of CO, diocese of
Cambrai; fr Benoît CASTELLAIN
800122

VERNASSAL, Marie de Chalvet de
Rochemonteix, Mlle de (born
c.1664). R's niece. Having lost
her mother in infancy and her
father in 1673, she and her two
brothers were brought up by
their paternal aunt, Gillette
(1639–1706), in Auvergne, near
Brioude. Her date of death is not
known, but she did not enter
religion as she had once
contemplated, instead marrying a
cousin, Amable de Bouillé du
Charriol seigneur de Saint-
Gérons. 800921
Gillette de ROCHEMONTEIX *or*
above 800129

VERTUS, Catherine-Françoise d'Avaugour de Bretagne, Mlle de, (1615-21 November 1692). Sister of Mme de Montbazon and Mlle de Goëllo. Mme de Longueville's companion from 1653, a devoted friend of Port-Royal, where she retired in 1671 in very frail health, for the last ten years bedridden and incurable. Dubois had access to original letters from R., kept in the Hecquet family at Abbeville, but no trace can now be found of these letters. ? 760217,? 760425, ? 760522,? 761007,780406, 821110a,? 840905,841106, 850328,850528,851104,851130, 860224,860404,860526,860908, 861121a,861230,87/1,870302, 870520,870522,870829,880422a, 880926,890302,890429,UD 80

VIALART DE HERSE, Félix (1618-80) Bp of Châlons 1642-80. Trained by Vincent de Paul. Encouraged pastoral work in schools and seminaries. Friend of Retz, and a much respected prelate, tolerant of Jansenism. 751100j,790722

VIBRAIE, Polyxène le Coigneux de Bélabre, marquise de (died 1705). Lady in waiting to Mme de Guise 1685, and as such came regularly to la T. in her suite. Patron of J-B Thiers, whom she installed as curé at Vibraie. 85/1

VIERGE, RM de la, Religieuse hospitalière, Place Royale, Paris 840720a

Visitation, Tours: apart from letters identified as being to the three following religious, it is virtually certain that all the letters to unnamed religious in M 1214 and A 2106 are to one or other of them. After May 1687 letters to RM d'Albon went to the Visitation at Riom. The only reliable source of information is the Archives of the mother house at Annecy, especially a precious collection of *Lettres circulaires*, many written by RM Rogier, from whom a single original letter (protesting vigorously against RM d'Albon's transfer) also survives there.

ALBON, RM Louise-Henriette d' (c.1646-27 December 1688). R's niece. Educated from c.1652 under the supervision of her great aunt, Mme Bouthillier, and great uncle, the Abp of Tours, at the Visitation of Tours, where she was professed in 1664. She was soon in serious trouble for insubordination, and at one time thought of moving to Port-Royal. Apparently at the urging of her sister, Mme de La Barge, she was elected superior at Riom, near ner sister in Auvergne, and took over in May 1687. She there saw a lot of her sister and her three La Barge nieces. Her efforts at reform were not popular and she might well have gone back to Tours had she not succumbed to a brief but violent illness in December 1688. Four original letters survive (at Utrecht) from her to Le Roy, all of 1677, from what was clearly a regular correspondence, and these show her to have had clear Jansenist sympathies, much personal respect for Le Roy, but also deep loyalty for R., whose dispute with Le Roy she bitterly regretted. Further original letters to Favier (at Clermont-Ferrand) written 1687–88, reveal her efforts to reform the house at Riom and also discuss her nieces' questionable vocations. 640210,660104,660622, 700216a,711104,711203, 730607b,740805,790306, 800106,800222,801121, 81/4,810831b,821102, 830224,830921,840606, 840628,841207a,850113, 850212,850522,850618, 851121,860707,861007a, 861016,870130,870529, ? 870620,870918,871006, 871218,880218,880308, 880404,880527,880818, 881130

LA ROCHE, RM Louise-Elisabeth Robin de (1637–1707). Daughter of a sister of RM Rogier. Brought up at the Visitation at Tours, professed 1653. She joined RM d'Albon in one of the letters to Le Roy, together with a third unidentified nun, and actually signed on their behalf 'the three sisters', which suggests considerable intimacy between them and, from the content of the letter, Jansenist sympathies. 810725,810728, 810922,820101,820704a, 821102a,830902,831102, ? 840902a,841022,841207, 850608,? 860314

ROGIER, RM Louise Françoise (1616–9 February 1707). Daughter of Lieutenant-criminel at Tours, she became mistress of Gaston d'Orléans in 1637, but he dismissed her in November 1639 after her admitted infidelity. In January 1640 she bore a son (later called comte de Charny, and protected by Mme de Montpensier, his half-sister) and she resolved to enter religion. She was professed at the Visitation in 1644, was elected superior 1652–55, 1667–73, 1683–89, and by 1701, having outlived all former superiors, she became novice mistress (at eighty-five). A woman of strong character, her style comes through strongly in her *Lettres circulaires*, and her personality clash with RM d'Albon needs no explanation. She was on very close terms with the Oratory (we owe surviving copies of her letters to the Oratorian Galipaud) and with Mme Bouthillier. R. had numerous reasons, local and personal, to know her, and her decisive part in his conversion is in no way surprising. 570604,58/1,58/2, 58/3,58/4,59/1,59/2, 590916,590900,600400, 600501,600509,600600, 600601,600620,600705, 600708,600723,600816, 600902,601217,601228, 610105,610113,610202, 610211,610228,610728, 611211,611217,620211, 620501,620600,620600a, 620703,620720,620816, 620818,620829,620922, 621101,630416,630430, 630615,630805,630816, 631129,640116,640227,

Index of Addressees

640614,640630,640809
640900,641030,641113,
641207,650608,650619,
650715,650818,650904,
950929,651015,651201,
660111,? 660202,660819,
660915,? 661120,690130,
690529,700900,700929,
701201,710129,710412,
710903,711104a,711200,
720104,? 730916,740302,
740800,? 740815,? 800607,
800730a,820825,821110,
830922a,831210,840902b

GENERAL INDEX

The following professed religious of la Trappe will be found under their family name in the index:

Abraham Beugnet	Jacques Minguet
Achille Albergotti	Jacques de La Cour
Alain Morony	Jean-Baptiste de La Tour
Alipe Audibert	Jean-François Cornuty
Anselme Gillet	Jean-François Fournier
Antoine Noel	Joseph Garreau
Arcise Le Guay	Joseph de Saint-Mesmin
Armand-François Gervaise	Louis Guérout
Arsène Cordon	Malachie Garneyrin
Arsène La Croix	Maur Aubert
Basile Anzoux	Muce Faure
Benoît Deschamps	Palémon des Essarts
Bernard Vingtain	Palémon des Arcis
Bernard Soyrot	Palémon de Santena
Bernard Le Mosle	Paul Hardy
Bruno Le Digne	Paulin de l'Isle
Charles Denis	Pierre Vincent
Claude Estrée	Pierre Le Nain
Colomban Plouvier	Placide Pérouse
Dorothée Vitry	René Pasquier
Dorothée de L'Epine	Rigobert Levêque
Dosithée Cathiény	Siméon Lambert
Etienne Compagnon	Théodore Faverolles
Euthyme Faverolles	Urbain Le Pannetier
Euthyme d'Esclaux de Mesplez	Zénon de Montbel
Jacques Puiperrou	Zozime Foisil

Religious of other houses will also be found under their family name if it is known.

Bishops are normally to be found by name rather than diocese; abbots and abbesses under the name of their house.

An asterisk (*) indicates an entry in the preceding Index of Addressees.

It is not possible to distinguish Strict from Common Observance in this index, since many individuals passed from one to the other; all Cistercian religious and houses, men and women, are designated by the abbreviation C. Similarly all religious of la Trappe are designated by T.

ABBAYE-AUX-BOIS, Paris, C, 831117
AGNÈS, RM, See ARNAULD,
BELLEFONDS
ALAN (dioc. Comminges), 880809
890719,900123,911013,930913
ALBERGOTTI, fr.Achille, T, 990200
ALBERT, RM Marie-Madeleine,
Abbaye-aux-Bois, C, 831117
*ALBON, Gilbert-Antoine, comte d',
451125,640227,650904,
690611,700216a,701101,
720608,740424,791220,
791220a,800106,800201
*ALBON, Charlotte Bouthillier,
comtesse d', 760829,800100,
830914,860613,890113a,900602,
920911
*ALBON, RM Louise-Henriette,
Visitandine, 611211,641030,
700900,700929,710701,710903
720104,740123,870703,871028,
880415a,880727,890726
ALENÇON, 780113, 81/8, 860225
870306,89/2,930929
ALET, 600501,600509 See also
PAVILLON
ALEXANDER VII, Pope, 641207
ALEXANDER VIII, Pope, 891000
ALEXANDRE, RP,OP, 890414
ALEXANDRE, dom Louis, Champagne,
C, 810221
ALIGRE, Etienne d', Chancellor,
771222,991010
ALIGRE, François d', abbot, Saint-
Jacques de Provins, 991010
AMBROSE, St, 831209
*AMELINE, Claude, 780324
AMELOT, RP, Cong. Orat., 761121
AMFREVILLE, marquis d', 830415,
921119
AMSTERDAM, 850422a,861003
ANACREON, 410110,920416
*ANDILLY, Robert Arnauld d',
630430,741000c
ANGENNES, marquis d', 781006,
800424

ANGERS, 830817 See also ARNAULD,
HENRI
ANISSON, M. (publisher), 880712,
900727
ANNE DE GONZAGUE See PRINCESS
PALATINE
*ANNONCIADES, Order of, 911125
ANZOUX, fr. Basile, T, 950200
ARNAUDIN, M. d', 870309
ARNAULD,RM Agnès, Port-Royal,
610728
ARNAULD D'ANDILLY See ANDILLY
*ARNAULD, Antoine, 440317,680200
72/6,730927,731004,790104,
820308,820706d,831231,
940902,941218,950112,
950130,960522,98/1
*ARNAULD, Henri, Bp of Angers,
580820,581126,651201,820921
ARNAULD de Villeneuve, Jules,
580104
ARRAS, 800100a,820115
ATHANASIUS, St, 720922,73/1
AUBERT, M., 820730b
AUBERT, dom Maur, T, 700101
700219,810825b,981123
AUDIBERT, fr. Alipe, T, 72/1
AUGUSTINE, St, 720718,760314,
760611,771223,800408,841004a,
880629,930103
AUSTERITY (for bishop), 820700,
820704,820706c,820810,871030,
871214; (for nuns) 840206
AUVERGNE See LA TOUR D'AUVERGNE
AVEILLON, RP, Cong. Orat.,
820706g

BARBARIGO, Cardinal, 920903,
930128,960715
*BARBEAUX, C, 80/3,851003,901224
BARBÉRY, C, 80/3
BARILLON, Antoine de See MORANGIS
BARILLON, Antoine (son of Paul),
911029,920718,940516,940618,
961011

BARILLON, Bonne (daughter of Paul), 911018,911029
*BARILLON, Henri, Bp of Luçon, 580910,620419,620816,630805, 81/8,830101,831207,851125
BARILLON, Jean-Jacques, 711120 840910
BARILLON, Bonne Fayet (mother of Henri, 820507,820507a
*BARILLON D'AMONCOURT, Paul, 630805,860812,861207,881229, 890117,890317,890414,891017, 891119,900102a,900710,910405, 910513,910528,910618,910625, 910629,910709,910718,910726, 910730,930108; Mme (his widow), 941025
BARONIUS, Church historian, 590211
BARRÉ, Nicolas, 880810a
BASIL, St, 580710,580920,580730, 720922,730128,730927,740903, 821222a,830131,84/2,900920
BEAUCHÂTEAU, Hippolyte, 751100a
BEAUFORT See Septfons
BEAUVAIS, 510312,711209,780305, 820730b,891200
BEAUVAIS, Saint-Symphorien, OSB, 580303,610928,620816,640116, 640227,650925,661022,670903, 710708,710803,720527,730209a, 800201,810622,821119a,841015, 890914,891002,891114,920204a, 920524,920824
*BEAUVILLIER, duc de, 810123a
BEAUVOIR-SUR-MER, 900920,930420
BÉCHAMEL, M., 930813
BELIN, comte de, 421200
*BELIN, Antoinette, comtesse de, 800828,930823,930929,940222
*BELLEFONDS, RM Agnès de, ODC, 770829,770903,770920,780711, 851125,870211,911001,911007
*BELLEFONDS, Bernardin Gigault, maréchal de, 750604,751100a, 751100j,760911,77/1

BELLEFONDS, RM Laurence de, OSB, 870211,870309
BELLEFONDS, Louis-Christophe, marquis de, 820921,900420, 920810,920826
BELLÊME, 860225
*BELLÉROPHON, M., 580727, 600510,700124
BELZAI, M. de, 921015
BENEDICT, St, 881022 See also Rule of St Benedict
BENEDICTINES, 810825B,890502, 891017,920709; anciens (unreformed), 930413,930527, 930726 See also Saint-Maur, Saint Vanne
BENEFICES, plurality of, 58/1, 790919
BENOÎT, RP, Camaldolese, 951018, 951126
BERNARD, St, 720120,720707, 720718,730927,750900,761028, 780307,781112a,820300a, 820827,820830,820910,821119a, 821222a,850624,880513,930413
BERRIER, Louis, 891228,90/3, 940830b,951018,990809
BÉRULLE, Cardinal, 730301,770321
BÉTHUNE, 800100a
BEUGNET, dom Abraham, T, 950317
BEUVRON, marquis de, 930511
*BLAMPIGNON, Nicolas, 940628
BLOIS, 591026
*BOCCONE, dom Paul, C, 800626, 860515,890914a,891103,891126, 910603,920928
BOISDAVID, M., 860812
BOISSARD, dom, Carthusian, 880408
BOIVIN, M., 961018,961112,98/1
BONNAIGUE, C, 711212
BONNECOMBE, C, 730510
BONNEVAL, marquis de, 840929
BONNIVET, comte de, 421200
BONPORT, C, 90/4
BOSQUILLON, Jean, 980108

*Bossuet, Jacques-Bénigne, Bp of
Condom, then (1681) Meaux,
750604,750922,770823,770914,
781130a,821225,821231,830101,
830112,830117,803131,830311,
830530a,841009,850409,870309,
881122,89/5,890414,891228,
900710,900824,920500,970200,
971003a,980818,990114
Bouchard, RP, Cong. Orat.,
630530a
Boucherat, Louis, Chancellor,
851129a,951214; Mme, 910709a,
97/2
*Bouchu, dom Pierre, abbot of La
Ferté, then Clairvaux, q.v., C,
760217,760522
Bouhours, RP Dominique, sj,
870211,870309
Bouillon, Cardinal de, 770925,
780611,930615,930823
Bouillon, Louise-Charlotte, Mlle
de, 830530
Boulogne, Bp of, 950317
Boulogne, Grandmontine priory
of, 590900,610928,620600,
620816,620829,621222,630805,
650904a,711026,720217
Bourée, dom Georges, Cîteaux, C,
710225
Bourgogne, duc de, 810123a
Bourgueil, 720501
Bournonville, duc de, 820906a
Bouthillier, Henri See Rancé
*Bouthillier, Marie de Bragelongne,
Mme, 581024,590616,730619,
730907
Bouthillier, RM Marie-Dorothée,
Annonciade, 620214,911125
*Bouthillier, RM Marie-Louise,
Annonciade, 911125
*Bouthillier, RM Thérèse, Les
Clairets, C, 79/1,790526,840214,
840216,840323,840400a,880509
*Bouthillier, Victor, Abp of Tours,
510212,58/2,600601,601217,

601228,610202,610211,610228,
630416,700900,700929,701201
Boyne, Battle of the, 900300,
901129
Brachet, dom Benoît, osb, 820400
Brachet de la Miltière, dom
Claude, Perseigne, C, 790610
*Brancas, comte de, 760900,
760928,761102,78/5
Bréval, François-Bonaventure de
Harlay, marquis de, 820512
Breviary, 800912
Brézeau, RP, Cong. Orat., 800108
Brienne, Loménie de, Bp of
Coutances, 751100j,760314,
870309
Brussels, 940902
Bruzeau, Paul, 891013
Buonsolazzo, C, 81/3,930613
Burnet, Gilbert, 900710
Buzais, (or Buzay), C, 801124
Buzenval, Choart de, Bp of
Beauvais, 821119a

Cahors, 730510,760827,800609
Calumny, 760100,761121,860121
Camaldolese, 910830,930831,
951018
Cambron, C, 720514a
Campion, St Edmund, 870211
Canada, 58/2
Cantorbie, abbé de, 881125
Cape of Good Hope, 891019
Capolade, dom Pierre, C, 730510
Capuchins, 800100a
Carmelites (men), 470516, 601228
Carmelites (women), rue du
Boulais, 761106
Carthusians, 760309,800208,
810913,830817,831203,860512a,
880408,890720,890809,891017,
920812,931026a,961018,980108,
980818
Casanata, Cardinal, 920630,
920901,990630
Cassian, 900920

General Index

CATANIA, 930316a
CATECHISM, 830401
CATHIÉNY, fr Dosithée, *T,* 880809, 881111,930913
*CAULET, Etienne, Bp of Pamiers, 800912
*CAUMARTIN, Louis-François Lefèvre de, 580910,830207a
*CELESTINES, 700615,710400, 760100c,810800c,871027
CENDON (?), M. de, 721025
CHABOT, Mme de (RM Claire du St-Sacrement, ODC), 910627
CHALOCHÉ, *C,* 751000
CHÂLONS-SUR-MARNE, 600600, 600601,610211
CHALYPE, fr Candide, Recollect, 900824,901022,901119
*CHAMPAGNE, *C,* 810221,810923
CHAMPROND *See* Thiers, J-B
CHANTAL, St Jeanne de, 840420,890400
CHANVIER, fr, *T,* 930613, 931130,97/2
CHAPTER, General, 720529,730104, 79/4,810831,820627,830112, 830426,830530a,850422a,990630
CHARENTON, 601228,851028
CHARLES Borromeo, St, 721223, 800701,820810,870504a
CHARMOIS (?), M. de, 920121 920423
CHARTRES, 900824
CHARTREUSE, Grande, 600510, 790400,841230
CHASTELLUX, comte, de, 951005
*CHÂTILLON, *C,* 720217,730700, 731000,770414
CHAVIGNY, François Bouthillier de, Bp of Troyes, 870614
CHERBOURG, 920609
CHEVIGNY, RP Nicolas, Cong. Orat, 770207,770218
*CHOISEUL, Gilbert de, Bp of Comminges, then (1671) Tournai, 590616,600705,600708,600730, 600908,630530a,730607,770823, 880509,880600
CHRYSOSTOM, St John, 720718
CHUR, Switzerland, 880809
CIBO, Cardinal, 771001,780803
CÎTEAUX, Abbot of;
   Claude Vaussin, 650608;
   *Jean Petit, 710226,751018, 760100c,810831,920125;
   Nicolas Larcher, 930831, 940830b,990630
*CLAIRVAUX, *C,* 780307,780803, 801124,801200,820423,830207a, 851125,870921,880509,990707
   See also Bouchu
   Clarifications See Rancé, *Eclaircissements*
CLAIRISSES, 730225b
CLIMACUS, St John, 640809, 720706,720718,800618,84/2
CLOISTER, glazing of, 760100c
CLOTHING of nuns, 820301
*CLUNY, 781208
COFFEE, 850328
COLBERT, Jean-Baptiste, 781006
COLBERT de Croissy, Charles-François, 910405
COLLÈGE des Bernardins, Paris, *C,* 660119,800120,901224
COLLÈGE de Saint-Bernard, Toulouse, *C,* 730510
COLLOREDO, Cardinal, 961011
COLOGNE, 851129a,861003
COLOMBAN, St, 821225
COMMENDATORY abbot, duties of, 820423,870904
COMMERCY, 610120,641113,73/6
COMMINGES, 880809 *See also* Choiseul, Rechignevoisin
COMMUNION, 750500,760200, 801212c,820323,820816, 840905,851104,88/3, 881017a,890302,930614, UD 109
COMPAGNON, fr Etienne, *T,* 740500,75/3,810831

CONDÉ, Louis, prince de, 740328 851129,861219,861219a
CONDOM See Bossuet
CONDREN, RP Charles, Cong. Orat., 770321
Conduite chrétienne See Rancé, Conduite
CONFERENCES, 800618, 830508,850624
CONFESSION, 801212c,820916, 831112,831226,851113
Constitutions de la Trappe, 711212 72/3,791203a,810525,901026
CONTES, Jean-Baptiste de, dean of Notre-Dame de Paris, 821012
CONTI, François-Louis, prince de, 851129
Conversi (lay-brothers), 741023, 770207,800613,821107,951018
CORDON, dom Arsène, T, 720723, 730405,800113,850214
CORNUTY, dom Jean-François, T (Tamié), 781105
COSMAS, Roger, Bp of Lombez, 710129
COTTIN, dom Joseph, prior of Longpont, C, 800131a
*COURCIER, PIERRE, 821012, 830400A,860121,860613,890718 891013,910709A
COURDIL, DAVID, 830817
*COURTIN, Honoré, 910604
COUTANCES, 751100j,760314, 761106
*COUTURIER, dom Robert, C, 851003,901224

DAUPHIN OF FRANCE, Louis de Bourbon, 880900
DAUPHINE, Marie-Anne-Christine of Bavaria (wife of above), 900300, 900420,900427
DAUPHINÉ, 920619b
*DAURAT, M., 801104
DENIS, dom Charles, T, 711103,750715

DES ARCIS, fr Palémon, T, 910830
DESCHAMPS, fr Benoît, T, 671106 680200,740800a,740825,750410
DESERT FATHERS, 630430
DES ESSARTS, fr Palémon, T, 790710
*DESLIONS, Jean, dean of Senlis, 810100
DESMARES, RP, Cong. Orat., 770321
DIJON, 930128,930207, 971003a,000304
*DIROIS, François, 770823
DISCRETION, 75/2
DIVINING ROD, 890829a
DOSITHÉE See Cathiény
DROUAS, abbé, 800325
DOCTORS OF MEDICINE, 770704, 781112,831207,850624
DU BUC, RP Alexis, Theatine, 930326
*DU CHARMEL, comte, 900824, 910405,930831,950103
*DUHAMEL, Henri, 711026,720411, 720723,821220,821222
DUMBARTON, Earl of, 910214
DU PERRON, Cardinal, 581024, 581126
*DU PLESSIS-GUÉNÉGAUD, Elisabeth de Choiseul, marquise, 730607,730702
*DU SUEL, François, 751003
DUTCH See Holland
DU VERNAY, RP, OP, 930420 930527,930831

ECCLESIASTICS, 730729, 730817,751100a,820101a
Eclaircissements See Rancé
EDMOND, fr, 730508,730611, 730802,731229,740424,760806
EFFIAT, abbé d', 880602
ELOI See Le Mosle
ENCLOSURE:
  Annonciades, 691218,691227, 840323;
  seculars in, 820813,820827, 821012,840529

ENGLAND, 870904,890117,890414, 890815,920609 *See also* James, Mary
*EPERNON, Mme d' (Sr Anne-Marie de Jésus, ODC), 740825,770914, 830415
EPHREM, St, 800914,870108
*ESSAI, OSA, 76/2,870304,980610
ESTRÉES, dom Claude, T, 800718
ESTRÉES, C, 980900
ESTRÉES, Cardinal d', 73/6,770823 800516,800701,810825b
*ETRECHY, M. d', 830402
EUSEBIUS, *Church History*, 580710 580910,581214
EVREUX *See* Maupas du Tour
EXCOMMUNICATION, 781112a
Explication de la Règle See Rancé

FABAS, C, 880809,930913
FAGON, Guy, 930914b
FASTING, 75/2,800100c,850624
FAURE, dom Muce, T, 890627 900720,901026,901114,910718a, 940505,950606
FAVEROLLES, fr Théodore, T, 770207a,770324,780123,780224, 780324,780410,780501
*FAVIER, Jean, 620816,800100 870130,890726,900420
FÉLIBIEN, André, 770414
*FÉLIBIEN,, Pierre, 641113,711104 711104a,900824
FÉNELON, François de la Mothe-Salignac, Abp of Cambrai, 930326,970200,970300,971003a, 980605,980818,990312,990630
FÉRET, Hippolyte, 770914
FEUILLANTS, 780501,851000
FEYDEAU, Mathurin, 730405
FICTIONS, 720706,720718, 760827,830909
FIEUBET, Gaspard, 860121,910604 910627,910830,910905,930831 940912
FIEUBET, Mme, 860121

FISH, 650820,80/3,860225
FLANDERS, campaigns in, 731113, 900420,900710,920609, 920619a,b,930820
FLORENCE, 641113,800325
*FLORIOT, 730927,821222A
FOISIL, dom Zozime, T, 950705 960103,960119,960313 960317,960404
FOIX, 73/5,751200
FONFROIDE, C, 800829, 801124,811214
FONTAINE-DANIEL, C, 851003
FORBIN-JANSON *See* Janson
*FORCOAL, Jean, Bp of Séez, 740702 740704,740909,750922,77/1, 770702,781006,781130a,800103, 800424,820308,820308a,820323, 820520
FORNARI, RM Vittoria, 691218
FOSSE (publisher), 89/5
*FOUCARMONT, C, Jacques Fleur de Montagne, abbot, 73/2,730207, 730723,751100f,760917, 770914a,771001,781105,800131a
FOUNDATIONS FROM LA TRAPPE, 710607,720307,720723a,73/5
FOUQUET, NICOLAS, 610218
FOURNIER, dom Jean-François, T, 780501
FOY, Raoul, 891200
FRANCISCANS, 890117,890317
FRANÇOIS DE SALES, St, 851113, 870918,880818,89/4,890400
FRÉMONT, RP Charles, Grandmontine, 730611

GANGRA, council of, 830131
GARNEYRIN, dom Malachie, T, 81/3, 810800,981123
*GARREAU. dom Joseph, T, 800829, 801124,801200
GAULTIER, Pierre see Le Pin
GEORGES, DOMINIQUE *See* Val-Richer

GÉRARD, M., 700124
*GERBAIS, Jean, 801219,900602,
    930725
GERBERON, dom Gabriel, OSB,
    830401
GERVAISE, dom Armand-François,
    T, 960317,960404,960512,
    961018,961112,980714,980900,
    981123,981226,990115,990709
GESVRES, duc de, 860225
*GIF, OSB, 830227,840210,901218
GILLET, dom Anselme, T, 810920
GILLY, David, 830817
*GOËLLO, Mlle de, 761007
GOHIN, fr François, C, Champagne,
    80/2,801231a
GONDRIN, Henri de, Abp of
    Sens, 850104
GONTIER, St, 821225
*GOURDAN, RP Simon, Saint-
    Victor, 971003a
GRAMONT, comte de, 930108
GRANDMONT, Order of, 620600,
    730611,770223
GREGORY, St, 880629
GRENADIER See Faure
GRENOBLE, 780827,781130,860131
    See also Le Camus
GRIGNAN, Mlle de, 870504a
GROSBOIS, Camaldolese, 910627,
    910830,930831,951018
GRUEL, dom Etienne, C,
    Perseigne, 801122
GUÉROUT, dom Louis, T,681227
GUESTS: stay restricted, 820101a;
    danger of, 88120
GUESTON, fr, Saint-Victor, 881014
GUIGNARD, Mlle, 930813,940830a
GUIGO[1] THE CARTHUSIAN, 831203
GUILLAUME DE SAINT-THIERRY,
    780307
GUILLEMINS, Liège, 80/9
GUILLERAGUES, Gabriel-Joseph,
    comte de, 980605
GUISE, Mlle de, 880226,880300
*GUISE, Elisabeth d'Orléans,
    duchesse de, 751003,761028,
    800828,871123,921015

HAMEAUX, comtesse des, 860121
*HAMON, Jean, 770704,850328
    87/1,870302,890826
*HARCOURT, princesse d',
    761028,761121
HARDY, dom Paul, T, 700216
    700405,720706,750410,
    750415,810600
*HARLAY DE CHAMPVALLON, François
    de, Abp of Paris, 710129,750410
    751000,820308,831025,860913,
    950812,950818
HARLAY, Nicolas-Auguste de,
    870407
HAUTEFONTAINE, C, 610120,720217
    730712,751100a
HEIDELBERG, 880900
HEISTERBACH, C, 720514a,
    720706,791205
HEMINA, 860130,861024,890914a
HERMITAGE, 790909,951203
HILARY OF ARLES, St, 750704
HOLLAND, 880628,880712,881013
    881017
HONDE (?), RP, 720602
HOSTUN, Gilbert d', 80100
HOUDAR DE LA MOTTE, Antoine,
    930914a
HUBERT, RP, Cong. Orat., 730729
HUGUENOTS See Protestants
HUMILIATIONS, 720706, 720718,
    761028,761106,770815,
    780305,780705
*HUXELLES, marquise d', 761106

*INNOCENT XI, Pope, 780113,
    891000,891002
Instructions morales See Rancé
In suprema, Brief, 730510,780206
    831039,890809,930726
IRELAND, 870904,890903,
    891000,900300

JACQUES DE SAINT-GABRIEL, fr,
    Feuillant, 851000
*JAMES II, King of England, 881100,
    881229,890105,890117,890208,

General Index

890414,890815,890903,900129
901224a,91/1,910110,910120
920609,920619b,930820,
930914b,960700
*JANNEL, dom André, OSB,
750900,820906c
JANNON, abbé Hugues, 920500
JANSENIUS, Cornelius, Bp of Ypres,
440317,800701
JANSENISM, Jansenists, 440317
580626,751003,751100a,751100j
760100c,760314,761028,770104,
770120,781130,820308,820706d,
831231,940902,970129,981123;
signature of formulary against,
581227,59/1,760813,761206
781130,790822
JANSON, Cardinal de Forbin, Bp of
Beauvais, 960103,961011
JANSON, abbé Bruno de Forbin, 90/3
JANSON, abbé Jacques de Forbin,
891114,920824
JARD, 781217
JARGHILLEN, M., 780827
JESUS, Society of, 440317,751100a,
761028,791109,870211,870309
JOLY, Bénigne, 000304
JOUAUD, dom Jean, Abbot of
Prières, C, 630530a,720307,
730600,730700,730900a,751018,
890117
JUBILEE, 770324
JURIEU, Pierre, 871016,900710

KERVICHE, dom Julien, C, Perseigne,
790904,801120b

*LA BARGE, Catherine d' Albon,
comtesse de, 701101,870130,
871028,880727,910903
LA BARGE, Mlle de, 81/4,
880810,890726
LA BRÉTÈCHE, M. de, 721025
LA BRIFFE, Pierre-Armand,
Procureur-Général, 911018,
911029,91108,920214

LA BROSSE, Philippe de, Dean of La
Rochelle, 741029
LA CHAISE, RP François, de, SJ,
940912
LA CHALADE, C, 81/2
LA CHAMBRE, abbé de, 870717
891103,900920
LA COLOMBE, C, 800900b
*LA COUR, RP, CR, Soissons, 83/1
LA COUR, dom Jacques de, T,
940830b,990114,990115,
990709,990915
LA CROIX, dom Arséne de,
T, 940830b
LA CROIX, Mlle de, 861207
LA FERTÉ, C,760217,760522
LA FERTÉ-GAUCHER, 83/1
LA FOUCHERIE, M. de, 891017
LA GRANGE, RP, Saint-Victor,
830914
LA HOUGUE, Cap de, Battle of,
920609,920619a,920619b,920705
LA HOUSSAYE, M. de, 770815
LAIGLE, 681227
LAIGUES, maréchal de, 740521
LAIZIÉRES, C, 810820
*LA MADELEINE, abbé Erard de,
700100a
LAMBERT, fr Siméon, T,
780315,820115
LAMOIGNON, Guillaume de, Premier
Président, 751083,771222
LAMY, dom François, OSB, 940528,
940606,940628,940718
LANCHAL, dom Jacques de, C,
Perseigne, 790909,811022,
880609,901213
LANGRES, 711010
*LAQUERRE, M. de, 951121
LARCHER, Pierre, Président, 891228
LA ROCHELLE, 890117 See also La
Brosse (dean), Laval (bp)
LA RONGÈRE, marquise de, 890113a
LARROQUE, Daniel de, 851129a,
860121,860131,860317,
861003,861022

LASNIER, M., 910627
*LASSAY, marquis de, 820911
LA TAIGNAN, M. de, 730607
LA TOUR, dom Jean-Baptiste de, T, 990709
LA TOUR D'AUVERGNE, RM Elisabeth-Eléonore, C, Les Clairets, 930615
LA TRAPPE, 580626,580710,600400, 610928,620816,620818,620829, 620922,621101,630530a, thereafter constantly, site of, 850624
LAVAL, Henri-Marie de, Bp of La Rochelle, 760522
*LA VALLIÉRE, Sr Louise de la Miséricorde, ODC, 740909, 750604,770914
LA VERNÈTE. M. de, 730702
LA VIEUVILLE. RM Anne de, C, prioress Leyme, 810820
LA VOVE, Mlle de, 850821
See also Tourouvre
LAY-BROTHERS *See Conversi*
LE BALLEUR, RP Joseph, OFM, 890117,930413,930726
*LE BOULANGER, abbé, 891228, 92/1,941117
*LE CAMUS, Etienne, Cardinal, Bp of Grenoble, 671106,680828, 711026,711125,770321,770720, 770920,800129a,800700,801126, 810917,820308,820831,820913a, 821222a,821225,821231,830131, 830311,831207,841230,850404, 851125,851129a,860131,860913, 861007a,861024,870304,871122, 890720,900710,920619a,920812, 930527
*LE CAMUS, Nicolas, 850124
LE CHEVALIER, Enguerrand, 780501,920428
LE CLERC, Daniel, 840802
Lectio divina, 681030,711212, 760100c,831207,850212
LE DIGNE, fr Bruno, T, 911001

LEFRANC, M., 950310
LE GUAY, dom Arcise, T, 800730
LE JAY, Henri, Bp of Cahors, 800730
LE LYS, C, 761028
LE MANS, 88/2,990809
LE MARÉCHAL, *See* Maréchal
LE MASSON, dom Innocent, General of Carthusians, 890720, 920812,831026a,961018
LE MOINE, M. 430900
LE MOSLE, dom Bernard (Eloi), T, 831206
*LE NAIN, Jean, 840220, 840304,940622
LE NAIN, dom Pierre, T, 681119, 681119a,690326,700124,900602, 90702,930826,931008,940128 940509,950430,950512,981123
LE NAIN DE TILLEMONT *See* Tillemont
LEO, St, 750704
LE PANNETIER, dom Urbain, T, 760314
LE PIN, C, Pierre Gaultier, abbot, 730600,821019
L'EPINE, dom Dorothée de, T, 941014
LÉRINS, 880712
*LE ROY, Guillaume, 590917, 591026,591108,591122,591225 610120,760827,761028,761106 770815,770823,780305,800618
LESCAR *See* Mesplez
*LES CLAIRETS, C,840216,861128, 880914,900911,900920,901026, 901213,910222,910800,92/1, 920122,920407a,920911,930615, 930726,940912,980900
LESDIGUIÈRES, duchesse de, 810602
LES ROBINIÈRES, 890117, 890317,930413
LE TELLIER, Charles Maurice, Abp of Reims, 821225,821231, 830117,830131,841009,850409
LE TELLIER, Michel, Chancellor, 851108; Mme, 910709a,97/2
*L'ETOILE, C, Bernard du Teillé, abbot, 751018,781105b,79/4

Lettres d'une religieuse portugaise,
980605
LÉVÊQUE, dom Rigobert, T,
730712,740206,790124,
800113,800131
*LEYME, C, 760425,761007
LIÈGE, 810629
LIMOGES See Urfé
L'ISLE, dom Paulin de, T, 870604a.
870614,870629
L'ISLE-MARIE, 740328,761106,
770420
LOMBEZ, Bp of, 710129
LONDONDERRY, 890903
LONGPONT, C, 800131a
LONJON, dom François, C,
730510,760100c
LORRAINE, Marguerite-Louise de
See Tuscany, Grand Duchess
LOUIS IX, St, 880200
*LOUIS XIV, King of France,
851129a,860913,861121,861205,
861216,861225,861230a,870130,
870211,881013,910403,940912.
950630,950705,950711
LOUIS, M., 790723,801126,940830c
LOUVOIS, François-Michel Le Tellier,
marquis de, 791203,
910730a,910920
LOW COUNTRIES, monastery in, 84/1
LUÇON, See Barillon, Henri
LUTHUMIÈRE, abbé, 741100j,760314
*LUYNES, duc de, 580404,580920,
581024,591108,591122,841130
*LUYNES, duchesse de, 841130
'LUZANCY', M. de, 751100a
LYON, M., 951203
LYON, 650608

*MABILLON, dom Jean, OSB, 780307,
830300a,831209,880603,890914a,
891103,910421,910603,910718a,
910830,911105,911126,920303a,
920322,920407,920421,920428,
920500,920519,920524,
920619a,c, 920709,920824,

920908,930527,930604,
930610,930725,930802,
930914,940606
MADAGASCAR, 800602
MAILLEZAIS, 930413
MAINTENON, Mme de,
740909,840929a
MAISNE, Charles, 981226
MAIZIÈRES, C, 930316a,930604
MAJEUR, RP, 930831
See also Camaldolese
MALNOUE, OSB, Marie-Eléonore de
Rohan, abbess, 810421,810421a,
810427,820223
MALTA, Knights of, 881202
*MARCEL, Louis, Saint-Jacques-du-
Haut-Pas, Paris, 810921a,
881013,910405,910709,941025
MARÉCHAL (OR LE MARÉCHAL),
dom, C,830826,90/4
MARIE-LOUISE See Bouthillier
MARIE-LUCE See Picot
MARIE-THÉRÈSE, Queen of France,
830501,830830,831024
MAROLLES, dom Vincent, OSB,
820400
MARTELOT, fr, 720706,721201
MARTIN, St, 850830
MARTIN, dom Claude, OSB, 820400
MARY OF MODENA, Queen of
England, 89/1,960700,970509
MASS:
Rancé says daily, 650708;
Cistercian usage, 730927;
in Rule, 890911,890914a
MASSON, M., 920712,940613
MATIGNON, comte de, 930511
*MAUBUISSON, C, 781105,
811123,820713
*MAUPAS DE TOUR, Henri, Bp of
Evreux, 77/1,771223
*MAUPEOU, PIERRE, 830211B,
860121,931026,931128
MAURISTS See Saint-Maur
Maximes See Rancé
MAZARIN, Cardinal, 610202,610328

*Mazarin, duc de, 751100a, 820921,830503,851129
Meaux, 750900 *See also* Bossuet
Mège, dom Joseph, osb, 880118a, 890113,890414,900720, 910121,910605
Melfort, Earl of, 920609
Mendicants, 761014
*Mesmes, Président de, 880115
Mesplez, Dominique d'Esclaux de, Bp of Lescar, 920303a, 920619a
Mesplez, fr Euthyme de, *T*, 920393a,920619a
Minguet, dom Jacques, *T*, 800113, 800131,800616
Mitigations, 730510,75/1,831231 851119,930726
Mixtum, 820627
Molé, Mathieu, 700100
Molinists, 751100a,781130
*Monchy, RP Pierre de, Cong. Orat., 711125,711209,76/1, 761121,780324,780711,780717, 791109,800129a,801126, 820913a,821231,861207
Monmouton, dom de, *C*, 760217 760425,760522
Mons, 910403
Montausier, duc de, 781006
Montbazon, duchesse de, 810421, 820723,851129a
Montbel, fr Zénon de, *T*, 940505
Montélimar, 940505
Montier-en-Argonne, *C*, 820423,851125
Montmartre, 991112
*Montpensier, duchesse de, 930412
Morale du Pater (by Floriot), 730927
Morale, Essais de (by Nicole), 751202,780315a,871228,890826
Morangis, M. (uncle of Barillon),650904a,720411
Morangis, Antoine Barillon de (brother of Barillon), 780113,

780922,821231,851129a,860523; Mme, 861207
Morel, M., 830400a
Mornay, Mme de, 861128, 920407a,920500,930823
Morony, dom Alain, *T*, 781105,810920,811123,820300, 820706a,820713
Mortagne, 801218,890703, 920124
Mouchamps, 830117,830131
Muce *See* Faure
Muguet, François, 820706d, 841009,850409,850611,89/5, 920928,921030,931128
Murmuring, 801120b

Namur, 920530,920619a,920626 920708,920709
Naval Activity, 881013,881017 *See also* La Hougue
Neerwinden, 930820
Nevoir, dom Alexis, *C*, Perseigne, 810923
*Nicaise, Claude, 891017
*Nicole, Pierre, 831231 *See also Morale, Essais de*
Nijmegen, Peace of, 79/4
Nilus, St, 900920
*Noailles, Louis-Antoine de, Bp of Cahors, then Châlons, then Abp of Paris, 800609,800730
*Nocey, M. de, 790104a,801122, 920224,920303
Noël, fr Antoine, *T*,810920
Noirmoutier, 930420
Noisy, 840929a
Nomasticon cisterciense (by Julien de Paris), 760827
Notre-Dame du Tard, 930207,990312
Nouvelles catholiques (female converts), 830829

Obedience, 711203a
Odouair (?), M., 711209

OLD TESTAMENT, unsuitable for nuns, 900911,900920, 920404,910121
OLONNE, 930413
ORATOIRE, Institution, de l', Paris, 630530a,730225,730914,751003, 800108,861229
ORATORIANS OF ROME, 650608
ORBESTIER, 930413
ORDINATION, 810213,810521, 850830
Original Spirit of Cîteaux (Premier esprit), 760827
ORLÉANS, Elisabeth of Bavaria, duchesse d', 751003
ORLÉANS, Gaston, duc d', 580626,591026,600208,600222, 600510,930412
ORLÉANS, Philippe, duc d', 930823,940900
ORON, M. d', 650904a
*ORVAL, C, 790710,790817,810911, 830112,830508
OUVRARD, M., 870601,931007

PAMIERS, 801210 See also Caulet
PARENTS OF RELIGIOUS, 73/7, 730927,780809,82122a,830131, 830311,830829,881122
PARIS, See Harlay
PARIS, Julien, C, Abbot of Foucarmont, 760827 See *Nomasticon* and *Original Spirit*
PASCAL, Blaise, 440317,580626, 710521,790607
PASQUIER, fr René, T, 80/2, 801231a,810221
PAUL, dom, C, Barbeaux and/or Perseigne, 790906,851003
*PAVILLON, Nicolas, Bp of Alet, 590616,590916,600620,600730, 600816,600822,601017,751005, 751200,751200a,751200b,78/1, 780807,970127
*PELLISSON, 800930,930208

PAYEN, RP, Cong. Orat., 730624,730725
PENSION, 82/3,820706, 820730, UD 60
PÉROUSE, dom Placide, T, 810600
PERRECY, OSB, 891228, 940830b,951126
*PERSEIGNE, C, 620818,630805, 640116,720409,781105, 790104a,901224
Petrus Aurelius (by Saint-Cyran), 580626,580710,580730,581214
PHILOSOPHY, 780206
*PICOT, RM Marie-Luce, Annonciade, 890623
PIERRE DE REIMS (Petrus Cantor), 730927
PICQUET, abbé, 720217,960103
*PINETTE, Nicolas, 70/2,750303, 780711,810602,820706f,820725, 830400a,830914,851122,861229, 880210,890317,920712,930326, 940222
PIROT, Edmé, 770914,870309
PLOUVIER, dom Colomban, T, 990915
*POMPONNE, marquis de, 711013,71227
PONS, Saintonge, 920812,930420
PONT-AUDEMER, 860225
PONTCHARTRAIN, comte de, 920705
PONTIGNY, C, 820524a
POOR, feeding the, 820104, UD 55
PORT-ROYAL, 580104,711203, 760100c,761007,830914,840905. 870211
PRAYER, 820916,830508
Préjugés ... contre le calvinisme (by Nicole), 850112
Premier esprit de Cîteaux See *Original Spirit*
PREMONSTRATENSIANS, 831206, 930120
PREUILLY, C, 711212
PRIÈRES, C, 80/3, 801224,810309
See Also Jouaud

PRINCESS PALATINE (ANNE DE
GONZAGUE), 731123,751100c,
780123,820510
PRIOR, right to elect at la Trappe,
771001,771223,780113,780804,
800211,830209a
PROCLAMATIONS, 770404,850608
PROCUREUR-GÉNÉRAL See La Briffe
PROTESTANTS, 821225,830117,
830131,830817,851028,851125,
851129a,860131,860225,860611,
860813,870227,870304,870316,
870526,870924,880424,890414,
910905a
PUIPERROU, dom Jacques, T,
680819,681027,750410
PUITS D'ORBE, OSB, 920416,920523

QUEBEC See Saint-Vallier
QUESNEL, François, 711006
QUESNEL, Guillaume, 691230,
700115,700224a,700917,701000,
701019,710117,780807
*QUESNEL, RP Pasquier, Cong.
Orat., 88123,891103,891126,
940902,941014,941216,950112,
950812,961112
QUIETISM, 871109,970200,970300,
970414,970500,970707,970803,
980417,980818,990630

RABELAIS, François, 930413
RAMBOUILLET, marquise de, 781006
RANCÉ, Armand-Jean de, works:
Conduite chrétienne, 97/3,970314,
980115;
Eclaircissements sur quelques
difficultés..., 850104,850409,
850422a,850512,850611,
850715,850722,850802,
851028,860130,860131
Explication de la Règle, 89/5,
890117,890414,890428,
890502,890630,890914,
891002,891017;

Instructions morales, 931128,
940108;
Maximes, 931026,931128,97/3,
970803,980115;
Relations de la vie et de la mort de
quelques religieux..., 750410,
760100b,781022,870520,
950103,951121,951126,
951214,960105,960414,
960922,970110;
Réponse à... Mabillon, 920303c,
920312,920330,920402,
920519,920619a,920630,
920709,920903;
Saint-Dorothée, Instructions de,
861121,861227,870520;
Sainteté (De la Sainteté et des devoirs
de la vie monastique), 820627,
821222a,821225,830311,
830400a,830401,830402,
830415,830430a,830530b,
830817,830826,830902,
831209,831231,840124a,
840802,841009,85/1,850104,
850802,851028,860328,
861003,870703,871005,
900911;
sermons preached by, 470516
RANCÉ, Denis Bouthillier de,
430325,430900,461016,
500219
*RANCÉ, Henri Le Bouthillier,
chevalier de, 650904,660915,
730802,771001,800129,
801000,970110
RANCÉ FAMILY, other members,
See Bouthillier
RANTZAU, RM Elisabeth de,
Annonciade, 670910
RAUCOURT, 830401
*RECHIGNEVOISIN DE GURON, Louis
de, Bp of Comminges, 880809
RECREATION, 78/3,860527
RECOLLECTS, 900824
REGNIER DES MARAIS, François,
860515,881213,920416

REGULATIONS OF LA TRAPPE,
  800131,800616,830207a,901026
Relations See Rancé
Réponse See Rancé
RETREAT, annual, 830914,
  831112,870202
*RETZ, Cardinal de, 481222,610120.
  641113,650608,650619,650715,
  650929,750922,790903,800127,
  810602
REVOCATION OF THE EDICT OF
  NANTES, 851125,851129a,860130
RHEINFELDEN, 930112
RICHELIEU, Cardinal de, 410110
RICHELIEU, marquis de, 820921
RIOM, 870130,890726
ROBERT, St, 881022
ROCHEFORT, comte de, 590804
RODRIGUEZ, RP Alfonso, SJ,
  870918,881213
*ROGIER, RM Louise, Visitandine,
  870130
ROMAGNÉ, fr Etienne, C,
  Perseigne, 801120b,801122
ROME, Rancé's stay in,
  641113,641207,650608,650929,
  651015,730723
ROUEN, 790607,870211,921015
ROULARD, M., 801219
ROUSSEAU, M., 81/9
ROUSSILLON, 840311
RULE OF ST BENEDICT, 770404,
  780206,780307,781112a,800618,
  801114,820300a,821119a,
  880118a,89/5,900108
RYE HOUSE PLOT, 831024

SABAIN, M., 920718,940618
SAINT-AIGNAN, duchesse de,
  880228
SAINT-AMOUR, Guillaume de,
  940211
*SAINT-ANTOINE, Order of, 81/3
SAINT-BARTHÉLEMY, Paris, 870717
SAINT-CLÉMENTIN, OSB, 580910
SAINT-CYRAN, Jean Duverger de
  Hauranne, abbé de, 580626,
  720125,930207
Saint-Dorothée, Instructions de
  See Rancé
SAINTE-AGATHE, Filles de,
  930813,970330
SAINTE-GENEVIÈVE, CR, Paris, 941014
SAINTE-MARTHE, RP Abel de,
  Cong. Orat., 721000,730118
SAINTE-MARTHE, dom Denis, OSB,
  930306,940211
Sainteté See Rancé
SAINT-EVREMOND, Charles de,
  930108
SAINT-GÉRAN, comte de, 810123a
SAINT-JACQUES-DU-HAUT-PAS, Paris
  See Marcel
SAINT-JACQUES, Provins, OSA,
  991010
SAINT-JULIEN, Le Mans, OSB,
  990809
SAINT-LAZARE, 481222
SAINT-LOUIS, M. de, 911018,
  930511
*SAINT-LOUP, Mme de, 58/4,
  861227,920626
SAINT-MARTIN-DES-CHAMPS, Paris,
  OSB, 810829
*SAINT-MAUR, Congregation of,
  71708,710723,720527,730209a,
  800408,820400,871027,890414,
  920619a,930629
SAINT-MESMIN, dom Joseph de,
  T, 810800c
SAINT-MICHEL-EN-L'HERM, 781217
SAINT-MIHIEL, OSB, 750922
SAINT-NICOLAS-DU-CHARDONNET,
  Paris, 770914
SAINT-PAUL, comte de, 720700
*SAINT-PÉ, RP François de, Cong.
  Orat., 770321,790607
SAINT-PIERRE, marquis de,
  760507,920705
SAINT-POL, 950317
SAINT-SACREMENT, RM du, 801115
SAINT-SAUVEUR, Laon, C, 880509

SAINT-SIMON, duc de, 810123a,
    920407a,930108
SAINT-THIERRY See Guillaume
*SAINT-VALLIER, comte de,
    910905,910007
SAINT-VALLIER, Jean-Baptiste de, Bp
    of Québec, 911007,920506
SAINT-VANNE, Congregation of,
    870614
*SAINT-VICTOR, Paris, 681119,
    681119a,690326,761115,801219,
    830914,860818,880417,881014,
    971003a
SALLERTAINE, Vendée, 900920
SANDERS, RP Francis, SJ, 920609
SANTENA, fr Palémon de, T,
    910830,910905,941110,950310,
    950430,950612,990200
*SANTEUIL, Jean-Baptiste, Saint-
    Victor, 831207,901224a,910405a,
    910603,970803,971003a
*SAVARY, Mathurin, Bp of Séez,
    820608,830131,860406,87/2
SAVONAROLA, Girolamo, OP,
    750704,750715,760130
SAVOY, duke of, 920619a,b,930223
SÉEZ, 780501,781006 See also
    Forcoal, Savary
SÉGUENOT, RP Claude, Cong.
    Orat., 58/1,600902,620703,
    620720,620816,760611a
SELF-LOVE, 751100,820223,830224
    840605,851121
SENAULT, RP Jean-François,
    Cong. Orat., 720817
SENEFFE, battle of, 740800a
SENS, 720723 See also Gondrin
*SEPT-FONS, C, Eustache de Beaufort,
    abbot, 670422,700817,760100c,
    760500,760827,761106,761121,
    770404,78/5,790300,790511,
    790817,800314,800918
SÉRAPHIM, RP, OSFC, 920317
SERRE, Madeleine, 880809,930913
SEVERITY IN A SUPERIOR, 781112a,
    790511

SÉVIGNÉ, marquise de,
    870504a,910405
SEVIN, NICOLAS, BP OF CAHORS,
    730510
SICK, treatment of the, 820627
    830805,940830b
SILENCE, 661120,790610,790710,
    810911,830805,84/1,850624a,
    851104, UD 68
SLEEPING IN COWLS, 760100c,
    800613
SLUZE, Jean, 810825b,840124a,
    860130,861024,870814a,871109
SOLMINIHAC, Alain de, Bp of
    Cahors, 800609
SORBONNE, 831203
SOYROT, dom Bernard, T, 801212a,
    810120,940606
SPAIN, Queen of (Marie-Louise),
    880100,890208
SPINOLA, RP Fabius Ambrosius, SJ,
    691218
STEENKERKE, battle of, 920810
STUDY, 780206,801005,870307,
    910307,920619a

TALON, M., 941202
*TAMIÉ, C, 660119,770914a,
    771000,771222,790817,791109,
    810100,820715
TARD See Notre-Dame du Tard
TERESA OF AVILA, St, 761102,
    781022,880229a,900911
TESSON, M., 880607
*TÉTU, abbé, 911018
THEATINES, 871027
THEOLOGAL See Courcier
THEOLOGY, 700419a,830508,
    870710,880629
THEONAS, St, 821225
THÉONAS, fr
    (Etienne Lyon), 951203
THIERS, 711215,730611,800100
*THIERS, Jean-Baptiste, 831231,
    841009,930306,940211,940308,
    940606,960119,980108,980417

General Index

Thomas Aquinas, St, 821222a,
  831231
Thorigny, C, 930615
Thou, RM Louise de, C, Abbess
  Les Clairets, 710930
Thouron, RP Jean-Baptiste, Cong.
  Orat., 940324,940516,941011
*Tillemont, Sébastien Le Nain de,
  700124,950812
Torbay, 881013,881017
Tourné, RP, 890718,891013
Touron See Thouron
*Tourouvre, marquis de,
  770829,820921,830415,
  831024,850821
*Tourouvre, marquise de, 800122,
  800424,81/5
Tours See Bouthillier, Victor
Tours, 880218,880727,881130
Tours, Mlle de, 910903
Tourville, comte de, 920609,
  920705
Translation of bishop, 900121
Treuvé, Simon, 81220
*Tréville, comte de, 720825,
  73/5,750227,751200a,
  751200b,761028,781130a,
  861022,890914a
Tripoli, Bp of (?), 890630
Tristan, M., 891114
Troisville See Tréville
Troyes See Chavigny
Turenne, maréchal de, 720501,
  750800,750422
Turin, 920619a,b,920626
Turkey, 831024,900102
Tuscany, Grand Duke of, 641113
Tuscany, Grand Duchess of,
  620922,641113,870924,88/3

*Urfé, Louis Lascaris de, Bp of
  Limoges, 781105a
Us (Usages) of Cîteaux, 711212,
  720514,721100,760827,
  770404,78/3

Vainet, M., 860812
Val, abbaye du, cr, 600400,
  610928,611211,821119a
Valant, Mme, 770208
Valence, 901026
Valognes, 751100j,760314
*Val-Richer, C, Dominique
  Georges, abbot, 641113,751100a
  77/1,870921,931110
Varese, Mgr, 781105
Vauclair, C, Louis Brulart,
  abbot, 830112
Vauguyon, M. de, 931207
Vaussin See Cîteaux
Véretz, 610928,611211,800602
Vernassal, comte de, 650904,
  730802,730907
*Vernassal Marie Bouthillier,
  comtesse de, 651015
*Vernassal, Mlle de, 740123,
  800930,810213a,810525
Vernassal family, 800129
Verrolles, fr Euthyme, T, 760314
*Vertus, Mlle de, 921200
*Vialart de Herse, Félix, Bp of
  Châlons, 730819,760106,
  760314,770815,800700
Vichy, 790526
Vienna, 831024,900102
Villandri, M. de, 740909
Villars, abbé de, 820423,851125
Villeneuve, M. de, 820608,
  930511,930820
Villeroy, maréchal de, 781006
Vincennes, 820608,930820
Vincent de Paul, St, 481222
Vincent, fr Pierre, T, 800900b
Vingtain, dom Bernard, T, 790710
Virville, M. de 941117
Vitry, dom Dorothée, T, 930316,
  930316b,930328
Vuillart, Germain, 720718

Waters, taking 79/1,790526,
  810923,811005,820720,820831,
  880115,880509,880600, UD 96

WEAKLINGS, admission of, 761014
WILLIAM III (OF ORANGE), King of
    England, 881013,881017,881100,
    890126,890414,890903,90/2,
    920619a,b,930820
WILLIAM OF ST THIERRY
    See Guillaume
WINE, 78/3
WINSLOW, M., 00620

ZANNONI, RP Bernardino, SJ,
    691218,840323

CISTERCIAN PUBLICATIONS INC.

TITLES LISTING

THE CISTERCIAN FATHERS SERIES

THE WORKS OF BERNARD OF CLAIRVAUX

Treatises I: Apologia to Abbot William,
On Precept and Dispensation . . . . CF 1
On the Song of Songs I–IV . . . . CF 4,7,31,40
The Life and Death of Saint Malachy
the Irishman . . . . CF 10
Treatises II: The Steps of Humility,
On Loving God . . . . CF 13*
Magnificat: Homilies in Praise of the
Blessed Virgin Mary [with Amadeus
of Lausanne] . . . . CF 18
Treatises III: On Grace and Free Choice,
In Praise of the New Knighthood . . . . . . CF 19
Sermons on Conversion: A Sermon to Clerics,
Lenten Sermons on Psalm 91 . . . . CF 25
Five Books on Consideration:
Advice to a Pope . . . . CF 37

THE WORKS OF WILLIAM OF SAINT THIERRY

On Contemplating God, Prayer,
and Meditations . . . . CF 3*
Exposition on the Song of Songs . . . . CF 6
The Enigma of Faith . . . . CF 9
The Golden Epistle . . . . CF 12
The Mirror of Faith . . . . CF 15
Exposition on the Epistle to the
Romans . . . . CF 27
The Nature and Dignity of Love . . . . CF 30

THE WORKS OF AELRED OF RIEVAULX

Treatises I: On Jesus at the Age of Twelve,
Rule for a Recluse, The Pastoral Prayer . . . . CF 2
Spiritual Friendship . . . . CF 5
The Mirror of Charity . . . . CF 17†
Dialogue on the Soul . . . . CF 22

THE WORKS OF GILBERT OF HOYLAND

Sermons on the Song of Songs I–III . CF 14,20,26
Treatises, Sermons, and Epistles . . . . CF 34

THE WORKS OF JOHN OF FORD

Sermons on the Final Verses of the Song
of Songs I–VII . . . . . . CF 29,39,43,44,45,46,47

OTHER EARLY CISTERCIAN WRITERS

The Letters of Adam of Perseigne, I . . . . . . CF 21
Alan of Lille: The Art of Preaching . . . . . . CF 23
Idung of Prufening. Cistercians and Cluniacs:
The Case for Citeaux . . . . CF 33
The Way of Love . . . . CF 16
Guerric of Igny.
Liturgical Sermons I–II . . . . CF 8,32
Three Treatises on Man: A Cistercian
Anthropology . . . . CF 24
Isaac of Stella. Sermons on the
Christian Year, I . . . . CF 11
Stephen of Lexington. Letters from
Ireland, 1228–9 . . . . CF 28
Stephen of Sawley, Treatises . . . . CF 36

THE CISTERCIAN STUDIES SERIES

MONASTIC TEXTS

Evagrius Ponticus. Praktikos and
Chapters on Prayer . . . . CS 4
The Rule of the Master . . . . CS 6
The Lives of the Desert Fathers . . . . CS 34
The Sayings of the Desert Fathers . . . . CS 59
Dorotheos of Gaza. Discourses
and Sayings . . . . CS 33

Pachomian Koinonia I–III:
The Lives . . . . CS 45
The Chronicles and Rules . . . . CS 46
The Instructions, Letters, and Other
Writings of St Pachomius and
His Disciples . . . . CS 47
Besa, The Life of Shenoute . . . . CS 73

* Temporarily out of print   † Forthcoming

Symeon the New Theologian. Theological
and Practical Treatises and Three
Theological Discourses..............CS 41
Guigo II the Carthusian. The Ladder of
Monks and Twelve Meditations.......CS 48
The Monastic Rule of Iosif Volotsky......CS 36

CHRISTIAN SPIRITUALITY

The Spirituality of Western
Christendom.....................CS 30
Russian Mystics (Sergius Bolshakoff).......CS 26
In Quest of the Absolute: The Life and Works
of Jules Monchanin (J.G. Weber)........CS 51
The Name of Jesus
(Irénée Hausherr)..................CS 44
Entirely for God: A Life of Cyprian
Tansi (Elizabeth Isichei)..............CS 43
The Roots of the Modern
Christian Tradition.................CS 55
Abba: Guides to Wholeness and
Holiness East and West..............CS 38
Sermons in a Monastery
(Matthew Kelty–William Paulsell).......CS 58
Penthos: The Doctrine of Compunction in
the Christian East (Irénée Hausherr).....CS 53
Distant Echoes. Medieval Religious Women,
Vol. 1..........................CS 71

MONASTIC STUDIES

The Abbot in Monastic Tradition
(Pierre Salmon)....................CS 14
Why Monks? (François Vandenbroucke)...CS 17
Silence in the Rule of St Benedict
(Ambrose Wathen).................CS 22
One Yet Two: Monastic Tradition
East and West.....................CS 29
Community and Abbot in the Rule of
St Benedict I (Adalbert de Vogüé)......CS 5/1
Consider Your Call: A Theology of the
Monastic Life (Daniel Rees et al.).........CS 20
Households of God (David Parry).........CS 39
Studies in Monastic Theology
(Odo Brooke).....................CS 37
The Way to God According to the Rule
of St Benedict (E. Heufelder)...........CS 49
The Rule of St Benedict. A Doctrinal
and Spiritual Commentary
(Adalbert de Vogüé)................CS 54
As We Seek God (Stephanie Campbell)....CS 70

CISTERCIAN STUDIES

The Cistercian Way (André Louf).........CS 76
The Cistercian Spirit
(M. Basil Pennington, ed.)............CS 3

The Eleventh-Century Background of
Citeaux (Bede K. Lackner)............CS 8
Contemplative Community............CS 21
Cistercian Sign Language
(Robert Barakat)...................CS 11
The Cistercians in Denmark
(Brian P. McGuire).................CS 35
Saint Bernard of Clairvaux: Essays
Commemorating the Eighth Centenary of
His Canonization..................CS 28
Bernard of Clairvaux: Studies Presented
to Dom Jean Leclercq...............CS 23
Bernard of Clairvaux and the Cistercian
Spirit (Jean Leclercq)................CS 16
Image and Likeness. The Mystical Theology of
William of St Thierry and St Augustine
(D.N. Bell)......................CS 78
Aelred of Rievaulx: A Study
(Aelred Squire)....................CS 50
Christ the Way: The Christology of
Guerric of Igny (John Morson)........CS 25
The Golden Chain: The Theological
Anthropology of Isaac of Stella
(Bernard McGinn).................CS 15
Studies in Cistercian Art and Architecture, I
(Meredith Lillich, ed.)...............CS 66
Studies in Cistercian Art and Architecture, II
(Meredith Lillich, ed.)...............CS 69
Nicolas Cotheret's Annals of Citeaux
(Louis J. Lekai)....................CS 57
The Occupation of Celtic Sites in Ireland
by the Canons Regular of St Augustine and
the Cistercians (G. Carville)...........CS 56
The Cistercian Way (André Louf).........CS 76
Monastic Practices (Charles Cummings)....CS 75
The Letters of Armand-Jean le Bouthillier,
abbé de Rancé (A.J. Krailsheimer).....CS 80,81

*Studies in Medieval Cistercian
History sub-series*

Studies I...........................CS 13
Studies II..........................CS 24
Cistercian Ideals and Reality
(Studies III)......................CS 60
Simplicity and Ordinariness
(Studies IV)......................CS 61
The Chimera of His Age: Studies on
St Bernard (Studies V)..............CS 63
Cistercians in the Late Middle Ages
(Studies VI)......................CS 64
Noble Piety and Reformed Monasticism
(Studies VII).....................CS 65
Benedictus: Studies in Honor of St Benedict
of Nursia (Studies VIII).............CS 67
Heaven on Earth (Studies IX)...........CS 68

* *Temporarily out of print*   † *Forthcoming*

THOMAS MERTON

The Climate of Monastic Prayer . . . . CS 1
Thomas Merton on St Bernard . . . . CS 9
Thomas Merton's Shared Contemplation:
A Protestant Perspective
(Daniel J. Adams) . . . . CS 62
Solitude in the Writings of Thomas Merton
(Richard Anthony Cashen) . . . . CS 40

The Message of Thomas Merton
(Brother Patrick Hart, ed.) . . . . CS 42
Thomas Merton Monk (revised edition/
Brother Patrick Hart, ed.) . . . . CS 52
Thomas Merton and Asia: A Quest for
Utopia (Alexander Lipski) . . . . CS 74

THE CISTERCIAN LITURGICAL DOCUMENTS SERIES †

The Cistercian Hymnal: Introduction
and Commentary . . . . CLS 1
The Cistercian Hymnal: Text and
Melodies . . . . CLS 2
The Old French Ordinary and Breviary
of the Abbey of the Paraclete: Introduction
and Commentary . . . . CLS 3
The Old French Ordinary of the Abbey of
the Paraclete: Text . . . . CLS 4

The Paraclete Breviary: Text . . . . CLS 5-7
The Hymn Collection of the Abbey
of the Paraclete: Introduction
and Commentary . . . . CLS 8
The Hymn Collection of the Abbey of the
Paraclete: Text . . . . CLS 9

FAIRACRES PRESS, OXFORD

The Wisdom of the Desert Fathers
The Letters of St Antony the Great
The Letters of Ammonas, Successor of
St Antony
A Study of Wisdom. Three Tracts by the author
of *The Cloud of Unknowing*
The Power of the Name. The Jesus Prayer in
Orthodox Spirituality (Kallistos Ware)

Contemporary Monasticism
A Pilgrim's Book of Prayers
(Gilbert Shaw)
Theology and Spirituality (Andrew Louth)
Prayer and Holiness (Dumitru Staniloae)
Eight Chapters on Perfection and Angel's Song
(Walter Hilton)

Distributed in North America only for Fairacres Press.

DISTRIBUTED BOOKS

La Trappe in England
O Holy Mountain: Journal of a Retreat on
Mount Athos
St Benedict: Man with An Idea (Melbourne Studies)
The Spirit of Simplicity

Vision of Peace (St Joseph's Abbey)

The Animals of St Gregory (Paulinus Press)
Benedict's Disciples (David Hugh Farmer)
The Christmas Sermons of Guerric of Igny
The Emperor's Monk. A Contemporary Life of
Benedict of Aniane
Journey to God:. Anglican Essays on the
Benedictine Way

* *Temporarily out of print*   † *Forthcoming*